Taxing for Development

CRITICAL FRONTIERS OF THEORY RESARCH AND POLICY IN INTERNATIONAL DEVELOPMENT STUDIES

Series Editors

Naomi Hossain, Briony Jones, Alfredo Saad Filho, Benjamin Selwyn, and Fiona Tregenna

The contemporary world is characterized by massive wealth alongside widespread poverty, inequality, and environmental destruction–all bound up through class, race, and gender dynamics of inequality and oppression.

Critical Frontiers of Theory, Research, and Policy in International Development Studies, the official book series of the Development Studies Association of the UK, was established to contribute to critical thinking about local, national, and global processes of structural transformation. The series publishes cutting-edge monographs that promote critical development studies as an interdisciplinary and applied field and shape the theory, practice, and teaching of international development for a new generation of scholars, students, and practitioners. As the series evolves, we wish to publish a diverse and inclusive range of authors whose work engages in critical, multidisciplinary, decolonial, and methodologically plural development studies.

Recently published in the series

The Rise and Fall of Neoliberal Rentier Capitalism
The Political Economy of the 20th and 21st Centuries
Luiz Carlos Bresser-Pereira

The Spectre of State Capitalism
Ilias Alami, Adam D. Dixon

Business of the State
Why State Ownership Matters for Resource Governance
Jewellord T. Nem Singh

Disrupted Development in the Congo
The Fragile Foundations of the African Mining Consensus
Ben Radley

Politics and the Urban Frontier
Transformation and Divergence in Late Urbanizing East Africa
Tom Goodfellow

Equity, Evaluation, and International Cooperation
In Pursuit of Proximate Peers in an African City
Gabriella Y. Carolini

They Eat Our Sweat
Transport Labor, Corruption, and Everyday Survival in Urban Nigeria
Daniel E. Agbiboa

Taxing for Development

Contested Ideas, the State, and Commodity Taxes in Argentina

Matt Barlow

OXFORD
UNIVERSITY PRESS

OXFORD
UNIVERSITY PRESS

Great Clarendon Street, Oxford, OX2 6DP,
United Kingdom

Oxford University Press is a department of the University of Oxford.
It furthers the University's objective of excellence in research, scholarship,
and education by publishing worldwide. Oxford is a registered trade mark of
Oxford University Press in the UK and in certain other countries.

Published in the United States of America by Oxford University Press
198 Madison Avenue, New York, NY 10016, United States of America

British Library Cataloguing in Publication Data
Data available

Library of Congress Control Number: 2025937395

ISBN 9780198923190

DOI: 10.1093/9780198923220.001.0001

The manufacturer's authorised representative in the EU for product safety is
Oxford University Press España S.A. of Parque Empresarial San Fernando de Henares,
Avenida de Castilla, 2 – 28830 Madrid (www.oup.es/en or product.safety@oup.com).
OUP España S.A. also acts as importer into Spain of products made by the manufacturer.

For David

Acknowledgements

This book wouldn't have been possible without the significant support I received, and I want to take the opportunity to thank those who have been essential to its completion. First and foremost, to Professor Jean Grugel. Jean initially offered unwavering support, constructive criticism, advice, and—above all—trust in her role as co-supervisor to my doctoral thesis, from where this book emerged. Since then, we have become colleagues and friends. I cannot thank her enough for everything that she has done, including reading many versions of earlier chapters with good spirit and with as keen an eye as there ever was. Huge thanks also go to Dr Alejandro Peña, my other co-supervisor and friend. Your support was invaluable both during and after my PhD. Your deep knowledge and interest in all things historical and political in Argentina significantly helped shaped the project. I look forward to seeing you back in Buenos Aires soon.

Thanks also goes to the Economic and Social Research Council and the London Interdisciplinary Social Science Doctoral Training Partnership, which funded the second period of fieldwork and the writing of this book as part of my post-doctoral fellowship: *Taxing for Development: Contested Ideas, the State, and Commodity Taxes in Argentina*. I would like to extend my sincere thanks to the Department of International Development at King's College London for hosting me during this period, and to Dr Ingrid Kvangraven and Dr Ewa Karwowski for mentoring me throughout. Thanks also goes to Professor Ben Richardson from the University of Warwick; Ben's insights were instrumental in framing both the book outline and the fellowship proposal, and I truly appreciate his input.

I also want to convey my gratitude to the Editorial Board of *Critical Frontiers of Theory, Research, and Policy in International Development Studies* and particularly to Professor Benjamin Selwyn who was incredibly supportive throughout the latter stages of the book's development.

I want to thank my colleagues and friends from the Department of Politics and International Relations at the University of York for their encouragement and support along the way. Thank you also to everybody at the Universidad Torcuato di Tella in Buenos Aires who made me feel so welcome during both my periods of fieldwork, especially Professor Enrique Peruzzotti and

Professor Carlos Gervasoni, but thanks go to the whole team in the Department of Political Science and International Studies. I would like to also thank all the interviewees who contributed towards this project; their hospitality and generosity made both trips a success and a pleasure. Many people have offered me advice and support with this book. There are too many to mention here, but particular thanks go to Dr Benjamin Hunter at the University of Glasgow—your support and well-meaning gentle pressure to *write* were very helpful and much needed over this past year.

Throughout this journey, I have received overwhelming support from friends and family. There are too many of them to mention here, but this support has meant the world to me: Mum and Dad and Gary and Julia, love you guys. And last but by no means least, thanks to David for your unwavering support throughout this entire process, including your (mostly) good humour whilst I've been working over weekends and holidays to complete the book and everything you have sacrificed to make this possible. Thank you – this is for you.

Contents

List of Figures xii
List of Tables xiii
List of Abbreviations xiv

1. Taxing for Development: Export Taxes as a Development Strategy 1
Introduction 1
Challenges of raising tax in developing countries 5
Extracting natural resource revenues 9
Export taxes in national development 10
Key arguments 13
Methodological approach 16
Structure of the book 18

2. Theorizing Tax Challenges in Resource-Rich Developing Countries 22
Introduction 22
Why tax matters: State-building 23
Taxing the interests of capitalists 25
Legitimizing taxes 27
Theorizing tax for development 30
Taxing the interests of Latin American wealth 34
The politics of institutional tax capacity 36
Deep political cleavages and tax ideologies 38
Natural resource management: Extracting and redistributing 43
Post-neoliberalism and the return of the state 48
Conclusion 50

3. Fiscal Extractivism: The Historic Politics of Raising Tax in the Global South 52
Introduction 52
Legacies of colonialism: Natural and fiscal resource extraction 53
Fiscal bargaining 55
The British Empire, 1583–1997: Extraction and conflict 56
Bargaining over British imperial trade taxes 59
The French Empire, 1630–1977 60
Belgium and the Congo Free State, 1885–1908 62
Dutch extraction in the Indio Pacific: Negotiated practices, 1595–1975 63
Commodity wealth in the New World: Portuguese imperialism, 1415–1822 64
The Spanish Empire, 1492–1898 66

Raising tax across Spanish America: Fragmented and negotiated 66
Tax for development after Iberian subjugation 70
Export-led growth through external economic shocks 74
Trade liberalization versus protectionism: A conflict of ideas 77
Conclusion 80

4. Extracting from *el Campo*: A Twentieth-Century Argentine Fiscal Puzzle 82
Introduction 82
Tensions in the countryside: *Estancieros* and *chacareros* 84
Peronism: The rise of the spending state 88
Fiscal policies to extract from the landed class 90
Public spending and indirect taxes 93
Deepening fiscal tensions 96
Post-Peronist politics: Low tax, social conflict, and growing debt, 1955–1989 98
The introduction of export taxes 99
Exacerbating the rural versus industrial cleavage: Debt dictating development, 1976–1989 105
The shift to market-led development: Debt rises still further, 1989–2001 108
Reduced conflict and rural-sector transformations 110
Conclusion 111

5. Taxing Exports for What?: Building and Losing Legitimacy 114
Introduction 114
Taxing out of financial crisis 115
The First Kirchnerismo: A return of the Peronist left 120
The consolidation of the redistributive 'emergency' state 121
Soybean and beef exports: A different tax logic 127
Tax for an interventionalist state? 129
Economic deterioration and commodity headwinds 132
Export tax reform and contested state visions 133
The end of the fiscal peace: Export tax conflict 136
Conclusion 142

6. Commodity Price Volatility and Fiscal Entrapment 144
Introduction 144
Redistributive tensions: Expansive policies and reducing headroom, 2008–2011 145
Federalism, extraordinary taxation, and conflict 149
Concessions through the soy fund 151
Deepening of the fiscal deficit, 2011–2015 153
Squaring the circle: The politics of redistributive commitments 157
Asignación Universal por Hijo: Universal child benefit 164
Export tax fatigue 166
Conclusion 170

7. Embedded Ideas of Taxation, Wider Conflict, and Political Polarization **172**
Introduction 172
Conflict around ideas of development: A confluence of factors aggravated by tax 173
Beyond taxes: A wide-ranging and muddled debate 178
Growing opposition and the offer of a different vision of state 185
Loss of legitimacy to govern 189
Conclusion 191

8. Conclusion: Contested Ideas of Tax and State **194**
Introduction 194
Limitations of the Argentine export tax regime 197
Theoretical contributions 203
Commodity dependence and challenges in the twenty-first century 208

References 212
Index 237

List of Figures

2.1 Modalities of natural resource revenue extraction 43

4.1 Direct versus indirect taxation, 1943–1955 97

4.2 Argentine fiscal deficit, 1956–1983 (%) 104

5.1 Government spending and fiscal balance, 2000–2015 122

5.2 Commodity prices and soybean tax levels, June 2001–July 2008 134

6.1 Total and emergency tax collection and public spending, 2008–2011 (% GDP) 148

6.2 Evolution of redistributed revenue via *Coparticipación Federal*, January 2009–2010 152

6.3 Total and emergency tax collection and public spending, 2012–2015 (% GDP) 157

6.4 Natural gas imports and exports, 2005–2015 160

6.5 Currency reserves and fiscal and current balances, 2008–2015 161

6.6 Gas production and consumption, 2010–2015 162

6.7 Argentine poverty levels, 2010–2016 (% of population) 165

List of Tables

3.1 Central government debt-to-export ratio, 1929–1935 (%) 75
3.2 Selected Latin American customs revenues, 1929 (% of total tax take) 76
4.1 Comparative contribution of the rural sector in Argentine GDP (%) 91
4.2 Average tax collection by decade, 1930s–1990s 94
4.3 Fiscal deficit percentage of GDP, 1945–1955 95
4.4 Export tax levels on major exports, 1965–July 1970 (%) 101
4.5 Volume of exports of goods, 1985–2000 (%) 109
4.6 Argentine foreign debt, 1993–2000 111
5.1 Key economic and social indications, 2001–2008 123
5.2 Evolution of the level of export taxes, 2002–2007 (percentage) 125
5.3 Resolution N.125 and the tax bands 133
5.4 Evolution of agricultural export taxes, 2002–2015 (percentage) 135
6.1 Key economic and social indicators, 2008–2011 146
6.2 Key economic and social indicators, 2011–2015 155
6.3 Evolution of Universal Child Benefit, 2009–2015 164

List of Abbreviations

AFIP	*Administración Federal de Ingresos Públicos* (Tax Collection Agency)
ANSES	*Administración Nacional de la Seguridad Social* (National Social Security Service)
APES	Argentine Panel Election Study
ARCA	*Agencia de Recaudación y Control Aduanero* (Revenue Collection and Customs Control)
ARI	*Coalición Cívica* (Civic Coalition)
AUH	*Asignación Universal por Hijo* (Universal Child Benefit)
BCRA	*Banco Central de la República Argentina*
CEPAL	*Comisión Económica para América Latina y el Caribe* (Economic Commission for Latin America and the Caribbean)
CFS	Congo Free State
CGT	*Confederación General del Trabajo de la República Argentina* (General Confederation of Labour)
CODELCO	*Corporación Nacional del Cobre* (National Copper Corporation of Chile)
CONINAGRO	*Confederación Intercooperativa Agropecuaria*
CRA	*Confederaciones Rurales Argentinas*
DGA	*Dirección General de Aduanas* (Argentine Customs Tax Agency)
DGI	*Dirección General de Impositiva*
DNU	*Decreto de Necesidad y Urgencia* (Necessity and Urgency Decree)
ECLA	Economic Commission for Latin America
ECLAC	Economic Commission for Latin America and the Caribbean
ENAMI	*Empresa Nacional Minera*
FAA	*Federación Agraria Argentina* (Argentine Agrarian Federation)
FAUNEN	*Frente Amplio UNEN*
FIEL	*Fundación de Investigaciones Económicas Latinoamericanas* (Latin American Economic Research Foundation)
FPV	*Frente para la Victoria* (Victory Front)
GATT	General Agreement on Tariffs and Trade
GDP	gross domestic product
IAPI	*Instituto Argentino de Promoción del Intercambio*
IDB	Inter-America Development Bank
ILO	International Labour Organization
IMF	International Monetary Fund
INDEC	*Instituto Nacional de Estadísticas y Censos de la República Argentina*
OECD	Organisation for Economic Co-operation and Development
PJ	*Partido Justicialista* (Justicialist Party)

PRO	*Propuesta Republicana* (Republican Proposal)
SAP	structural adjustment programme
SDGs	Sustainable Development Goals
SQM	*Sociedad Química y Minera*
SRA	*Sociedad Rural Argentina* (Argentine Rural Society)
UCA	*Universidad Católica Argentina* (Catholic University of Argentina)
UCR	*Unión Cívica Radical* (Radical Civil Union)
UIA	*Unión Industrial Argentina* (Industrial Union of Argentina)
UIF	*Unidad de Información Financiera* (Argentine Financial Information)
UN	United Nations
YPF	*Yacimientos Petrolíferos Fiscales*

1

Taxing for Development

Export Taxes as a Development Strategy

Introduction

Whilst the importance of tax collection for sustainable development cannot be overstated, deep-rooted structural, political, and social factors have presented significant barriers to growing the tax burden in low- and middle-income countries. Many of these factors—discussed in this book—have meant that in lieu of higher tax receipts, revenues from natural resource exports remain significantly more important to the political economies of developing countries across the Global South. Moreover, in situations where governments lack autonomy into specialized natural resource-exporting sectors, and other taxes are low, export taxes are essential because they represent one of the only pathways for states to mobilize domestic resources from these industries. They have been effectively utilized as a fiscal strategy to extract revenues from sectors benefiting from high commodity prices to redistribute to other areas of the economy as a tool to depress domestic prices or to strengthen food security (Richardson N., 2009; Shama, 2011). But they are polemic and generate contention and are emblematic of development dilemmas in developing countries that rely on natural resource exports. This book sets out to explore the critical but understudied role export taxes play in these projects of national development.

Two vignettes, from 2008 and 2022, drawn from the country case that forms the empirical core of this book, show how taxes over exports are profoundly contentious, deeply political, and have the ability to generate opposition outside of the extractive and export sectors over which the taxes fall. Export tax strategies can have a significant impact on fiscal policies and set the course for conflict between governments and specialized exporting sectors, creating a barrier to mobilizing domestic resources and impeding national development. Furthermore, opposing ideas and ideals shape ideologies surrounding the use of export taxes. Opposing visions of extraction and redistribution of natural resource revenues through export taxes can

Taxing for Development. Matt Barlow, Oxford University Press.
DOI: 10.1093/9780198923220.003.0001

generate discord in wider society because export taxes are emblematic of an interventionalist state. Moreover, the contention around their use demonstrates the salient role that natural resource exports still occupy in many developing countries following decades of attempts to modernize economies through structural change.

In May 2022, the conflict that export taxes could induce was evident when Argentine president Alberto Fernández (2020–2023) presented the case for increasing the level of export taxes levied over wheat exports to try and slow the growth in commodity prices, which were skyrocketing within the Argentine domestic market. The domestic policy over a commodity that was worth $2.71 billion to the Argentine economy in 2021 (OEC, 2024) was a direct response to the spike in international prices that had been driven by the 2022 Russian invasion of Ukraine. The Russian naval blockade of Ukrainian ports in early 2022 created a major disruption to grain exports from two of the world's largest agricultural exporting countries, resulting in a 35 per cent drop in global wheat exports, 18 per cent drop to maize markets, and sunflower exports reduced by 14 per cent (The Seam, 2022). The invasion increased pressure on global food supplies, threatened global food security for millions, and pushed up the price of the remaining commodities in the market. However, high food prices in Latin America's third largest economy already represented a major challenge for President Alberto Fernández's administration, with inflation hovering around 50 per cent in 2021 (before surpassing 100 per cent by February 2023: a three-decade high; La Nación, 2023), it was having a devastating impact on livelihoods and dominating opposition political attacks (Página 12, 2023; Clarín, 2023). In the immediate aftermath of the invasion, the reduced supply of grains to global markets pushed wheat prices up by 15 per cent (March–April) on the previous month, but it represented an increase of 80 per cent on the previous year (Baffes and Temaj, 2022). Moreover, this situation was layered on top of already high global commodity prices in other food groups; even before the invasion, the United Nation's Food and Agricultural Organization estimated that during 2021, supply-chain constraints and surging demand meant that food prices globally rose at their fastest rate on record by 23.1 per cent (IMF, 2022).[1]

President Fernández presented the tax increase as a way to respond to the steep upwards trajectory of wheat prices, isolating domestic from international wheat prices by increasing the level of export taxes known in Argentina as *retenciones*—withholdings in English—that were levied over wheat. The President argued that the taxes were a mechanism that would decouple

[1] Food prices that were tracked were meat, dairy, cereals, oils, and sugar.

the domestic from the international price because it would help dissuade wheat producers from selling internationally and favour the domestic market. Moreover, the implementation of export taxes also represented a fiscal pathway for the government to increase revenue collection from exporters who were benefiting from high prices driving extraordinary, unexpected profits. Speaking about the prices rises, the President pointed out that

> Suddenly something happens in the world, and someone begins to earn much more money than they anticipated and unexpected wealth is produced. We ask for it to be redistributed another way (La Nación, 2022).

However, the President mooted the increase in an understandably tentative manner with the caveat that it was the preserve of Congress to raise export taxes and not that of the president. And, rather tongue-in-cheek, he acknowledged that ‘whilst some people would be happy at the tax rise, others would not’ (La Nación, 2022), an understated reference to the mobilization on 23 April 2022 by farmers and rural actors protesting in the Plaza de Mayo in central Buenos Aires at state intervention into agricultural markets through (now abolished) quotas and export taxes. But it was also a reference to memories of 2008 when a major tax revolt against export taxes spilled out from a conflict between the government of Cristina Fernández de Kirchner (2007–2015) and landowners, producers, and farmers in the agricultural sector (known in Argentina as either the rural sector—the term that I use in this book—or *el campo*, ‘the countryside’ in English) to a conflict that completely polarized Argentine society and generated social conflict in groups that were not directly impacted by the tax but that mobilized nonetheless. In doing so, it created a deep political and enduring cleavage, which has meant that these taxes have become an Achilles heel for Argentine governments since the revolt and a barrier to mobilizing domestic resources (Barlow and Peña, 2022).

Following a decade where they had been abolished in Argentina’s neoliberal experiment in the 1990s, export taxes were reintroduced in 2002 because the state’s access to international financial markets had been completely severed as a result of the International Monetary Fund (IMF) debt default in December 2001 (Datz, 2009). They consequently became an essential fiscal tool for the emergency governments of Eduardo Duhalde (2002–2003) and Néstor Kirchner (2003–2007) to help fund state emergency obligations and crisis response. And because of the crisis, it created a temporary truce between the government and agricultural producers over whom the taxes were levied because it was underpinned by the fact that national crisis required the government to raise revenue quickly and through strategies which had generated conflict for much of the twentieth century (Ondetti, 2023).

However, this fragile peace came under increasing strain by late 2007, when the export tax rate over some agricultural exports was hiked twice, coinciding with strong growth in global commodity prices and, crucially, at a moment when the country had clearly emerged from the crisis. Simultaneously, discussions of increasing welfare provision and redistributive policies were at the fore of policy commitments by the newly and emphatically elected President Cristina Fernández de Kirchner.[2] In her 2007 presidential election campaign, Cristina Kirchner promised an ambitious expansion of the social redistribution programme offered first by her husband and that had now become firmly associated with the development model of the Kirchners known as *Kirchnerismo* (Grugel and Riggirozzi, 2012; Wylde, 2018), a proposal that could only be funded realistically though export tax rises.

Following the two earlier hikes, the final straw for producers came in early 2008, when the government introduced a tax reform that would peg a progressive export tax rate to the price of international agricultural commodities. This suggested that tax reform was the catalyst for a major revolt. It instigated social conflict, national strikes, a lockout of Buenos Aires, and food shortages that lasted three months (March–June 2008) and that critically permeated from the rural sector into other sectors of Argentine society. The tax reform—Resolution N.125—was a watershed moment in the presidency of Cristina Kirchner and a defining moment in Argentine tax strategy and governance. At the time of the conflict, it completely polarized Argentine society and moved the tax conflict from an argument about export taxes—that had historically been confined to landowners and agrarian elites and the Argentine presidents seeking to redistribute away from the sector—to embedding ideas of export taxes in a wider fiscal conflict but one that was framed by tax ideology and opposing visions of state that were being funded by this tax, a point that would be referred to throughout the president's eight years in office.

Moreover, the tax revolt put this expansive social redistribution programme in jeopardy because ideas of the tax became directly associated with ideas of state spending, which permeated into other areas of fiscal policy, extending beyond the tax but underpinned by an idea of the tax, a point that

[2] President Fernández de Kirchner was elected with a landslide victory in October 2007. Cristina Kirchner captured 45 per cent of the vote, beating her closest rival Elisa Carrió of the ARI (Civic Coalition) (23 per cent) and the outgoing president's former finance minister and the UCR (Radical Civil Union) candidate, Roberto Lavagna (17 per cent) (Ministerio del Interior, 2007).

Alberto Fernández was all too cognizant of when mooting the idea of raising taxes again to cool the rising price of wheat because this had been so polarizing, historically, which presented an ideological barrier to raising them. This also highlights an enduring development challenge regarding how governments in export-dependant countries can extract revenue and raise the tax burden from specialized sectors over which the state does not have control and redistribute them in wider society.

This book therefore seeks to understand why a progressive export tax strategy that was levied over grain exports in 2008 generated an intersectoral and countrywide tax revolt that entirely polarized Argentine society and led to a bruising government defeat in Congress and challenged the social redistribution programme that was being pursued. Moreover, it asks why these taxes remained so contentious in a context where they were not levied over the majority of citizens but generated a profound response anyway. In exploring these export taxes, the book situates them in a wider political economy of development debate and highlights their salient position in development and the deep political cleavage that exists about both the appropriate role of the state versus the private sector and the place of commodity production in national development, which directly affects the tax capacity of the state. It offers a novel understanding of the place of commodity production in development and, in particular, the commodity bonanza that occurred in Argentina, and Latin America, in the first twenty years of the twenty-first century. This has the potential to make a major contribution to understandings of both resource dependency and the challenges of revenue-raising in Latin America, and, more widely, for low- and middle-income countries in the Global South.

Challenges of raising tax in developing countries

Strengthening and increasing the effectiveness of tax systems in developing countries is deemed by the IMF, World Bank Group, Organisation for Economic Co-operation and Development (OECD) and United Nations (UN) as essential to meet the Sustainable Development Goals (SDGs) and to promote inclusive and equitable economic growth (UN, 2024). Indeed, the importance of raising tax for development within an uneven global economy has spawned an extensive and increasingly *fashionable* corpus of research seeking to offer policy advice to governments in developing countries on how to better mobilize domestic resources. At the time of finalizing this book (2025), poor global tax governance and its negative relationship with development is a fulcrum of debate. At the UN, in 2023, the Africa group of nations tabled proposals for a framework Convention whose 'Terms of Reference' provided a blueprint for strengthening tax cooperation and compliance by moving governance away from the OECD to the UN to 'ensure fair and equitable taxation of multinational enterprises, the digital economy, cross-border services, tackling Illicit Financial Flows and Base Erosion and Profit Shifting' (ATAF, 2024). This proposal was supported by the African Union, 120 other member countries, and influential groups such as the Tax Justice Network, all of whom sought to ameliorate the weaknesses in existing tax governance by promoting 'inclusive and effective international tax cooperation' with developing countries central to the debate (ATAF, 2024).

As I finalize this chapter, these discussions are, of course, ongoing, and have attracted significant opposition, including from interest groups within the OECD and the European Union. International political economy of development scholars—me being one of them—are under no illusion of the need to make these changes, but we are also aware of the scale of the challenge to rewrite the global architecture of tax governance to get states to buy into the Convention to ultimately mobilize domestic resources to support the financing of development strategies, including the SDGs. However, this focus on international tax governance comes with an underlying assumption that governments in developing countries have the capacity, political will, and autonomy to raise the taxes advocated for by these discussions—a point about which I am less sanguine.

The current focus on international tax governance, whilst fashionable, eschews domestic political economy factors. But the strengthening of tax systems in the Global South has proved to be a complex and contentious task with structural economic factors, limited tax administration capacity, incomplete information of taxpayers, and political instability meaning that, in many cases, tax policy has often been the 'art of the possible rather than the pursuit of the optimal' (Tanzi and Zee, 2000: 300). And, as Adebayo, Lashitew, and Werker (2021) argue, in countries that rely on tax revenues from natural resource exports, the political economy of taxation has significant influence over government tax take. Pointing to the scale of this challenge in a post-COVID-19 pandemic context, the OECD (2021b) highlights that whilst 'tax plays a central role in promoting development [. . .] those developing countries face significant challenges in developing their tax capacities and mobilising their domestic resources'.

I argue throughout this book that these challenges to raise tax for development should be considered in a longer historical arc because they have their deepest roots in colonialism. Wealth and power that were concentrated in exporting sectors, and thus with exporting elites, have shaped tax collection capacities to this day because, in many cases, building tax capacity was subsidiary to extractive forms of economic production. Low levels of legitimacy to collect tax in colonies, lengthy processes of tax bargaining, and an overreliance on revenues from natural resource exports set in motion a framework for weak and fragmented tax collection in economies where wealth is highly concentrated and tax reform options limited.

Existing studies exploring the challenges of fiscal policy reform in developing countries tend to privilege interest-based and materialist analyses or utilize arguments of weak institutional capacity as key explanatory factors for low levels of taxation (Sánchez-Sibony, 2019). Interest-based accounts are grounded in the political power and the resources that groups can wield and how they bargain to protect their interests. In these arguments, the centrality of economic interests of political, business, and landowning elites that are impacted by reforms impact to what extent tax reforms are implemented or not, and thus creates a barrier to tax collection (Schneider, 2013; Fairfield, 2015). These literatures demonstrate how exporting elites from specialized sectors have an ability to influence economic production, therefore impinging their interests could present major obstacles to domestic resource mobilization; as has been well documented, the owners of capital wield significant power (Przeworski and Wallerstein, 1988).

But the difficulties of raising tax in developing countries are not just attributed to actors whose interests have been negatively impacted; institutional-based accounts argue that weak and fragile tax administration is a barrier to tax collection. In this body of work, tax is approached as a technical and administrative process that focuses on the strength of a state's institutions as both a driver and constrainer of fiscal design (Torgler, 2005; Fjeldstad, 2005). In these literatures, weak institutional capacity has been conflated with poor tax administration and low levels of tax collection through a number of issues: partial taxpayer information (Vom Hau, Peres-Cajías, and Soifer, 2021); uneven application of tax rules; lack of enforcement (Brinks, Levitsky, and Murillo, 2020), and corruption and frequent political intervention, including through the use of mechanisms to bypass legislative processes (Fjeldstad, 2005; Von Haldenwang, 2010).

However, the extent to which these administrative challenges impact upon tax strategies is up for debate, with other authors instead pointing to the importance of politics. Bird (1989) argued that administrative limitations to tax more generally can be overcome if the political will is there to do so. And the importance of the politics of tax collection in developing countries is a conclusion that Nicolas Kaldor (1962) came to when he asked, '[W]ill underdeveloped countries learn to tax?'. Kaldor concluded that raising tax is difficult because tax is overwhelmingly political, a tax system reflects its political institutions, and 'political will' is the *sine qua non* in tax reform. And even if it is a time-consuming and costly process to implement tax reforms, if the political will is there to reform taxes, governments will find the capacity, a point that foregrounds the importance of politics within tax reform.

Therefore, whilst interest- and institutional-based approaches are load-bearing, they fail to take ideational factors and ideas fully into account when evaluating the driving forces of fiscal policy design and reform. But the politics of taxing for development are shaped by ideologies that are highly polarising. Castañeda and Doyle (2019: 597) highlight the influence of left- and right-wing political ideologies to tax strategies with divergent tax designs implemented to both 'pursue economic growth *and* satisfy governments core support'. Ideas of tax have historically reflected opposing ideas of the role of tax, with right-leaning governments choosing to place the tax burden on labour and the Left choosing to increase the tax over capital (Beramendi and Rueda, 2007). What this means is that, broadly speaking, a tax strategy for the Left based on lower indirect taxation in the form of consumption taxes but higher rates of direct taxes, is levied on income and corporation taxes. All of which is inverted as a strategy for right-wing governments with an expansion of indirect taxes while the direct tax burden is reduced (Castañeda and Doyle, 2019).

In governments from the Left, or what Hibbs (1977, 1992) and Alt (1985) define as social democratic governments, the interests of labour (which they are expected to promote) are associated with policies—including tax—both on the expenditure and the revenue side. Taxes are redistributed to lower socio-economic groups from 'upscale groups' that are associated with greater levels of wealth and control of the means of production (employers, upper-middle classes, and the business and financial community) (Rueda, 2005: 62). And in doing so, interventionalist states and class become embedded in these tax strategies because tax ideologies are inextricably linked with both the governments taxing business and financial elites and the tax strategy used to redistribute to popular classes. Navarro (2007) thus argues that not only is class conflict embedded in leftist tax strategies but also that class ideology becomes embedded in fiscal policies where right-wing governments have reduced taxes for the wealthiest in favour of an expanded tax burden across popular and middle classes. Introducing class ideology into development tax strategies paints an even more complex picture as questions of class become enmeshed with the conflict around state interventionism.

Extracting natural resource revenues

In natural resource-exporting countries, in situations where wage tax collection is low, export taxes become even more important to governments. Whilst indicative of a function of high levels of inequality that the state needs to redistribute, export taxes fit directly with the idea of an interventionalist state because expanded redistribution is mainly funded through taxation (Castañeda and Doyle, 2019), and greater redistribution is contingent on governments collecting higher levels of taxation from these resources. But taxing these resources represents a key challenge because the taxes fall—inevitably—over some of the most influential and powerful business and individual elites.

Historically, and notwithstanding the inevitable revenue generation from industries where governments lack other means to extract from specialized sectors, export taxes have been utilized widely across the Global South for a number of reasons: to encourage value added processing, to adjust domestic prices, as a diplomatic tool to align favourable trade, and as a mechanism to ensure food security (Richardson N., 2009; Shama, 2011). Moreover, they have been levied over a heterogenous basket of commodities across developing countries: gold in Uganda; ferrochrome and diamonds in South Africa; animal hides in Ethiopia; leather, wood, crude palm oil, and raw cocoa in Indonesia; unfinished agricultural products in Brazil; and minerals in China, all of which have attracted varying levels of export taxes (Tanzi, 2008). However, some of the most famous and polemic examples of their utilization are undoubtedly over grain exports in Argentina.

Along with Paraguay and Brazil, Argentina is one of the South American countries that is blessed with some of the most fertile lands on the planet, and therefore, its grain export contributions are both essential to global food chains and a key facet of its national economic development. Collectively, Latin American agricultural exports are so important globally that the Inter-America Development Bank (IDB) labelled Latin America (albeit using older terminology) the 'breadbasket of the world' because of both its position as the largest net food-exporting region in the world and its untapped potential for agricultural technological expansion and logistics modernization to support both regional consumption and global exports (Zeigler and Truitt Nakata, 2014).

Soybeans, maize, and wheat are some of the principal crops that are exported from across the continent (Hora, 2001). Whilst Brazil dominates production and export of soybeans, accounting for 44.7 per cent of the global market share, Argentina is the third largest exporter after the United States

(OEC, 2024). However, Argentina is the largest exporter of wheat in the region, which accounts for 7 per cent of the total global exports (75 per cent of which is exported to Brazil) (Colussi, Schnitkey, and Cabrini, 2022). This underlines the importance of these exports both to global food chains and to Latin American economies, while pointing towards the influence that agricultural elites may wield in these countries. In relation to export taxes, it is these agricultural producers and exporters who are the taxpayers that the government needs to extract from to support state spending, and it is this relationship that is tested through the levying of export tax strategies, especially when the prices of commodities are high.

Therefore, in times of commodity booms, where there are excess revenues to be captured, it is these export taxes that fund the redistributive type of state and exacerbate the conflict between opposing ideologies when the state intervenes in specialized export markets to redistribute to other sectors of society. And this is deeply political because this intervention is associated with left-wing governance, and historically opposing ideas generated by the tax reform have contributed towards political instability and resulted in failed tax policy implementation and consolidation. But rather than being solely a symptom of a Left-versus-Right governance, it is illustrative of a more profound development challenge: how to build a social consensus around natural resource revenues to fund national development and the purpose of the role of the state within these debates.

Export taxes in national development

In Argentina, the contention around export taxes that permeated into other sectors of society in 2008, thus becoming a barrier to domestic resource mobilization, raises important questions that are relevant beyond the case of Argentina to all natural resource export-led countries where states have little autonomy to extract through other measures: (i) why is raising revenue from export taxes so contentious, (ii) how do the export taxes fit in wider arguments of tax for development, (iii) how did the idea of export taxes permeate into other societal groups creating widespread polarization in 2008, and (iv) to what extent are these ideas of tax relevant when discussing tax collection challenges for development? In short whilst the OECD, IMF, and World Bank argue that tax is essential for development, what role do export taxes play in the challenge to increase the tax burden, especially in situations where commodity exports are a driver of economic development, and these commodities are benefiting from an upwards trajectory in their prices?

This book offers various answers to questions of the role of export taxes in national development by exploring the extreme but illustrative case of the use of export taxes in Argentina. In doing so, it illustrates the contention of raising revenues from influential industries where the state may lack sufficient autonomy to extract from them through other means such that it needs to rely on export taxes. I argue, first, that export taxes exemplify a long-standing development debate, one which speaks to class conflict and opposing visions of state versus markets across the Global South. In Argentina, this debate is grounded in the relationship between agrarian actors and governments seeking to extract from the sector, and I use this example to demonstrate the conflict that coalesces around export tax strategies. On the one hand, the taxes represent an unacceptable government intervention into an industry when there are excess revenues to be extracted when commodity prices are high; on the other, a legitimate taxation regime from a specialized and privileged sector to redistribute to other areas of the economy to support national development and social spending (Burchardt and Dietz, 2014). These taxes sit at the intersection of this debate, which extends beyond Argentina in a region that overwhelming remains integrated into the global political economy through natural resource exports.

Moreover, because the Argentine state lacks sufficient embedded autonomy into the rural sector, it lacks pathways through which to extract extraordinary revenues during times of high prices that do not involve the application of export taxes over producers and exporters. Therefore, the tax design becomes contentious because it represents a 'anti-business' and rent-seeking perspective that becomes embedded with state management of revenues from an influential sector. In doing so, it ignites the argument about who the owners of natural resources are in Latin American countries and what role the state plays in managing this capitalist relationship, what Gudynas (2016) calls the role of the *compensatory state*.

Second, in the early 2000s, the emergency context that Argentina found itself in bestowed a *temporary* legitimacy upon export taxes for actors in the rural sector. The emergency acted as a critical juncture, which opened additional space for policies that would have previously been thought of as inordinate to be implemented. Moreover, the relative fiscal consensus that was evident from 2002 to early 2008 was, in fact, not the normal state of affairs, but the conflict that erupted in March 2008 was a return to conflict over export taxes, which was a demonstration of a loss of legitimacy when the taxes were viewed as supporting an interventionalist form of redistributive state rather than being for crisis response. This shift became a fault line in this current iteration of export taxes.

Third, ideas of tax became conflated with contested conceptualizations of the state by becoming embedded within the highly polarizing state vision that the Kirchners built. Therefore, as the Kirchners' redistributive model was associated with export taxation, both facets became interlinked, and opposition to the interventionalist state model could not be separated from the opposition to export taxation, which translated into deepening political polarization. There was a confluence of factors that was driving political polarization, and sitting underneath this confluence was a fundamental dispute about who should have to pay tax and how much. It is a normative fault line between supporters of liberal and interventionalist types of state and economy and one that deepened with the imposition of Resolution N.125. But importantly, as an idea of export taxes permeated into, and polarized, other groups of society, it went beyond solely institutional and interest-based explanations to show a more complex picture where ideas of tax can play a significant role in accounting for the effectiveness of tax reforms. In doing so, it highlighted a development dilemma illustrative in low- and middle-income countries still dependent on natural resource commodity exports.

In short, this book demonstrates that the interventionalist role of the Kirchnerist state into economic and social life fed into a profound social and political cleavage, of which export taxes and Argentine tax-sharing mechanisms were the fault line. The book argues that first, there was a failure to create a social consensus around these tax ideas and then, second, this fed into a debate about contested state visions. This created resistance to wider tax collection and presented limitations to state spending and social redistribution. In this scenario, tax ideas generated conflict, as this occurred in a context where institutions had capacity to collect revenue and interests were not always impinged, but conflict ensued nonetheless. In presenting the salient role of export taxes and foregrounding their role in an ideological debate between state and markets and tax ideologies, it offers much needed insights into the extant political economy of development literatures where, in relation to taxation, impinged interests are the overwhelming framework through which scholars and policymakers have sought to explain challenges in domestic resource mobilization. By situating export taxes in an ideological debate of state versus markets, this book demonstrates a more complex picture than interests alone can fully account for.

In Argentina, this conflict of ideas occurred under a progressive government whose economic programme was underpinned by a particular set of favourable circumstances that led to increases in exports: strong commodity prices, high Chinese demand for Argentine agricultural products, and inflows of foreign direct investment. This progressive governance in

Argentina fitted squarely with the progressive shift throughout Latin America where left-of-centre governments increased intervention into natural resource-exporting industries (at varying levels). This, Gudynas (2016: 106) argued, demonstrated that while there were heterogenous explanatory theoretical perspectives and disparate political slogans, in practice, these governments agreed on 'a resource nationalism that should be in the hands of the state'. Therefore, the push back against export taxes that were funding this progressive governance, which was endemic within the region at the time, was a push back against this idea of resource nationalism or what was also termed neo-developmentalism because the state was using natural resource revenues to try and actively improve citizen's lives and development outcomes.

But the polarization surrounding state intervention and redistribution in Argentina isn't new. Historical embeddedness of opposing ideas about commodity-led development has meant that contestation around opposing state visions runs deep on both sides of the debate—one with its deepest roots in colonialism (Giraudo and Grugel, 2022). The lasting impact of Western European colonization has framed historical development narratives throughout Latin America, where landed elites that control the means of production have sought to demonstrate their relevance to the nation's prosperity and its future (Hora, 2001), a prosperity that would be detrimentally impacted if their profits were taxed. These relationships, which played out in Argentina post 1940s between landowners in the fertile Argentine Pampas and progressive Peronist governments, have influenced ideas that have endured and influenced political economic narratives well into the twenty-first century, a point that gains academic support from Sanchez (2006) and Tanzi (1997), who argue that the ideational environment of any historical period has overwhelmingly influenced tax policy reform.

Key arguments

These answers are grouped together into two substantive arguments. The first argument that the book offers is that the tax revolt that was instigated by the variable tax mechanism in 2008 actually returned relations between producers and exporters in the rural sector and governments seeking to extract from them to their normal state of contentious affairs. It argues that the crisis situation that beset Argentina post 2001 IMF debt default created a temporary tax consensus and fragile peace. The crisis legitimized the export tax strategy for agrarian producers for a number of reasons: the crisis context meant that producers were aware of their position in Argentina's most specialized industry and its role in helping rebuild the state following deep economic and political instability. Moreover, because commodity prices began their early 2000s super cycle, producers who were taxed were able to ameliorate their economic position somewhat because the growth in commodity prices was offsetting the tax lost to the government. So, whilst initially the taxes were perceived as necessary, as they continued to be levied and importantly not increased, they did not impinge any further on the economic interests of the producers.

It argues that factors that have historically called into question the legitimacy of tax strategies in Argentina and the wider Latin American region and have caused conflict—procedural legality of tax reforms, the value of services that the tax purchases, and a tax burden falling over a more concentrated pool of taxpayers—were temporarily put aside because of the crisis situation with which Argentina was faced. Whilst there is a range of competing interests from heterogenous groups and associations in the Argentine countryside, overwhelmingly—and fitting with the moto of the oldest and most prestigious of the Argentine rural associations, the *Sociedad Rural Argentina* (Argentine Rural Society) *'cultivar el suelo es sirvir a la patria'* ('working the land is serving the fatherland')—the producers and exporters accepted their role in national response to emergency with little resistance to the taxation strategies that were levied under the emergency government of Eduardo Duhalde and remained levied under the subsequent presidency of Néstor Kirchner.

However, while the government had legitimacy to tax exports for emergency response, when the emergency context diminished and was left behind, but the taxes were increased to support an expansion of an interventionalist state through the augmentation of social policies and welfare redistribution, the legitimacy was abruptly lost, and questions of the role of the state in markets once again came to the fore. For many producers, the taxes were now viewed as correcting problems of growth that were needed for expansive redistribution, a point that was unacceptable to the producers. Opposition to the suggested export tax reform was so strong that it managed to unite the historically opposing interests of landowners' associations and cooperatives from across the sector as it was universally viewed as rent-seeking and opportunistic on behalf of the government because it occurred at the same time as strong growth of international soybean prices and strong Chinese demand (Giraudo and Grugel, 2022).

The level of dissatisfaction is difficult to significantly convey, but following five years of a tax strategy that overwhelmingly placed the burden on agricultural producers and their exports, Resolution N.125 completely unified previously fragmented actors across the sector, who argued that the tax was no longer legitimate because it had ceased to be used for supporting emergency response but instead was being used to support social redistribution and the wider vision of the Kirchnerist state.

The second and interrelated argument that the book presents is that an idea of what this tax represented became embedded in the model of state that the government was building and became inseparable from the government and wider government policies. Therefore, the contention that the taxes engendered within the agricultural sector extended beyond the sector; not because it impacted upon the interests of actors in other sectors but because of an idea of what the tax—and crucially, the redistribution—represented: a state intervening into markets and redistributing to its core supporters.

Export taxes are emblematic of Kirchnerist governance, but they became viewed very differently over the decade by supporters and opponents of the Kirchners. They were simultaneously evidence of an extractive form of taxation for actors in the rural sector and conservative politicians, whilst also being symbolic of state funding of a generous programme of subsidies and welfare distribution for government supporters. Export taxes were politically polarizing precisely because they aggravated and amplified wider socio-economic tensions and conflict that then became embedded in debates about the Kirchnerist tax design. These socio-economic tensions themselves added to growing political polarization. Therefore, the debate spilled over from one centred on just tax to becoming muddled in a wider political and economic debates where the statist model of Kirchnerismo itself became the source of conflict. Taxes became part of a bigger political cleavage that polarized politics and hardened positions.

In this light, the tension around export taxes permeated into other sectors of society and indeed into other areas of Kirchnerist policies because of an idea of what the taxes were associated with. Tension was underpinned by a politically polarizing reading of the *retenciones* by both supporters and opponents of the government. The increase in export taxes became the fault line around which wider political polarization hardened because it reflected fundamentally different views of the role of the state. As a result, tax became embroiled in wider redistributional conflicts. The debate around tax thus became more than a tax conflict between the Kirchners and agricultural producers. It spread out to other social sectors and was accompanied by a regrouping and hardening of the Kirchnerist opposition.

Export taxes became the cleavage around which a new regrouping of the right coalesced. We cannot therefore consider the *retenciones* as a separate or technical narrow fiscal issue because they are so embedded within Kirchnerismo. Tax remained a prominent focus of attack for the growing opposition, along with the model of the Kirchnerist state because they were considered part of the same argument. Conversely, for the government, tax was defended because it made its redistributional policies possible. However, sitting underneath this expanded argument is the fact that, once again, export tax questions had not been addressed. The question of the legitimation of this taxation model was not fully resolved: no consensus was formed, either with the sector in question or with opposition actors. They therefore remained unresolved and remained contentious.

Methodological approach

Empirically, the principal aims of the book are to foreground the role of export tax collection to national development under the Kirchner presidencies in Argentina (2003–2015). Theoretically, the book seeks to critically engage with dominant political economic accounts and contribute to wider debates about tax and development by demonstrating the multifaceted ideological components of export taxes, which build from interest-based accounts. As such, the book is situated within political economy of tax and development debates in order to explore the interplay between global and national economic systems and politics through the lens of state society relationships, using Argentina as a case study. In particular, the book examines the tensions between the fiscal needs of the state (especially under a government committed to increased social spending); the limitations of a tax and development system based on the predominance of export production; and competing social, economic, and political ideas and interests in relation to tax and spending. Therefore, the interactions between state and non-state actors are central to the book's arguments, which in turn guided the methodological approach. As it approaches tax ideas, tax ideology, and questions of tax legitimacy, a qualitative analysis is employed throughout the book, which is supported by the exploration of a wide range of statistical data within a mixed-methods research design.

By combining elements of qualitative and quantitative data analysis in a methodological approach, the research design moves towards the overarching purpose of increasing the breadth and depth of understanding of the research project (Schoonenboom and Johnson, 2017). Mixed methods enable the development of rich insights into certain works that would not be possible by solely utilizing qualitative or quantitative methods (Venkatesh,

Brown, and Bala, 2013). In this sense, it enables triangulation of data and provides a wider optic to a research project. Ideally, the researcher is looking for a 'convergence of the data collected by all methods to enhance the credibility of the research findings' (Hesse-Biber, 2010: 3) or contradictions and tensions between data sources that might require analysis and discussion.

This combination of methods is typical of those utilized in the field of political economy of development, with a whole tradition of qualitatively led political economy of development research supported by macroeconomic statistical data. Phillips (2017) highlights that in conducting political economy research, she has

> Sought to embrace what might be described as a 'magpie' approach which involves pursuing a variety of methods for collecting information taking insights from wherever they are to be found and relying on the cumulative results of research for building my account of the political economy of [. . .]
>
> **(Phillips, 2017)**

This research utilized a cumulative approach to data collection. It does lead with qualitative data collection and draws from a variety of quantitative data sources in a 'magpie' approach, and through the process of triangulation, it builds a political economic account to answer the research questions. Therefore, in doing so, it joins a long tradition of qualitative research supported by quantitative data. Triangulation of data helps increase the persuasiveness of evidence, and it can elaborate understanding and confirms the accuracy of many data sources (Downward and Mearman, 2007). By utilizing triangulation of both quantitative and qualitative data collection, the research is able to test the validity of qualitative insights, or it is able to use qualitative insights as preparation for quantitative work to 'elucidate a phenomenon in as much detail as possible' (Danermark, Ekström, and Karlsson, 2019: 153).

Qualitative methods were employed to explore understandings, perceptions, and interpretations that enabled the research to engage with the underpinning reasons and rationales behind the nature of the tax regime and compliance with it. To do this, a series of semi-structured elite interviews were carried out across two periods of field work in Buenos Aires in Spring 2019 and Spring/Summer 2023. Interviews are essential to mixed-methods research design (King, 2004). First, they allow the researcher to access primary data, which may challenge 'official' government narratives or accounts and therefore highlight areas for analysis and discussion. Second, they are fundamental to gain more insights into underlying contexts, inter-governmental workings, and state–society relationships, which would enrich the research (Lilleker, 2003; Morris, 2009). Furthermore, the insights gained from interviews can make up for any scarcity of information and limitations in documentary evidence (Tansey, 2007).

Quantitatively, the research uses government data documentation that includes archival tax policy documents, national accounts, and treasury records demonstrating changes to tax design and the results of their implementation. These documents were analysed against wider macroeconomic figures from a range of national and international sources. While this quantitative data is used extensively throughout the book, I did not carry out any advanced quantitative analysis; instead, these macroeconomic indicators were used to trace the impact of the tax design and alongside the semi-structured interviews to assess the different rationales behind this.

Quantitative data were utilized and compared to build up a framework to understand the effects that tax had following reforms and the level at which the reforms actually took place. A descriptive design enabled the research to employ longitudinal methods, including triangulation and process tracing, to evaluate the data (Odell, 2001). It was not only official documents that were created by the national tax agency or central bank or by other official government institutions that were analysed, but also data contained in reports that may have been collected for another reason were also analysed through the triangulation process, highlighting the potential value of secondary data to this research (Masefield, Megaw, and Barlow, 2020; Omukuti, Megaw, and Barlow, 2021).

Structure of the book

This book is divided into eight substantive chapters. This introduction is followed by a presentation of the theoretical framework that critically foregrounds the role of export taxes in national development and the contention that they engender in the state-versus-market development debate (Chapter 2). First, I ground the book in a theoretical development discussion that explores classical development studies literatures, analysing why tax matters for development. It then introduces the role of the state and draws from Gudynas's conceptualization of the 'compensatory state', situating export taxes within this debate. It highlights the contested role of the state within capitalist production in these discussions and demonstrates how export taxes can be understood in relation to them. It builds from dominant frameworks in extant political economy of tax for development literatures that is underpinned by solid, interest-based accounts grounded in materialist arguments and utilizes these as a launching point to demonstrate how visions of export taxes can crystallize around a contested vision of state, which, in turn, can conceptually impact upon tax strategy design and implementation. To do so, it draws from literatures in historical sociology and new fiscal sociology that highlight the importance of the bargaining process between state and society around tax where tax legitimacy is a central tenet that influences tax design. It therefore approaches legitimacy in a critical manner and explains why legitimacy is important conceptually, even in situations where governments may have strong mandates and there are institutional pathways to push through reforms, but bargaining is essential nonetheless.

In Chapter 3, I historically analyse the challenges that leaders have faced when trying to raise tax in resource-rich countries in the Global South. The chapter contextualizes the experiences of developing countries that are heavily reliant on revenues from natural resource exports and concomitant tax systems characterized by high levels of evasion and informality, which therefore rely on programmes of indirect taxation. It shows how the utilization of commodity taxes have their deepest roots with colonial narratives, and it foregrounds the importance of tax bargaining within these narratives. The chapter demonstrates how this bargaining process not only helped shaped wealth and power but also framed the ideological politics of domestic resource mobilization. By exploring how, historically, ideas and the contentious politics of tax have become associated with a vision of state, crucially, it sets the scene for the presentation of the politics of tax challenges in Argentina, whose empirical case study will be introduced in a historical context in Chapter 4.

In Chapter 4, I empirically introduce the Argentine case study, it traces the evolution of export taxes and political tensions that emerged during the mid- and late-twentieth century to finance the Argentine state (1946–2001). It introduces the deep political cleavage that exists around Peronism in Argentina and shows how ideas of export taxation over the rural sector and wider extraction mechanisms became synonymous with the type of redistributive state left-wing Peronist governments were trying to build. The chapter argues that opposition to government price fixing and export taxes was characterized by a number of factors, among them being interest group politics, a failure to build social consensus around the tax design, opposition to the erosion of political influence, and as a symptom of more profound disagreements about what national development should look like. It traces the politics of these taxes until 2001, and in doing so, it grounds the theoretical and more general historical narratives discussed in the previous two chapters in an Argentine political economy of development challenge.

The following chapter, Chapter 5, explores the process of both building and losing legitimacy around an export tax design that was initially presented as a response to emergency but whose rationale changed in the eyes of those over whom the burden fell. Ideas of export taxes in this period were temporarily seen as legitimate because of the crisis, and this period represents a temporary consensus, both around the tax and the vision of the state that was being built. However, the chapter introduces that fact that when the context of emergency faded, the sustainability of export taxes began to be questioned by actors in the rural sector because ideas of tax were no longer for crisis response but for building the capacity for an interventionalist state. This chapter tells the story of a seminal moment in the political economy of development in Argentina and of growing opposition to Kirchnerist governance. The chapter argues that opposition to export tax rising out of an emergency context was so strong that it enabled associations within a normally fragmented sector to bridge traditional differences and come together to instigate a cohesive response, which then transcended the sector to envelop other societal groups, exacerbating a deep political cleavage.

The wider political economic implications for the loss of export tax legitimacy are the focus of the following chapter, Chapter 6, which explores how the government responded to the loss of export tax resources and what this meant for the expansive social redistribution programme that Cristina Kirchner had been elected to deliver less than a year earlier. It also engages with uneven redistribution of export tax revenues and demonstrates how existing mechanisms to redistribute export taxes fuelled the conflict around tax ideas. To do so, it engages with the *Coparticpación* mechanism through which tax is collected and shared, and through which concessions were made post tax revolt. It explores the tensions that this mechanism created between business and regional political actors in wealthier agrarian provinces and the federal government in Buenos Aires. It does so to demonstrate how perceptions of this tax mechanism fed into the conflict around ideas of state, especially when this mechanism was deemed to be underpinning ideas of interventionalist state capacity that the government of Cristina Kirchner was building.

How these contentious ideas around tax crystallized around an idea of state is the substantive focus of Chapter 7. This chapter extends the tax and development discussion beyond tax. It highlights how politically polarizing and conflict-inducing tax can be and, in turn, highlights how this polarization can impact upon wider tax for development questions. The chapter shows that these taxes became politically polarizing not only because they were the cause of conflicts over material interests but also because of opposing ideas of development and, more explicitly, the state's role in this development.

The debate spilled over from one centred on just tax to becoming muddled in a wider political and economic debates where the statist model of Kirchnerist governance itself became the source of conflict. Taxes became part of a bigger political cleavage that polarized politics and hardened positions, which led ultimately to political change.

The final chapter presents the conclusions of the book. It draws together the findings from the earlier chapters and set out what we can learn from the case study of Argentina and how ideas of tax of tax should be considered when thinking about tax designs for development. The conclusion highlights the wider implications for development that tax ideas can have, especially in natural resource export-dependent economies with a powerful landed elite and where the role of the state is contentious. The book concludes that some of the limitations of the export tax regime was underpinned by a politically polarizing reading of the export taxes by both supporters and opponents of the government. The increase in export taxes became the fault line around which wider political polarization hardened because it reflected fundamentally different views of the role of the state. As a result, tax became embroiled in wider redistributional conflicts. We cannot therefore consider the export taxes as a separate or technical narrow fiscal issue because they are so embedded within ideas of Kirchnerismo and state interventionism.

2
Theorizing Tax Challenges in Resource-Rich Developing Countries

Introduction

This chapter explores the ideational relationship between natural resource exports, export taxes, state interventionism, and the politics of redistribution. It builds a theoretical framework that accounts for how tax ideologies around export taxes and redistribution can generate wider societal tensions than just in the exporting sectors over which they are levied and become a barrier to raise tax for development. Mainstream theories that offer explanations for the challenges to raise tax in the Global South have overwhelmingly argued that negatively impacted interests of political and business elites and weak institutional capacity are the principal barriers to mobilizing tax resources. Drawing from a materialist school of thought, scholars have pointed to the motivations and desires of potential taxpayers to hold on to as much of their money as possible, to protect their interests (Schneider, 2004; Centeno and Portes, 2006; Fairfield, 2015; Ondetti, 2015, 2017). They see detrimentally impacted interests as being *the* overarching rationale for creating tensions between taxpayers and governments seeking to raise revenues from them.

Other theoretical explanations for low levels of tax collection in developing countries have focused on institutional weaknesses and a lack of state capacity to collect tax (Haggard and Kauffman, 1994; Torgler, 2005; Fjeldstad, 2005; Brinks, Levitsky, and Murillo, 2020). However, from both these perspectives, the focus is grounded either in the desires of taxpayers to avoid paying taxes or in insufficient administrative processes to mobilize domestic resources. Less weight is afforded to the politics of the role of the state, the ideological cleavages that tax can generate, and how opposing visions about the mechanisms the state uses to intervene into socio-economic life through tax shapes these politics. Moreover, much less scholarly attention has been afforded to the ideological cleavages that exist around commodity tax regimes that governments have utilized to extract revenue from natural resource exports—when these are the principal drivers of economic

Taxing for Development. Matt Barlow, Oxford University Press. © Matt Barlow (2025).
DOI: 10.1093/9780198923220.003.0002

production—when governments lack autonomy to benefit from 'commodity price booms' through other mechanisms.

This chapter builds a theoretical framework that enables the book to redress some of the theoretical lacuna in a number of literatures: political economy of taxation, development studies, and post-neoliberal and neo-extractivism literatures. It both highlights the contentious role of export taxes and demonstrates how export taxes can be viewed ideologically. And because of this, it shows how contested tax ideologies have the power to generate tensions that extend beyond interest- and institutional-based explanations for low levels of tax collection to embed tax ideology in a conflict of state versus markets when taxes are rejected by other societal groups over which the taxes may not be levied, but tension is generated in that group nonetheless.

The chapter proceeds through an exploration of the study of taxation and its role in the very creation of the state, before exploring questions of taxation in development through a focus on export-dependent countries. It then introduces theoretical arguments of extractivism and raising tax in natural resource-dependent Latin American countries. It concludes by situating the theoretical debate in Latin America in the early 2000s, in the period that forms the theoretical and empirical core of this book, what is commonly understood economically, socially, and politically as post-neoliberalism (Grugel and Riggirozzi, 2012).

Why tax matters: State-building

The role of tax for development has been fundamental to scholars working across disciplines in economics, the social sciences, and humanities. Before being directly conflated with economic and social development, the transformative processes of taxation have been associated strongly with the very formation of the state and state-building. The fundamental role of taxation in state-building has long attracted academic attention in extant world history and historical sociology literatures. In her seminal work, which builds from Mann's (1986) characterization of a state as the centralized regulation of all important aspects of territorially bound social life, Levi (1988: 1) argued that 'the history of state revenue production is the history of the evolution of the state'. Within this centralized regulation, tax compliance, understood as the ability of the state to persuade or coerce citizens to comply with taxation frameworks, is seen as a measure of state capacity, a core link within a positive cycle where tax is needed to increase state autonomy and chances of survival, and states need capacity to collect tax (Mann, 1984, 1986; Skocpol,

1985; Tilly, 1985). Tax therefore supports the basic functions of an effective state (Prichard, 2010) and is a key indicator of what the state can do:

> A state's means of raising and deploying financial resources tell us more than could any other single factor about its existing (and immediately potential) capacities to create or strengthen state organisations, to employ personnel, to co-opt political support, to subsidise economic enterprises, and to fund social programs.
>
> **(Skocpol, 1985: 17)**

Scholars in world history, historical sociology, political science, international relations, and development studies see taxation as essential for governments to finance expenditure (Burgess and Stern, 1993), which in turn lays the foundations for growth and development (Prichard, 2010). In these fields of study, tax is broadly understood as a tool for transformations and transitions across societies, cultures, and periods. In some, it has held a dominant and defining role. In world history literatures, war, and the need to respond has been embedded in the very creation of the state (Tilly, 1985; Mann, 1988; Moore, 2004; Fjeldstad and Moore, 2007). Schumpeter (1991) argued that the growing expenses of warfare acted as the foundations of the modern state (Schmidt, 2006). The general argument surrounding this perspective is that powerholders in the pursuit of war initiated the extraction of resources from the populations over which they had control, and in the process, the framework of the modern state was created.

Supporting this argument is Tilly's influential (1985) 'war made the state' claim. In his paper, he argued that the state creation was a consequence of going to war with the goal of overcoming competitors and thus expanding power and/or territory. Tilly posited that war and the need for taxation came first, with the modern state being a consequence of this. The financing of these conflicts, first through coercive methods and later through taxation and borrowing, became embedded in the formation of states (Tilly, 1985). While it may be self-evident to say that wars required financing and that tax was central to the mobilization of domestic resources, the crisis context that conflict engenders led to declines in social constraints, which allowed opportunities for further revenue extraction and bestowed legitimacy on the tax strategy when war was the rationale: taxation was legitimized by the threat of external violence, a point that was foregrounded by Centeno (1997: 1567): 'Wars generate greater needs for resources whilst also providing temporary declines in the state's social constraints.'

And the concept of legitimacy of taxation is a major conceptual focus of historical sociologists and new fiscal sociologists who, in significant corpora of works, argue that through taxes, the infrastructural power of the state intersects with society (Bräutigam, 2008) in a delicate relationship where both sides seek to leverage the balance in their favour (Martin, Mehrotra, and Prassad, 2009). Whilst these concepts in relation to development are explored in greater depth later in the chapter, this bargaining process between state and society, where the state amasses revenues but spends and redistributes this on behalf of society, is critical to understanding the challenges that governments face when trying to raise taxes because of a complex sociological relationship that can impact how taxes are levied; who bears the burden; and ultimately how it affects state, society, and economic relationships.

But while world history and historical sociology scholars have debated the role of taxation in state-building and state–society relations, in what is a somewhat axiomatic statement, tax has been central to political economic authors, who have explored its utilization and impact in capitalist production and development. Some of the earlier seminal works within political economy sought to unpack the concepts of labour, capital, class, 'the state', and (directly or indirectly) tax: Adam Smith's *An Inquiry into the Nature and Causes of the Wealth of Nations* (1776), Karl Marx's *The Economic and Philosophical Manuscripts* (1844, published 1932) and Max Weber's *The Protestant Ethic and the Spirit of Capitalism* (1904–1905). Although Smith, Marx, and Weber had different views on the specific role of tax—Smith arguing that it would be a catalyst for ingenuity on behalf of capitalists who seek to protect profits, Marx viewing it as both a tool of proletariat oppression (a burden on the poor) and as a trigger for political change (Ireland, 2019), and Weber concentrating on the importance of the state bureaucracy to collect this—where they did agree was that taxation was intrinsic to the state (as we currently understand it), and it had a fundamental role in economic development. These capitalist development narratives and critiques demonstrated a shift in the understanding about the role of tax across disciplines, but they highlighted that the role of interests, albeit different interests—material, ideal, and religious (in this case, the interests of capitalists and capital)—was a prominent factor in tax debates. But the interests of capitalists would crystallize into a concept that would dominate a rich field of scholarly enquiry seeking to explain for challenges in raising the tax burden.

Taxing the interests of capitalists

Interests have held a dominant position throughout social science disciplines, especially as a critique of enlightenment scholars, who argued that men were, above all, rational thinkers, but when it comes to interests, intellectual enquiry has pointed to desires and motivations as a driver that supersedes rationality, which (when conflated to tax) relates to desires and motivations to avoid paying it (Vaisey, 2009).

Much of nineteenth-century social thought—through different approaches—was pervaded by the notion that the capacity of men to reason and act rationally was ascended by their selfishness and desire to protect and enhance their own interests. For Schopenhauer and Nietzsche, this came down to men's will, a will that drives men to desire 'everything for themselves and will do anything to possess this'. For Schopenhauer, who wrote about this will in relation to power, it challenged the notion of Western rationality and the rational choices of men because the will for power was greater (Janaway, 1998), whilst, for Nietzsche, the supremacy of will surpassed intellect (Nietzsche, 1977). This anti-rationalist tradition was further drawn upon by Weber in his essays exploring the sociology of religion. In these, he argued that above all else, material and ideal interests govern men's conduct (Lizardo and Stoltz, 2018). Whilst the debate about the distinction between Weber's ideal and material interests remains an enduring element of his theoretical legacy (Swidler and Arditi, 1994; Swedberg, 2003), Weber utilized the concept of interests to explore the passion that is involved even in the most esoteric religious beliefs. He argued that it was not *only* because of economic interests that influences men's conduct but also because ideals and beliefs explain situations where economic interests failed to offer answers (Swedberg, 2018). He argued that motives and ideals can shape interests.

This was Weber's own critique of Marx's concept of material interests that had formed the foundations for a long tradition of Marxian strands of historical sociology. For Marx, material interests were understood as economic interests or, more specifically, as both greed and the accumulation of riches within the ruling classes (Marx and Engels, 1970), and critically, the pursuit of the ruling classes' interests would deny the proletariat its own material interests. Moreover, these material interests in this Marxian tradition are the drivers of capitalist activity that has historically created the foundations and framed all institutions of human society: government, religion, class. So, in a materialist perspective, interests are underpinned by motivations, which, as Parsons (1937) argued, inspired motivations of action meaning that actors do things because they *want something* or *want to keep something* that they like, and desires and wants are drivers before cognition and action. Therefore, in relation to taxation, interests would be centred in the economic motivations and desires of taxpayers to keep more of their money rather than paying this to the state apparatus. Thus, these motivations to keep more income to protect interests become a barrier to governments that try to implement tax reforms because they are not motivated to pay these. But there are pathways that governments can, and have, used to ameliorate for interests being negatively impacted through taxation, principally through the value of the tax spend. Whilst initially in feudal England, very early tax procured protection (Ames and Rapp, 1977), the evolution of taxation meant that in capitalist societies, tax bought access to public service provision, including, latterly, a welfare state.

In developed countries, the provision of these services is supported by relatively well-established and professionalized tax systems that can broadly permeate into society to tax the interests of a range of businesses and workers at varying levels in order to generate the domestic fiscal resources required to finance state obligations and provide these services. Moreover, they are less contentious because of the significant reach of the tax collection system, which means that the burden of taxation (and therefore the impinged interests) are, theoretically, more diffused (Von Haldenwang, 2008). Moreover, fiscally mature states have managed to achieve a higher degree of legitimacy around taxes whereby interests that have been impacted are ameliorated through what the tax purchases.

Legitimizing taxes

And it was the essential role of taxation that underpins the provision of public goods provided by the state on behalf of society that led Bräutigam (2002: 1) to argue that

> Raising revenue is the most basic task of the state. Before a state can protect its citizens, before it can provide justice or administer a bureaucracy, it needs to raise money. Through its key role as the tie that binds the ruler and the ruled, taxation supports representation, accountability, and state capacity.

How states raise these revenues through this tie—binding the ruler and the ruled—has been the focus of literatures in historical and new fiscal sociology, which have explored the evolution and characteristics of the distinct institutional arrangements through which tax collection and compliance are implemented as well as the conflicts and social relations associated with these arrangements, given that 'states tax societies but they do not tax all their citizens equally' (Bräutigam, 2008: 25). How governments legitimize taxation strategies is an important analytical question because it directly impacts upon tax-level compliance; tax evasion; and ultimately, the fiscal revenues that are available to the state. Therefore, how to create a tax system that is legitimate and complied with is both essential and complex. It is a multi-faceted challenge that is shaped by the opposing views of legitimate for what and legitimate for whom.

Tax can generate links of accountability between taxpayers and rulers that impact on how responsive governments are (Paler, 2013). An increased dependence on the part of governments on taxation generates a *governance dividend* between the state and taxpayers. This dividend describes a state–society relationship that is constructed vis-à-vis negotiation between governments and society that coalesces around what citizens expect to receive for their taxes: what the taxes purchase. In this sense, in democracies, society has a significant influence over higher domestic tax collection and its utilization by the state, a point Moore (2004: 310) highlights is achieved with substantial 'quasi-voluntary compliance'. Levi (1988) also points to the importance of the fact that this quasi-voluntary compliance does not involve coercive tenets of tax compliance but that it only occurs in a situation when taxpayers have confidence that (i) rulers keep their side of the bargain and (ii) other taxpayers keep theirs. Tax becomes embedded within the state–society contract as it concerns politics and power and the manner in which authority is exercised in a nation through its formal and informal institutions. This embedded taxation relationship and state–society contract is fundamental to tax reform within classic development literatures and in more contemporary development writing; however, the fiscal contract is multi-layered and complex because vertical exchanges between state and citizens do not affect all citizens equally, and some groups share a greater responsibility for the burden. Therefore, when the state intervenes in the socio-economic lives of its citizens through taxation, the collection and redistribution of resources impacts societal groups unevenly and therefore has contrasting impacts.

In this sense, taxation is central to the relationship that states have with society; a perspective argued by Martin, Mehrotra, and Prasad (2009), for whom taxation 'enmeshes us in the web of generalised reciprocity that constitutes modern society', a relationship of necessity as the state depends on taxes to function, which are spent on behalf of society—members of which are the recipients of public goods and services. As such, this relationship can generate contention because government officials and taxpayers are expected to try and 'renegotiate this relationship to their advantage' (Martin, Mehrotra, and Prasad, 2009: 3–4). Therefore, whilst taxation constitutes a key nexus between states and society, it is a nexus that is far from equal, and because of this, it can be counted upon to generate tensions. Academic studies (Mann,

1984, 1988; Levi, 1988; Bräutigam and Knack, 2004; Bräutigam, Fjeldstad, and Moore, 2008) have explored how different types of state manage these tensions and are able to adopt more legitimate and efficient forms of tax collection, recognizing that the same taxes will not be viewed as legitimate and efficient by all groups. In general terms, theories of tax compliance can be distinguished between contractual or vertical 'fiscal exchange' models, and horizontal 'political community' ones (Von Haldenwang, 2010; D'Arcy, 2011). Fiscal exchange models argue that taxpayer compliance increases when they expect the state to deliver services and public goods in return for their taxes. A classic argument here is that representative government emerged as part of the democratic legitimation of the fiscal contract, which allowed the state to appear as 'fairer' vis-à-vis its citizens and collect more from more people (Levi, 1988). At the same time, democracies are expected to tax more efficiently because they trade taxation for more inclusive forms of representation (Ross, 2004; Bräutigam, 2008).

The horizontal exchange models argue that the willingness of citizens to pay taxes is not only influenced by the level of trust in the state or government but also by levels of horizontal solidarity existing among 'tax citizens'. In this situation, taxpayers would be willing to accept a higher tax burden if considering taxes benefits 'in-groups' in the political community, and tax systems that strengthen social cohesion and equality would be expected to enjoy higher levels of legitimacy (Lieberman, 2001; D'Arcy, 2011). Legitimacy is thus an important concept for understanding tax compliance, but it is also a concept that can become complex when building these solidarity bonds becomes disputed in terms of political actors and affiliations and also opposing interest groups. This point is one that decants further into a 'solidarity hypothesis', which highlights that social heterogeneity can curtail political possibilities in terms of redistribution policies as it requires extending sympathy to outsider welfare recipients. So, the high trust and solidarity that is not extended to migrant communities may require active state policies to address this weakness in solidarity (Ervasti and Hjerm, 2012). This and other factors can cause limitations to legitimacy-building.

Tax legitimacy has historically been associated with three arguments. First, fiscal policy that strengthens social cohesion garners higher levels of legitimacy. Second, dependence on taxes (in place of other revenues) will eventually lead to fiscal contractualism between governments and citizens. Finally, a tax system based on transparency, technical capacity, and procedural legality may garner its own level of legitimacy (Von Haldenwang, 2010).

However, in relation to tax reforms in developing countries that have low levels of tax collection, legitimizing taxes becomes even more complex because of structural factors where wealth is heavily concentrated in extractive and natural resource-exporting sectors and the value of what the tax purchases is deemed to be less than in developed countries, with partial and fragmented public services along with lower levels of transparency in tax reform processes; all of which shape fiscal tensions that can impede domestic resource mobilization and associate developing countries with poor tax collection capacity. What this all means is that while there was an association of a professionalized tax system with 'developed' country status, conversely, poor tax collection and weak tax systems became an indicator of underdevelopment across the Global South, a point that gained prominence with economists, political economists, and development scholars at the end of World War II.

Theorizing tax for development

Conceptual tax discussions fed into a growing number of more contemporary development theories that accompanied the end of World War II and the fall of European colonialism that, post 1945, generated a 'busy but fashionable field of intellectual enquiry' (Payne and Phillips, 2010: 56), a period understood widely as the 'Golden Age' of development theories (Payne and Phillips, 2010: 56). As part of this scholarship, it gave to birth to modernization theory, which held that underdeveloped countries are proceeding along a linear process that developed countries have previously traversed to attain 'developed' status through a shift from agricultural and natural resource exporters to industrialization (Bernstein, 1971; Lerner, 1968; Bock, 1979; Ellis and Biggs, 2001). At the time, the process of industrialization was understood by many as an engine that would push developing countries from natural resource exporters towards 'modernity' and was an indicator of developed status. Kaldor (1962: 412) wrote that an inability to tax progressively was a rubric of underdevelopment: 'the shortfall in revenue is thus largely a reflection of failure to tax the wealthier sectors of the community effectively'. And this point of efficient and progressive taxation as development is embedded in Rostow's (1959) seminal paper, 'The Stages of Economic Growth', where one of modernization theory's most famous protagonists highlights, in the penultimate of his five stages, that

> the choices made by the society are determined by the existence of independently powerful political and social processes where effective influence is not weighted by property ownership; and, notably when maturity is reached, these

> areas of influence help determine how, and in what sequence, the resources of the mature economy will be used, including the possibility of a welfare state based on progressive taxation.
>
> **(Rostow, 1959: 15)**

Therefore, not only was development understood in the Global South in terms of industrialization, but also, in modernization theory, economic maturity was viewed in terms of a professionalized tax system that could first collect tax through a wide (and low) tax base and then redistribute these revenues to support the provision of public services.

However, at the same time, a more critical view of development was taken by scholars who argued that rather than developing countries being further behind in a linear temporal process towards modernity as modernization theory would argue, instead, development theories needed to take into account the negative relationship between developed and developing states, which led to situations of underdevelopment (Roxborough, 1979). This critical approach created the conceptual space for the theories of structuralism, neo-Marxism, dependency theory, and world systems theory to critique the core foundations of modernization theory's temporal and linear appraisal of development (Payne and Phillips, 2010), seeking instead to offer answers for poor levels of development through concentration on the exploitative relationships between developed and developing countries, which coalesced around the supply of natural resources to developed states and low levels of industrialization in developing states.

The process of moving from natural resource exporters to industrialized status was not rejected by these theories as a pathway to modernity and development, but they offered critical analysis of why industrialization was problematic for developing countries by focusing on the uneven relationship between developed and developing countries and offered policy prescriptions to address this imbalance. Beginning in Latin America, before finding purchase in resource-rich states across Africa (Mendes, Bertella, and Teixeira, 2014), the perspective of an overreliance on natural resource exports, coupled with poor international terms of trade, led the Argentine economist and former head of the Argentine Central Bank, Raúl Prebisch (1996) to champion a theoretical pathway to break dependence on this system of primary resource exportation through his own and latterly the Economic Commission of Latin America's (ECLA's) and the Economic Commission for Latin America and the Caribbean's (ECLAC's—*Comisión Económica para América Latina y el Caribe* (CEPAL) in Spanish) advocation of import substitution industrialization (ISI).

Structuralism was the term deployed to this period of industrial development during the period from 1950 to the 1970s, which offered an alternative to the vicissitudes of neoclassical economics' specialization in natural resource exports and instead promulgated for industrialization through the promotion of the domestic production of previously imported manufactured goods. Bértola and Ocampo (2012) argue that in the structuralist school of thought, following an economic strategy underpinned by the export of primary commodities—which, at the time, was considered a condition of economic backwardness (Sikkink, 1997)—was the principal reason for the region's failure to grow more rapidly, and ISI was a pathway to break this.[1] For structuralists who were part of the growing Latin American Development School in the 1950s, orthodox economic pathways were of limited value to address the development needs of Latin American countries because these orthodox programmes were built in and for developed and industrialized economies and therefore were of little value for Latin American states (Seers, 1963; Sunkel, 1969; Kay, 1989).

ISI offered a framework of policies that were constructed to favour the process of industrialization at the expense of natural resource-extracting and exporting industries. However, and importantly, a point that is much underexplored in this period was the role that export taxation played to the process of ISI. Prebisch argued that export taxes should be levied for a specific purpose, to discourage primary commodity exports to instigate a shift towards manufacturing; it was key to the development model (Kay, 1991). Whilst theoretically underexplored within structuralism, it fitted with the contentious role of an interventionalist state, which pitted commodity-exporting sectors that were shouldering the burden of the tax, against industrialists, who were the beneficiaries of the redistributions as the taxes were being utilized to support the industrialization process. In doing so, it also highlighted an interventionist role for the state in development—in contrast to the minimal state advocated by neoclassical economists—but it also reinforced the notion that wealth was, and remains, concentrated in natural resource-exporting sectors and therefore, questions of what role the state should take in these sectors to

[1] At its core, Prebisch argued that deteriorating terms of trade meant that increases in production in core countries did not result in price drops for imports to peripheral countries because wages and costs increased in developed countries faster than the relative increases in production—partly explained by strong unions and organized labour (Prebisch, 1996). Furthermore, with the value and share of Latin American primary commodities deteriorating in the mid-twentieth century, it was affecting capacity to import and industrialize due to deteriorating terms of trade (Skidmore, 1978). Moreover, because of this imbalance and the high cost of imports, it would manifest in a way that primary commodity production and exports would remain the main mode of production and integration of Latin American countries into global markets as they were causing limitations to industrialization.

support public spending to move towards developed status was integral to this golden age of development theories.

Tax was en vogue in several of these economic and development theories when Nicolas Kaldor (1962) asked, '[W]ill underdeveloped countries learn to tax?' And when he did, it was underpinned by an understanding that tax was, and is, essential to moving countries from a state of underdevelopment through a process of modernity to a stage of development concomitant with a professionalized tax collection and away from natural resource dependency. Kaldor began his paper pointing to the aphoristic fact that 'the importance of public revenues to underdeveloped countries cannot be exaggerated if they are to achieve their hopes of accelerated economic progress' (Kaldor, 1962: 410), thus conflating economic progress and increased tax collection with the notion of development. It is a question that remains largely unanswered, but its salience is one that finds widespread purchase across today's mainstream multilateral economic institutions and development agencies and forms part of the United Nations' Sustainable Development Goals (SDGs), especially through SDG 8 Decent work and Economic Growth (UN, 2024). Moreover, the Organisation for Economic Co-operation and Development (OECD) highlights both the importance of augmenting tax collection and the challenges that exist:

> raising tax revenue is especially important for developing countries. Strong tax systems are central to financing development [. . .] and whilst there has been significant progress over the past two decades, in many countries revenue collection remains well below the levels needed to achieve the SDGs and secure robust and stable growth.
>
> **(OECD, 2023)**

But whilst taxation is a key fiscal policy tool, which provides developing governments with a stable revenue stream, and improvements and efficiencies in tax systems can enhance their revenue generating potential (ODI Global, 2023), Kaldor alluded to the scale of the development puzzle related to the politics around the mobilization of domestic resources. Writing in the 1960s, when the advice of neoclassical institutions was for developing countries to focus on growing the income tax base, to tax more, and to *tax better* (Bird, 2010), Kaldor (1962) questioned whether or not low levels of tax collection were an ineluctable feature of countries with high levels of poverty. Elucidating the fact that taxation can only be paid out of the surplus of income over the minimum of subsistence needs of a population, he pointed to mainstream views at the time that the proportion of national income that could be redistributed without causing social tensions was lower than in developed countries. Approaching this perspective critically, Kaldor argued that this mainstream approach didn't tell the whole story and perhaps missed the overriding explanation for low levels of tax collection (which, up until this point, had focused on consumption) and trade taxes with low levels of tax over income. Kaldor suggested that the politics of tax collection in developing countries was a major factor in an inability to raise domestic resources but emphasized how important trade taxes had been, thus far, to low- and middle-income countries.

Getting the politics of tax right has proved a somewhat Sisyphean task in developing countries. A point that Bird and Zolt (2004) highlight becomes even more complicated when developing countries pursue other pathways for growth, including donor-led development, debt-led development, and profiting from natural resource bonanzas. Therefore, politicians, who are sensitive to their political standing and future prospects, will usually be happy to pursue these easier pathways, to expand the public sector, and will avoid asking politically difficult questions, which have the ability to generate conflict between the state and some of the most influential businesses and individuals in society. In short, turning back to agricultural and extractive industries to support state spending means that many tax questions in developing countries remain unasked, and the addressing of fiscal challenges is *kicked down the road*. Literatures in political economy of taxation and political economy of development group these challenges under three principal approaches: interests, institutions, and the much underexplored, ideas. The following sections explore these concepts by centring the chapter's focus on Latin America. But whilst doing so, they also offer a couple of conceptual vignettes, which illustrate the shared nature of these development challenges across the Global South.

Taxing the interests of Latin American wealth

The rationale for this book is overwhelmingly to show both the relevance of export taxes for projects of national development and to critically engage with the dominant interest-based theoretical frameworks by foregrounding the role of tax ideas and ideologies. Taxes, as Martin, Mehrotra, and Prasad (2009: 4) highlight, is one of 'the most widely and persistently experienced relationships that individuals and businesses have with their government', and because of this, this is also the one policy domain that can be counted on to generate conflict and resistance. Therefore, this relationship between state and citizens—where taxes are collected by the state but spent on behalf of taxpayers—led Flores-Macías (2019: 3) to ask how we make tax 'politically palatable' for development. And in asking this question, it grounds questions of political economy in a tax-for-development debate. Political economic approaches have explored how politics influences tax strategies in developing countries, but while both *interests* and *ideas* are variables that sit within this approach, overwhelmingly, accounts draw from interest-based analyses (Schneider, 2013; Flores-Macías, 2014; Fairfield, 2015).

Interest-based accounts are grounded in the political power and the resources that groups can wield and how they bargain to protect their interests. In these arguments, the centrality of economic interests of political, business, and landowning elites that are impacted by reforms determines whether tax reforms are implemented or not, and thus can create a barrier to tax collection (Fairfield, 2010; Schneider, 2013). In a vast corpus of work, existing scholarship gives precedence to the same interest-based arguments where, in export-led developing countries, taxes have fallen over a more concentrated pool of actors, who, in many cases, are the owners and business leaders associated with natural resource commodity exports and whose economic interests are being impinged by extraction schemes (Sánchez-Sibony, 2019).

Writing in (2003: 1)—and using African countries as empirical examples—Fjeldstad and Rakner highlighted that powerful interest groups have significantly influenced government tax collection across the African region, acting as a barrier to tax reforms and to domestic resource mobilization:

> whilst there is an urgent and obvious need for more revenues to enable resource poor states to provide and maintain even the most basic public services. The reality is, however, that those with political power and economic ability are few and do not want to pay tax. And those without political power are many, have almost nothing to tax, and do also resist paying taxes.

In Latin America, business and landowning elites have benefited from control of the means of production across a number of natural resource-exporting sectors since the Wars of Independence and have framed development trajectories and challenges to this day (Bethell, 1993; Bulmer-Thomas, 1995; Hora, 2001, 2020). And therefore, when talking about businesses interests in Latin America, we are discussing some of the most established and historically salient natural resource-exporting companies' interests in both the region and the planet (Schneider, 2013). In many cases, governments have strategically relied on the same natural resource-exporting sectors because of the challenge of impacting the interests of influential actors through tax reforms.

But because of an historic overreliance on these sectors, Von Haldenwang (2008: 2) points out that this represents a 'structural factor that shapes fiscal legitimation tensions' in Latin America. He elucidates that, compared to developed countries, taxation in Latin America is concentrated on a narrow pool of individuals and sectors with excess income to be captured. Therefore, while developed economies draw fiscal revenue from the income of their citizens and businesses, Latin American countries put a heavier burden on consumption and economic activity, representing half of their fiscal take in comparison to one-third in developed countries (OECD, 2020: 47–48), pointing both to the challenges in legitimizing resource mobilization from natural resource-exporting industries and the importance of these industries to Latin American economies.

The politics of institutional tax capacity

Importantly, these interest-based arguments are premised on the assumption that governments have the capacity to levy and collect taxes in the first place. And it is this assumption that is explored critically by authors who take an administrative approach in their analysis of tax collection. These approaches explore the institutional capacities of developing states to collect and redistribute tax revenue. In this body of work, tax is approached as a technical and administrative process that focuses on the strength of a state's institutions as both a driver and constrainer of fiscal design (Fjeldstad, 2005; Torgler, 2005). Institutional weaknesses, theoretically defined as the difference between the way that social interactions should be structured by institutions and the actual way that social actions occur, is a point of departure for scholars, who argue that this institutional weakness directly impacts upon the ability of states to collect taxes for development.

Haggard and Kauffman (1994: 12) argued that across Africa and Latin America, progressive tax reforms would 'encounter strong opposition from powerful upper-income groups as well as daunting administrative obstacles'. In Latin America, these obstacles have been explored in literatures that converge around the premise that formal institutions in regional democracies are weak, unstable, and have limited capacity to shape actors' behaviour, including to pay taxes (Fernández-Milmanda and Garay, 2020). Weak states and institutional capacities have been associated with fragmented tax administration, which creates barriers to tax collection and leads to low levels of domestic resource mobilization. Reasons explored for weak tax administration include uneven application of tax rules (Brinks, Levitsky, and Murillo, 2020) and subnational disparities within countries, which present a real challenge (Fernández-Milmanda and Garay, 2020). Another scholarly argument is that imported institutions in Latin American countries are innately inferior to their indigenous counterparts (Evans, 2004). Vom Hau, Peres-Cajías, and Soifer (2023) point to a lack of taxpayer information as another obstacle to raising taxes in the region, whilst uneven and politically motivated or selective enforcement (Amengual and Dargent, 2020; Saffon and González Bertomeu, 2020) is also conflated with weak institutional capacity, which all attributes to high levels of tax evasion, which is synonymous with the region (Bergman, 2019a).

And building from earlier literatures on tax and state-building, it is these institutions and their ability or lack thereof to both levy and enforce tax collection that authors point to when conflating poor levels of tax collection for development with weak state capacity. For Amengual and Dargent (2020: 161) a lack of enforcement in countries with weak institutions points to a 'deficit of state capacity in institutions', a state capacity that Skocpol defined in her (1985) seminal work as the ability of states to implement their policies. Effective enforcement of policies is therefore associated with high levels of state capacity. Whilst enforcement in itself is a contested framework, many authors have highlighted that an inability to collect tax or enforce tax laws is the direct result of fragmented institutions and state weakness (O' Donnell, 1993; Grindle, 2009), which, when inverted, demonstrates the positive relationship between strong state capacity and enforcement through strong institutions. And these weaker institutions have been used to conceptually account for problems in legitimizing Latin American tax reforms. In OECD countries, governance is broadly viewed as more transparent and more grounded in procedural legality than in Latin America, where political authority is more vertical and often heavily centralized in the executive branch—with most constitutional arrangements granting presidents significant emergency and decree powers, even over taxation matters (Malloy, 1993; Cheibub and Limongi, 2011).

However, to what extent domestic resource mobilization is influenced by weak state capacity and institutions has itself initiated widespread scholarly debate, especially in relation to the how politics influences these institutional weaknesses. The politics of these institutions has been used as a conceptual framework to critically analyse administrative perspectives that have drawn heavily from institutional weakness and state capacity arguments when offering explanations for weak tax collection. Amengual and Dargent (2020) and Saffon and González Bertomeu (2020) introduce politics into debates of enforcement and highlight that a lack of tax enforcement is not always due to weak state capacity but can, instead, reflect a political decision to prioritize one fiscal law over another to benefit a particular societal group or political supporters. Whilst weak institutional capacity presents the space for leaders to proceed through selective enforcement, in this perspective, it is the politics that is the driver, a point echoed by Bird (2010), who highlights that institutional capacity is not the problem but political will, and if the political will is there to pursue a policy, then leaders would find a way. These arguments demonstrate a further complexity of the tax-for-development challenge by introducing the salience of politics to administrative explanations of low tax collection through weak state capacity. Moreover, they point to a pathway for political leaders to favour a class of social actors through perspectives of selective non-enforcement vis-à-vis tax administration.

What all of this means is that weak institutional and limited state capacity, or the politics of non-enforcement in relation to tax administration, reduces the feasibility of direct taxes as a reliable source of revenue and limits the total tax take in developing countries (Tanzi and Zee, 2000). In other words, states remain reliant upon regressive consumption taxes and taxes on trade, including imports levies and, in some cases, export taxes. A failure to grow the tax base has meant that specialized natural resource-exporting sectors continue to bear the burden of being the motor of economic production within developing states, but this increases the risk of tension within them because the legitimacy of this strategy is questioned by actors impacted by the taxes where they have been viewed as iniquitous, especially because of the tension centred around the politics of redistribution from influential taxpayers to other societal groups.

Deep political cleavages and tax ideologies

When asking rhetorically whether or not underdeveloped countries will learn to tax, Kaldor concluded that tax was overwhelmingly political, that a tax system reflected its political institutions, and that 'political will' was the *sine qua non* in tax reform. If the political will was there to reform taxes, governments would find capacity (Kaldor, 1962), a point that foregrounds the importance of politics within tax reform but, in a Latin American theoretical context, points to the politics of taxes on trade, including on the taxes on exports. But these exports and exporters and their revenues sit at an ideological intersection in Latin America political economy and development debates because it is through these exporting sectors that Latin America intersects with the global political economy.

Whilst interest-based arguments are load-bearing, alone they fail to fully explain why tax reforms are challenged by actors across sectors of society over whom the taxes are not levied and whose interests are not impinged, but conflict is generated nonetheless. Moreover, interest-based theories have been challenged for not considering the evolving interests of influential actors and business sectors over time (Schneider, 2004) and how this evolution impacts upon tax collection. An interest-based perspective does not sufficiently take into account other intrinsic factors, such as political ideologies and for what reason the state is collecting taxes. However, and perhaps more importantly in the Latin American context, a critique of the model is that it is ill suited when applied to areas where the redistributional effects are wide and varied, and it is the role of the state which is ostensibly attracting criticism, not the tax specifically. In these cases, a focus on ideas of tax provides a deeper understanding to the wider challenges of tax reform and revenue generation and points to a more complex ideological political economic picture: one where the interventionalist role into markets fuelling the redistributive role of the state engenders tensions in wider society.

But, despite these insights, how exactly ideas play into tax for development is an understudied area. Bird (2010: 4) pointed to the limitations of the debate when he argued that when evaluating the driving forces of fiscal policy design and reform, 'tax ideas are overwhelmingly overlooked'. And this is a significant omission because the role of ideas in the policymaking process more widely has a long history that has generated rich scholarly debate centred on how ideas are central to policymaking and the processes through which they are operationalized (Hall, 1993). Writing in (1974: 305–306), Heclo argued that policy finds its sources not only in power but also in the discursive process of 'wondering what to do'. Expanding on this a few years later, Anderson (1978) cited in Hall (1993: 279) pointed to the value of ideas in the discourse of policymaking:

> the deliberation of public policy takes place within realm of discourse [. . .] policies are made within some system of ideas and standards which is comprehensible and plausible to the actors involved.

The process of how these ideas become embedded in policy is the focus of Hall's (1993) seminal article, and whilst related to British economic policymaking, his framework provides an analytical lens that elucidates how ideas frame policies. Hall argues that there are three processes through which social learning translates into policy, defined as first-, second-, and third-order changes. These steps illustrate a trajectory from incremental changes (first order), through strategic action (second order), to punctuated equilibrium changes (third order). First- and second-order changes are what Hall defines as the 'normal' policymaking processes, where policies reflect a set of ideas and judgements that are less scientific and more political, which lead to incremental changes, whereas third-order changes are illustrative of more radical changes associated with a 'paradigm shift'. These changes can occur in response to a particular set of socio-political and socio-economic circumstances, including crises that shift ideas and in turn, impact policies. But importantly, it is not just the state or ruling elite that is the sole driver of policy in these steps; a more diverse group of actors' ideas in society influences the policymaking process, pointing to a much more complex sociological picture, a point also highlighted by Steinmo (2003), who foregrounds a heterogenous and interrelated nexus of ideas, beliefs, values, and interests that influences policy trajectories.

By failing to engage with ideas, authors have neglected to see the importance of how ideas of tax sit at the intersection of opposing ideas of state, governance, and class. In Latin America, the ideational politics of tax has contributed to inconsistent tax regimes over time and historically led to high levels of regional indebtedness; governments have frequently preferred to borrow for development in order to avoid contentious domestic debates about tax as well as the challenges of managing the leverage of major corporate investors (Peralta-Ramos, 1992; Gerchunoff, Rapetti, and De León, 2020). Leaders have chosen the politically easier route out of asking the smaller pool of taxpayers to contribute more.

And as Castañeda and Doyle (2019) highlight, the influence of left- and right-wing political ideologies to tax strategies is significant because, whilst aimed at mobilizing domestic resources, these strategies have been designed to ameliorate the burden to political supporters and interest groups. Ideas of tax and tax ideology have historically reflected differing and opposing ideas of the role of taxation as a growth strategy and political strategy. Traditionally, right-leaning governments have chosen to place the tax burden on labour with broad-based income taxes and the Left choosing to increase the tax over capital with the aim of extracting from concentrated wealth (Beramendi and Rueda, 2007). Tax ideologies therefore sit squarely with opposing political visions but are overwhelmingly anchored in the debate between a minimal state and economically liberal and low direct tax strategy versus high direct taxation and redistribution in state-interventionist approaches.

What this means is that, for the governments from the Right, generally, indirect consumption taxes are favoured to enable them to follow a low direct tax strategy, creating a favourable environment for businesses. However, this approach is inverted as a tax strategy for the Left based on lower indirect taxation in the form of consumption taxes, but higher rates of direct taxes are levied on income and corporation taxes (Castañeda and Doyle, 2019).

An increase in capital mobility, brought about by globalization, meant that for governments that levied taxes over capital, they risked increased capital flight and thus aligning a low tax on capital strategy (from the Right) with the conceptualization of a market-friendly neoliberal state (Boix, 1998). And this approach fits squarely with tax for development policies advocated for by the International Monetary Fund (IMF) and the World Bank's structural adjustment programmes (SAPs) where, through fiscal policy prescriptions, the SAPs are designed to curtail state interventionism and reduce the size of the state. Within these programmes, tax is viewed 'as part of a wider reform agenda of state capacity-building that was seen as a technical exercise in administrative reform' (Di John, 2006: 2). Reducing the tax burden would create a more market-friendly environment and build stronger economies, crystallizing an idea of low tax with both politics from the Right and a neoliberal state.

But whilst the interests of capital have dominated the policy preferences of right-wing parties, conversely, government policies from the Left seek to protect the interests of labour and the popular classes at the expense of capital. These interests are foregrounded within policies that place the burden of tax collection on both capital and production, while the redistribution of state revenues is for the benefit of lower socio-economic groups.

Left-wing tax policies have become associated with the process of redistribution to these lower socio-economic groups from what Rueda (2005: 62) denominated 'upscale groups', which include the economic and business elites and upper and middle classes, where wealth is heavily concentrated in Latin American countries. Therefore, the tax strategies that underpin this process of extraction from these groups and provide the fiscal capacity for governments to redistribute to lower socio-economic groups then become embedded within connotations of class but also within an idea of an interventionalist state. In doing so, the tax that has been used as an administrative tool becomes ideologically associated with a form of state and a mechanism that aggravates class tension because, through redistribution, it is used to the detriment of the upper classes and directly benefits lower socio-economic groups.

Moreover, tax ideologies from the right become embedded in those strategies that offer greater relief to business and economic elites, but as Navarro (2007) points out, these also sit at the intersection of class conflict because these strategies reduce taxes for the wealthiest in favour of an expanded tax burden across lower socio-economic groups. What is axiomatic is that introducing social purpose into development tax strategies paints an even more complex picture for governments needing to mobilize domestic resources to support the development process because class becomes enmeshed with the conflict around state interventionism, which ultimately generates ideological tension.

And in natural resource-exporting countries, it is the extraction strategies that fit squarely with the idea of class conflict and the idea of an interventionalist state because expanded redistribution is mainly funded through revenues extracted from these natural resource industries. Castañeda and Doyle (2019) highlight that greater redistribution is contingent on governments collecting higher levels of revenue from these resources. But not all extraction schemes are the same, and the forms of extraction that governments use to appropriate surplus profit are framed by the degree of state ownership into natural resource-exporting industries (Nem Singh and Chen, 2017). In state-owned enterprises across the region, governments can intervene into natural resource-exporting sectors vis-à-vis royalty and special share schemes. When these businesses are externally owned, taxes at the site of extraction are widely utilized, including metals and hydrocarbons extracted in Peru and Bolivia, respectively (Barlow, 2023), but are packaged up in longer-term fixed capital investment programmes (Ponce and McClintock, 2014). However, in cases where private domestic elites control the means of production, export taxes are utilized as a mechanism to extract resources to take advantage of increased prices because of a lack of other mechanisms to do so.

What all of this means is that when commodity prices are in an upwards trajectory in the cycle, there are excess revenues to be captured; it is these export taxes strategies that underpin the fiscal capacity of a redistributive type of state and exacerbate the conflict between opposing ideologies when the state intervenes into specialized export markets to redistribute to other sectors of society, which aggravates the deep class cleavages that exist in Latin American countries and which has contributed historically to political instability and conflict, in part because of a lack of state legitimacy to redistribute to other areas of society. Utilizing tax to support other socio-economic groups means that the quality of what contributors' 'purchase' with their taxes is low in terms of public goods and services (Von Haldenwang, 2008).

Export taxes are overwhelmingly emblematic of these tax and legitimacy challenges, and by taking the conceptual threads discussed in this and the previous sections, the framework shown in Figure 2.1 elucidates how ideas and ideologies of export taxes have the ability to generate wider contention than negatively impacted interests because where an idea is contested, it can move contention beyond the boundaries of interests and become embedded within the governing party carrying out the policies, which, in Latin America, has often been related to contested ideas around the extraction and management of natural resource revenues.

Natural resource management: Extracting and redistributing

The state as an actor of development (as demonstrated earlier in this chapter) has long been recognized by authors who argue that the state is *the only* actor that has the capacity to implement the structural reforms that are necessary to move towards an idea of economic development (Prebisch, 1996; Sunkel, 1969; Sunkel and Paz, 1976), but when natural resource revenues are a driver of many of these development programmes in developing countries, the debate about who controls national natural resources is

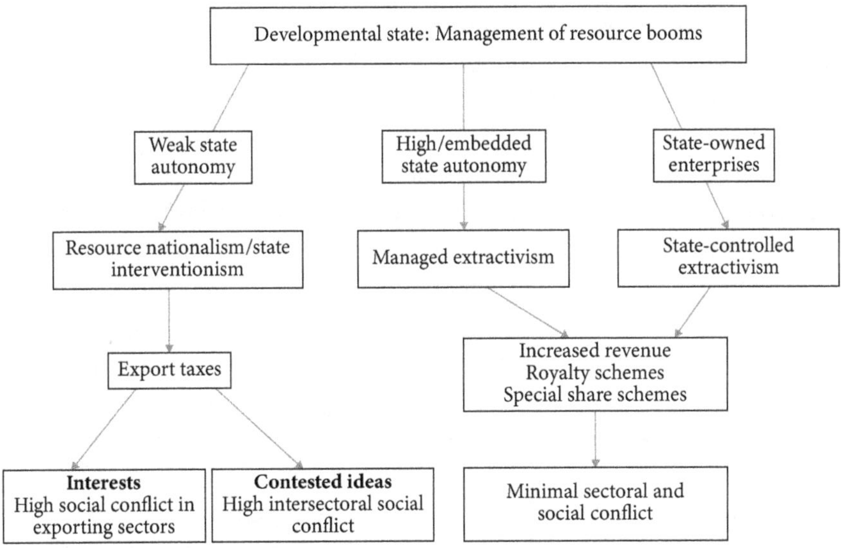

Figure 2.1 Modalities of natural resource revenue extraction

Source: Author.

both a long-established and an unresolved facet in many theoretical debates (Gudynas, 2016). Therefore, in situations whereby historically fragmented and weak tax systems have led to lower and wider tax collection, states have relied more heavily both on these resources and on the consequential debt-funded development programmes to fund development. Whilst this book engages more fully with the empirical consequences of debt-based development pathways in the following chapter, it is important to highlight here that it is an option that has been favoured to avoid asking conceptually difficult and politically contentious tax questions and also to ameliorate for weak tax collection, but growing debt fits squarely with theoretical vicissitudes of natural resource-based development programmes. And in situations where the state lacks autonomy to extract through other means, export taxes are a pathway to benefit from commodity booms.

Export taxes are contentious; they are contentious both as a policy for exporting elites and they are contentious theoretically. In orthodox economic literatures, they are viewed with some degree of scepticism because they affect the competitiveness of exporting firms (Martin and Trannoy, 2019). Moreover, in these literatures, they adversely affect production through both the distortion of domestic prices and the suppression of domestic demand. For this reason, Tanzi (2000) labels them a 'bad tax'. This distortion leads to producers either withholding exports or increasing domestic prices to offset the depressed purchase prices from export firms. Therefore, it is domestic consumers who pay the final price of the export taxes as the cost of the tax is passed on to the producer who sells domestically at an inflated price to recoup international losses. But this perspective itself relies on the somewhat dominant assumption that the prices that are set by the markets are the correct ones, a point that is refuted by progressive Latin American governments, which have sought to intervene through export taxes and price controls to ameliorate prices within domestic markets and to help alleviate poverty and hunger, which the market prices have failed to address sufficiently.

Therefore, the neoclassical perspective has both been challenged and reframed to demonstrate how, economically, export taxes can be a valuable fiscal tool. N. Richardson (2009) argues that export taxes work in times of emergency because they insulate the domestic market from changes in the external sector. Therefore, 'by driving a wedge between domestic and international prices, export taxes mitigate the inflationary pressures caused by rising export prices, whether resulting from currency devaluation or from exogenous factors' (Richardson N., 2009: 241). Moreover, export taxes represent a mechanism that can dissuade exporters from selling internationally and, thus, strengthen food security whilst depressing the prices of staple foods in the domestic market (Bouët and Laborde, 2010). In short, they act as a decoupling mechanism between markets and consolidates domestic prices.

But because of this intervention, the role of the state in socio-economic life and the contention that surrounds this is brought to the fore in a traditional development debate of state-led versus market-led and interventionism versus anti-statist development policies. However, and importantly, this is a contentious debate that many developing countries need to navigate with extreme caution, especially when the state relies on natural resource revenues because of low tax collection but lacks sufficient autonomy into natural resource-exporting sectors to compensate for fiscal deficits. Therefore, these states rely on export taxes as an extraction scheme to benefit from spikes in commodity prices, but in doing so, they fit squarely with tensions surrounding both a left-wing tax ideology and the conceptualization of an interventionalist, redistributive, and less business-friendly state, but one that crucially relies on the revenues from natural resource exports and sits in a wider and long-standing Latin American development debates.

The theoretical utilization of volatile natural resource revenues—including those collected vis-à-vis export taxes—to support programmes of development across Latin America has principally been approached as a motor of underdevelopment where a wealth of literature attributes the drastic fluctuations of international prices to the creation the foundations of a fiscal barrier for medium- and long-term sustainable spending and borrowing (De Janvry, 1981; Mendoza and Oviedo, 2009; Cornia, 2013). In countries that are endowed with minerals, hydrocarbons, and petrochemicals, the challenge is labelled as the resource curse or paradox of plenty, which refers to ineffective government policies that sufficiently benefit from these resources while responding effectively to public welfare needs (Bebbington and Humphreys Bebbington, 2011; Acosta, 2013).[2] Political scientists and political economists have explored how these resources have generated internal conflicts with groups seeking control over them and governments (Sachs, 1989; Rasch, 2017; Mcneish, 2018).

While the resource curse idea is generally understood to apply in states that are endowed with minerals and hydrocarbons and is not directly attributed to agricultural-based exporting economies, some of the conceptual threads that have shaped these theories are prevalent in agricultural-exporting countries all the same, namely the boom-and-bust nature of the commodity markets (Sinnott, Nash, and de la Torre, 2010), but rather than an argument over who

[2] For discussions on Dutch disease, see Bresser-Pereria (2008) and Acosta, Lartey, and Mandelman (2009).

controls the commodities, in Latin America, it is centred on who controls the land on which they are cultivated (Goldfarb and van der Haar, 2017). Moreover, how the state can appropriate from these agricultural resources, which in some cases are in the control of landed elites that have held prominent positions in society since before the Wars of Independence in the 1800s (Centeno, 2002), is a complicated task when states lack sufficient autonomy to extract (Giraudo, 2020), but one of the most effective ways to extract from these elites has been through export taxes.

Who controls the revenues from these resources is a salient and, in some cases, an unresolved question, which has underpinned decades of class tension between landed elites, states (which, in some cases, are captured by the landed elites), bourgeoise, and popular sectors (Berins Collier and Handlin, 2005; Robinson, 2008; Schneider, 2012). However, these revenues and their role in development, as highlighted earlier, were elevated to another level in Latin America in the mid-twentieth century when state–society tensions would shift fundamentally when the previous repression of the working classes gave way to new modes of state–labour relations—from repression to institutionalization, from exclusion to incorporation—that occurred at the same time as wider political shifts and the decline in political power of old oligarchic powers, which gave way to newer 'elites' that were drawn from the middle sectors (Collier and Collier, 2002: 6). This shift saw strengthening popular classes under Perón in the 1940s and 1950s in Argentina, under Ibáñez in Chile post 1952 (Grugel, 1992), and latterly (post-dictatorship), in the early-1980s in Brazil (Pereira, 1997).

The changes were accompanied by the introduction of corporatism into wider Latin American society (Collier and Collier, 1979); a new set of structures for the vertical integration of society but one that produced two broad new sectors, the working class and the middle classes, which began to be integrated into political life in a subordinate and dominate position (Collier and Collier, 2002). At the same time, the state assumed new social welfare responsibilities over economies that, in some cases, saw a shift from a laissez-faire state to a more interventionalist state. Collier and Collier (2002: 7), argue that

> within its new economic responsibilities, the state began to establish a regularized system of labour relations—with trade unions the main representative of labour—and acted as a mediator of class conflict whose overarching goal was to harmonize the relationship between labour and capital.

With a shift in salience towards the middle and working classes, the state's responsibilities for providing social welfare became a factor that was more salient than before.

Funding these new social and welfare responsibilities from the mid-twentieth century onwards required significant revenue and therefore, with generally weak tax systems, revenues from natural resources became all the more important for the delivery of expectations of this nascent popular class. Inevitably, these revenues extracted by the state, to be redistributed and reutilized in support of other sectors of society, caused tension. Conceptually, the extraction schemes used negatively impact upon the interests of elites that control the means of production in these areas. But the contention runs deeper than interests; it is embedded in the ideological role of the state extracting from wealthy actors to redistribute to other sectors. Simply put, the extraction schemes are illustrative of a clear ideology of an interventionalist state and a state that is impacting upon the interests of one sector and class for the benefit of another, therefore the tax not only represents a debate about state versus markets but also illustrates class tensions within this redistribution.

Redistribution is conflictual. But Teichman (2008) argues that conflict is not inevitable if states can reach compromise over redistribution between influential actors and workers. She argues that the countries with the lowest levels of inequality in Latin America are those that compromise over the redistribution of rents. However, she does caveat this with an acknowledgment that opposing interests not only from business elites but also from upper- and middle-income groups and, in some cases, trade unions can present limitations to this redistributional compromise. Furthermore, Gough (2004: 21) expands on the challenges and complexities of this compromise and argues that it is difficult for a state to achieve redistributive compromise in Latin America if it is not deemed as legitimate or autonomous, or it is deemed as being unduly influenced by particular societal groups. So, it is the role of the state to manage these redistributional conflicts and to sufficiently embed itself into industries to extract without being viewed as predatory (Evans, 1995).

However, during the 1980s and 1990s direct state interventionism into natural resource-exporting industries fell out of favour both empirically in relation to policy and theoretically when the neoliberal doctrine of minimal state involvement of the Washington Consensus and market-led development programmes dominated Latin American development pathways for two decades (Panizza, 2009). During this period, natural resources remained essential to the development paradigm, but the theoretical responsibility for management was acquiesced to the market. Classical extractivism explored the privatization of raw materials during the final two decades of the twentieth century. As highlighted by Burchardt and Dietz (2014), there are two key factors within this theoretical approach: (i) the leading role of transnational corporations in the exploitation of raw materials and the appropriation of profits and (ii) the fact that the state was tasked with preserving this model internally. It was the role of the state to ensure access to commodity markets and not to intervene in them. But it was a model that would ultimately be short-lived, and the role of the state would return to try and ameliorate high levels of poverty, unemployment, inflation, and low growth, which has plagued much of the region since the 1980s into the early 2000s.

Post-neoliberalism and the return of the state

At the turn of the millennium, deteriorating Latin American development indicators led to the political pendulum swinging away from right-wing market-led programmes to Left and centre-Left state-led governance development agendas, which in the early 2000s, occurred in a very particular context. Regionally, strong prices across many primary commodities converged in a period of strong demand for these resources, and strong foreign direct investment resulted in significant economic growth (Gudynas, 2016). In a period of development that is conceptually and widely known as post-neoliberalism[3] underpinned by strong export revenues, progressive governments of what became known as the *pink tide*[4] increased both the number and expanded existing social redistribution programmes to meet major development challenges and to provide welfare assistance to citizens made invisible by the years of neoliberal governance. It was a paradigm that was supported by a new type of extractivism: neo-extractivism (Burchardt and Dietz, 2014; Girvan, 2014). In this theoretical reconceptualization, the state is the principal actor, and progressive governments regulate the appropriation of resources and their exports by 'nationalising companies and raw materials, revising contracts and increasing export duties and taxes' (Gudynas, 2016). It represented a return of the state in these markets, which became central to this shift in development, where the scale of development crisis was such that national crises legitimized extractive patterns of economic behaviour into the neo-extractivism development project.

This progressive development project led academics, including Panizza (2005), Wylde (2012a, 2012b), and Grugel and Riggirozzi (2012, 2018), to

[3] Neostructuralism is a conceptual framework also associated with this period but whose theoretical foundations are in political economy and development economics (Nem Singh and Ovadia, 2020).

[4] Left or left-of-centre governments promising progressive redistributive policies to improve citizens lives and reduce poverty were elected in Venezuela, Brazil, Bolivia, Argentina, Ecuador, Mexico, and Chile.

argue that in the search for social justice, post-neoliberalism represented a rewriting of the social contract between state and society, with the state using the natural resource bonanza to deliver expanded programmes of social welfare to its citizens. Tussie (2009: 80) highlighted that within this theoretical approach, there was a 'pragmatic belief in a role for coordinated state management'. Moreover, it was a state that was relying on extracting profits from natural commodities, or what Gudynas (2016: 106) points out as nationalist extractivism that is 'considered indispensable for capturing part of the profits from these exports, and therefore to finance the state', a state that came to be understood as a developmental state through interventions into specialized markets to redistribute to other areas of the economy.

In post-neoliberalism literatures, whilst export revenues are deemed essential for this shift in development model, their collection and availability to governments for redistribution are overwhelmingly assumed. But given the contentious nature of taxing these resources, the assumption does not elucidate the full social and political challenge that exists to raise these revenues through tax strategies before they can be redistributed. It is the role of the state to mediate between influential industries and businesses to legitimize the extraction that is being appropriated to underpin development programmes, a task that is not easy and sits squarely in the debate of state versus market-led development, which are at the core of tax for development questions under progressive governments.

Gudynas (2016, 2018) goes some way towards pointing to the balance and contradictions that exist in South American progressive governments that rely on interventions into capitalist markets to extract profits to fund these programmes. He calls this progressive state the compensatory state and points to the fact that, under resource nationalism, the state is characterized by at least three different aspects: contradictions, equilibria, and compensations: contradictions because the state seeks to ameliorate the tension between 'promoting and liberalizing capitalist processes and attempting to regulate these dynamics and iron out their most negative aspects'. The second analyses the challenge to achieve an equilibrium between 'the concessions offered to, and the limitation imposed upon, capital', while finally, the compensatory state 'alludes to the overwhelming importance of economic compensation within this dynamic, which is used to reduce the level of social conflict and maintain electoral support'.

However, in the characterization of the compensatory state, the theory focuses on the state's role as a harmonizing force in the tension that exists between capital and the state's interventionalist role into natural resource markets and its wider programme of compensations. The importance of extraction schemes is foregrounded within the narrative but as a tool within a model of state that helps provide the funding for the compensations discussed, and the autonomy of the state to collect these, and therefore the legitimacy of the schemes, is assumed within the context of a state providing compensations for liberalizing markets. But within the compensatory state, the ideological contention around what the tax strategy itself represents is not a feature. Moreover, its theorization does not account for when the compensations themselves are contested, even by groups that are in receipt of compensation, especially in situations where an ideological reading of the extraction scheme presents a barrier to development.

Conclusion

The theoretical challenges to raise tax for development have principally been explored through questions of interests or institutions, with ideas receiving scant focus. The theoretical framework (Figure 2.1) offered in this chapter provides a deeper layer of analysis and demonstrates the salience of export taxes to Latin American development frameworks by demonstrating the pathway through which ideological readings of export taxes can impact on development by causing social conflict outside of the exporting sectors over which they are levied. In doing so, it builds a connection between the rich theoretical scholarly works discussed throughout by shining a light on how tax ideologies can become embedded in profoundly political cleavages that are centred on the state's interventionist role in natural resource extraction and redistribution. Export taxes can become embedded in an ideological framing of the interventionalist state, and because it is an ideology that is contentious, and representative that more than tax (wealth, class, and political preferences), it has the ability to move this polemic from interest groups to wider groups in society.

Furthermore, the chapter clearly situates the politics of tax collection within a rich body of post-neoliberalism literatures that recognizes the importance of natural resource revenues as essential for the provision of new social welfare responsibilities under the Left turn but whose collection is assumed. While the empirical core of this book centres on the use of Argentine export taxes and the conflict that erupted post 2008 as part of the *pink tide*, by drawing from historical and new fiscal sociology and using the concepts of legitimacy, interests, ideas, and ideology, the book demonstrates that this framework has a much wider theoretical relevance for other developing states and regions that remain reliant on natural resource exports but where states lack the autonomy to extract, making a significant contribution to theoretical tax-for-development discussions that have failed to fully convey why extraction schemes that are levied over influential exporting sectors can generate tension within the recipients of redistributed wealth or compensations but whose interests are not negatively impacted by the tax burden. In these cases, a focus on ideology of tax provides a deeper understanding of the wider challenges of tax reform and revenue generation and points to a more complex ideological political economic picture. In Chapter 3, I discuss the historical challenges to tax for development and discuss the role of export taxes within these frameworks, drawing out their salience and that of natural resources more widely to programmes of national development.

3

Fiscal Extractivism

The Historic Politics of Raising Tax in the Global South

Introduction

This chapter explores some of the historical challenges that governments faced when trying to mobilize domestic resources in Global South settings. In doing so, it contextualizes the experiences of developing countries that seek to fund the state and public services through tax systems typically characterized by high levels of evasion and informality and low levels of direct tax collection. One consequence may be increasing or unintended reliance on strategies of indirect taxation. Another may be that governments can collect direct taxes but only over a limited pool of actors—in many cases, from the highly specialized extractive industries.

The chapter also shows how tax design and low levels of collection are shaped by the same colonial legacies that have framed development trajectories for centuries. Whilst concentrating wealth in lucrative exporting sectors, colonial administrations also concentrated influence and, in many cases, power, which has made the contemporary taxing of exporting elites and export industries more politically contentious than in typical high-income countries. This has led to the domestic avoidance of debates about tax in place of the adoption of debt-led development strategies, alongside a continuation of indirect tax strategies in place of a progressive direct taxation strategy where there is state capacity to tax.

Historically, the need to raise tax across the Global South has taken a back seat in debates about development, in contrast to dependence on resource extraction, the challenges of building legitimacy between the state and taxpayers, and the need for bargaining around what tax purchases in terms of services. This is important, and the chapter seeks to foreground these points for several reasons: first, it sets the scene for the later chapters by demonstrating the extent to which natural resource revenues have been instrumental in development across the Global South. Second, it introduces how fiscal extraction has historically been closely related to trade in natural resources and

Taxing for Development. Matt Barlow, Oxford University Press. © Matt Barlow (2025).
DOI: 10.1093/9780198923220.003.0003

that critically, even in colonial times, raising tax was contentious; there was a crucial bargaining process around the levels of taxes levied and collected, and the legitimacy of the tax strategy was key to this. Third, it looks in increasing detail at the Latin American experience, especially how natural resources and fiscal extraction strategies shaped up after the nineteenth-century Wars of Independence and became embedded within ideological debates over who controlled the resources and what role the state should play in redistribution away from exporting elites to wider society (Bértola, Lana, and Martínez, 2023). In other words, there is nothing new in the fact that tax, as well as resource distribution, has generated intense conflict between different societal groups and rulers in the region.

The chapter first proceeds through an exploration of colonial approaches to taxation and the legacies left in place, which have framed revenue extraction across the Global South, drawing from examples in Africa and Southeast Asia before engaging more explicitly with these fiscal legacies in Latin America. It explores Latin America's historical integration into the global economy as a provider of extracted resources, and because of this, the mobilization of domestic tax resources has been subsidiary to programmes of natural resource export-led growth and the concomitant borrowing—explored throughout the chapter (Bethell, 1991). Finally, it highlights the regional tensions that existed in Latin America around the contested role of the interventionist state in terms of redistributing resources from exporting industries to services for domestic groups (Munck, 2003).

Legacies of colonialism: Natural and fiscal resource extraction

The extraction of natural resources from Global South colonies was absolutely critical to all Western European empires. Early integration into global trading patterns for countries in the Global South was through exploitative extractive relationships with colonizing forces. While Western European empires' military, political, and economic power waxed and waned with the wars that they fought between other empires and indigenous populations over whom they held fragile dominion, one central pillar of imperialism was the salience of natural resources that were extracted to support the imperial homeland, and which also formed the bedrock of the imbalance in the trading relationships between motherland and colony. Moreover, it elucidates the salient role of the indigenous merchant class, which facilitated access into extractive industries, built strong relationships with colonizing forces, and—crucially—benefited from the extractive behaviour of colonial administrations (O'Rourke, de La Escosura, and Daudin, 2010a; Walker, 2016).

Access to the abundance of natural resources from Global South settings significantly underpinned Western European empires' wealth accumulation, provided export opportunities, cemented trading relationships and imperial expansion, and latterly supported industrialization processes, which deepened dependence on colonies and protectorates. Yet, after independence, the abundance of natural resources across much of the Global South did not translate into equitable development, and the very commodities that were so desirable to Western European empires continue to anchor developing states to their historic role of natural resource exporters, subordinating their role in the global political economy (Veltmeyer, 2012). This can be said to have begun more than 500 years ago, when

> the world economy—the capitalist system—began to be structured with the conquest and colonisation of the Americas, Africa, and Asia. This extractivist mode of accumulation has been determined ever since by the demands of the metropolitan centres of nascent capitalism.
>
> **(Acosta, 2013: 62)**

While the term 'extractivism' became more widely utilized in the 1970s in relation to market-versus-state changes in the oil and mineral industries (Gudynas, 2018), the core understanding of 'development as growth and Nature as a basket of natural resources to be exploited [. . .] has maintained a remarkable permanence' (Gudynas, 2018: 74) since colonial times, when agricultural commodities dominated many extractive economies. Extractivism as a development strategy (Munck and Wise, 2018) is so deeply embedded in Global South political economies and economic histories that Gudynas (2020: 203) argues a world without extractivisms (including an active state role in redistribution from these industries) would be almost 'unthinkable'. And it is these deep-rooted patterns of natural resource extractivism that have framed the development trajectories of many countries across the Global South, which continue to rely on extractive strategies today because colonizing empires had built their wealth on the extraction of valuable natural resources and thus embedded this pattern of development in early trading relationships. This has consigned developing countries to an overreliance on volatile commodity markets and anchoring them into a cycle of boom-and-bust development, where extractive economies are overexposed to price fluctuations and global economic shocks when reduced demand quickly pushes extractive and export-led countries into recession and presents a major barrier to sustainably financing state obligations and projects of national development (Greco, 2020).

European empires were initially involved in a variety of mercantilist policies that were designed to 'enrich both the [imperial] state and the local merchant class' (O'Rourke, de la Escosura, and Daudin, 2010b: 4). These policies formed the bedrock of imperial trading relationships and early dependent integration of Global South economies into a global trading system, the foundations of which were built on the extraction of abundant natural resources for Europe (Bulmer-Thomas, 1995) and for which the empires provided labour, protection from competition, and security in return. But these mercantile systems heavily constrained the colonies, through regulatory processes, including from trading with each other and elsewhere:

> Empires yielded financial benefits by providing control over precious metal supplies (in Latin America); giving access to abundant supplies of slaves (Africa); allowing the cultivation of warm-climate crops such as tobacco and cotton, or trapping furs in colder climates, and selling these on to consumers in Europe (the Americas and North Asia); or allowing control over trade routes, or better yet the sources of supply of scarce commodities such as spices (in Asia).
>
> **(O'Rourke, de La Escosura, and Daudin, 2010b: 4)**

But maintaining access to these markets was costly, and raising taxation was a way for empires to fund the bolstering of security in their colonies from external threats, while simultaneously providing an opportunity to maximize capital extraction from them. However, there was a myriad of factors that shaped tax strategies and, ultimately, how much revenue they could mobilize through them. Much of this was influenced by a lack of capacity and legitimacy for direct taxes, which led to bargaining with influential indigenous leaders and the utilization of indirect trade taxes, which colonial administrations believed, while still subject to some bargaining, were less likely to engender conflict.

Fiscal bargaining

Empires levied taxes in their colonies, but the nature of the fragile relationship between colonial administrators and indigenous populations meant that strategies that were less likely to provoke domestic conflict were often preferred. Economic historians have highlighted unifying threads that shaped fiscal strategies across empires, which included questions of capacity

(Manse, 2022); legitimacy (Frankema, 2010; Gardner, 2012); and crucially, whether or not there was strong domestic opposition (Swain et al., 2003; Bush and Maltby, 2004; Sheild Johansson, 2018). Tax legitimacy and strong domestic opposition were inextricably linked, especially in situations where colonial officers were 'either using colonial revenue to finance metropolitan expenditure or targeting colonial expenditure to European settlers and firms' (Cogneau, Dupraz, and Mesplé-Somps, 2021: 444). To avoid strong opposition translating into conflict, colonial administrations often bargained with indigenous elites—large farmers, local chiefs, and plantation owners—offering direct tax exemptions and other dispensations while simultaneously choosing to pursue strategies of indirect taxation over sales and trade. And while the process of European colonial powers forcefully taking over territory might suggest that little bargaining was necessary, the reality discussed in the following sections presents a more nuanced account and points to the requirement for tax bargaining across empires in order to facilitate tax reform and to minimize internal conflict (Grafe and Irigoin, 2006; Gardner, 2012; McClure, 2023).

In the following sections, starting with the British Empire—followed by the French, Belgian, and Dutch Empires[1]—I explore some of the extractive strategies but also contextualize the way that extractivism framed tax collection, which, in many cases, created fiscal frameworks that remained in place after independence. This exploration sets the scene for a more in-depth analysis of the Spanish and Portuguese imperial extractive strategies in the 'New World' and that provides the opportunity to discuss how early independence in Latin America in the 1800s led to a deepening of both these natural and fiscal extractive strategies.

The British Empire, 1583–1997: Extraction and conflict

The British Empire (1583–1997) was the largest European empire; it gained much of its riches from materials extracted and then traded from across Africa, South Asia, Southeast Asia, Australasia, the Caribbean, and (for a shorter period) the Americas. Precious metals, diamonds, minerals, rubber, cocoa, cotton, opium, and sugar were extracted and traded to support wealthy influential elites within the British Empire. British interests in Africa were not only confined to extracting their abundance of natural resources but also exploited its vast labour resources; the lucrative African slave trade

[1] Other Western European empires: the Danish Empire (1620–1979), Swedish Empire (1638–1663, 1733, 1784–1878), Italian Empire (1882–1960), and German Empire (1884–1920).

became essential to the viability and profitability of British sugar production through its plantation economies in the British Caribbean (Richardson B., 2009) to such an extent, that by the 1650s, Barbados had become the most profitable, and the most densely populated, British colony in the Americas (Dunn, 1969).

The British Empire sought to mobilize domestic resources in its colonies, primarily because one of the overarching principals of British colonial rule held that 'the colonies had to be financially self-sustaining' (Frankema, 2010: 449). Domestic revenue generation through tax was extremely important to officials in London, to such an extent that 'governors' salaries were highly dependent on the amount of revenue they were able to extract from their respective colonies' (Broms, 2017: 271). The principle of self-sufficiency was consolidated after the British-Franco imperial wars (1756–1763), where, although successful for the British, the weaknesses of the metropolis/colony governance framework had been laid bare in a seven years' war fought across thirteen colonies in North America and India. The cost of defending the colonies with the British Navy was extremely expensive and pushed the level of British debt from £75 million in 1756 to £133 million by 1763. This debt led to a process of imposition of local direct taxes within North American colonies, which, the British argued, would help finance permanent garrisons to provide security (Young, 1994). But this raised important questions around the legitimacy of the British levying taxes in its colonies and highlighted one of the major challenges that imperial rulers faced when trying to extract fiscal resources because the tax design had to be sufficiently legitimate to maintain stability and political control over territories and populations.

The complexities of raising direct taxation in its colonies was highlighted by the attempt by the British Parliament to impose the Stamp Act (1763–1767), which was designed to raise revenue for security and to protect the territory that it had seized from the French.[2] But while stamp duty was already levied in Britain, when it was attempted in North America, it engendered significant violent conflict. Local elites argued on two fronts—ideologically and constitutionally—that 'there should be no taxation without representation' (DuRivage and Priest, 2014: 876). The Stamp Act was eventually repealed after months of conflict, causing significant damage to British trade. The cost of providing security in British American colonies actually

[2] 'On 17 February 1765, the British Parliament passed an act "granting and applying certain stamp duties, and other duties, in the British colonies and plantations in America," intending to defray the expenses of troops stationed in North America since the end of the Seven Years' War. The taxes were designed to be light, spread evenly throughout the colonies, requiring anyone who participated in civil society—from graduating college students to lawyers writing a last will and testament—to pay a small fee to the British State' (Edwards, 2017: 337).

led to an inverse tax relationship between Britain and its North American colonies, with British taxpayers subsidizing the security of the colonies rather than fiscal resources being mobilized domestically to provide security or extracted back to Britain (Frankema, 2010). A point upon which proponents and opponents of wider British imperial expansion agreed was that 'most colonies would require significant subsidies from the imperial treasury before they were able to raise sufficient revenue to cover their own costs' (Frankema and Buelens, 2013: 134). This revolt foregrounded the challenge that the empires faced to extract fiscal resources because of questions of legitimacy, which meant that latterly, in Africa, the British employed lower indirect tax strategies as they associated positively with stability:

> Colonial governments needed to anticipate the responses of the native population when pursuing fiscal reforms, and low tax rates could provide a more stable political economic equilibrium when they served to prevent social unrest and political disorder.
>
> **(Frankema, 2010: 451)**

Gardner (2012) corroborates and expands this point by pointing to difficulties that colonial administrations in Africa faced in reforming taxes after the bargaining process. Discussing attempts to implement tax reforms post 1918, he argued,

> In attempting to increases collections of direct tax from Africans, colonial administrators were confronted by the weaknesses of the tax system they had established in the first decades of imperial rule. The system of exemptions negotiated through local intermediaries established before the war was entrenched and made the revision of tax rates and the closer enforcement of tax collection exceedingly difficult.
>
> **Gardner (2012: 95)**

And because of these challenges, Frankema (2010) argued that, rather than colonial administrators extracting and transferring fiscal revenues from its colonies, the British Empire did not, in fact, 'institute any systematic interstate transfers of tax revenues from the colonies to the metropolis', and the 'redistribution of revenues between colonial states, hardly ever occurred' (Frankema, 2010: 449). Broms (2017: 271) agrees, suggesting that the colonies had their own budgetary constraints and struggled to be self-sufficient, and while there was a 'hunger for revenue, the individual colonies were in reality far from cash cows for the metropolitan government'.

The British, then, like other empires, struggled, in practice, to collect direct taxes, especially in its colonies in Africa, and in British India, where taxes were often decentralized and collected through informal institutions before the arrival of the British (Gardner, 2012). Local elites and the merchant class were entrusted with collecting these taxes on behalf of the British, but there was always an awareness of the risk of 'reviving fears of tax revolts and disturbances' if direct taxes were levied in any significant way (Gardner, 2012: 95). To reduce the bargaining capacity of local elites, the British—not dissimilar to the state after independence, in fact—frequently turned to indirect trade taxes.

Bargaining over British imperial trade taxes

Trade taxes were understood to be a way of circumventing the direct tax conflicts seen in British colonies and, because of booming exports, a way to generate significant amounts of revenue. However, they were still subject to a level of bargaining between the British colonial administrators and local elites, and their utilization was not universal. For landlocked British African colonies, customs revenues were comparatively low (between 20 and 30 per cent), which meant that the 'native hut, head or poll taxes constituted the main source of government revenue' (Frankema, 2010: 465–466). However, in the coastal colonies in British West Africa, for example, customs taxes represented up to 79 per cent of public revenue, and the growth and importance of agricultural exports, including cocoa from the Gold Coast and palm oil from southern Nigeria, meant that there was less requirement to levy more modern direct taxes (Austin, 2007). The export of raw sugar, which was fundamental to British imperial trade operations in the Caribbean, also provided a source of domestic resource mobilization for the governors of Jamaica, Barbados, and other British colonies in the Lesser Antilles. An export tax levy of 4.5 per cent was negotiated between plantation owners and colonial administrators and levied on all raw sugar exported from the Caribbean to Europe (Aworawo, 2010). But as Dunn (1969) points out, even this export tax, whist indirect, was also susceptible to a delicate bargaining process that took place between colonial administrators and indigenous planters. He highlights that in Barbados, the British Governor Atkins of the Plantation Office was in an 'awkward spot' and 'if he wanted to elicit a decent income from the Barbadians, he had to cooperate with them'. Part of this cooperation was raising the planters' opposition to Crown representatives over regressive strategies, including the 4.5 per cent duty that was levied over commodities exported from the island (Dunn, 1969: 6), all which points to the power that was held by merchants across colonies and the delicate process of legitimizing any fiscal generation strategies.

In summary, tax strategies in the British Empire were shaped by a myriad of factors that set the scene for fragmented and partial colonial tax collection, and rather than the pursuit of the optimal, tax strategies more closely reflected the implementation of what was possible. The bargaining processes that the British followed to avoid conflict in its colonies were instrumental in other empires.

The French Empire, 1630–1977

The French Empire extracted vast natural resources from its colonies in West Africa (along with French Indochina protectorates): fossil fuels; minerals; and agricultural products, including banana, cotton, groundnut, rubber, palm produce, coffee, maize, cocoa, and wood. Tens of thousands of enslaved Africans were displaced by the French in support of their plantation economies in the French West Indies, where lucrative sugar, cotton, and cocoa extraction made Martinique, Guadeloupe, and Haiti (Saint Domingue) some of its most important overseas territories (Kelly, 2017). The subjugation and extraction from Africa by the French was so deeply embedded that it has evolved into a contentious relationship that endured after the fall of the Empire (1977), with the French continuing to provide security vis-à-vis military support to fragile African democracies for continued access to natural resources (Martin, 1985; Gordon, 1993). The uneven extractive economic relationships that were in operation during the height of the empires was summed up by Albert Saurrat, Colonial French Minister (1920–1924 and 1932–1933):

> economically, a colonial possession means to the home country simply a privileged market whence it will draw the raw materials it needs, dumping its own manufactures in return. Economic policy is reduced to rudimentary procedures of gathering crops and bartering them.
>
> **(Fofack, 2015: 282)**

In relation to the mobilization of taxes, geography and capacity were major factors in framing French fiscal strategies in its colonies. For its North African colonies, whose trading relationships with Mediterranean states were more established, the French approached these with more modern, direct taxes, which placed a greater fiscal burden on indigenous populations.[3] But the value of specialized natural resource sectors to fiscal collection in North Africa was already evident with the bulk of modern taxation in Morocco, pre-1940, collected through taxes levied over agricultural income called *tertib* (Cogneau, Dupraz, and Mesplé-Somps, 2021).

In areas where French imperial administrative capacity was lower, France relied on pre-existing informal institutions to collect taxes. One of the major taxes, the *capitation* or head tax—a blunt direct tax already utilized in France that collected a fixed amount from every individual that could work—represented a significant amount of tax collected (Huillery, 2014), but was simultaneously emblematic of low fiscal capacity because it did not require colonial administrators to collect this and was, instead, administered by local chiefs (Zucarelli, 1973 cited in Cogneau, Dupraz, and Mesplé-Somps, 2021). But it had the capacity to be contentious because of its regressive approach whereby the arbitrary amount payable was the same regardless of economic means, thus challenging any notion of progressive social justice, a strategy that Adam Smith labelled as 'either arbitrary and uncertain or inquisitorial and tyrannical' (Gross, 1993: 81).

In many West and Central African French colonies, the level of capitation tax collected represented around 1.5 per cent of gross domestic product (GDP) but was overtaken by the utilization of indirect trade taxes (Cogneau, Dupraz, and Mesplé-Somps, 2021). Trade taxes had several benefits: they were viewed as less regressive than the head tax so fitted squarely with attempts to reduce fiscal tensions with indigenous populations. They were also an important source of revenue where French colonial capacity was weaker in collecting direct taxes. And while many of these taxes were levied over imports, before World War II, tax revenues from exports were also significant in some colonies outside of the African mainland. Taxes were levied by French administrators over rice exports from Indochina and vanilla, hides, and other commodity exports from Madagascar. Cogneau, Dupraz, and Mesplé-Somps (2021) highlight that the opportunity for financing colonial states through trade taxes was influenced by several factors. The intensity of international trade was one reason but, simultaneously, the creation of a customs union between France and some of its colonies (Algeria, Madagascar, and Indochina) meant that trade taxes were abolished through this customs union. However, it does foreground the importance of extracting primary commodities to finance colonies and their utilization as a pathway to avoiding conflict.

[3] Income taxation was introduced in 1919 in Algeria and 1928 in Tunisia (Cogneau, Dupraz, and Mesplé-Somps, 2021).

Belgium and the Congo Free State, 1885–1908

This voracious appetite for natural resources and imperial competition to control them meant that most European states sought to enhance their economic reach and influence through extractivist strategies. Under King Leopold II (1865–1909), the Belgian forces focused on central Africa and extracted large quantities of ivory and natural rubber from the Congo while under the King's private 'ownership' of the Congo Free State (CFS) (1885–1908) (Frankema and Buelens, 2013). Leopold's impatience to substantiate his belief of the Congo's economic value to the Belgian Parliament meant that he initiated violent and brutal extractive methods: forced labour, rape, torture, executions, hostage taking, and surprise raids, all of which would become the hallmark of the CFS under Leopoldian rule but which underpinned the value of these commodities to Europeans (Hoffmann, Vlassenroot, and Marchais, 2016).

To try and ensure fiscal viability of the colony, 'the CFS was divided into two categories—*terres indigenes* ("native land") and *terres vacantes* ("vacant land")—and all vacant land was assigned to the state for exploitation' (Hoffmann, Vlassenroot, and Marchais, 2016: 1438). Both categories were administrated by local chiefs, who were allied with colonial administrators and who operationalized the pillaging of resources. Such was the extent of rubber extraction that the export value of rubber in relation to other commodities between 1896 and 1901 increased from 53 per cent to 87 per cent of total value of exports (Ndaywel e Nziem, 1998: 332, cited in Hoffmann, Vlassenroot, and Marchais, 2016). However, this extensive extractivism of finite commodities meant that, all too quickly, rubber reached a point of exhaustion, which was compounded by geographical and labour factors that precluded the colonizers from diversifying to coffee production, therefore, trade tax revenues on imports and exports became even more salient, which, by 1897, represented 21 per cent of total revenue (Frankema and Buelens, 2013). And while these figures were relatively low in comparison to other African colonies, Clarence-Smith (1983: 6) 'suggests that the lack of investment in building a tax base' was a major contributing factor because low wages had led to low imports and a reduction in trade taxes.

Post 1908, in the Belgian Congo,[4] the network of local chiefs that had supported the extraction of rubber under Leopold II would now be fundamental for the implementation of wider fiscal extraction through the bargaining processes that brought around the implementation of head taxes.

[4] The rule of the CFS transferred from Leopold II to the Belgian government (1908–1960).

These pre-existing local elites would collect taxes through informal institutions to redistribute to administrators, which would support revenue generation in the context of diminishing natural resource supplies, low levels of trade, and lightly administered colonies.

Dutch extraction in the Indio Pacific: Negotiated practices, 1595–1975

Similarly, extractive processes were pursued in the Dutch East Indies, a colony comprising much of modern-day Indonesia, where the Dutch colonizers benefited from the extraction of lucrative cash crops: tea, coffee, and palm oil, all harvested through the exploitation of Javanese labour (De Zwart and Van Zanden, 2015).

The wealth of natural resources that today underpins much of Indonesia's economic output were the exact resources that were so sought after by the British (1811–1815) and the Dutch during its control of the Dutch East Indies (1815–1941): cash crops that, under the cultivation system (1830) mandated indigenous agricultural producers to assign at least 20 per cent of their land to lucrative export crops—indigo, coffee, rubber, and sugar. However, and once again foregrounding the pitfalls of overreliance on volatile natural resource markets, the revenue from these crops dropped dramatically during the decade of the Great Depression (1929–1939),[5] and to try to ameliorate the decline in revenues, the Dutch instead turned to the wider application of trade taxes, an approach that formed a central plank of the later fiscal design for the Dutch in Indonesia and that would fall hardest on indigenous farmers and especially those from the Outer Islands, where tax administration was weaker, and so export taxes represented an appropriate fiscal strategy to raise tax collection.

At the turn of the century (1901–1905), export taxes, import taxes, and excise duties represented 31 per cent of total revenues collected, but due to hikes in tax levies, their relative share of the fiscal burden grew to 51 per cent of all tax revenues by 1936–1940 (Booth, 1980). Moreover, the use of export taxes increased dramatically, by 300 per cent, over the same period, but while 90 per cent of this tax burden fell on indigenous producers and not Dutch companies (Manse, 2022), this increased burden was not shared equally amongst producers, and the farmers who were not located on the

[5] Total average revenues fell from 730.6 million guilders in 1925–1929 to 433.5 million guilders by 1935–1939 (Creutzberg, 1976, cited in Booth, 1980).

island of Java were taxed almost twice as heavily as those located on the island because of an inability to collect the land taxes that were collected on Java.

But these were not the only tax inequalities; autonomy granted to village chiefs—promoted landowners—by colonial administrators to tax villagers created opportunities for deepening inequities in fiscal collection: 'the precepts on which services and taxes were levied were largely determined locally, based on the discretion of indigenous elites' (Manse, 2022: 424). Therefore, it was local elites that decided what and who were to be taxed, reinforcing both the political power of this landowning and merchant class and simultaneously highlighting the continued utilization of negotiation between the Dutch and indigenous elites. Such was the extent of negotiations required to collect tax that Manse (2022) suggests that the *only* way that the Dutch were able to collect any fiscal revenue, because of the gap between tax strategies and collection capabilities, was through negotiations with local elites. In light of this, tax bargaining was used to 'negotiate and sometimes defy the terms of hegemonic discourse' of the colonial state (Van der Meer 2020: 5).

Thus far, the sections have highlighted common threads that shaped fiscal strategies and challenged the autonomy of the Western European empires (O'Rourke, de La Escosura, and Daudin, 2010b): a lack of legitimacy, weak capacity, and bargaining processes with indigenous representatives over the collection and redistribution of revenues (Davis and Huttenback, 1986; Austin, 2008). The discussion now introduces Portuguese and (in more detail) Spanish interventions into Latin America, where initially, the overarching focus on extracting precious metals meant that taxes were subsidiary, fragmented, and fell overwhelmingly on trade transactions rather than any significant other direct taxes. Crucially, however, even these taxes were negotiated.

Commodity wealth in the New World: Portuguese imperialism, 1415–1822

The Portuguese Empire assumed a network of costal trading centres from Madeira to the Azores stretching as far as Japan via India, Sri Lanka, China, and Malaysia, through which gold, ivory, pepper, cinnamon, and cotton were traded. But a significant economic dynamic and wealth accumulation of their empire had a focus on the Americas and the production of sugar in its biggest colony, Brazil. Supported by displaced labour from the Atlantic slave trade, sugar and other plantation commodities became some of the most valuable resources during the period from the sixteenth to the eighteenth centuries, to such an extent that from 1580 to 1680, Brazil was the largest producer and exporter of sugar in the world (Schwartz, 1987).

Across Latin America, early colonial tax systems were weak and fragmented and were not implemented through a centralized and comprehensive tax framework. Therefore, taxes on production and trade in the sixteenth and seventeenth centuries were at the forefront of Portuguese colonial tax collection. These taxes were collected through methods that had previously proved successful in the Azores and Madeira whereby plantation owners 'had agreed to pay the Crown a portion of the taxes and revenues collected' (Calogeras, 1939: 50). In Brazil, from the second half of the sixteenth century,

> [the] most important tax [was] constituted by the *dízimo*, (the tenth) of the [sugar] crop that the *senhor de engenho* [the plantation owner had] to pay to the Order of Christ, whose estate [was] administered by the crown.
>
> **(de Paiva Abreu and do Lago, 1997: 7)**

It was expanded to a wider basket of products such as manioc (yuca), bananas, potatoes, sheep, goats, and poultry (Johnson, 1987) and was later followed by customs taxes on trade into Portugal. In the late sixteenth century, Brazilian products exported to Portugal were levied with a 10 per cent *dízima* ('customs duty') and 10 per cent *sisa* ('sales tax'), a total of 20 per cent taxation to export to Portugal. However, highlighting the bargaining that was also evident, some sugar mill owners were able to obtain exemptions for several years from these taxes (de Paiva Abreu and do Lago, 1997). And bargaining was important because, increasingly, merchants were attempting more elaborate methods to avoid the payment of customs duties, which 'were a cause for concern in the [colonial] administration' (Pedreira, 2000: 855), as were the close bargaining relationships between colonial administrators collecting the *dízimo* from producers (Azevado, 1973).

The Portuguese also levied taxes on the extraction of minerals but especially on precious metals. The Imperial State taxed the extraction of gold, which represented 10 per cent of Portuguese public revenue by 1716. However, as pointed out by O'Rourke, de La Escosura, and Daudin (2010b: 11), by the 1760s, 'just before the gold and diamond mines started to decline, it provided a fifth of state receipts'. Demonstrating how important tax over gold had become to the Portuguese, at the time of the Marquis of Pombal (1756–1777), tax from Brazil accounted for a staggering 40 per cent of government tax returns (O'Rourke, de La Escosura, and Daudin, 2010b), but this also points to the finite nature of natural mineral resources and thus the importance of the cash crops and the taxes on their trade.

The Spanish Empire, 1492–1898

The Spanish Empire (1492–1898)[6] was the other major colonizing force in the Americas. It colonized much of Latin America, and, initially, the extraction of gold and silver was a driving force in the Conquest (Marichal, 2006). However, very quickly, Spanish *conquistadores* widened their focus from the abundant gold and silver discovered in the Andean countries and Mexico to concentrate on new commodities and the extraction of iron, copper, tin, and salt. Sokoloff and Engerman (2000) discuss the divergent development pathways between the United States, Canada, and Latin American countries post-imperial subjugation, and they argue that the wealth of minerals was a major factor endowment in Latin America. But the preponderance of minerals was not the only factor endowment; the enforced slave labour brought across the Atlantic (Sanjurjo-Ramos, 2021) and fertile lands meant that some of the Spanish Empire's most lucrative colonies in the Americas were those with plantation economies in the Spanish Caribbean.

On Columbus's second voyage (1493–1496), the sugar cane he transported from the Spanish Canaries came to be cultivated in what is now the Dominican Republic (Richardson B., 2009) and would form the bedrock for phenomenally lucrative sugar plantation economies that thrived in the Greater Antilles region of Puerto Rico, Cuba, and the Dominican Republic. Sugar was one of the most profitable extractions from the Spanish Caribbean, and countries that engaged with its production had the highest per capita income in the New World (Sokoloff and Engerman, 2000), thus shining a light on how important extractivism of Latin American natural resources was to support Spanish imperial ambitions. In the following section, I discuss Spanish colonial attempts to maximize revenue through the extraction of taxes across Latin America. It shows how the taxes were applied in a fragmented and decentralized way, which created early inequalities in tax collection that led particularly to an overreliance on indirect taxes over trade.

Raising tax across Spanish America: Fragmented and negotiated

In line with Portuguese strategies, the Spanish taxed the extraction of precious metals. While a tax of 20 per cent tax was levied over all minerals, it was especially associated with the extraction of silver and, in common

[6] Spanish colonial rule in South America ended much earlier than in Cuba and Puerto Rico. Peru was the last territory under Spanish rule, which came to an end in 1824.

refrain, is known as *el quinto real* (the royal fifth) because of the value that the Crown would appropriate from mining. More widely, taxes in Latin America were a combination of both direct and mainly indirect taxes (Marichal, 2006). Moreover, they are characterized as being regressive, fragmented, uneven, and collected throughout the region on a subregional basis with no overriding central authority (McClure, 2022). Since the mid-2000s, a body of literature has become more prominent that has added to these adjectives describing tax design as also *negotiated* through tax bargaining, thus challenging the dominant canon that the Spanish Empire governed through absolutist rule (Grafe and Irigoin, 2006; Irigoin and Grafe, 2008; McClure, 2022, 2023). Connecting some of the key facets of Spanish American tax design, McClure (2022) highlights how intertwined they are by pointing to the fragmented nature of tax design as enabling the necessary space for bargaining between tax officials and local elites—wealthier farmers, producers, and plantation owners—a point she highlights is emblematic of Iberian tax structures but one that creates an uneven and inconsistent tax burden. It was precisely because there was no single authority that was responsible for collecting taxes and it was administered in a fragmented nature that this framework allowed for easier bargaining with local elites, where their co-optation was necessary for fiscal stability (Irigoin and Grafe, 2008).

Ruling and taxing people differently—through a strategy of exemptions and favours—was already the norm in Spain. And the replication of this strategy across Spanish America, coupled with the lack of legitimacy that colonial rule engendered, meant that the requirement for bargaining between colonial administrators and indigenous elites was essential for collecting taxes. And this bargaining process is one that McClure (2023) argues is deeply rooted in the Iberian constitutional tradition, which framed tax strategies in Latin America:

> Iberian Peninsula was made up of a patchwork of different polities and the political and economic trade-offs that facilitated the conquest and consolidation of the Christian kingdoms engendered a particular constitutional arrangement [. . .] the medieval Iberian constitutional arrangement, underpinned by the *fueros* (law codes) and *cortes* (parliaments) gave Spanish sovereignty a more contractual and negotiated nature than is typically recognized.
>
> **McClure (2023: 150)**

This negotiating and bargaining structure in the Spanish Americas has even led historians to argue that there was a social contract because while 'people transferred sovereignty to the ruler', they had representation in the *cortes* because the Crown had to consult with them to levy taxes (Ortiz, 1971: 8).[7] The negotiations were influenced by both the collection and the redistribution of collected resources, with the monarch expected to uphold justice to provide protection and welfare. But as pointed out by McClure (2023: 150–151), it created the foundations for unequal exchange and fiscal inequality throughout the region as 'welfare was not orientated towards equality but a form of distributive justice that upheld equity, distributing goods proportionately according to status and perceived merit'.

And this early tax inequality, where status and merit would form a central plank of shaping inequalities, would begin to form the bedrock for contentious tax design because the *fueros* had fiscal freedom and autonomy to raise taxes and to bargain for them, leading to inequalities in tax design and damaging future tax capacity and legitimacy because those with higher social statuses often received exemptions. One of these was a direct tax or *servicios*, which was payable to the Crown and was applicable in both town and countryside. But towns, which were represented by the members of the *cortes*, could bargain for better terms in relation to the *servicios*: 'As many individuals, and sometimes whole towns, had been granted tax exemptions, the tax burden often fell to those in the countryside who could least afford it' (McClure, 2023: 151), thus creating an inequality and hierarchy in tax design that would add to the contestation around imperial direct taxes and begin to embed an idea of unfairness because landowners, military officials, and those connected to the church were often given exemptions (Marichal, 2006).

But direct taxes were not the most important form of tax, and low levels of capacity and weak and fragmented tax collection more widely meant that there was an overreliance on indirect taxes; especially the *alcabala* (sales tax) and *aduanas* (customs duties). And while indirect taxes made a significant contribution, their collection was nonetheless complex and fragmented.

The *alcabalas* were levied and collected by Crown representatives for utilization and redistribution within the wider empire through a system of transfers and credits (Grafe and Irigoin, 2006). Domestically, early collection of any sales taxes was arranged in *cajas* (treasury districts), which, in turn, were redistributed under the auspices of the *Hacienda Real* (Royal Treasury) but in a more complex domestic resource mobilisation system because there were two authorities responsible for the collection of taxes as they were levied by either royal officials or by representatives of the Catholic Church—which, whilst showing the strong ecclesiastical bond of the Spanish monarchy into

[7] It was a particular model of sovereignty, one framed by paternalistic ideas, where subjects were under the protection of the monarch.

Spanish America, blurred the lines between revenue collection for the state and for the Church. Therefore, 'no single authority was responsible for the assessment and management of tax revenues throughout Spanish America' (Grafe and Irigoin, 2006: 10). This would become problematic because without the uniformity of the tax system, there were systematic differences in the treatment of taxpayers with taxes for similar activities in different territories levied at different rates, which added to perceived unfairness and inequalities in the design. There was no single fiscal constituency guaranteeing uniformity of treatment of taxpayers, and subjects were divided into indigenous populations: the *República de Indios* and the European *República de Españoles* (Grafe and Irigoin, 2006), once again foregrounding inequalities in imperial taxes and uneven collection across the region.

But sales taxes did make a significant contribution to the Crown (McClure, 2023), and by the end of the eighteenth century, the sales taxes represented 14 per cent of total revenue extracted from Peru, 24 per cent from Chile, and 6 per cent from *Alto Peru*.[8] While the sales taxes were increasing, they were simultaneously becoming more contentious as they were levied over a wider range of products and at different levels of burden across the continent. The fact that they were not applied in a uniform manner by a centralized authority meant that the legitimacy of these was questioned, and the taxes became contentious because of a lack of tax for representation. This dispute manifested through conflict and indigenous tax revolts that were instigated following the application of different sales taxes in different areas. Grafe and Irigoin (2006) point to the asymmetries between these rates, which, by the late eighteenth century, were levied at 4 per cent in Buenos Aires, 6 per cent in Peru(s), and 8 per cent in Mexico. Furthermore, they point to the conflict and revolt that ensued when the Crown tried to levy taxes on wheat and maize—following earlier (1776) sales taxes over staple foods, which were further increased to include tobacco and sugar. This perceived unfairness fed into the contention around heterogenous tax levels for the same products and highlights early conflict around regressive tax design.

However, these elites would not have it all their own way, especially the landowning class, which represented a significant source of tax revenue for the Spanish administrators. Coatsworth (2008: 557) described this landowning class as the 'colonial elites', and he used the term to describe wealthier farmers/producers or plantation owners, but he highlights that even this class had to endure a burden of high excise taxes and endless regulations for fiscal and other purposes to export its products. He argued that this class

[8] Now modern-day Bolivia.

acquiesced in colonial trade monopolies that forced all trade to pass through the Iberian Peninsula, to secure protection from the state that would protect the elites from worker revolt—which had been seen on plantations and slave farms across the Americas (Coatsworth, 2008).

Aduanas were increasing in importance for several reasons. First, like the sales taxes, it required little capacity to mobilize these revenues because customs and export taxes were collected in the port districts themselves. Second, geography played a hugely significant role, with major ports located in prime positions on the Atlantic coast for export of the myriads of primary commodities back to Spain, but they also served as the gateway to taxable imports from Europe. Because of its location on the *Rio de la Plata* (River Plate), the port of Buenos Aires became one of the most influential viceroyalties of Spanish America and one of the most lucrative for raising customs revenues (Phelan, 1960; Grafe and Irigoin, 2006). But this trade also engendered conflict because it raised questions of who controls natural resource wealth, who has the right to tax it, and what that rate should be. And while it has its deepest roots in colonial narratives, these questions continued to shape tax strategies after the Latin American Wars of Independence (1808–1826) and the region's nascent relationship with debt.

Tax for development after Iberian subjugation

This section introduces the evolution of extractivism and taxation in Latin America, following the fall of the Iberian empires in the 1800s, pointing to a deepening of both extractivism and indirect taxation, combined with an increasing reliance on debt-led development.

Following Napoleon's invasion of Spain in 1808, the deposition of Ferdinand VII, and with Spain allied with the British and Portuguese forces against Napoleon in the Peninsula War (1807–1814), the independence movement across South America gathered impetus (Bulmer-Thomas, 1995). Napoleon's invasion was the catalyst that ultimately led to the independence of Latin American territories.[9] The 'Wars of Independence led to fragmentation of political power, militarization of society, and mobilization for war of resources and men' (Donghi, 1985: 321). This would set in motion a tumultuous period in the region when the process of nation-state building from former colonies into republics collapsed under the pressure of the challenges of forming new states (North, Summerhill, and Weingast, 1999): 'Political

[9] Cuba and Puerto Rico were the last colonies in the Americas that the Spanish ceded to the United States in 1898.

turmoil did not end with independence [. . .] national boundaries inherited from Spain and Portugal were often up for dispute' (Bulmer-Thomas, 1995: 20). In short, following the subjugation by Iberian empires, former colonies entered a turbulent period of political conflict, with rival elite factions vying for power and territory in the vacuum created by the withdrawal of imperial forces. Instability was a dominant feature where, throughout the process of nation-state building, power was defined by 'military force, under the influence of significant de facto national and international powers' (Bértola, Lara, and Martínez, 2023: 27).

These wars needed financing, and the financing of them across Latin America tells a very Latin American story whereby revenue to support belligerent states in the region was operationalized through the consolidation of the customs taxes used during colonial trading, but now supported by external debt. Colonial rule set the foundations for tax design and borrowing after independence and concentrated wealth and power in the natural resource-exporting sectors, which were essential to imperial economies but which had bypassed the process of building an effective tax-collecting capacity and the legitimization process. So, whilst war supported economic expansion across the region, state-building for Latin American republics followed a different pathway to the European expedited state-building process through taxation (Tilly, 1985). Direct taxes were not levied in Latin America in the same way as they had been in Western Europe, and states relied instead upon the region's integration into the global economy as providers of natural resources. Trade revenues, customs taxes, and borrowing are more emblematic of the financing pathways of Latin American states than of a strong tax-collecting state (Centeno, 1997). For Phelan (1960), lower levels of domestic tax collection and a simultaneous increased dependence on customs taxes (and debt) was a consequence of the failure of Spanish and Portuguese rule to implement a robust and strong administrative framework for tax collection, which meant that the tax burden remained concentrated on the export and import sectors.

Drawing on the examples of Chile and Brazil, Centeno (1997) suggests that while the United Kingdom was collecting one-third of its taxes from customs revenues during the early nineteenth century—even less in France—they represented two-thirds of collection in Chile and Brazil. Therefore, whilst fiscal collection was heavily concentrated on trade, it was overly exposed to fluctuations in commodity markets. Furthermore, with a lack of capacity to extract tax from wider domestic social sources, regionally, countries turned to debt (both domestic and international) to complement these customs revenues (or, in the case Mexico, in lieu of) in place of attempting to raise this through direct taxes over citizens. Debt ballooned throughout the region during the nineteenth century and as highlighted by Centeno (1997: 1585): Argentinian debt rose from £19 million (currency equivalent) in 1865 to over £26 million by 1886, which represented at least four times the size of the state (Randall, 1977: 215); in Mexico, debt had increased to 102 million pesos by 1840, which then compounded to 165 million by 1867 (López Cámarra, 1967: 171–172; López Gallo, 1967: 98). In Brazil, debt ballooned from £4.5 million in 1863 to £9.3 million by 1871 (Buescu, 1974: 119, 126). In Uruguay, the pattern of indebtedness continued. By 1830, a debt of two million pesos had already been accumulated by the newly independent Uruguayan government which, by 1858, had risen to 106 million pesos—in contrast, the government's annual budget was estimated to be around 2 million pesos (Reyes Abadie and Romero, n.d.: 339). And while borrowing to fund wars—and to pay down pre-existing debt—had been utilized hitherto in Europe, in the aftermath of these belligerent periods, what followed was a period of increased mobilization of domestic resources through increased direct taxes to pay down debts. But, as highlighted by Centeno (1997: 1586), the problem in Latin America was that this 'fiscal reckoning' never came, and an overriding factor of this was that the availability of external finance meant that rulers didn't have to mobilize domestic resources and thus bypassed the bargaining process and potential conflict of raising taxes domestically. As a result, direct fiscal collection throughout the region in the nineteenth century was low:

> taxes on wealth and production [in Brazil] contributed less than 4% of ordinary revenue even during the war years'. [. . .] The most significant [tax in Chile] was a colonial tithe used to support the Church that represented less than 3% of all revenues by the 1860s. Early Argentinean governments did attempt to impose a *contribución directa* capital tax with rates of 1%–8%, but this never functioned and was not obeyed. Land rents never accounted for more than 3% of total receipts.
>
> **(Buescu, 1974: 89–91; Rock, 1987: 99; Cavalcanti, 1989: 326; Alemann,1989: 61; all cited in Centeno, 1997: 1578)**

Furthermore, societies were left much poorer following the Wars of Independence and therefore, taxing social sources of revenue would prove fruitless as the wars had left little base on which to build a fiscal state (Coatsworth, 1978). As pointed out by Bértola and Ocampo (2012), growth had been poor across the region from 1820 to 1870, where GDP per capita dropped by 20 per cent from just over 50 per cent to just over 30 per cent in relation to industrialized Western countries. In the prevailing context of 'frequent civil wars and de facto challenges to property rights, economic activities were difficult to carry out and sustain' (Munck and Luna, 2022: 128). For Bethell (1991), it was not only a period of economic stagnation and widespread violence but also one defined by growing ideological conflict, where avoiding difficult tax questions circumvented, albeit temporarily, this conflict of ideas.

And therefore, the availability of international debt eschewed the need to grow the domestic tax base because difficult tax questions could be avoided by borrowing. But by doing so, it simultaneously deepened states' reliance on natural resource exports throughout the region and the taxes that accompany this type of economic production; all of which created the foundations for an enduring relationship between Latin American states and the global economy based on three areas: (i) foreign debt, (ii) commodity provision, and (iii) customs (Centeno, 1997).

In the aftermath of the Wars of Independence and the Napoleonic Wars in Europe—but during the numerous civil wars throughout the region[10]—the significant levels and value of Latin America's natural resources were again foregrounded, but this time to markets outside of the Iberian Peninsula. The restrictive mercantilist trading framework that had been operationalized by the Spanish and Portuguese was now ruptured, which meant that new republics and the short-lived empires of Brazil and Mexico (the latter lasting only nine months under Agustín de Iturbide) followed pathways of export-led economic growth, which would first need to be rebuilt following decreased production during the battles for independence (Bethell, 1985; Bulmer-Thomas, 1995). Latin American states needed foreign capital to reinstate many extractive operations (Franko, 1999), and because of the early end to colonial rule, these nascent states opened their markets to a wider range of global interests. British capital alone financed twenty-five mining operations (1824–1825) throughout the region from Mexico to Chile, and while much of this investment did not yield the expected returns, exports increased significantly throughout the mid-nineteenth century. First, in mining, both Peruvian gold production in the 1830s and Mexican gold production in the 1820–1840s doubled, while Chilean silver extraction surpassed colonial levels of production (Bulmer-Thomas, 1995). Moreover, Latin American countries were also to the fore, with production of commodities that were essential drivers of the Industrial Revolution, including copper from Chile and wool from Argentina (Bulmer-Thomas, 1995).

The period of nation-state formation was a period of consolidation for some Latin American states, where differences deepened between the new republics in favour of those republics that had 'greater political autonomy, that had suffered less from the Independence wars, that had exploitable

[10] See Centeno (1997) for a comprehensive list of these conflicts.

resources, and that were well located in respect to transport routes' (Bértola, Lara, and Martínez, 2023: 27). What this deepening instigated was the centring of economic and political power in those exporting elites that had held power and land during imperial times and throughout the nation-state building period; the lack of diversification away from natural resource export-led growth consolidated both factors. Wealth became concentrated and where taxes on trade had previously been levied by colonial administrators, they were now levied by rulers of these new republics. Excise taxes continued to be the principal method of collecting fiscal revenues within a natural resource export-led productive strategy, but with the proponents of extractive operations shifting from imperial officers to rulers of the new states. And because of the ease of collection, 'a few soldiers in the main ports could provide significant income' and trade taxes would remain the dominant fiscal framework into the early twentieth century (Marichal, 1989: 17).

Export-led growth through external economic shocks

By the eve of the World War I (1914), most Latin American states had been undertaking a programme of export-led unrestricted trade for nearly a century. But as Bulmer-Thomas (2003: 146) highlights, whilst 'each republic had become more closely integrated into world markets for commodities, capital and even labo[u]r', there were greater regional variances related to economic performance than at the beginning of the nineteenth century. The different rates at which long-run exports per head expanded and differences in the rate of transfer of productivity gains from exporting sectors to non-exporting sectors are cited as factors that influenced this heterogeneity and thus impacted upon living standards.

The vicissitudes of an overreliance on export-led growth, during what widely became known as the agro-export model period (1880–1930) of Latin American development (Munck and Luna, 2022; Bértola, Lara, and Martínez, 2023) came to the fore during the same period. Through the pursuance of this model as a national strategy, it exposed economies to strong and volatile cycles in commodity prices, which in turn impacted upon non-export areas of the economy, including 'financial systems, exchange rates, prices, and nominal incomes' (Bulmer-Thomas, 2003: 171). The fragility of Latin American countries' integration into the global economy through procyclical export-led pathways—whereby a rise or fall in international prices was linked to a subsequent increase or decrease of the net output of sectors that relied on the export sector, including commerce and transport—was highlighted in World War I, and again in the late 1920s and early 1930s, with the collapse in demand of primary commodities that was driven by the Great Depression (1929–1932/33). This period saw a precipitous drop in both demand and prices, affecting growth and forcing Latin American economies to deepen their relationships with debt-led pathways for funding state obligations. This, Fehling and Burchardt (2023: 3) argue, demonstrated the problem with a 'single revenue resource dependency that exposes government finances to the volatility of world market prices'.

Table 3.1 highlights the growth in debt-to-export ratios in Latin American states. The growth in this ratio shows both the drop in export levels and the growth in debt to account for it. However, Latin American countries were not able to service this debt because of the deep drop in commodity prices. Terms of trade deteriorated throughout the 1920s—with falling natural resource commodity prices—which, as Eichengreen and Portes (1989: 10) highlight, 'dropped like a stone with the onset of the Depression'. The index of prices entering world trade fell from 1929–1932 by 56 per cent for raw materials, 48 per cent for foodstuffs, and 37 per cent for manufactured goods. These deteriorating terms of trade led to debt defaults that underpinned economic and social crises throughout the region.

This increase in debt and deteriorating terms of trade helps explain a shift in economic thinking and allows us to trace the regional shift away from market-led development models, which hitherto had been dominant throughout the region, to the economic models characterized by state intervention that were discussed in Chapter 2. This period of high debt reduced global demand, and drops in commodity prices forced many Latin American states to look inwards to domestic markets and underpinned attempts at import substitution industrialization (ISI) to alleviate dependency on natural resources exports. Towards the end of the 1930s, there was a regional shift away from previous laissez-faire policies towards ideas of active state involvement into economies. Getúlio Vargas's *Estado Novo* ('New State')

Table 3.1 Central government debt-to-export ratio, 1929–1935 (%)

Year	1929	1931	1933	1935
Argentina	49	73	113	81
Brazil	153	163	215	127
Chile	102	327	842	573
Colombia	58	101	123	67
Costa Rica	96	130	174	158
El Salvador	106	153	183	157
Uruguay	147	185	212	148

Source: Eichengreen and Portes (1989).

dictatorship in Brazil (1937–1945) and the Popular Front and Colorado Party's 1938 election victories in Chile and Uruguay, respectively, increased active state involvement into economies, and the overexposure of export-led economies into the global economy led to space for rulers to promulgate for structural change through domestically fostered state-led industrialization (Bak, 1985).[11]

What did this shift in development strategy mean for fiscal collection? There was a deepening of the form of domestic resource mobilization that had been implemented in many cases during the colonial period, which became the dominant framework thereafter. Table 3.2 shows the level at which customs taxes dominated fiscal collection throughout the region by the start of the Depression. However, crucially, they also clearly show at this point that the majority were collected from imports, and these were levied principally over manufactured imports (textiles from Britain), and less over direct exports, so were therefore anodyne in their domestic strategy for fiscal accumulation. This design did not challenge the powerful exporting elites, which still represented wealth and power in the region.

Table 3.2 Selected Latin American customs revenues, 1929 (% of total tax take)

	Import duties	Export duties	Direct taxes*	Income taxes
Argentina	45.7	2.4	3.6	0
Bolivia	32.3	13.7	9.0	n/a
Brazil	43.9	0	4.0	3.1
Chile	30.0	24.3	17.7	12.6
Colombia	54	0.5	4.9	3.6
Costa Rica	56.8	7.9	2.8	0
Ecuador	32.9	6.4	6.6	1.8
El Salvador	50.7	11.9	5.2	0
Guatemala	47.4	13.6	1.3	0
Mexico	37.7	3.5	6.7	6.7
Paraguay	49.3	10	6.9	0
Peru	27.7	6.5	10.3	6.0
Uruguay	40.8		19.2	1.2
Venezuela	51.1	0	20.1	0

Note: * Includes income taxes, which are shown separately.
Sources: Council of Foreign Bondholders (1931); League of Nations (1938), cited in Bulmer-Thomas (2003).

[11] The 1938 elections in Uruguay brought an end to the Terra presidency (1934–1938) that began as a dictatorship in 1931 until the Constitution was rewritten in 1934. In Chile, there had been military intervention into politics in 1932 (Lowy, Sader, and Gorman, 1985).

Table 3.2 clearly shows that whilst there is divergence in fiscal collection between states, in every case, import and export duties represent the principal source of revenue for governments. Tax collection, across Latin America, in other words, reflected that fact that trade taxes dominated, with very little direct tax. There was an overwhelming over-reliance on natural resources extractivism, both for commerce and to maximize fiscal resources. Moreover, the need for governments to move away from trade taxes was compounded by the burgeoning debt burden, and because external debt obligations were denominated in currencies linked to gold, trade taxes could also be paid in gold.

Whilst World War I and the Great Depression highlighted the vulnerabilities of Latin American economies to global price fluctuations, the arrival of World War II in 1939 was the third major shock to regional governments that occurred while the benefits of turning away from market-led and export-led economic pathways to state-led interventionalist development (Knight, 1996) were being seriously explored in Mexico, Argentina, Chile, and Brazil. A point that led Bulmer Thomas (2003: 232) to argue that this crisis was 'qualitatively and quantitatively different'.

Not only were traditional European markets eviscerated, but also a growing sense of nationalism was accompanying this shift in ideas of development, with the expropriation of oil rights from foreign entities occurring in Bolivia (1937) and Mexico (1938). Poor terms of trade, the loss of major markets, growing debt, and low tax takes all converged and pushed many states in the Southern Cone to reject export-led growth in favour of a pathway that held the manufacturing of products domestically under protections as key (Knight, 1996). And with this *desarollo hacia adentro* ('inward-looking development'), governments pitted themselves against the arguments of the Bretton Woods institutions, whose role post 1945 was to facilitate the rebuilding of Europe and whose trade and fiscal arguments would be in direct tension with state interventionism and, critically, crystallized an understanding that the role of an interventionist state was inefficient in relation to market processes and that the trade taxes that had, up until this point, been a central plank of fiscal policy (Table 3.2) should be abolished as part of trade liberalization.

Trade liberalization versus protectionism: A conflict of ideas

The approach of reducing trade taxes where applicable to international markets became a central canon within the General Agreement on Tariffs and

Trade (GATT) in 1948, where the multilateral deal that regulated trade between 153 countries sought to deepen trade liberalization and accelerate global trade during the post-World War II reconstruction period. But while the GATT and the newly created Bretton Woods institutions were advocating for a deepening of laissez-faire economics, concomitant trade liberalization, and a reduction of the role of the state, Latin American states doubled down on trade protectionism. Now, many Latin American economists and politicians drew the conclusion that it was exactly an overexposure to global markets and the subsequent financial crises of the 1930s and 1940s that they saw as representative of a 'failure of the world economic order' and only through selected protectionist policies and state intervention could governments insulate themselves from further economic shocks (Griffith-Jones and Sunkel, 1986).

So, while the GATT's framework centred on the premise of unobstructed free trade, natural resources from across the Global South, including from Latin America, were central to the provision of raw materials for processing and manufacturing in the industrialized wealthier countries. Regionally, this was at tension with many Latin American governments, which had seen their terms of trade plummet during the Great Depression, sometimes by as much as 50 per cent—Brazil, Colombia, and Chile—and following protectionist policies implemented in the United States and Britain in the 1930s (Edwards, 1994). As a response, Diaz-Alejandro (1979: 340 cited in Edwards 1994) points to the protectionist policies that Latin American governments implemented as a reaction to these failures of the global economy, which included the devaluation of currencies and the imposition of tariffs: 'Exchange rate devaluations were not the only measures undertaken [. . .] there were also increased tariffs, import and exchange controls, bilateral clearing agreements and multiple exchange rates.'

So, what this meant was that many Latin American governments from the Left chose to follow state-led policies and attempted to initiate structural change through an economic productive shift from extracting and natural resource-led export growth to the domestic processing and manufacturing of goods—accompanied by the construction of welfare states and wider social redistribution. And this process was widely engaged with and sought to address some of the vicissitudes that governments in the region had encountered through their integration into the global economy through extractive processes. Taylor (1991: 119) highlights that in the post-war period, for many states in Latin America, the 'trade liberalization strategy [was] intellectually moribund' and that there was value in inward-facing development strategies. In reality, many Latin American states would abandon ISI by the 1960s and 1970s and embrace the narrative of trade liberalization and neoliberal economics from the 1980s onwards, but in the immediate post-war period, Latin American states rejected ideas of liberalism for protectionism, with the state the principal actor.

The heterogeneity in the outcomes of the Latin American ISI strategies of the mid-twentieth century spawned a corpus of theoretical work that has sought to understand these outcomes, and that formed the basis for discussions in development economics, development studies, dependency theories, and political economy. However, empirically, while country-specific domestic socio-economic complexities, including interchanging military and civilian governance and state autonomy, impacted upon the successes of ISI as a development tool, which will be discussed in relation to Argentina in some depth in Chapter 4, there were some unifying threads that governments had to contend with. Fishlow (1990) argues that where the import substitution strategy worked,

> it was at the expense of growing disequilibrium in three dimensions [. . .] first policy-induced exchange rate overvaluation discriminated against exports, especially non-traditional ones [. . .]. Second an increase in government expenditure was not matched by increased tax revenues giving rise to growing deficits [. . .] Third that the emphasis on industrialisation frequently occurred at the expense of inadequate agricultural development.
>
> **Fishlow (1990: 63)**

So, while ISI was a state-led strategy, it pitted governments from the Left against some of the most influential extracting and exporting elites because of the focus on economic structural shift. Moreover, fiscal extraction continued from highly specialized industries when commodity prices were high and funds were redistributed towards other sectors of the economy and to the growing incorporation of formalized labour and the new working classes that were finding their political expression through the popular Latin American leaders coming to power at the same time. So, taxes that were being levied over extractive and agricultural industries were being redistributed both to support the ISI process and to support social redistribution of the new working classes, including through welfare and health care.

And with this, the fiscal schemes that supported these processes; export taxes and royalty schemes became ideologically associated in the region with state intervention and redistribution, which was contested by influential elites, but taxes, redistribution, and ISI became embedded with each other and with left-wing governance. Now, a century after fiscal extractivism was associated with imperial coercion, this became associated with a new form of fiscal extractivism through state intervention, one that intervened in markets to redistribute for welfare and development.

Andersson (2023) points out that left-wing governments are expected to implement more progressive, redistributive economic policies than centre or right-wing governments but that the burden of tax to support this redistribution would be drawn from tax strategies levied over capital. These left-wing governments would minimize the burden over the popular classes—the historic supporters of left-wing parties—and would, instead, seek to extract from the profits of natural resource-exporting elites, which is squarely associated with left-wing state interventionist policies, with parties from the Right advocating for a different strategy, a business-friendly strategy with higher income but low businesses taxes (Mares and Queralt, 2015).

The shifting of the fiscal burden to the profits of exporting and influential elites is, in some circles, the antithesis of development because appropriating profits from natural resource exports has framed an idea of development—with heterogenous commodities converging into 'development imaginaries' (see Giraudo and Grugel, 2022 for a discussion on soybean imaginaries)—whereby, in situations where commodity prices are high, those commodity owners or the controllers of the means of production stood to reap significant financial rewards.

And because these commodities were so sought after, the association with development becomes clear, but the role that the state intervened in markets crystallized into an idea of development, and an idea of what the state taxed for became closely associated with a type of state intervention, one that would generate conflict between elected left-wing governments in the region and the influential elites that had historically benefited from export-led development and presented major challenges for Latin American states to raise taxation to fund state obligations and reduce dependency on debt.

Conclusion

The wealth of natural resources across the Global South has been sought after for centuries. The extraction and export of valuable commodities, first to fund the wealth of empires and latterly for the profits of elites and to fund national projects of development have been central to these narratives. But while the extraction of agricultural products, minerals, and other natural resources have concentrated wealth across many regions of the Global South, fiscal extractivism and the mobilization of domestic resources have lagged far behind. This chapter points to some of the historical factors that framed this weak fiscal extraction, with lack of capacity and lack of legitimacy to tax indigenous populations as major barriers. In doing so, it has joined with critical voices that have challenged the concept of 'absolutist' imperial rule (Irigoin and Graf, 2008; McClure, 2022) to highlight that bargaining and negotiations between colonial administrations and indigenous elites were central to the collection of fiscal revenues, principally head taxes across much of Africa and trade and customs taxes across Latin America. But these tax systems favoured both the colonizers and wealthy and powerful elites in these countries, and high fiscal capacity was not transformed into high redistributive capacity because of oppressive colonial governance, and thus bypassed the process of building a fiscal contract between tax collectors and taxpayers and acted as a form of repression.

The chapter points to these specific processes in Latin America and explores the fragmented nature and lack of uniformity with which the Iberian imperial forces extracted fiscal revenues, and critically, it has argued how imperial tax strategies created the foundations for fiscal design post the Wars of Independence. By doing so, it not only demonstrates how these weak tax frameworks, which were overwhelmingly reliant on customs taxes, underpinned tax strategies during the formation of the new Latin American Republics, but also relates the funding of civil wars post Independence with the region's long relationship with international finance and debt but also as an exporter of primary commodities (Centeno, 1997). And who the elites were that would control the means of production after these wars has been foregrounded throughout the chapter because this is an incredibly salient point. The lack of building of a social contract meant that, in many cases, it was difficult for new rulers to extract from this wealth of resources, which has led to challenges of legitimacy to collect taxes that have endured until the 2020s, impacting upon many of the socio-economic challenges faced by low- and middle-income countries, which has created ideological fault lines in states that seek to extract from these specialized industries when commodity prices are high because of what the redistribution is utilized for. The swathe of left-wing governments that implemented ISI strategies to move towards industrialization and manufacturing was pitted directly against these landed elites when policies, fiscal and otherwise, were to the detriment of natural resource-exporting sectors, to the benefit of a new urban working class, and the taxes that supported this extraction became embedded with an idea and ideology of a heavy taxing and redistributive state, which would frame political economic tensions throughout the region and create a barrier to domestic resource mobilization. The case of Argentina is one of the most emblematic of these ideological challenges and is explored in Chapter 4.

4

Extracting from *el Campo*

A Twentieth-Century Argentine Fiscal Puzzle

Introduction

This chapter introduces the Argentine case and explores in depth the contention that extractive schemes engendered in the twentieth century in an economically and politically turbulent time in Argentine development. It introduces some of the key actors in these extractive processes and demonstrates the barriers that the Argentine government had throughout the twentieth century to raise revenue from agricultural specialized exporting elites because of a lack of state ownership and influence into the sector but also the pitfalls of an over-reliance on commodity revenues to fund public spending.

The chapter has several aims, first to demonstrate the reliance that Argentina had upon agricultural commodity exports for funding state obligations. Rather than being bestowed with mineral riches, its fertile lands have presented consecutive governments with opportunities to extract significant revenue from the Argentine Pampas.[1] But in doing so, this strategy has pitted redistributive governments against some of the most influential and powerful large landowners in the Argentine rural sector, the *estancieros*.

Second, the chapter demonstrates the difficulties that Argentine governments have faced in extracting from this historic landed elite, principally because of a lack of state autonomy into the rural sector, which meant that state interventions into the sector were viewed as extractive and, in many cases, illegitimate by members of this oligarchy. Third, it introduces the contention that exists around the implementation of export taxes in Argentina and explores how, historically, they have been at the centre of a deep political cleavage between left-leaning Peronist governments and landowners

[1] The Argentine Pampas are 'immense, grassy plains blessed with favourable natural resources, unique in the world for their fertility and their proximity to ocean ports' (Hora, 2001: 1).

Taxing for Development. Matt Barlow, Oxford University Press. © Matt Barlow (2025).
DOI: 10.1093/9780198923220.003.0004

and producers in the Pampas. And critically, it points to the development challenges faced by all governments that rely on volatile commodity markets because of the boom-and-bust nature of these export-led strategies.

The chapter shows how export taxes represented a fault line around which fiscal and political tensions have historically coalesced in Argentina. It traces the evolution, pathways, and political tensions that emerged during the mid- and late twentieth century to finance the Argentine state. And through this exploration, I demonstrate that there was a confluence of factors—interest group politics, a failure to build a consensus around tax, opposing ideas of development and state, and power politics—that presented barriers for subsequent Argentine governments to sufficiently legitimize this type of fiscal extraction, which therefore led to increased tensions around the utilization of export taxes.

However, the chapter also shows that because of volatile commodity prices and inconsistent export volumes, external borrowing took the place of tax collection. Therefore, this type of tax collection was never fully legitimized or accepted by the rural producers because, in many instances, debt was used by governments to avoid the contentious process of extracting this tax, and crucially, contention around the strategy remained unresolved by the end of the twentieth century. When the taxes were levied, they instigated conflict, which was sustained by a complex and politically polarized relationship between organized influential Argentine actors, social actors, and a state apparatus that needed funding but had limited options to raise income.

The chapter begins by introducing Argentina at the end of the nineteenth century to contextualize the extent to which wealth was concentrated in the Pampas and to demonstrate the salience of agricultural commodities to Argentine development. It then discusses the specifics of the shift in development thinking towards state-led development and interventionist policies through the arrival of its most famous political movement in 1946: Peronism. This alternative vision of the state and development would ultimately feed into a highly politicized, and unresolved, set of redistributive class conflicts that converged around the use of state revenues, to which export taxes were central. This tension around different visions of the state formed the bedrock for politicized development debates that would endure throughout the twentieth century and resurface in the first two decades of the twenty-first. Tax was central to these different visions of state, and this chapter traces the journey.

Tensions in the countryside: *Estancieros* and *chacareros*

By the late nineteenth century, early independence, which had opened new European markets for Argentine primary commodities alongside an increase in political stability that followed the creation of the unified Argentine Republic (1861) and reforms implemented by its first president, Bartolomé Mitre (1861–1868), converged to create an environment that strengthened the economic influence of landowning elites in the rural sector.[2] Access to new markets and the growing requirement for natural resource inputs to fuel the Industrial Revolution boosted Argentine prosperity and channelled transnational flows of capital, (some) technology, and labour to the Pampas (Bulmer-Thomas, 1995). From a very early date, the large Pampas landowners, the *estancieros*, became the 'main beneficiaries of liberal economic development and Argentina's integration into the global economy' (Hora, 2010: 1). As a result, production in the Pampas was more advanced (i.e. more capitalist) than other areas of the country as early as the mid-nineteenth century, based on the rapid expansion of sheep breeding, which would later be supplanted by cattle breeding and crops for producing grains (Bethell, 1993). These changing patterns of land use reflected both domestic and international market opportunities (Lewis, 2002). Demand in Europe for Argentine primary products was at such a level that by the early twentieth century, 'Argentina's per capita foreign trade was three times higher than the average foreign trade in the rest of the Latin American countries, and its income per head was five times higher than either Brazil or Colombia' (Bulmer-Thomas, 1995: 433, 439).

The landowning class driving this growth was made up of the most prestigious and influential people in Argentina, able to exert political 'clout' over the ruling elite (Hora, 2001). The most dynamic of these large landowners formed the *Sociedad Rural Argentina* (Argentine Rural Society) (SRA) in 1866—an association created to represent the corporate interests of its members. And whilst initially fragmented, by the twentieth century, it would be a formidable voice for wealthy, influential, and prestigious large landowners, which would ultimately become synonymous with the association of the Argentine upper class (Ondetti, 2021): 'A period of exceptional growth and stable government, the 1880s permitted *estancieros* to improve both their rural establishments and their position in Argentine society' (Hora,

[2] The landowning elites are the large landowners in the Argentine pampas with the largest number of hectares and who are the landlords of smaller tenant farmers. They are often referred to interchangeably as rural producers, landed oligarchy, landed elites, the landed class, and large landowners.

2001: 68). By the late 1880s, the Barings banking crisis would help consolidate this standing further. The Barings Crisis was the first major economic emergency faced by the Argentine Republic. The crisis led to a precipitous drop in investment. It was the catalyst for major social unrest, whose economic ramifications were so deep that it would depress investment into Argentina that would prolong the crisis until the-mid 1890s (Ford, 1956).[3] But it was the rural sector that acted as the motor for recovery from crisis, and in doing so, consolidated the standing of rural elites. Between 1893 and 1899, agricultural exports almost doubled (Hora, 2001). And with it,

> The Sociedad rural and its exhibitions thrived after the 1890s [. . .] the agrarian sector alone proved capable of pulling Argentina out of its economic crisis. This achievement helped consolidate the prestigious position farming had acquired in the 1880s and had profound consequences for the consolidation of the landowning ethos as a defining feature of the social elite.
>
> **(Hora, 2001: 72)**

But as highlighted by Ocampo (2015: 12), because of the underlying structure of the Argentine economy, 'agricultural commodity price booms [driving growth] inevitably led to higher inequality and thus more power to the landed elite'. And while undoubtedly some of the most influential actors in the Pampas, these landowners were just one of a heterogenous group of actors whose opposing interests would underpin a growing social conflict within the sector, framed by a view that although influential, they were simultaneously regarded as greedy and exploitative by other actors within the rural sector, including farmer tenants and smaller landowners, who were squeezed by larger landowners, especially during times of low commodity prices. In these instances, falls in international commodity prices and export levels were recouped by the landowners by forcing *chacareros* ('smaller farmers') to pay for the market adjustment (Hora, 2001).

Conflicts between large landowners and small- and medium-sized landowners and tenant farmers intensified during the early twentieth century because of worsening terms of leases, price increases—due to the rapid valorization of land from diversification towards grain—rent increases, and

[3] The British Investment Bank, the House of Baring, had invested heavily into projects infrastructure and capital projects in Argentina throughout the 1880s. The Barings Crisis refers to the economic fallout in 1888–1889 when economic slowdown, stagnant commodity prices, and slow-maturing investments translating into an increase in tax receipts meant that the Argentine government could not service its debt liabilities, triggering the crisis (Ford, 1956). Whilst the Bank of England intervened to support the House of Baring to prevent a widespread banking crisis in Europe, it did nothing to support interests in Argentina or Latin America.

worsening conditions for tenant farmers. All these factors were instrumental in the creation of another agricultural society, the *Federación Agraria Argentina* (Argentine Agrarian Federation) (FAA) in 1912[4] but also underpinned a major agrarian rebellion and general strike that began in Alcorta in the southern province of Santa Fe before spreading across the entire Pampas (Hora, 2020). Protagonists in the *Grito de Alcorta*, many of whom were Spanish and Italian immigrants, demanded better pay and conditions (and succeeded in obtaining them), which also included better lease terms from their landlords.[5] But what this demonstrates was wider societal class resentment of this landed oligarchy because the conflict between large landowners and tenants spilled over into the growing urban centres, where farmers and tenants gained popular support from nascent industrial workers, thus deepening political cleavages between popular-class workers and the landed elites.

During the farmers' rebellion, relationships between landowners and the Argentine government would also come under pressure when the government tried to intervene in the rural sector vis-à-vis the levying of higher rural real estate taxes in Buenos Aires province. This was a catalyst for a political stand-off between a Conservative government and the landed oligarchy (Hora, 2020). Tensions would increase further in the aftermath of World War I, when US investment into Argentina would outstrip British investment by two to one and US capitalists became active lenders to the government and active investors in local industry (Hora, 2001). This was a structural shift because British investment had thus far concentrated on supporting the export of natural resources and those in the rural sector, but US investment was offered in support of industrialization, and government policies made this investment more appealing. This meant that big enterprises were of growing importance, which influenced the industry, and big business took firm control of the manufacturers' organization the *Unión Industrial Argentina* (Industrial Union of Argentina) (UIA).

Tensions between business leaders and the oligarchic agrarian industry started to manifest around this time because of this shift in investment, leading to the scenario where industrial business leaders now openly criticized

[4] There were two more associations created in the twentieth century: *Confederaciones Rurales Argentina* was founded in 1943 and represented large landowners with less hectares than SRA members and *Confederación Intercooperativa Agropecuaria* was founded in 1956 as an association representing cooperatives of smaller producers (Fairfield, 2011).

[5] Rents increased from one-fifth of the crop value to one-third between 1904 and 1912 (Hora, 2001).

rural landowners and producers.[6] The argument from the UIA and its president, Luis Colombo (1925–1946), was that the landowners were

> a burden rather than a force for progress and they do not interest themselves with the country's progress, only their own well-being, provided by rents that they spend in Europe.
>
> **(Hora, 2001: 187)**

This tension would form the bedrock for domestic structural 'class' conflict that would remain prevalent throughout the 1930s and the early 1940s, with criticism of the SRA from the UIA described as relentless. Moreover, with the onset of World War II in 1939, Argentine exports to Europe declined drastically, and the ruling government known as the *Concordancia* ('Concordance') (1931–1943) government(s) tried to implement land taxes on the largest landowners, with over 20,000 hectares to finance the process of industrialization, and thus exacerbated tensions within this group.[7] The industrialization process had benefited from mass migration of workers from the Pampas to Greater Buenos Aires—Buenos Aires attracted 1.1 million migrants, of which two-thirds came from the Pampas (Rock, 1987)—and as Hora (2001) argues, it was an acknowledgment that a society would emerge post-World War II, where 'social justice' would become a major political issue because of growing demands from this class. In short, there was a recognition that governments would need to look after the growing working classes, and revenue was needed to do this. The tax was presented by some conservative legislators as a tax on greedy, self-centred individuals who were out of touch with the times (Bethell, 1993).

The tax debate itself was contentious because although the centre-Right government had originally supported the rural sector and its influential actors, some were breaking ranks to argue against the privilege of the landowners. Tax and redistribution were at the intersection of class conflict between a growing working class and the landowning elites, one that was being mediated by the state but would become exacerbated further with the arrival of Juan Domingo Perón as part of a military coup in 1943 before he was elected president in 1946. With Perón's arrival came an alternative vision

[6] Failed attempts to permeate into the US beef market meant that the rural producers had focused on rebuilding the sluggish beef trade through calls for bilateral deals with Britain (Bethell, 1993; Lewis, 2002). Leaders in the manufacturing industry feared that policymakers would be influenced by the landowners to give British importers preferential treatment, thus damaging their relationship with US capitalists and stalling industrialization (Hora, 2001).

[7] The *Concordancia* was a political alliance under which three presidents ruled Argentina: Agustín Justo (1932–1938), Roberto Ortiz (1938–1942), and Ramón Castillo (1942–1943).

of state and development, a vision that was at direct odds with that of free markets and the landed oligarchy.

Peronism: The rise of the spending state

This section introduces the arrival of Peronism in Argentina and traces the policies that were synonymous with extracting wealth from the landed elites and redistributing to the popular classes. It foregrounds the extractive choices pursued by the Perón government in the context of low tax collection while also highlighting the political and economic limitations of funding Argentine development through natural resource exports in the mid-twentieth century.

The military regime that seized control of the republic in 1943 ended a period of governance that was widely labelled as the *década infame* ('infamous decade') because of widespread claims of institutionalized fraud and corruption under the *Concordancia* (James, 1988; Hora, 2001). And with it, the coup brought an end to the disillusionment with the ruling political class that had failed to convince the Argentinian citizens of their legitimacy after a decade of instability (Sánchez Román, 2012). Following the military coup, the rights and protections of the growing working class were expanded under Perón's tenure as secretary of labour, which began in October 1943. During this period, Perón set about addressing some of the basic concerns of the emerging industrial labour force. He rearticulated the role of the state into one that oversaw unionization, and collective bargaining between the state and society and underpinned this by law (Gerchunoff and Llach, 2010). The extensive expansion of union organization assured working-class recognition as a social force in Argentine production, and this shifted the importance towards industry from the rural sector—which fitted in with wider patterns of development in the region. Furthermore, Perón recast citizenship within a new social context that assured their rights to political citizenship—which had been further eroded under the infamous decade (James, 1988).[8] Within this newly found political participation, Perón, as head of the *Partido Laborista* (Labour Party) (1945–1947) formed by new and empowered trade union leaders in 1945, mobilized the enormous support base that he had constructed with the Argentinian urban working class in the 1946 elections and argued for social justice and economic independence and against the previous elitism in Argentina that was associated with the landowners:

[8] Peronism changed the terms of citizenship by establishing the *pueblo*, consisting of unionized workers, the urban poor, and the lower-middle classes as a political actor with rights to social and economic inclusion (Grugel and Riggirozzi, 2007; Wylde, 2012a).

> The old traditional parties have ceased to be the voice of the people, in order to act instead in small circles of clear unpopular character, deaf and blind to the worries of the mass whose aid they only think to call upon when elections come around.
>
> **(James, 1988: 15)**

'Peronism' became the term deployed to the movement that represented the political, social, and economic agenda of Juan Perón and the *Partido Justicialista* (Justicialist Party) (PJ).[9] Social justice was one of the two central tenets of the Peronist movement—the second of which I shall address in a later section—and was one that altered the distribution of wealth and power within Argentinian society, creating tensions with former political and economic elites (Murmis and Portantiero, 2004).[10] The urban working class that had rallied around the President in the 1946 election was rewarded in the years following his ascension to power through the creation and the implementation of the Argentinian welfare state and a succinct focus on the augmentation of wages through labour policies. Under Perón, 'workers ameliorated their economic position and gained unexpected social recognition and symbolical salience' (Sánchez Román, 2012: 83). A raft of policies that was targeted towards the fledging industrial sector and its workers would, however, increase costs for the state. The real wage rises that increased by 62 per cent in Argentina between 1945 and 1949 would outstrip the rate of industrial productivity (Sánchez Román, 2012). Furthermore, these wage rises were accompanied by expansions to social security, health systems, and pension provisions (480,000 people were enrolled in the pension system in 1943, which figure had reached 2.3 million by 1947 and 4.6 million by 1954), a freeze on rents, and the abolition of evictions were all emblematic policies that were implemented with a social focus at the beginning of the Peronist era (Sánchez Román, 2012). However, it was a social focus through an interventionalist state, which pitted the traditional powerful Argentine landowners with their conservative political elite supporters against the PJ, that would form the bedrock for a conflict around the ideas of the form of state, a conflict that remained unresolved into the twenty-first century.

[9] Formed in November 1946 as the previous Labour Party was disbanded.

[10] While defining the Peronist ideology is a matter of deep scholarly debate and one beyond the scope of this book, it has often been described as a form of leftist-populist nationalism (Panizza, 2005) or as a nationalist, expansionary redistributive project, one that favoured urban wage labour over agro-exporting, landowning elites (Weyland, 2001; Vellacott, 2007) and which presented a broad political appeal as it redefined citizenship within a social context (James, 1988).

Fiscal policies to extract from the landed class

To pay for the social policies of the PJ, Perón turned towards the export revenues of the rural sector, which placed the President and the landed elites in direct conflict with each other, as the government sought to extract profits from the sector to redistribute to other areas of the economy and other sectors of society. Whilst attempts to raise land taxes had been a contentious issue for rural producers in 1912, and again under the Concordance government in the 1930s, there had been a real absence of consistence tax levied over these actors outside of these attempts. However, the reappropriation of profits from agricultural exports to support industrialization would exacerbate deep political cleavages, which would become associated with Peronism (Lewis, 1975; Peralta-Ramos, 1992; Ramos, 2019). The redistribution of revenues from agricultural producers meant that the power of the 'great landowners was diminished by Perón's pro-industrialization economic policies' (Craig, 1976: 711). Argentina was enjoying a post-war boom, owed in part to its neutrality during World War II, which had consolidated its position as a major provider of food to Britain (Craig, 1976). It was from these agricultural revenues that President Perón sought to extract. To do so, his government expanded and centralized the *Junta Nacional de Granos* (Grain Regulatory Board) that had been created in 1933 to form a single state grain purchaser, the *Instituto Argentino de Promoción del Intercambio* (IAPI), in 1946, whose role was to buy grain at state-fixed prices to sell to the exporters (Sourrouille and Ramos, 2013). The prices that were paid by the IAPI to the producers were significantly less than market value, with the state appropriating and redistributing the difference. This detrimentally affected their interests, and therefore the process was a matter of political contestation as it was seen by rural producers as openly discriminatory (Gerchunoff and Llach, 2010). Sánchez Román (2015) argued that the creation of the IAPI institutionalized state appropriation from rural-sector exports and was contentious because the state redistributed these to other areas of the economy—especially in a landscape of high commodity prices. Craig (1976: 711) points out that these interventionist extractive policies led to the landowners viewing Peronism and its supporters as 'huge sectarian hordes, fired with vengeance'. Table 4.1 highlights the years following the implementation of the IAPI and illustrates how the producers were worse off (by 100 per cent), with the government setting the prices and redistributing the profits to other sectors of the economy.

Table 4.1 Comparative contribution of the rural sector in Argentine GDP (%)

Period	At current prices	If domestic prices would have followed international prices
1925–1929	33	33
1935–1939	26	28
1947–1949	16	32

Source: Díaz-Alejandro (1975), cited in Gerchunoff and Llach (2010).

The deep political cleavages between landowners and Peronists reflects asymmetrical visions of the role of the state. The role of the state was politically disputed, not only because of ideas about the state but also because it was affecting large landowner interests. It was through the IAPI that the government intervened significantly into the economy, causing contention. But as Gerchunoff and Llach (2004) highlight, the Argentine export economy had generated significant inequalities, so to achieve social justice and obtain greater levels of equality, the power of this sector required moderating and wealth needed to be redistributed. Therefore, for Perón, reducing the authority of the landowners through fixing the prices of grain would generate a double-positive effect. Fiscal resources could be redistributed to support higher wages and pension payments, whilst allowing the government to fix the domestic price of grains would stabilize the price of bread, which was a staple of the 'Argentine Consumption Basket'.[11] Both measures would address the demands of the urban working classes by providing increased wages and pensions while implementing price controls on some major domestic food items.

However, this wealth redistribution was targeted towards supporting not only the drive for social justice but also the second central tenet of Peronism: the concept of national economic independence. To move towards this goal, the government proceeded with a programme of nationalization that was planned to both reduce Argentina's dependency on natural resource exports and develop the autonomy of the Argentine state. The strategy was to actively promote the shift towards industrialization to achieve

[11] The consumption basket is widely understood to mean the affordability of staple foods, which is used as a measure of poverty in Argentina. It includes food items that satisfy a minimum level of calories needed to survive and also includes non-food essential items, such as clothing (Porto, 2010).

a greater share of manufacturing in the overall production matrix, all of which would need significant funding. Perón would pay off the remaining debt liabilities and nationalize major foreign-owned Argentine industries—with compensation—including transportation and shipping.[12] Furthermore, Perón was suspicious of multilateral finance agreements through the Bretton Wood institutions, which meant that to achieve his government's goal of economic independence, he favoured bilateral deals, which the president argued would 'not damage national self-determination' (Skidmore, 1978: 7). What all of this meant was that the state was spending big to achieve both central tenets of the Peronist narrative. And extracting wealth from the rural sector was central to supporting his agenda (Skidmore, 1978; Bulmer-Thomas, 1995).

Attacks by the government on the landed elites were woven into the narrative of Peronism. These attacks, whilst aiming to reduce the highly inequitable income concentration that had been created under the export development model, negatively impacted the interests of the large landowners. The Argentinian wealthiest 1 per cent saw their share of national income drop from 26 per cent in 1943 to 15 per cent in 1953 (Alvaredo, 2010), partially through rent freezes that shifted income from proprietors to tenants, which while redistributive, was not an official tax, but the tax burden would rise to contribute towards funding a higher-spending state (Gerchunoff and Antúnez, 2002). Furthermore, to curtail an exodus of lower-paid workers from the Pampas to manufacturing jobs in urban centres, the producers had to raise the wages of their employees, pushing up their costs and squeezing profits further (Gerchunoff and Llach, 2010). This agrarian reform from above (Hora, 2001) instigated a permanent animosity towards the government from the landed oligarchy. It was not seen as a legitimate process as agrarian producers were not 'purchasing' anything for this state extraction; it was being redistributed to other sectors and funding policies that did not align with the producers' interests. It was therefore, never consolidated into any form of fiscal contract. This generated significant tension between the Perón government and landed elites because it was an extractive process that was not legitimate because of where the resources were being redistributed.

Under Perón, the Argentine state was spending on welfare and on policies aimed at ameliorating the lives of the working classes that had brought the PJ to power. However, these programmes required significant financial

[12] All remaining debt was transferred into internal securities, meaning that pre-war foreign obligations had been redeemed in full by 1949 (Bulmer-Thomas, 1995).

resources, and an inability of earlier governments to address tax questions meant that tax systems in Argentina at this point remained regressive and overwhelmingly reliant on indirect strategies.

Public spending and indirect taxes

The coup that brought the military to power in 1943 was not the first occasion during this contemporary period of Argentine history where tax debates had come to the fore. Structuralists (including Prebisch) believed that the 1930 military coup that supplanted the government of Hipólito Yrigoyen with José Félix Benito Uriburu presented the perfect opportunity to implement tax reforms in the country as there was a lacuna of political interference, and the treasury was in a critical situation. Although a few emergency tax measures were introduced, there was a reticence from Uriburu surrounding the implementation of progressive income tax implementation due to animosity he feared would be created between conservative supporters and the landed oligarchy (Sánchez Román, 2012). The landowners presented an obstacle to tax reform. The Concordance government that followed did not challenge the landed oligarchy's influence through taxation until the final years of its rule, and then, unsuccessfully. Table 4.1 demonstrates how the largest percentage of tax take in 1932–1940, was based around indirect taxes on consumption at a level of 37.3 per cent, and the reluctance of Uriburu and the subsequent government to directly tax the powerful landowning elites meant that the level of direct taxation was at a level of 10 per cent of the total tax burden (Cetrángolo and Gómez Sabaini, 2010).

Up to this period, indirect taxes had dominated Argentine fiscal strategies. However, direct progressive taxes presented opportunities to tap into income that was strongly concentrated at the top level of society; they constituted an important fiscal tool both for reducing this concentration and for ensuring that the state has resources for its redistribution (Antía, 2019). But direct taxes can be contentious when their rationale is contested. Therefore, by imposing reforms from above, Hora (2001) and Sánchez Román (2012) argue that price-setting through the IAPI—although not a direct tax in the traditional sense—was not legitimized in the eyes of the rural producers. It was highly exacting, and therefore contentious, because it affected their interests, and as the monetary difference between the prices paid to the producers and the international prices of commodities was being utilized to support a different sector, it fitted with opposing visions of development and of state.

Table 4.2 Average tax collection by decade, 1930s–1990s

Decade	1932–1940	1941–1950	1951–1960	1961–1970	1971–1980	1981–1990	1991–2001
Percentage of GDP							
Income: benefits and capital gains	0.95	2.56	3.37	2.35	1.37	1.02	2.54
Assets	0.32	0.25	0.47	0.54	0.61	0.54	0.35
Taxes on goods and services	3.52	3.69	4.73	4.85	5.47	6.17	8.74
Taxes on international trade and transactions	3.27	1.03	0.44	1.77	1.83	1.73	0.92
Social security contributions	1.37	3.01	4.86	4.2	4.51	2.94	4.31
Others	0	0.06	0.12	0.15	0.17	0.4	0.49
Federal gross tax revenues	9.43	10.6	13.99	13.86	13.96	12.8	17.35

Source: Cetrángolo and Gómez Sabaini (2010).

The Perón government did manage to increase the overall tax burden, as shown in Table 4.2, but while the tax burden was increasing, importantly, public spending also continued to expand—as highlighted in Table 4.3—which meant that the Perón government would spend more than it collected in each year of this first mandate (Gerchunoff and Díaz-Alejandro, 1989). Therefore, although the government mobilized more in taxation, it could not keep pace with government spending, highlighting a rising fiscal tension that would become endemic in Argentina from this point onwards—which I shall explain later in the chapter. In 1946, 33 per cent of total national government expenditure was funded through taxes—both direct and indirect.[13] By 1955, this level had increased to 55 per cent (Cortés Conde, 1956; Sánchez Román, 2012). As Sánchez Román (2012: 86) argues,

> for a government that was committed to greater wealth distribution in society, one may expect greater use of taxation, yet the distributive policies were not underpinned by direct taxation but upon the maintenance of full employment and high wages in industry and increases of public expenditures that were funded by alternative sources including social security taxes and foreign trade profits.

That said, there was some tax reform. The tax burden overall had increased (Gerchunoff and Antúnez, 2002), aided in part by the strengthened capacity to tax through the centralization of tax collection under the newly created institution: *Dirección General Impositiva* (DGI). And some tax levels were

Table 4.3 Fiscal deficit percentage of GDP, 1945–1955

Fiscal deficit as percentage of GDP	
1945	4.6
1946	6.9
1947	5.8
1948	13.4
1949	9.8
1950	5.5
1951	4.5
1952	5.6
1953	8.8
1954	8.5
1955	8.9

Source: Gerchunoff and Díaz-Alejandro (1989).

[13] Excluding social security taxes (Cortés Conde, 1956).

increased substantially between 1946 and 1955 (corporation tax from 10 to 24 per cent, the top bracket of personal income tax from 22 to 40 per cent), and the continued reapplication of taxes on extraordinary profits, a strategy initially levied as an emergency policy during World War II, was repeatedly renewed with the justification of aiming to achieve a more equitable income distribution.[14]

However, for all the progressive rhetoric and policies, it was indirect taxes and not progressive direct taxation that was the hallmark of Perón's fiscal strategies post 1949 (Sánchez Román, 2012). Significant increases in direct taxation were, by and large, avoided. Figure 4.1 shows that direct taxes increased slowly during the early years of the Perón premiership, where it peaked in 1947, at a level of 48 per cent of the total tax burden before receding. This is because the implementation of new sales taxes in 1948 changed this trajectory, and the level of direct taxes had fallen by 9 per cent to 39 per cent of the total burden in 1955; the implementation of the sales tax was, in part, a policy to encourage industrialization (Sánchez Román, 2012). Therefore, to shift the Argentine economy towards an industrialized mode of production, and with it, greater state autonomy—one of the underpinning tenets of Peronism—the state would require greater tax collection because of the financial burden of industrialization (Skidmore, 1978). As time progressed, indirect taxes, which are exactly the taxes that exacerbate inequalities in the lowest paid, conversely, became more important to the Perón regime than direct taxes.

Deepening fiscal tensions

Not raising the tax burden above 14 per cent of gross domestic product (GDP) (Table 4.2) would, for several reasons, become problematic for the President, who was pursuing both a redistributive agenda and simultaneously a programme of industrialization (Andrenacci, Falappa, and Lvovich, 2004). First, although Perón had managed to crystallize the shift towards industrialization seen through rises in manufacturing employment, real year-on-year percentage increases in both manufacturing and agricultural economic output were weak or contracting from 1948 to 1954 (Gerchunoff and Llach, 2010). Second, between 1946 and 1949, the redistribution that had thus far been pursued by the Peronist government had been driven by strong commodity prices, but from 1949, the international prices of Argentina's

[14] Tax policies under Perón were embedded into the constitutional reform of 1949, which stated that 'equity and proportionality are the basis of taxation and public burdens'. The reform was aimed at legitimizing fiscal discrimination and progressiveness (Sánchez Román, 2012).

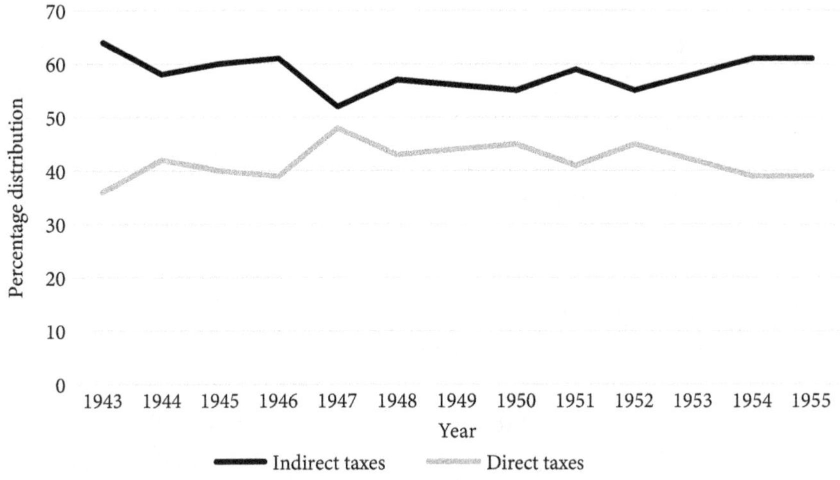

Figure 4.1 Direct versus indirect taxation, 1943–1955

Source: Sánchez Román (2012), Graph author's own.

main agricultural export commodities (corn, wheat, and flax) dramatically dropped (Ocampo, 2015). Third, net terms of trade plummeted in 1951 because of the Central Bank's currency devaluation, which led to an exhaustion of foreign currency reserves—which had been utilized to buy imports for the industrialization programme, stabilize the exchange rate, and control inflation—and would become emblematic of the redistributive fiscal and balance-of-payment problems that would besiege Argentina throughout the twentieth and into the twenty-first centuries (Cortés Conde, 1956; Skidmore, 1978; Gerchunoff and Díaz-Alejandro, 1989; Gerchunoff and Antúnez, 2002).

Under Perón, the government consistently spent more than it collected, with the fiscal balance anchored in a deficit (Table 4.3). Gerchunoff and Llach (2009: 402) attribute this growing fiscal deficit to 'Perón's spending away of exceptional terms of trade in the immediate post-war'. Moreover, this redistribution strategy exacerbated the deteriorating level of currency reserves. With the increase in real wages, this, in turn, initiated an increase in import requirements that was driven by a working class with more disposable income, which would paradoxically drive up inflation and erode the real-term wage gains. Increased demand for imports would erode the foreign currency reserves needed to purchase imports required for industrialization and to give confidence to attract investment, laying bare a key developmentalist puzzle—growing inflation and a negative balance of payments account.

Considering these factors, the government instigated the *Plan de Emergencia* in 1952, which was a stabilization strategy underpinned by enhanced agricultural exports and greater fiscal responsibility, and a reduction in welfare redistribution. However, sluggish growth in traditional sectors—whose competitivity had suffered through national focus on the industrialization process—an inability to raise the tax burden, a growing fiscal deficit, and growing inflation meant that, with the vocal support of the landed oligarchy, the military stepped in and deposed President Perón in 1955.

Post-Peronist politics: Low tax, social conflict, and growing debt, 1955–1989

In this section, I highlight that following the overthrow of Perón in 1955, the contested idea about the role of the state continued to frame development debates in Argentina. Failure to implement tax reforms and increase domestic resource mobilization meant that debt became the principal way to fund the Argentine state for much of the twentieth century. At the same time, this was a period of relative fiscal peace—until President Perón returned from exile in Spain in 1973—between governments and landed elites because commodity prices were enduring a period of low value and, therefore, the extraordinary profits were not there to be extracted. In this case, the interests of the landed elites were less negatively impacted than under the IAPI fixed-price framework.

This period in Argentina—as with much of Latin America—was characterized by extreme political instability, with governance frequently interchanging between military and civilian rule. This context meant that confronting the structural macroeconomic problems that existed to finance the Argentine state remained largely unaddressed and the political cleavages opened up under Peronism, deepened further.[15] While there were attempts to navigate a middle ground between the interests of the landed elites and the urban working classes—in a few isolated cases[16]—this period is illustrative of a struggle between those who sought to end economic interventionalism and return power to the markets and those who sought deeper state intervention into the Argentine economy. In relation to taxation, the debate became more convoluted, with questions of democratization an additional factor within

[15] Following the overthrow of President Perón, the military excluded the PJ from taking part in elections—the interests of the working classes were effectively excluded from the formal political arena—which would exacerbate tensions, especially as real-term wage cuts were a 'conditionality' of the International Monetary Fund borrowing required to fund the state.

[16] Presidents Illia (1963–1966) and Onganía (1966–1970) both sought to navigate a more central development trajectory, with President Illia implementing a minimum wage and promoting heavy industry (Tedesco, 1994).

an already contentious policy framework. But now, taxing the wealth of the rural sector would be approached differently, with the disbanding of the IAPI in favour of export tax strategies operationalized for the first time in the twentieth century.

The introduction of export taxes

In the decades after the overthrow of President Perón, there were no major reforms to Argentine tax design; those implemented under Peronism, for the most part, endured until 1976. One of the principal reasons that major reforms were avoided was because of the costs involved in implementing reforms. Therefore, the average tax burden as a percentage of GDP remained consistent for three decades: in the 1950s—13.99 per cent, 1960s—13.86 per cent, and 1970s—13.96 per cent (Cetrángolo and Gómez Sabaini, 2010). However, although the overall burden remained stagnant, Table 4.2 demonstrates a shift back towards indirect taxation from direct taxes on income. The protracted social and political conflict that is illustrative of this period deeply undermined the chances to implement a more progressive direct tax strategy, and therefore the overall burden remained flat. Furthermore, by maintaining an indirect taxation strategy, the political conundrum over who to tax would be avoided by governments with limited legitimacy. One tax reform that was implemented, however, was the levying of export taxes over agricultural exports. And while it may seem counterintuitive for the military to tax the landowning oligarchy that had pushed for it to overthrow Perón, they too were in a difficult socio-economic position. The government needed revenue, and while it was unpopular with rural producers, it was less costly to them than the IAPI and represented a policy that was the lesser of two evils (Barsky and Dávila, 2008; Sánchez Román, 2015).

The IAPI, which had been central in extracting revenue from the rural sector under Peronism, was disbanded on 16 September 1955 (Sánchez Román, 2015). The following year, *retenciones* were first levied on agricultural exports (Barsky and Dávila, 2008), the utilization of which would be applied at varying levels between 1956 and 1976, dependent on several factors, not least the price of commodities. Taxes were first imposed at a rate of 15 per cent over cereals, including maize and wheat. This early implementation of the export tax regime created tension between the government(s) and landowners, with the SRA arguing that these taxes were discriminatory towards the sector, demonstrating that these taxes were beginning to instigate contention between the producers and government as soon as they were levied.

This would form the bedrock for contention, which would last into the twenty-first century—at varying levels (Gerchunoff and Llach, 2010; InfoAgro, 2024). However, by and large, they were initially, and reluctantly, accepted because there was an understanding on the part of the producers that this was a temporary measure that was used intermittently by governments (Barsky and Dávila, 2008), deemed necessary due to the political and economic instability that characterized this period (Sánchez Román, 2015). And because the producers and the associations of the rural sector felt that they had been *maltratados* ('very badly treated') by President Perón, to them this tax represented a better scenario than the price-fixing mechanism of the IAPI (Sánchez Román, 2015).

Furthermore, the producers' interests were not as negatively impacted as high profits were not there to be collected due to falls in commodity prices, which began a downwards trajectory following a price boom in the late 1940s. The price of corn in December 1947 had reached a high of US$295 per bushel, which by 1956, had dropped to US$136 and by 1968 to US$119 (World Bank, 2021a).[17] Therefore, the surplus profit from high commodity prices that had been present for redistribution during the Peronist decade was no longer there, and so, for now, a moot point. As such, the producers were not losing this profit as international prices dictated that these gains were not there for collection anyway. However, the tax still created tension, but this was through a different logic. Producers and exporters claimed that the export taxation regime penalized production and deterred exports in times of a sluggish market with low commodity prices. Since the price that the producers receive was based on the world market price of commodities, the return to the producers after taxes ended up below the international commodity prices (Hutchison, 1972). Therefore, this directly affected the levels of commodities that the producers exported as they chose to hold on to their products. Over the course of the 1960s, agricultural exports as a share of total exports fell from 98 to 85 per cent (Hutchison, 1972).[18] Sánchez Román (2012) argues that when the low commodity prices in the late 1950s and early-to-mid-1960s were coupled with reduced exports, it meant that the tax was viewed as pointless. Whilst not expanding on whether or not it was viewed by the government or producers as pointless, this highlights that these taxes were less polemical because prices were lower, and therefore, there was less to be collected from export taxes and less for the producers to lose.

[17] A bushel is equivalent to 56 lbs.

[18] This was also affected by poor harvests in 1961, which contributed to a lower export level (Conklin and Davidson, 1986).

Table 4.4 Export tax levels on major exports, 1965–July 1970 (%)

Date	1965	March 1967	November 1967	April 1968	October 1968	July 1970
Wheat	13	25	18	6	6	17
Corn	6.5	25	25	18	8	19
Sorghum	–	25	25	18	8	19
Beef	9.5	25	18	18	15	20

Source: United States Department of Agriculture (1972).

Table 4.4 shows how these taxes were reintroduced between 1965 and 1970. While it traces that they were levied at a low rate in 1965 by President Illia's civilian government, they did not attract contention, with prices remaining low. When these were hiked across all products in 1967 under military governance, it was done in a different context. Export taxes this time were imposed on practically all exports of grains and livestock products as well as live animals, but they were imposed so to avoid exporters' windfall peso gains during a major devaluation of the peso—that was a requirement to access International Monetary Fund (IMF) loans (Hutchison, 1972).[19] These hikes were then followed by systematic decreases in tax levels in 1968 before being hiked again in 1970, but as producers had benefited from a weaker peso to aid exporting and the tax level was intermittent, by and large, these did not generate the tensions that were seen under the IAPI.

Another explanation for reduced tension between governments and the producers over export taxes during this period can be drawn from the fact that now, the rural associations had formal channels into government, enabling them to advocate for the producers' interests. Schneider (2004) highlights that between 1955 and 1983, seventy-four SRA members were appointed to ninety-four government positions, also offering a possible explanation as to why tax did not change dramatically during this period as the rural sector had political influence. However, this political influence would be short-lived; between 1973 and 1976 under both President Juan Perón's second presidency (1973–1974) and the presidency of his wife and successor Isabel Martinez de Perón (1974–1976), no members of the SRA

[19] The peso was devalued from 250 to 350 per US$1 as part of the IMF's conditions for securing finance. The plan also required the reduction of import duties and lifting of import restrictions and the elimination of export subsidies, increased utility charges for public services, higher internal taxes, higher taxes on exports, wage controls, and increasing credit to the private sector (IMF, 1967).

were appointed to government positions when the export taxes would be reintroduced in a progressive mechanism that would increase taxes based on prices (Schneider, 2004).

This would again generate conflict with the producers, not least because taxes were reimposed as prices had started to rise and therefore, as argued by Gerchunoff and Llach (2010), the tax was once again deemed by the producers as an attack on profits and a further example of the perceived maltreatment by President(s) Perón towards the rural sector. Since the return to power of President Perón in 1973, the sector had lost its political influence, and under the mobile tax mechanism, the sector's interests were being adversely affected by tax hikes because commodity prices were on the ascendence and profits were being eroded by the taxes. The price of a corn increased from US$128.5 per bushel in 1970 to US$382 by 1974 (World Bank, 2021a). This increase was accompanied by strong growth in other commodity prices, including wheat and soybeans, and therefore taxes on cereals and oilseeds were hiked to just under 40 per cent in 1974, while taxes were applied at lower levels on meat (20 per cent) and dairy (10 per cent) (Brambilla, Galiani, and Porto, 2018).[20]

However, throughout the 1960s and 1970s, the imposition of these taxes did not raise the overall Argentine tax burden, which meant that increased government spending would need to be met with hikes in borrowing. During the 1960s, the overall tax burden actually dropped as a percentage of GDP from the previous decade (Table 4.2), with direct taxes showing the largest deterioration. This drop was attributed in part to two interrelated factors that were endemic during this period of Argentine development. There was a linkage mechanism between inflationary pressures, which impacted upon economic production and increased incidences of tax evasion. During this period, inflation was high, and prices increased every year (apart from 1969) by over 10 per cent (Gerchunoff and Llach, 2010). In some years, this skyrocketed: 129.5 per cent in 1959, 182.4 per cent in 1975, and 444 per cent in 1976 (Sánchez Román, 2012). As inflation moves taxpayers from one tax bracket to another, their real incomes do not increase, and in many cases, taxpayers defer paying tax, which increases the pressure on other taxes and other taxpayers (Mayer, 1962). Sánchez Román (2012) correlates high inflationary pressures to increases in tax evasion estimated to reach 63 per cent in 1959 and over 75 per cent in 1975. This decrease in direct taxes and an increase in

[20] Part of the oilseed group now incorporated soybeans, which Argentina began to export in 1973. Within six years, exports had grown from 1,000 tonnes to 2.84 million tonnes (FAOSTAT, 2021).

indirect taxes is traced in Table 4.2. However, the inability to expand the tax base is not only an economic challenge but also, overwhelmingly, a political one.

Bergman (2019) argues that it is political because governments do not want to damage their political support bases by increasing tax over groups whose votes they rely on, and Kaldor (1962) himself pointed to political will as a key driver of tax strategies. In this light, popular democratic rulers across much of Latin America, including Argentina, opted to avoid broadening the income tax base to fight tax evasion because such a strategy would damage political support. However, while this is a salient point and demonstrates one theory of how politics is enmeshed with tax collection, I want to draw attention again to the fact that the tax spend remained contentious during this period because it sits squarely with the tension surrounding the idea of the role of the state. Following the overthrow of President Perón in 1955, government spending was reduced from 30 per cent of GDP to 25 per cent by the Frondizi government (1958–1962), which was cut further by subsequent military governments to 23 per cent. On re-election, President(s) Perón returned government spending to 30 per cent by 1975.[21] However, this level of spending was problematic because the government was again collecting less in tax revenue than it was spending. Therefore, debt increasingly became the fallback option to meet these demands and to plug the recurrent fiscal deficits (Figure 4.2). This tension became even more acute following 1973, when spending increased by 7 per cent in a year, and so did the fiscal deficit. Moreover, it highlights how reliant Argentina had become on foreign debt because, by 1975, with such a low tax burden, only one out of every three pesos spent by the government was raised from taxation (Conklin and Davidson, 1986); all other financing was through a programme of quantitative easing or borrowing, which meant that debt was being used to eschew difficult political tax questions.

Owing to the repeated fiscal deficits, Argentina's debt liabilities had grown exponentially since 1955. At the time of President Juan Perón's death in July 1974, the increased spending programme since his return to office led the IMF to decline any requests to extend medium- and long-term loans further (Conklin and Davidson, 1986). At this point, it would only issue short-term aid. The level of public-sector debt that was required to be repaid in 180 days grew from US$379 million in 1974 to US$717 million in 1975. By 1976, US$1.1 billion in short-term loans were due for repayment. However, this

[21] Isabel Perón succeeded her husband as president of the Republic following Juan Perón's death in 1974.

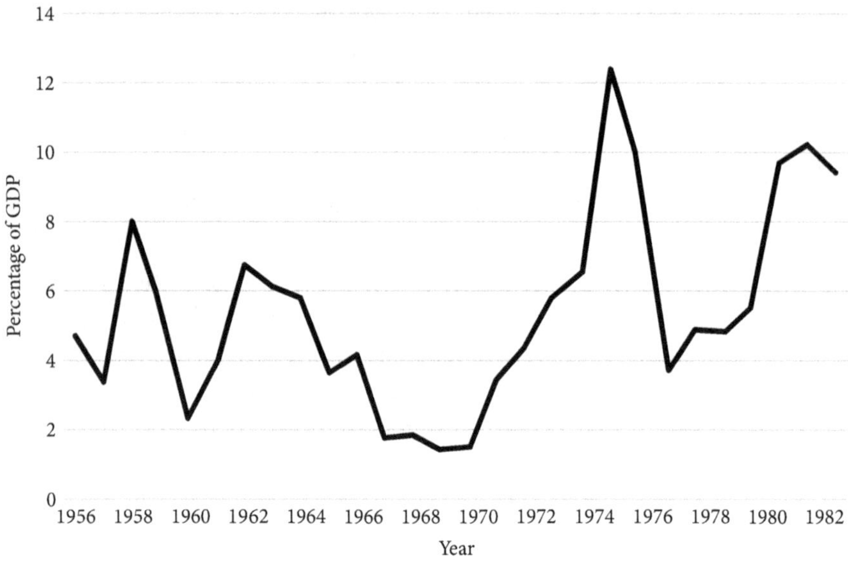

Figure 4.2 Argentine fiscal deficit, 1956–1983 (%)
Source: Gerchunoff and Llach (2010). Graph author's own.

debt, too, had a class dimension because when both Peronist presidents attempted to reverse some earlier military policies—which formed part of the loan conditions by the IMF in 1967—the policies they were reversing were policies that had placed the burden of debt servicing on the working classes because real wages had fallen by 11 per cent in 1968 and a further 7.6 per cent in 1969. In the light of growing debt and a narrow tax base, the hikes in export taxes presented an opportunity to redistribute once again away from the rural sector in support of the working classes. But this time, it was no less contentious and by 1976, it was met by calls for strikes from the rural associations (Manzetti, 1992).[22] As debt had been used to circumvent tax questions, and spending was increasing, foreign creditors insisted that Argentina stabilize its finances, but before President Isabel Perón could renegotiate with the IMF, she was deposed by the military junta of Jorge Videla in 1976.

[22] Economic tensions during this period extended beyond those between the government and the rural sector. A package of economic policies known as the *Rodrigazo* was implemented by economy minister Celestino Rodrigo in May 1975. Its aim was to address the growing fiscal deficit and improve productivity through a 150 per cent currency devaluation, a 100 per cent hike in transportation and utility prices, a 180 per cent rise in the price of fuel, and a 45 per cent hike in real wages (Clarín, 2005). The inflationary pressures that followed meant that prices increased by around 30 per cent per month, which would lead the largest labour union, the CGT (General Confederation of Labour), to call for the first general strike under a Peronist government demanding wage rises of between 125 and 150 per cent (Kiguel, 2015).

Exacerbating the rural versus industrial cleavage: Debt dictating development, 1976–1989

Following the overthrow of Isabel Perón, Argentina was ruled by a military government through state terrorism (Peralta-Ramos, 1992). The state apparatus was entirely under the autonomous control of the junta and the seven de facto presidents who would represent it between 1976 and 1983. Under the first president, Jorge Rafael Videla, the military exacerbated the tension between the landed elites and working classes by implementing policies that would favour the rural producers and negatively impact the working classes. Economic policies headed by the economy minister José Alfredo Martínez de Hoz (1976–1981) included a dramatic cut to real wages and a shift in the direction of the economy through a swing back towards natural resource exportation and the removal of the export taxes. The junta initially sought to 'harmonise the development of farm [rural] and industry by stripping the latter of its privileges that it had acquired and restoring the former to its lost economic power' (Peralta-Ramos, 1992: 72). Although the unions were not disbanded, real wages were cut by 32 per cent in 1977, and then, until 1983, increases were controlled at 0.23 per cent cumulative growth per annum (Peralta-Ramos, 1992: 72). In contrast, production grew over the same period at a cumulative annual rate of 4.97 per cent, sending the ratio of wages to productivity plummeting.

The cessation of economic interventionalist policies and the move towards the liberalization of the economy was attributed to a rapidly growing debt burden. Before the military assumed power in 1976, the level of external debt had reached US$7.8 billion. The following year, it had reached US$9.6 billion, and by the end of the dictatorship in 1983, Argentinian external debt had risen to a level of US$46 billion (Peralta Ramos, 1992: 143), an increase of 364 per cent during seven years of military governance. In line with regional economic patterns at this time, state financing in Argentina had become dangerously dependent on continuous borrowing from foreign banks and had maintained a constant fiscal deficit. Further loans were needed to pay existing debt, debt was financing debt, and interest rates were skyrocketing—adding further downwards pressure as debt was becoming more expensive.[23]

[23] The Interbank interest rate (Libor) increased by 28 per cent in real terms from 1979 to 1982; in short, any borrowing that Latin American administrations implemented to fund the state during this period would cost much more than in the preceding years (Armendáriz and Larraín, 2017).

These state financing challenges meant that the military itself now turned to the rural sector and reimposed taxes of 25 per cent on exports of cereals and oilseeds in the early 1980s (InfoAgro, 2024). However, this was not enough to address the government's macroeconomic problems, which were simultaneously coming under increasing pressure from mass capital flight to the United States. This, in turn, was adding to growing domestic instability, which was brought about, partially, by numerous administration changes and meeting the strengthening demands of the working classes, which were protesting at the deteriorating state of the economy, which had contracted by 6.2 per cent in 1981 and 5.2 per cent in 1982. All of this culminated in a return to democratic elections and the electoral victory of Raúl Alfonsín of the *Unión Cívica Radical* (Radical Civic Union) (UCR) in December 1983.[24]

President Alfonsín had the task of rebuilding the country, both politically and economically. Prices had soared under the preceding three years of military rule. The index of wholesale prices rose by 180 per cent in 1981, 311 per cent in 1982, and 411 per cent in 1983. Investment in Argentina had been stifled, brought about in part by instability and lack of confidence in previous administrations. This level had fallen from 23.2 per cent of GDP in 1980 to 14.1 per cent in 1983. Exports fell by 20 per cent from 1982–1983 (Kedar, 2013). Alfonsín and his government inherited a situation characterized by the acceleration of the struggle of the appropriation of income between rural and industrial sectors. And as such, the administration attempted to implement a *Pronagro* ('national agricultural programme'), whose aim was to increase rural production over a six-year period. However, as it was a programme that called for significant state intervention into the sector through government-controlled prices, credit policies, and land taxation, it was rejected by two of the major rural associations—the *Confederaciones Rurales Argentina* (CRA) and the SRA—and received limited support from the FAA and *Confederación Intercooperativa Agropecuaria* (CONINAGRO) (Manzetti, 1992).

The SRA called instead for the abolishment of all export taxes—which had remained from the previous military government—and demanded that the government should focus its support on agricultural exports over industrial production, instigating protests from the UIA. However, this situation was not borne out, and the level of extraction from the rural sector in the early and mid-1980s was significant, with the World Bank estimating that '45 per cent of the sector's GDP was transferred via taxation to the public sector and other parts of the economy' (Manzetti, 1992: 613). One of the policies that

[24] The Argentine invasion of *Las Malvinas* (the Falkland Islands) in April 1982 instigated a short but expensive war with Britain, and the Argentine defeat was a catalyst for the return of elections as it had eroded any remaining regime legitimacy.

this supported was an increase in industrial wages, this time not to appease powerful trade unions but in a nod to earlier distributionist models to stimulate domestic demand through the availability of finance available to citizens (Kedar, 2013).

This revenue redistributed from the rural sector was an essential source of finance for the government because the enormous growth of foreign debt had drastically diminished the resources available to the state. This, in turn, made it more difficult to continue the programme of state-managed subsidies. The traditional patterns of 'subsidies to agricultural and industrial sectors would now be transformed under pressure from international debt repayments' (Peralta-Ramos, 1992: 87). Addressing contradictory interests of industry and the rural sector was becoming a Sisyphean task for the government (Teichman, 2019). Falling prices of commodities, including beef and grains in the mid-1980s, further exacerbated the rural sector's position. The deteriorating economic environment was at such a level that it managed to unite ten of the most influential representatives of agriculture, finance, and industry along with the *Confederación General del Trabajo de la República Argentina* (General Confederation of Labour) (CGT), which was calling for reduced government intervention into the economy, which was deep in recession and, by 1985, suffering under hyperinflationary pressures above 2000 per cent (Dornbusch and Carlos De Pablo, 1989).[25]

While attempts to address hyperinflation and interrelated deteriorating macroeconomic indicators through the Austral Plan were received positively by actors in the rural sector, there remained rising tensions between the sector and the government because price controls remained and there was a continued use of export taxes.[26] As a concession, the President appointed an SRA member to be minister of agriculture, and because of low international prices, export taxes on maize and wheat were abolished in early 1987 (Manzetti, 1992). However, continued macroeconomic pressures and further borrowing led to national debt levels reaching US$51.5 billion by the end of 1987. There was an attempt to address this through the implementation of a two-part *Plan Primavera* ('Spring Plan'), whose target was the stabilization of the economy to control hyperinflation. However, part of this plan would

[25] In order to exercise greater pressure on the government, in 1984, the SRA, CRA, and CONINAGRO joined with the so-called group of 11, which represented the country's ten major interest groups in industrial, agricultural, commercial, and financial fields and were joined by the CGT in order to negotiate a pact among themselves to overcome the crisis (Manzetti, 1992).

[26] The Austral Plan was introduced as an attempt to address the deteriorating economic landscape in a period when agricultural prices remained relatively low (OECD, 2019). The fundamental tenet of the Austral Plan was a currency change. The Austral Plan replaced the peso at a rate of 1:1000 and was accompanied by a freeze on prices and wages, an increase of state utility prices, and a commitment not to carry out a programme of quantitative easing.

exacerbate political cleavages around interventionalist policies further as it included the reimposition of export taxes in May 1989 at levels of 30 per cent, withholding on each commodity. This reintroduction of taxes instigated immediate opposition from the SRA and its members, who protested during their annual conference, labelling the tax, once again, as discriminatory (InfoAgro, 2024).

These taxes and the wider Spring Plan were not enough to control the growing hyperinflation. This cycle of debt-fuelled state funding continued, and the economic instability beset upon Argentina became more complicated because, due to non-compliance with earlier agreements, finance options were withdrawn from the IMF and later the World Bank (Kedar, 2013). The President left office early in July 1989, with hyperinflation having pushed consumer prices up by 3,610 per cent and wholesale prices by 5,062 per cent in eleven months (Kedar, 2013), and power returned to the PJ with the election of President Carlos Menem (1989–1999).

The shift to market-led development: Debt rises still further, 1989–2001

In this section, I shift the chapter's focus to what is the final period of Argentine development explored in this chapter to show how the debate about state intervention shifted in this period and was characterized by an absence of state and the return of the market. However, the debate would not be resolved, and conflict around market-led policies and an absence of state intervention would culminate in the largest debt default the world had ever seen (at the time) and, ultimately, a rejection of earlier neoliberal reforms. When a period of continued low commodity prices converged with a new pro-market state vision, there was less redistributive conflict between the government and the actors in the rural sector. Now, taxes on agricultural exports became subsidiary. However, because of an overvalued peso and skyrocketing debt, mostly borrowed locally in dollars (Feldstein, 2002), tensions began to build throughout wider areas of society through wide-ranging deteriorating macroeconomic indicators.

A Peronist, Menem had the task implementing a reformist agenda to counter the economic conditions that had led to Alfonsín's resignation. However, the reforms that were implemented demonstrate the wide scope of ideas within the PJ itself surrounding the role of the state within the economy. Policies were simultaneously implemented to control hyperinflation—including the instigation of the Convertibility Plan, which stipulated free convertibility of the Austral into US$—while sitting squarely in the 'Washington Consensus' neoliberal narrative of 'macroeconomic stabilization, trade liberalization, privatization, deregulation, and related market-orientated policies' (Bambaci, Saront, and Tommasi, 2002: 76),[27] called by Smith (1991: 53) 'the assault on the state'.[28] However, as Panizza (2005) highlights, this was not only an economic shift but also an ideological one. Neoliberal policy prescriptions offer broad guiding principles that highlight the benefits of reducing state intervention into economic affairs, therefore, they sat squarely within an ongoing ideological debate around the characterization of the Argentine state.

Starting immediately after his inauguration in 1989, President Menem's plan was to restructure the state apparatus as rapidly as possible to reduce the public sector's intervention in, and regulation of, the economy (Smith, 1991; Antía, 2019).[29] Menem aligned Argentina with the economic doctrine of the prevailing Washington Consensus, which subsequently allowed for the reintroduction of IMF drawing rights. However, tax reforms to reduce marginal rates and broaden the tax base were part of the doctrine of the Washington Consensus (Panizza, 2009). Trade liberalization generated an increase in the level of exportations throughout Menem's tenure as president (1989–1999) and led to the creation of the regional body MERCOSUR.[30] Table 4.5 highlights the continued upwards trajectory in export levels until 2000. However, the production matrix of these demonstrates a shift back towards a comparative advantage with natural resource exportation one that benefited the

Table 4.5 Volume of exports of goods, 1985–2000 (%)

Year	1985	1990	1995	2000
Percentage	49.3	70.3	100*	136.2

Note: *1995 = 100.
Source: CEPALSTAT (2021).

[27] At a rate of 10,000 Australs to US$1.

[28] Through economic shock measures, inflation fell from 200 per cent in July 1989 to 5.6 per cent in November 1989. Austerity policies included increasing government-controlled prices of petroleum products, electricity, and transports from 200 to 640 per cent and suspending tax breaks, along with promotional business incentives and the devaluing of the currency by 170 per cent (Smith, 1991).

[29] A major privatization programme included state-owned electricity, water, gas, pension system, and the national oil refinery (Smith, 1991).

[30] The Southern Common Market or MERCOSUR (the Spanish acronym) is a regional economic trading bloc that was established in 1991 through the Treaty of Asunción and initially comprised four full members: Argentina, Brazil, Paraguay, and Uruguay. Venezuela would later join and be expelled in 2016 because of a failure to follow democratic processes. Bolivia became a full member in July 2024.

rural sector, especially following the abolition of export taxes under Menem's administration (InfoAgro, 2024).[31]

Reduced conflict and rural-sector transformations

Although President Menem was elected from the PJ, under his presidency, relationships between the government and the rural sector were much improved. Manzetti (1992) argues that the president's commitment to free market policies, rolling back the state, and privatizations found its biggest supporter in the SRA. Early tensions surrounding the currency overvaluation—brought about by the Convertibility Plan—had been addressed between the government and representatives of the FFA, CRA, and CONINAGRO through a 'fiscal pact'. In this pact, economy minister Domingo Cavallo (1991–2001) agreed to abolish taxes on exports on the understanding that the associations urged their members to increase production and pay the new VAT, property, and land taxes. Moreover, the minister conceded to long-standing demands by the rural associations by creating joint commissions of government and representatives of the rural sector to negotiate new taxes, transports, and credits (Manzetti, 1992). Tensions during this period were reduced.

Importantly, the overvalued currency and low international prices during the 1990s impacted on the composition of actors in the rural sector, and this led to a race for productivity and economies of scale that benefited those medium-to-large producers with the financial capacity to invest, the entry of large foreign entities, and the expansion of the agricultural frontier through processes like genetically modifying soybeans (Gras and Hernández, 2009). These changes supported a disarticulation of the sector as a coherent political actor, as landowners and family businesses were now sharing the market with foreign businesses, planting pools, trust companies, and professionalized tenants (Gras and Hernández, 2016; Hora, 2020). Furthermore, during the 1990s, the rural sector became more heterogenous in its composition, with the type of roles associated with agricultural production diversifying to include other activities such as contractors, consultants, service providers, local machinery and chemical producers, and transport companies, most of whom no longer lived 'on' the land but in nearby small towns and cities

[31] The top five exports by volume in 1989 were cereal and vegetable oil (21 per cent), meat and eggs (11 per cent), machinery (8.3 per cent), chemicals and health products (8 per cent), and metal products (5.6 per cent). The level had shifted following a decade of compliance with neoliberal policies championed by the Washington Consensus, and by 1999, the top five exports were represented by cereal and vegetable oils (30 per cent), oil (12 per cent), machinery (12 per cent), chemicals and health products (7.8 per cent), and food processing (4.7 per cent) (OEC, 2019).

Table 4.6 Argentine foreign debt, 1993–2000

Year	1993	1994	1995	1996	1997	1998	1999	2000
US$ billion	72	87	99	110	124	141	145	146
Percentage of GDP	32.5	33	37	40	44.5	49	51	52

Source: Ministerio de Hacienda (2019).

'strongly linked to their surrounding environment' (Craviotti, 2008: 9; Gras and Hernández, 2016). In short, a wider range of businesses were enmeshed within the sector, which meant that interests outside of those of the traditional producers became important. However, the associations remained key players in the 'fiscal pact' between the government and the rural associations, and the export taxes were not reimposed. President Menem's reforms to increase the tax base yielded only moderate results. By the end of the 1990s, the total Argentine tax burden was less than 22 per cent. This was well below other countries in the region, and well below the Organisation for Economic Co-operation and Development (OECD) averages of between 35 and 40 per cent at the end of the same period (OECD, 2021).[32] But debt had continued to increase as it had been used as a vehicle of state financing instead of addressing tax questions (Table 4.6).

Following the completion of President Menem's two terms in 1999, Argentina descended into a tumultuous period of social, economic, and political instability that resulted in deteriorating macroeconomic indicators, including high inflation, growing unemployment, poverty, and rising social conflict.[33] An inability to address tax questions eventually led to Argentina defaulting on its debt liabilities in December 2001 and plunged the country into a social and economic crisis.

Conclusion

This chapter introduced the Argentine case study. It demonstrated the importance of agricultural commodities to consecutive Argentine governments and highlighted that historically, the producers of these agricultural commodities were the landowning elites, whose exports brought them significant wealth

[32] Brazil and Uruguay had a tax burden of above 30 per cent in this period (Acuña, Galiani, and Tommasi, 2007).

[33] Fernando de la Rúa was elected as Argentine president in 1999 and was president until his resignation on 23 December 2001. His successor, Adolfo Rodríguez Saá, announced that Argentina would not repay the $18 million that was due [to the IMF] the following day, and Argentina defaulted on its huge sovereign debt liabilities on 24 December (Kedar, 2013: 178).

and power through the nineteenth into the twentieth centuries. Moreover, it has shown that for any government to extract revenues from this highly specialized export-led sector, it meant taxing the interests of a landed oligarchy that had been responsible for Argentina's integration into the global economy and had benefited significantly from this integration.

It has thus shown that attempts to structurally shift the Argentine economy towards industrialization through import substitution strategies placed the government of Juan Perón in direct tension with these landed elites for several reasons. First, post 1946, the government directly intervened in the rural sector to extract revenues and redistribute these to the nascent industrial sector, directly impinging upon its interests. Second, the process of intervention into specialized sectors and the redistribution from one sector to another by the state was deeply embedded within opposing ideas about what role the state should take in national economies. In short, the intervention, first through price-fixing vis-à-vis the IAPI and latterly through the utilization of export taxes, created tensions around opposing visions and characterizations of the state; these were initially underpinned by the fact that Perón's government was associated with heightened state intervention in the economy, which, in Argentina, had a deep class dimension because the redistribution was used to ameliorate the socio-economic conditions of a growing industrial working class at the expense of a landed oligarchy.

Peronism created a deep political cleavage around the strategies to extract and redistribute from agricultural producers, but the politics and tension surrounding this extractivism continued throughout the various civilian and military administrations of the twentieth century, albeit at different levels. Subsequent governments were unable to address these tax questions because of a number of interrelated factors that converged to present barriers to the legitimization of export taxes strategies, which in turn increased tensions. Among other factors, opposition to the export taxes influenced by the fact that the taxes negatively impacted upon the interests of the producers and a deteriorating political influence of the landed oligarchy were symptoms of more profound disagreements about what ideas of the state and national development should look like—which is illustrative of continued failures to build social consensus around the tax strategy.

Furthermore, with the sector's profitability also dependant on external markets, fluctuating commodity prices meant that tax was not consistently levied across these periods, and therefore, this tax was never fully legitimized and never fully accepted by the rural producers as it was utilized sporadically. In many instances, debt was used by governments to eschew the contentious process of extracting this tax, and crucially, it remained unresolved. By circumventing these questions, borrowing became a more important pathway for funding Argentine state obligations, especially because of the volatility of agricultural commodity prices and export levels. Therefore, twentieth-century Argentine development was funded by growing debt, which, by the end of the 1990s, had become unsustainable. This led to the ensuing economic, social, and political crisis that would create space to legitimize the taxes that had been so contentious previously. Chapter 5 introduces the culmination of this debt mountain and the aftermath of the Argentine financial crisis, when export taxes were essential to the rebuilding of the Argentine state following the debt default of 2001, but legitimacy would once again prove to be fragile.

5

Taxing Exports for What?

Building and Losing Legitimacy

Introduction

This chapter has two aims: first, to demonstrate how the Argentine financial crisis bestowed temporary legitimacy to a tax strategy that had been historically contentious between Peronist governments and agrarian elites in Argentina; and second, to explore the circumstances under which legitimacy to tax was lost in a process that was so polarizing that it enabled tension to permeate into other areas of Argentine society and conflict to embroil other classes. To elucidate the first aim of the chapter, I argue that the deep crisis in which Argentina found itself after a decade of compliance with the neoliberal doctrine of the Washington Consensus created the conditions for the emergency government of Eduardo Duhalde and the subsequent government of Néstor Kirchner to gain a temporary consensus and garner temporary legitimacy around export taxes for emergency response. It shows that, in this context, exports taxes were a fiscal tool for a crisis when there was no possibility for the state to borrow to build out of the debt default. I am therefore arguing that in this post-crisis period, there was a suspension of conflict around these taxes because the emergency environment created the necessary legislative and fiscal space to bridge the historical divide that existed between left-wing Peronist governments and organized actors in the rural sector.

However, the chapter's second aim is to demonstrate that when the context of emergency fades, the sustainability of export taxes began to be questioned by the same rural actors as these taxes were seen to be funding a redistributive welfare programme and were no longer for crisis response. The catalyst for social conflict came while commodity prices were growing strongly, and the government implemented an export tax strategy that was pegged to these growing international prices; now export taxes became associated with an extractive and redistributive interventionist form of state that was overwhelmingly rejected by the producers and their associations. The cleavage

Taxing for Development. Matt Barlow, Oxford University Press.
DOI: 10.1093/9780198923220.003.0005

that the tax revolt created was so deep that it permeated into other areas of Argentine society, where it would become a fault line and crystallized an association of this tax strategy directly with the ideology of Kirchnerismo and its brand of state-led development, which would endure beyond the export tax debate.

Taxing out of financial crisis

Following over a decade of compliance with neoliberal economic development policies under President Menem, by the end of the 1990s, the deteriorating economic environment and ballooning debt liabilities had reached such a level that capital in Argentina was scarce, the value of the peso was plummeting, and creditors were reluctant to lend more to the government, all of which created a situation whereby taxation in Argentina became all the more important as a pathway to financing state obligations and to trying to ameliorate the vicissitudes of the looming crisis for citizens. But, with low levels of income taxation and high levels of tax evasion (Mahon, 2015), export taxes would represent a fiscal lifeline to Argentine administrations.

Initially as a policy to address the scarcity of hard currency, and to avoid a 'run on the banks', on 1 December 2001, the economy minister, Domingo Cavallo, implemented a freeze on all bank-held deposits when it became clear that banks did not hold enough US$ to cover deposits: a policy named *El Corralito*. The response from Argentinians to this policy was instantaneous. With citizens unable to access their savings, *El Corralito* resulted in widespread social uprisings and mass civil unrest across the country which left thirty-seven people dead by 19 December (Vilas, 2006). Moreover, the implementation had wider implications for the value of the peso. *El Corralito* rendered the ten-year Convertibility Plan untenable as its core tenet was the accessibility to exchange pesos for dollars freely at a rate of one to one (Feldstein, 2002).[1] The civil unrest spread across the country and reached such a level that President De la Rúa was forced to resign on 21 December 2001, destabilizing further an already precarious situation.[2] During December 2001, Argentina witnessed a series of extraordinary events:

> in the space of 15 days, Argentina saw five presidents, the largest debt default the world had ever seen (at that point), the abandonment of the ten-year-old currency

[1] To give credibility to the 'Convertibility Plan', the government had to guarantee that for every peso in circulation, this would be backed by a dollar or another hard currency at the Central Bank, the so-called currency board system (Feldstein, 2002: 8).

[2] *El Argentinazo* as it was referred to by the Argentine Left.

> exchange regime which had formed the contractual basis for the whole Argentine economy since its inception in 1991, and the devaluation by three-to-one of the peso.
>
> **(Wylde, 2012a: 86)**

As part of this political turmoil, the congressionally appointed interim President Adolfo Rodríguez Saá announced that Argentina had defaulted on its sovereign debt liabilities to the International Monetary Fund (IMF). While this was celebrated by a majority of members of the chamber of deputies, it would exacerbate the socio-economic indicators and lived experiences of Argentinians, which had followed a precipitous pathway since entering recession in 1998. Following the debt default, in 2002, Argentine economic output contracted by 10.9 per cent (World Bank, 2019). This economic contraction contributed further to the already growing levels of poverty, which had increased drastically following the debt default. This index, which had risen from 28 per cent in May 1998 to 38 per cent by October 2001, now reached 57.5 per cent in early-2002 (INDEC, 2020). Inflation that was measured at four per cent in 2001 rose to 41 per cent in 2002, and unemployment reached 19.6 per cent, up from 17.3 per cent in 2001 (INDEC, 2020), all of which pointed to a deep financial crisis and a monumental challenge for the newly appointed President Eduardo Duhalde.[3]

In an attempt to stimulate the Argentine economy towards recovery and to meet the level of crisis, emergency legislative powers that had been bestowed on the President by Congress led to the implementation of a raft of sweeping macroeconomic policies in early 2002 (Giraudy, 2007; Wylde, 2011).[4] Among the emergency policies was the termination of the Convertibility Plan, under which the peso had been pegged to the dollar, as a measure to avoid the hyperinflation seen in both 1989 and in early 1990. This shift laid the foundations for the President to intervene more successfully into the Argentine rural sector because, through a three-to-one devaluation of the peso, it increased

[3] Eduardo Duhalde was appointed president on 2 January 2002, following the eight-day presidency of Adolfo Rodríguez Saá (22–30 December 2001) and the three-day presidency of Eduardo Camaño (30 December 2001–2 January 2002).

[4] There were two pathways through which President Duhalde could enact these emergency policies: first, the continuation of emergency 'superpowers', which were earlier granted by Congress between March and December 2001 to try and reduce budgetary constraints in times of crisis (Becerra and Mastrini, 2010; Clarín, 2010; Frers, 2017); second, another legislative tool through which he could also implement policies—the implementation of an executive urgency decree. Enshrined in Article 99 of the Argentine Constitution since 1994, the *Decreto de Necesidad y Urgencia* (Necessity and Urgency Decree) (DNU) gave the president(s) powers to enact decrees that were underpinned by the force of law and would come into effect immediately. Although the decree was enshrined in the Constitution in its present form in 1994, before this, decrees were still utilized in constitutional governance. In 1985, Raúl Alfonsín utilized decree 1096/85 to shift the national currency from the peso to the Austral (Dalponte, 2009).

the competitiveness of Argentine exports on the international market, while presenting favourable conditions for the reintroduction of export taxes, which, serendipitously, coincided with strong growth in the prices of many agricultural commodities (Salvia, 2015). All of this highlighted the continued importance of agricultural exports to Argentina at this most critical time. Moreover, it foregrounds the importance of export taxes as a mechanism for the Argentine government to penetrate the rural sector to benefit, through extraction, from high commodity prices.

An increase in export revenues was even more important in Argentina in a period where options to borrow internationally were severed. And because of the crisis and seeking ways to recover state welfare capacities, the taxes were presented differently from previous administrations: an emergency tax for crisis response. Furthermore, these were not the first taxes that had been administered in this way; emergency taxes had already been attempted in the run-up to the debt default by Minister Cavallo.[5] Taxes on financial transactions had been levied when debt was rising, capital was scarce, and options to borrow had diminished (De la Torre, Yeyati, and Schmukler, 2002). Therefore, emergency taxes had recent precedent in Argentina because, in the context of mounting and unsustainable sovereign debt, tax reforms represented one of the few remaining options to raise revenue in what was an increasingly volatile socio-economic landscape and would represent one of a limited number of pathways to rebuild following the crisis.

Following a decade under which they had been abolished as part of Argentina's neoliberal project, Decree 310/02, published on 14 February 2002, established a tax on the sales value of major agro-export crops, including soy and derivatives, sunflower seeds and derivatives, wheat, and corn. To begin with, the government levied these at a rate of 10 per cent tax on this basket of agrarian products, which was collected from export companies that passed on the burden to producers through depressed purchasing prices (Kosacoff, 2007; Fairfield, 2015). For the government, the tax design had the benefit of being a relatively quick pathway to collect revenue, with minimal tax capacity needed. Export tax collection does not need complex infrastructures in place. Moreover, as this tax design had been utilized previously, the collection of these export taxes could be operationalized through

[5] Taxes on bank transactions had been implemented when debt was rising and options to borrow had diminished (De la Torre, Yeyati, and Schmukler, 2002). Minister Cavallo targeted the banking sector through the implementation of a *Ley de Competividad* ('financial transaction tax') (Law No. 25413)—in the context of an emergency tax (Cetrángolo and Gómez Sabaini, 2010; Rossignolo, 2016), raising the equivalent of 1 per cent of gross domestic product in 2002.

existing frameworks. Therefore, it presented an easier mechanism to fund the state's obligations in a time of national crisis. A former president of the National Foreign Trade Commission highlighted that

> Export withholdings are easy to collect and as they are collected at the point of export [in the ports] they represent a tax that helps in the fight against tax evasion. They are difficult to evade. And, with the price of agricultural commodities increasing and as the system was already in place to collect the tax, understandably there were many in government in favour of it.
>
> **(Interview, former president National Foreign Trade Commission, 2019)**

This reintroduction of export taxes would form the bedrock for a fiscal policy that would become a cornerstone policy throughout subsequent administrations. The level of tax on agro-export crops was quickly augmented by President Duhalde's administration during 2002, and the policy was expanded to incorporate export taxes over a larger basket of commodities. Major export rights were applied in March 2002 and then increased, in some cases by between 10 and 15 per cent by April 2002, which covered some of the major primary Argentine commodity exports (Kosacoff, 2007). However, what was different this time was that, overall, the imposition of taxes over the sector was not challenged as strongly as previously. There was currently space for change through a 'post-crisis consensus', a consensus that was sustained by several factors, including that the crisis gave legitimacy to increasing taxes, and as borrowing was not an option, there was a logic around increasing taxes. Furthermore, commodity prices were high, which, along with the currency devaluation, gave space to implement the taxes.[6] Therefore, as pointed out by an interviewee who writes for the United Nations Economic Commission for Latin America and the Caribbean (CEPAL), the level and utilization of extraordinary taxation was generally accepted by producers in the rural sector as a necessary response from the state to collect revenues at a time of emergency (interview, CEPAL, 2019). In this sense, emergency taxation enabled the state to build legitimacy in the midst of crisis because it allowed the government to respond to immediate social needs. In an interview with the chief economist at the think tank *Fundación de Investigaciones Económicas Latinoamericanas* (Latin American Economic Research Foundation) (FIEL), he highlighted that

[6] The devaluation and the imposition of export taxes differentiated Argentina from other Latin American states, where, in many cases, there were existing revenue extraction mechanisms in place, including royalties and state-owned enterprises where the state could easily extract surplus profits.

> In the situation where over 57 per cent of the population was classified as living in poverty and with unemployment at a level of 25 per cent, the space to introduce taxes that were thought of as inordinate and unsustainable before, was dramatically increased.
>
> **(Interview, chief economist FIEL, 2019)**

And, further underpinning this position in another interview with a tax expert, 'these changes were initiated in response to emergency and because of the economic landscape, on the whole, they were accepted as such' (interview, former secretary of public revenue, 2019). Cetrángolo and Gómez Sabaini (2010: 23–24) argue that this emergency tax measure responded to the federal government's need to 'engage with the peso's extraordinary devaluation' that occurred after the crisis and that the increase in the tax burden was driven by increases that arose from temporary taxes—export duties and banking transactions. However, actors in the rural sector did voice some low-level opposition to the implementation of taxes as a 'concept', particularly because President Duhalde had promised not to raise taxes in January 2002, but ultimately, the scheme was accepted as being a *necessary* but temporary measure. Furthermore, the *Secretario de Hacienda de la Nación Argentina* ('Treasury Secretary') at the time, Oscar Lamberto (January–April 2002), acknowledged that, in his opinion, export taxes were a 'bad tax' but were needed to help with the fiscal deficit [–2 per cent]. At the same time, a *Federación Agraria Argentina* (Argentine Agrarian Federation) (FAA) representative conceded that even 'if the sector can't get the country out of the crisis alone', sacrifices were needed (Río Negro, 2002; interview, Anon., 2002). However, in a recent interview, the former economy minister Jorge Remes Lenicov (January–April 2002) commented that prior to the implementation of the export taxes, a *Sociedad Rural Argentina* (Argentine Rural Society) (SRA) representative approached him voluntarily to offer 5 per cent of its export revenues to the government, demonstrating an awareness of the crisis situation from the landed elites' association (Perochena, Rodríguez Rey, and Judzik, 2020). While Minister Lenicov recounts this period indicating, with laughter, that the government would be asking for much more, it demonstrates that the crisis had given temporary legitimacy to the export taxes in the eyes of the oldest producers' association. What this tax was 'purchasing' for the producers was the rebuilding of the Argentine state following debt default. Emergency had substituted the earlier conflict and bargaining that had been present around the taxes.

Post crisis, the extraordinary taxation (as it was called in Argentina) contributed to a growing tax burden, and when this was coupled with reductions in overall government spending, even though redistribution policies (including energy subsidies) were implemented across society (Bril-Mascarenhas and Post, 2015), it led to significant improvements in the state of the Argentine public accounts (Cetrángolo and Gómez Sabaini, 2010). There was an immediate drop in government spending seen post crisis that was equivalent to 3.3 per cent of gross domestic product (GDP). Spending cuts were primarily attributed to the 'reduction in the real value of public-sector wages, pension payments, and debt interests' (Cetrángolo and Gómez Sabaini, 2010: 9).[7] These austerity spending measures, coupled with an increased growth of tax revenues, set in motion a framework that would deliver the highest tax burden in Argentina's history (at that point), of 25.6 per cent of GDP by 2004 (OECD, 2017).The government of President Duhalde had managed to put into place short-term measures that helped return Argentina to growth and had raised tax collection over an influential sector while reducing spending, which translated into a fiscal surplus. This surplus would be important and was a salient factor supporting increased social spending and the expansion of the welfare state, key policy pledges made by Néstor Kirchner when he was returned as president through popular elections in May 2003.

The First Kirchnerismo: A return of the Peronist left

Kirchnerismo began in its first iteration in Argentina in 2003, when Néstor Kirchner became President Duhalde's choice to represent the *Partido Justicialista* (Justicialist Party) (PJ) and to challenge Carlos Menem's re-election bid in the 2003 elections.[8] He stood as candidate for the *Frente para la Victoria* (Victory Front) (FPV), a centre-Left faction of the PJ. Néstor Kirchner was elected with only 22.2 per cent of the vote share after Carlos Menem withdrew following the first round of voting.[9] Whilst ex-President Menem had represented a more conservative side of the PJ through his adoption of wide-reaching neoliberal reforms, Néstor Kirchner was elected on a mandate that championed economic nationalism and a state-led development model: a return to interventionalism (Manzetti, 2014). Although, under Menem,

[7] The reduction in the real value of wages and pensions was a direct result of the depreciation of the exchange rate when the convertibility was abandoned.

[8] Duhalde negotiated with Carlos Reutemann, José Manuel de la Sota, Mauricio Macri, Adolfo Rodríguez Saá, Felipe Solá, and Roberto Lavagna prior to choosing Néstor Kircher as the candidate to repel the challenge of ex-President Carlos Menem (Levitsky and Murillo, 2003).

[9] Menem was returned with a majority in the first round of voting, with 24.5 per cent of the vote. However, he withdrew following a deterioration in his public image.

the PJ had shifted away from being solely a labour-orientated party (Levitsky, 2003a), the FPV's victory demonstrated the ideologically flexible appeal of the Peronist brand (Calvo and Murillo, 2012). Under President Menem, there had been changes within the PJ itself, changes that had broadened the party's appeal, which meant that the middle classes and independent voters in metropolitan areas took on a level of importance, alongside the traditional support base of the working classes.[10] Therefore, during the presidency of Menem, these two voter groups were represented by choices within the same party showing the breadth of political ideology within the PJ: 'Never has the broad-church appeal and the breadth of political ideology within the PJ, been so evident as [the choice] between Menem and Kirchner' (interview, ex government minister, 2019).

The winning percentage represented the lowest vote share for any president in Argentine democratic election history, one that did not afford the new president a strong mandate to implement policy changes, nor did Néstor Kirchner have control of Congress when he assumed the office of president of the Republic (Ministerio del Interior, 2003). However, President Kirchner had space to maintain the redistributive agenda because of the continuation of emergency governance, which meant that the extraordinary taxes that were still levied over the rural sector were not rescinded. There remained a temporary legitimacy and suspension of hostilities around export taxes, which continued into President Kirchner's mandate.

The consolidation of the redistributive 'emergency' state

What this meant for export taxes was that under the presidency of Néstor Kirchner, they remained a salient fiscal tool, and their collection and, importantly, redistribution that had begun timidly under President Duhalde was consolidated. As demonstrated in Table 5.1, the Argentine tax burden increased strongly under President Kirchner from 18.4 per cent in 2002 to 26.4 per cent by 2006. And the emergency tax burden grew from 1.2 per cent in 2001 to 4.7 per cent by 2006. This helped finance the FPV's redistributive agenda, and the evolution of public spending is highlighted in Figure 5.1,

[10] The turn towards a neoliberal state was not enough to instigate an exodus of support from the PJ by the working classes, for reasons of continued voting for Peronist identities (Ostiguy, 2000) and because of support for an initially recovering economy (Gervasoni, 1998). However, clientelism was another salient factor and, more explicitly, the consolidation of clientelist linkages, which also helped the PJ maintain its support from low-income working classes without the influence of powerful unions (Auyero, 2000; Levitsky, 2003b).

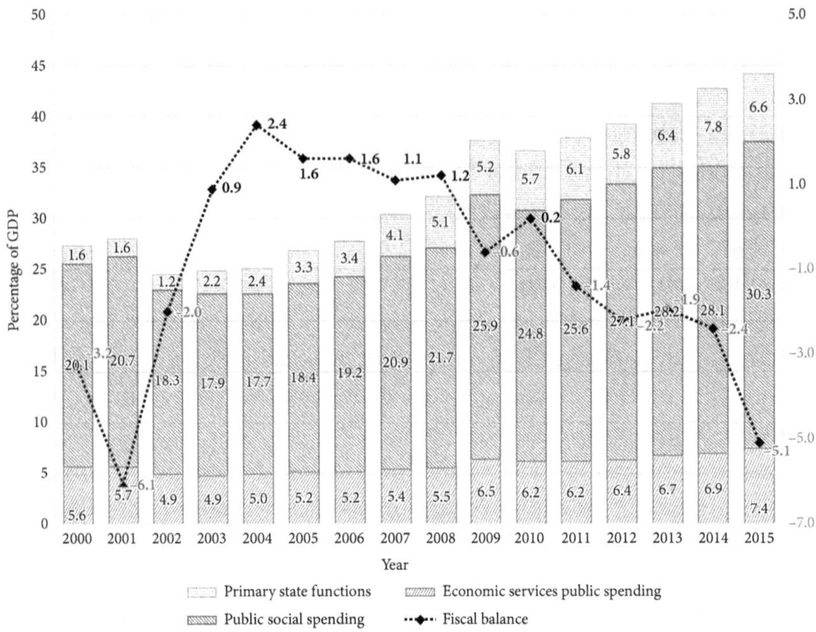

Figure 5.1 Government spending and fiscal balance, 2000–2015

Source: Ministerio de Hacienda (2021); Barlow and Peña (2022).

where the upwards trajectory of public spending can be clearly seen increasing from 24.4 per cent of GDP in 2002 to 30.4 per cent of GDP by 2007—when the President's term ended (Ministerio de Hacienda, 2021).

These emergency taxes, which represented 4.4 per cent of GDP, were driving the fiscal surplus, which (as Figure 5.1 demonstrates) reached 2.4 per cent at its peak in 2004. Why this is important is that it enabled President Kirchner to maintain social redistribution because there was the fiscal capacity to do so; emergency taxes had created fiscal space to continue an interventionalist state model. Following his assumption to the presidency in May 2003, President Kirchner consolidated this emergency discourse, highlighting the fact that the state needed to recover lost capacities and become 'an active economic actor'—promoting public investment; domestic consumption; and the growth of industry, employment, and salaries—whilst rejecting neoliberal austerity and dependence on foreign debt (Kirchner, 2003; Levitsky and Murillo, 2008).

This perspective was further reinforced three months later, when the President made a rare appearance at the headquarters of the SRA; the President and his ministers acknowledged that the export tax design was a necessary measure to finance social assistance programmes but 'not a state policy

Table 5.1 Key economic and social indications, 2001–2008

Year	2001	2002	2003	2004	2005	2006	2007	2008
GDP (US$) (1999 = 100) *Source*: World Bank	95	34	45	58	70	82	101	128
GDP growth increase (percentage) *Source*: World Bank	−4.4	−10.89	8.84	9.03	8.85	8.05	9.01	4.06
Poverty rate urban conglomerates (percentage of the population) *Source*: National Institute of Statistics and Census of Argentina (INDEC)	38.3	57.5	47.8	40.2	33.8	26.9	*20.6*	*15.3*
Inflation (percentage) *Source*: INDEC	4.0	41.0	13.4	6.1	12.3	9.8	*8.5*	*7.2*
Unemployment (percentage) *Source*: International Labour Organization (ILO)	17.3	19.6	15.4	13.5	11.5	10.1	8.5	7.8
Current account balance (percentage of GDP) *Source*: World Bank	−1.4	9.0	6.4	2.0	2.7	2.8	2.1	1.5
Fiscal account balance (percentage of GDP) *Sources*: Circular Economy Innovation Communities (CEIC), Organisation for Economic Co-operation and Development (OECD)	−6.1	−2.0	0.9	2.4	1.6	1.6	1.1	1.2

continued

Table 5.1 *continued*

Year	2001	2002	2003	2004	2005	2006	2007	2008
Total tax revenue (ARSm) (1999 = 100) *Source*: Ministration de Economia de la Republica Argentina	97	108	155	256	322	322	428	578
Total tax burden (percentage of GDP) *Source*: OECD	19.3	18.4	21.6	24.3	24.5	25.1	26.4	27.6
Emergency tax burden (percentage of GDP) *Source*: Ministration de Economia de la Republica Argentina	1.2	4.1	4.5	4.4	4.5	4.4	4.7	5.7
Emergency tax (percentage of total tax revenue) *Source*: Ministration de Economia de la Republica Argentina	6.4	22.2	21.0	18.3	18.2	17.6	17.8	20.6
Export tax (percentage of total tax revenue) *Source*: Ministration de Economia de la Republica Argentina	0.2	12.6	12.8	10.5	10.3	9.8	10.3	13.4

Note: the INDEC was intervened in 2007.

that had arrived to stay', recognizing that it affected the profits of a sector coming out of a long period of high costs and low prices (Varise, 2003). When presented through the context of emergency, the emergency logic was, on the whole, accepted by members of the association, however, with certain caveats: the SRA's president, Luciano Miguens (2002–2008), indicated that export taxes were only justifiable if they addressed 'exceptional Argentine problems', such as hunger, although he warned against viewing the sector as an economic lifeguard because there was an economic advantage to exploit (La Nación, 2003). While in 2004, the leader of the *Confederaciones Rurales Argentina* (CRA) highlighted that although they conceptually opposed export taxes, removing them was 'impossible', given the serious problems still faced by the country (Infobae, 2004), again, foregrounding the emergency context in which the export taxes had legitimacy in the eyes of rural actors. However, there were other factors that came into play that strengthened the validity of the tax design (to begin with) and re-enforced the legitimacy that the crisis had bestowed upon them. Export tax collection was strengthened by the fact that President Kirchner neither increased the taxes during the first half of his mandate (Table 5.2) nor deepened the programme of redistribution. To begin with, Kirchnerist governance did not increase challenges against the interests of rural sector actors; there was more compromise than conflict.

Although the government continued the emergency policies implemented by President Duhalde, on the whole, they were not expanded—with overall government spending virtually stagnant until 2006, as highlighted in Figure 5.1. Redistribution under President Kirchner was not as holistic as under Peronism. Grugel and Riggirozzi (2007) argue that one of the differences between (early) Kirchnerist rule and Peronism was the nature of

Table 5.2 Evolution of the level of export taxes, 2002–2007 (percentage)

Date	1 March 2002	1 April 2002	1 July 2005	1 March 2006	1 January 2007	1 November 2007
Sunflower seeds	13.5	23.5	23.5	23.5	23.5	32
Soybeans	13.5	23.5	23.5	23.5	27.5	35
Corn	10	20	20	20	20	25
Wheat	10	20	20	20	20	28
Beef	5	5	5	15	15	15

Source: Kosacoff (2007).

the link between citizenship and social welfare. Where Perón provided social protection and political patronage for the working classes as a whole,

> [Néstor's] Kirchnerismo represented more a neoliberal safety net style of social welfare with a more targeted provision seen through the 'running down of *Plan Jefes y Jefas* and the implementation of more targeted [smaller] *Planes Familias* and *Planes Trabajar* in its place.
>
> **(Wylde, 2012a: 110)**

This meant that it was not as progressive as targeting a whole class and, therefore, less contentious. This was favoured particularly where wider distribution could engage the government in conflict with influential sectors. This is a point that Panizza (2005: 730) also highlights within the context of the wider Left turn in Latin America, where he argues that policies during the *pink tide* were less radically *Left*; in many cases, they were less conflictual because they were only 'bending and moulding' the existing political institutions and free market economic models rather than attempting radical political and economic reforms.

With this in mind, a perspective that also came to the fore during interviews was that because President Kirchner was elected with a weak mandate, it acted as a barrier in the pursuit of a deeper interventionalist state model. The former head of the *Unidad de Información Financiera* (Argentine Financial Information) (UIF) and former director general of the *Dirección General de Aduanas* (Argentine Customs Tax Agency) (DGA) highlighted that the mandate of Néstor Kirchner directly affected the 'conflicts' with which he would engage. He explained,

> Néstor [Kirchner] continued with the export taxes as these had been implemented already under Duhalde; he was a president with little power. He needed to concentrate on debt restructuring and not engaging with the powerful Agricultural Cereal Cooperatives, he didn't have the power to do this. Néstor had to be more of a negotiator.
>
> **(Interview, former director general customs tax agency, 2019)**

This was a point that became less prominent after Néstor Kirchner emphatically gained control of Congress in 2005.[11] Following this landslide for the

[11] There were 127 seats up for election in the Chamber of Deputies; out of these, the FPV won 69 seats (54 per cent) with the PJ obtaining a further 11 seats (9 per cent). The FPV claimed seventeen of the twenty-four Senate seats up for election, with other Peronist parties claiming four during the 2005 mid-term elections (Ministerio del Interior, 2005).

FPV, there was a hike in public spending—especially in public social care, which had dropped slightly in 2004—see Figure 5.1, which demonstrates that post 2005, after the FPV took control of Congress, there was an expansion of social redistribution.[12] What all of this means is that in the early part of his presidency, Néstor Kirchner did not push the export tax burden over the rural sector any further, so the government did not increase negative impacts on their interests. Furthermore, the producers benefited dually from the currency devaluation and from strong commodity prices. So, for now, there was relative peace surrounding the tax strategy. However, the warning from the SRA's president that the taxes were only justified in emergency situations offered a vignette of what was to come and again demonstrated that the crisis was the only factor that legitimized the tax strategy in the eyes of the associations. This would become all the more contentious as the price of soybeans continued its upwards trajectory.

Soybean and beef exports: A different tax logic

The salience of agricultural export-led development fuelling growth in Argentina was undeniable and underpinned, in part, by high international market prices of soybeans—and their derivatives. In 2003, the price of a tonne of soybeans exceeded US$300, an increase of 50 per cent on 2002 prices.[13] The price then continued its upwards trajectory to surpass US$400 per tonne by 2008 (Bianchi and Szpak, 2017). Driven by Chinese demand for soy and high international market prices, Argentina witnessed a diversification in the composition of its agriculture matrix (Richardson N., 2009). Space where traditional crops (wheat, sunflower, and maize) were previously cultivated was now being replaced throughout the countryside by the more profitable soybean (interview, former president National Foreign Trade Commission, 2019; interview, former secretary in the Ministry of Agriculture, 2019). Cultivation and production of soybeans inordinately expanded, and exportation levels increased in line with production. During the period 2003–2007, Argentina witnessed augmented 'exports of soybeans (8.7 million tonnes (mt)–11.8 mt), soybean meal (18.5 mt–26 mt), and soybean oil (4.2 mt–6.4 mt)' (Richardson N., 2009: 8).

The soybean value chain was an important actor within the agro-export industry, and because of the growing prices, it became ever more important

[12] Investment targeted towards infrastructure and housing, which saw a gargantuan increase of 30 per cent in 2007, which was an election year.

[13] Post crisis, in 2002, soybean prices were US$200 per tonne (Bianchi and Szpak, 2017).

to President Kirchner. The soy sector estimated that it contributed an average of 7.3 per cent of the Argentine total fiscal collection during the years of the first Kirchner administration. Of relevance is the fact that soy has a certain 'distributive' benefit as, while important within the Argentine export matrix, it has no domestic market in Argentina, so its domestic price is not affected by the imposition of export taxes (Richardson N., 2009: 8), which should represent a tax that is more acceptable in a domestic context. However, because of a lack of domestic market, taxes on soy exports could only serve to increase government revenue and not to reduce domestic prices. Thus, a tax on soy was principally a fiscal tool to support redistribution.

However, not all export tax impositions followed the same logic. In November 2005, export rights on beef were levied at 15 per cent; this was augmented from a level of 5 per cent earlier that year. The initiation of this tax reform was, on the other hand, not instigated with the same rationale as one to solely bolster fiscal collection; this fiscal policy was a reactionary, state-led initiative intended to manipulate domestic market prices of beef through targeted price control measures. In 2005, beef prices were responding to extraordinary international beef demand, including from Russia and Chile (with other traditional suppliers suffering from the effects of mad cow disease), and increased domestic demand through an improvement in the level of real wages (Rossini, Arancibia, and Guiguet, 2017).

The tax hike on beef exports had been instigated following the failure of earlier policies to curb growing prices. In March the following year, an initial ban of 180 days on all exports of beef was enacted through a presidential decree.[14] As beef was a key product in the family consumption basket, protecting the price of this commodity was sociologically important. The price of the consumption basket was inextricably linked with the capacity of working-class and low-income workers to purchase its contents and, thus, politically crucial to leaders in the Peronist party. Historically, beef and wheat were the primary consumption goods of urban workers (Richardson N., 2009). Here, tax reform under President Kirchner was utilized in a different way, ameliorating against the growing price of a key Argentine commodity. It also represents the first occasion that the President intervened into beef markets through quotas and export taxes that directly negatively affected the interests of the producers, while improving those of the popular classes. This simultaneously shored up the President's core political support and enhanced his

[14] This was modified so that only beef that was surplus to the demands of the domestic market should be exported. This initiative led to a reduction in Argentina's market share from being the third largest global exporter in 2005 at 775,000 tonnes to eleventh position in 2014 at 197,000 tonnes (Rossini, Arancibia, and Guiguet, 2017).

government's political space to govern. However, four years after the debt default and approaching the final year of President Kirchner's mandate, the rationale of the export taxes began to be questioned. The consensus between actors in the rural sector and the government, which had previously been built around emergency, would start to show signs of fragility when the context of tax hikes changed.

Tax for an interventionalist state?

Since coming to power in 2003, the level of the majority of export taxes over commodities had remained consistent—aside from the hikes on beef. The Kirchner government announced two export tax rises in January and November 2007, increasing the rate for soybeans by 12.5 per cent and for sunflower and wheat by around 8 per cent (Table 5.3) (Kosacoff, 2007). However, the context in which these tax rises were levied represented a significant shift from the emergency rationale that underpinned the tax strategy in 2002. Table 5.1 highlights the strong economic growth between 2003 and 2007, where the country had surpassed its pre-crisis GDP levels, whilst the key indicators of poverty and unemployment levels substantially reduced—unemployment had dropped by half and poverty by just under half (Bergman and Gray, 2007; Kosacoff, 2007). Moreover, debt restructuring had lowered the burden of interest payments from 22 per cent of the fiscal intake in 2001 to 9 per cent in 2007, and the government had enjoyed several years of twin surpluses in both its fiscal and current accounts, allowing the constant expansion of public spending (Figure 5.1), which had grown 25 per cent in GDP terms since 2002—with major increases in subsidies to energy and transport, education and science, and social assistance programmes, amongst others (Filc, 2008).[15] Prior to the latest tax rises, emergency taxes accounted for 17.6 per cent of the total tax take, and the recovery of the economy had reinforced the government's fiscal position—although it had not widened the tax base—which resulted in an increasing tax burden that reached 25.1 per cent in 2006, but one that was heavily concentrated over the rural sector.

However, this time, the context had changed. The government no longer justified the export tax increases as due to an emergency response, but this time highlighted 'problems of growth' and the effects of inflation, which had been 12.5 per cent in 2005 and, by early 2007, had accelerated to a 20 per cent annualized rate, albeit the national statistics agency, *Instituto Nacional*

[15] Energy and fuel-related spending grew by 350 per cent in this period, while transport increased by 200 per cent.

de Estadísticas y Censos de la República Argentina (INDEC) had reported 8.5 per cent, but the institution was subject to widespread accusations of government intervention from 2007 (Gerchunoff and Kacef, 2016). Government officials, including chief of the Cabinet (and later president from 2019 to 2023) Alberto Fernández (2003–2008) and the economy minister Miguel Peirano (July–December 2007), therefore declared that the tax rises did not pursue a fiscal goal but were rather required to mediate the effect of rising international prices over the purchasing power of citizens, while also underlining the intent 'to preserve adequate levels of profitability' in the rural sector—in short, they were needed to keep the price of the consumption basket at a level that citizens could afford it (Cufré, 2007; El Economista, 2007).

Arbitrating long-term domestic prices for the working classes was a policy that had not been agreed upon outside of the emergency context. Here, the justification from the government was no longer one of emergency, which was temporary and short-term, but pointed towards a longer-term, consolidated redistributive vision. The government did not have legitimacy to tax for this, and it instigated opposition from rural and political opposition actors, who considered that the export taxes were 'confiscatory' and were being utilized for political reasons.[16] Elisa Carrió, presidential challenger from the *Coalición Cívica* (Civic Coalition) (ARI) and leading opposition figure, claimed that the government was trying to finance its 'fiscal disorder' because of a lack of foreign investment and external finance options (Perfil, 2007a; Página 12, 2007). The SRA's perspective was that the government was following short-term interests rather than the long-term promotion of production and investment, arguing that some producers within the sector were in trouble due to the export taxes (Perfil, 2007b), while the CRA and FAA not only advocated for minor protests but also considered their legal options due to the impact the increase would have on smaller producers, with lower productivity and tighter margins (Cufré, 2007; interview, former president National Foreign Trade Commission, 2019).[17]

In this sense, both the government and the rural sector acknowledged the changing status of export taxes. As highlighted in Table 5.1 and Figure 5.1, by 2007, the contribution of emergency taxes (4.7 per cent of GDP) was higher

[16] Indeed, much of the rise in public spending, including cash-transfer programmes, transport and energy subsides, housing projects, and additional rises in salaries—with real wages estimated to have increased around 70 per cent since 2002—benefited the governments' support base (Etchemendy and Collier, 2007; Richardson N., 2009; Interview former secretary of public revenue, 2019).

[17] As export taxes were determined by price and not by earning, smaller producers and those located in less fertile provides faced a higher fiscal burden and higher tax per hectare (Rodríguez and Arceo, 2006).

than the fiscal surplus.[18] This meant that the fiscal contract between the state and the rural sector could no longer be assumed as temporary because export taxes were a fundamental pillar in the long-term viability of the government's redistributive economic model.[19] What all of this meant was that the taxes that had been accepted as an emergency measure had changed rationale and were becoming more contentious, while representing an important funding stream for the redistributive governance of Kirchnerismo, a movement that would move into its second iteration with the emphatic election of Cristina Fernández de Kirchner for her first term as Argentine president in 2007.

The first period of Kirchnerist rule (2003–2007) closed with Néstor Kirchner leaving office as the most popular president in modern Argentine history, with approval ratings above 50 per cent (Bergman and Gray, 2007; Levitsky and Murillo, 2008). Underpinning this popularity were favourable macroeconomic indicators that had been prevalent in the post-crisis period: GDP (current US$) had grown from $97.72 billion in 2002 to $287.53 billion in 2007 (World Bank, 2021b), unemployment was down from 41.0 per cent in 2002 to 8.5 per cent in 2007, real wages had increased dramatically, and poverty was reduced from a high of 47.8 per cent recorded in the crisis aftermath in 2002 to 20.6 per cent by 2007 (INDEC, 2020).[20] Furthermore, the successful completion of debt negotiations, which had ameliorated the government's fiscal position, was also an attributing factor to the popularity of the outgoing president.[21] However, after presiding over four years of export-led consistent growth—rooted in a competitive exchange rate and soaring commodity prices (Etchemendy and Collier, 2007)—Néstor Kirchner did not seek re-election.[22] Instead, the transition from the first to second period of Kirchnerismo occurred with Cristina Fernández de Kirchner, a well-known public figure, assuming the candidacy of the FPV. President Fernández de Kirchner was elected with a landslide victory in October 2007, providing Cristina Kirchner with a mandate that had eluded her husband.[23]

[18] Also observed by Dborkin and Feldman (2008: 34).

[19] Bonvecchi and Giraudy (2007) indicate that the public sector would have been in deficit already in 2007 if it were not for the contributions of emergency taxes and transfers from the recently reformed pension system.

[20] By 2007, the Argentine GDP (US$ current value) surpassed its pre-crisis 2001 value of US$268.95 billion (World Bank, 2021b).

[21] The debt 'haircut' that was negotiated represented 30 per cent of the defaulted debt amount in 2001. A majority of creditors agreed to lose 70 cents in the dollar (Seager, 2005).

[22] Widely cited speculations in the media include health reasons, the impending energy crisis, and as a way to circumvent the restriction on the number of consecutive mandates that could be served.

[23] Cristina Kirchner captured 45 per cent of the vote, beating her closest rival, Elisa Carrió of the Civic Coalition (ARI) (23 per cent) and the outgoing president's former finance minister and the *Unión Cívica Radical* (Radical Civic Union) (UCR) candidate, Roberto Lavagna (17 per cent) (Ministerio del Interior, 2007).

Economic deterioration and commodity headwinds

During this period, in which President Fernández de Kirchner was elected emphatically, there were already signs that the strong economic indicators that had supported a redistributive programme so far were starting to abate, a factor that would become problematic as the President's economic and fiscal policies became more expansive. The Argentine economic landscape was changing, and there were growing indicators of problems that would beset the next president, which, in turn, would affect the space available to govern. In a point of departure from the previous administration, where Néstor Kirchner assumed power with both a growing economy and fiscal surplus, when Cristina Kirchner assumed the presidency, although Argentina was officially posting a fiscal surplus, this level was following a different trajectory from the one in 2003. This was now falling, and it was being further eroded by growing inflation.[24] The fiscal surplus that reached 2.4 per cent of GDP in 2004 (Figure 5.1) would enter negative territory between 2008 and 2009, showing the scale of the changing macroeconomic environment in Argentina during this period (Thomas and Cachanosky, 2016).

The fall in the fiscal balance was not only attributed to increases in the programme of public spending, but also, in part, it was attributed to the growing level of inflation that was impacting upon the cost of redistribution—Argentina's perennial macroeconomic challenge. In the aftermath of the 2001 crisis, inflation reached a level of 41.0 per cent (INDEC, 2019), and although this rate reduced sharply to a low of 6.1 per cent by 2004, it had started to creep upwards again and would ultimately present a barrier to the continuation of an interventionalist, state-led, redistributive model. Furthermore, along with the level of inflation itself, the validity of the inflation data (and other indicators) would start to become both contentious and political.[25] Higher rates of inflation, a diminishing fiscal surplus, and the global financial slowdown of 2007/2008 (affecting export levels) converged into a different economic environment for President Fernández de Kirchner, which translated into a tighter fiscal space for the continuation of widespread redistribution. However (and demonstrating the importance of export taxes as a

[24] Inflation has historically affected the Argentine economy, with an annual average of 22.85 per cent in the 1960s, 138.93 per cent in the 1970s, 565.70 per cent in the 1980s, and 252.92 per cent in the 1990s (World Bank, 2019).

[25] From 2007 onwards, there were widespread accusations of government intervention into the INDEC. The institution that is responsible for all official statistics in Argentina was embroiled in accusations of data manipulation after 2007. There was a sense among the economic establishment both in Argentina and internationally that, from around 2007, the figures had been subject to government intervention through an underestimation in the published official level of inflation (Cavallo, Cruces, and Perez-Truglia, 2016; Gerchunoff and Kacef, 2016).

fiscal tool), with the price of some of Argentina's major exporting commodities on the increase, the government chose to implement a tax strategy that would peg a variable tax rate to the international prices of some of Argentina's key exports. This policy was a catalyst for a major tax revolt and conflict that would come to be one of the most polemic and defining episodes of Argentine political economy under Kirchnerismo.

Export tax reform and contested state visions

To accompany the strong growth in global commodity prices (Figure 5.2), the newly appointed minister for finance, Martín Lousteau (10 December 2007–24 April 2008) implemented *Resolución 125/2008* (Resolution N.125) on 15 March 2008, which pegged a variable tax rate to the international price of commodities known as *retenciones móviles* ('mobile witholdings') (Table 5.3). The resolution was initially targeted at two commodities: soy and sunflower. At the time of implementation, it would have imposed an export tax at the rate of 44 per cent on soy and 41 per cent on sunflower (CEPAL, 2014; Regúnaga and Tejeda Rodriguez, 2015), which would have superseded the level of export taxes levied under the previous Kirchner administration of 35 per cent for soy and 32 per cent for sunflower, respectively (Kosacoff, 2007).

Resolution N.125 was a progressive tax mechanism insofar as tax applicable would increase alongside the price of the commodity increases. However, a point that was strongly argued by the government was that should prices fall, then the amount of export tax applied to the commodities would fall proportionately with this. Table 5.4 demonstrates the level of export tax for which the producers would have been liable under the suggested reforms if

Table 5.3 Resolution N.125 and the tax bands

Price range (US$/tonne)		VB (US$)	AM (percentage)	VC (US$)
0	200	0	20	0
200	300	40	32	200
300	400	72	48	300
400	600	120	79	400
600	>	278	95	600

Source: Ministerio de la Economía (2021).

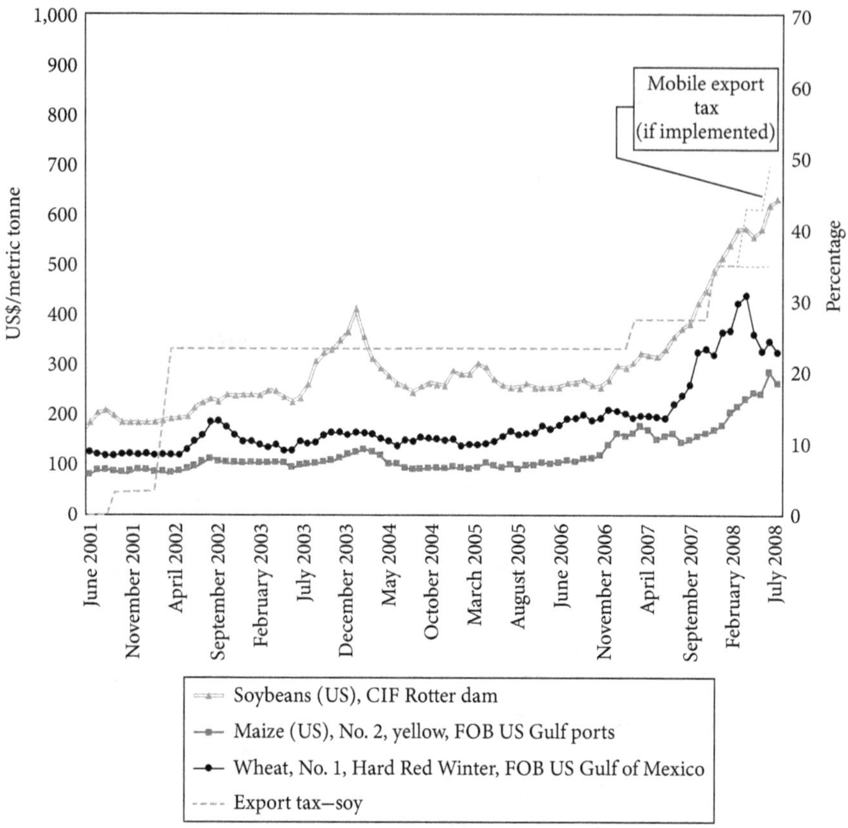

Figure 5.2 Commodity prices and soybean tax levels, June 2001–July 2008
Source: World Bank Commodity Price Data (2021). Graph by M. Barlow and A. Peña.

the resolution were to have been enacted. However, because of the profound tension that it generated, in the end, it was not.

The implementation of Resolution N.125 was a watershed moment in Argentine political economy, whose contention instigated a strong and near-instantaneous response from the rural sector. The logic utilized by Minister Lousteau for the implementation of this resolution was that these taxes had been levied to achieve 'a better equilibrium within agrarian activity, a greater decoupling of international and domestic prices [. . .] while guaranteeing domestic supply at reasonable prices for Argentine families', while underlining their importance in sustaining a developmental model based on low energy prices and a high and competitive exchange rate that also benefited the rural sector (Lousteau, 2008)—an argument the President would soon use to highlight the contribution towards foreign reserves generated by rural exports (Fernández, 2008).[26] However, it would set in process a period of conflict between the government and actors in the rural sector that would bring into question the legitimacy of the tax and the capacity of the state to collect the export taxes. The response to the tax hike, which would have augmented both soy and sunflower taxes by 9 per cent with this new resolution but which represented a hike of 16.5 per cent in fifteen months for the former and 17.5 per cent for the latter, was instantaneous and enabled the historically fragmented sector to reply with a cohesive response.

Moreover, what this resolution did was to reignite tensions between the Peronists and the rural producers, which laid bare historic tensions that were so polarizing that the argument and the response in Argentina was famously denominated by a journalist, Jorge Lanata (and widely known thereafter) as *la grieta* ('the crack'). The consensus and compliance that had been evident up to this point had been there because of emergency response, and now that the context of taxes was changing, this fed into the argument of rent appropriation by Peronist governments from the rural sector and its exports.

It was a tax policy that exacerbated the political cleavages around Peronism that existed between the working classes and elites in the rural sector. Politically, these export taxes sat squarely within that debate, and while achieving popular support from urban working classes, as one of the main recipients of export-led redistribution (Richardson N., 2009), it would be strongly challenged by the rural producers. Therefore, while popular with the government supporters, a CEPAL official highlighted that there was a high level of mistrust remaining within the rural sector about a Peronist government. The official argued that 'simultaneous Peronist policies of wealth redistribution targeted at the wealth of landowning elites, made Peronism more hated in

Table 5.4 Evolution of agricultural export taxes, 2002–2015 (percentage)

Date	March 2002	April 2002	January 2007	November 2007	March 2008*	2008–2015
Sunflower	13.5	23.5	–	3	41	32
Soybean	13.5	23.5	27.5	35	44	35
Corn	10	20		25	27	25
Wheat	10	20		28	28	28

Note: *Approximated rate if mobile scheme would have been implemented.
Source: InfoLeg (2021).

[26] The exchange rate would be kept around three pesos per dollar until mid-2008, when it started devaluing.

that group, than Stalin' (interview, CEPAL, 2019). This level of conflict was one that the President sought to highlight; in support of the mobile tax system, Cristina Kirchner focused on the class perspective by arguing that 'the international price of soy should not benefit a few producers; but all Argentinians [. . .] the burden of development should be shared by all' (Página 12, 2008). This argument was presented in the context that the continuation and the rearticulation of the export tax strategy was necessary for national development with the knowledge that inflation was eroding earlier gains and that macroeconomic indicators were generally deteriorating. However, as the taxes were funding an interventionalist model of the Argentine state, they became inextricably linked with wealth redistribution and associated with cash transfers and subsidies, whose recipients were the growing voter share of the President.

Although the implementation of the resolution was operationalized initially through presidential decree, it was underpinned by the legislative security of an FPV-controlled Congress and knowledge of weak institutionalized representation from the rural sector (Freytes and O'Farrell, 2017; Fairfield, 2015)). As the sector lacked effective institutional channels to protest the hikes, this meant that a groundswell of public support and collective action was required to try and overturn the mobile tax strategy. Put succinctly, one of the only ways for farmers, producers, association members, and other rural actors to protest the tax hikes was by mobilizing and taking to the streets.

The end of the fiscal peace: Export tax conflict

By this time, the export tax revenues had become a significant funding stream for the Kirchner governments. By 2007, they made up the lion's share of emergency taxes, which represented 4.7 per cent of the 26.4 per cent tax to GDP burden (Ministerio de Hacienda, 2021). Emergency taxes had become entrenched in the Kirchnerist tax policy basket: they represented 58 per cent of the emergency tax collection, which equated to 10.3 per cent of total revenue collected by the Argentine Treasury in 2007. However, when the export taxes were hiked in March 2008, this happened out of an emergency context. Argentine output had been growing at around 8 or 9 per cent for several years, whilst poverty and unemployment levels halved, which (as alluded to earlier) granted President Kirchner approval ratings above 50 per cent towards the end of his term and assured the electoral victory of Cristina Kirchner in October 2007 (Bergman and Gray, 2007). The context of these taxes had now changed, which was a change too far for the producers, and as such, it was no longer acceptable to them.

As alluded to earlier, the justification for the increases no longer pointed to the crisis and conditions of economic emergency but rather to 'problems of growth', particularly around the effect of inflation, which, in 2007, neared a 20 per cent annual rate—albeit the INDEC reported a level much lower at 7.2 per cent (Gerchunoff and Kacef, 2016). Officials therefore claimed that the hikes did not pursue a fiscal goal but were needed because the rise of international prices exposed the local consumption basket to 'imported inflation' and lowered the purchasing power of citizens (Cufré, 2007). At the same time, the economy minister declared that the hike 'preserved adequate levels of profitability' of the sector (EFE, 2007). But these arguments were rejected by rural and political actors, who increasingly viewed the taxes as 'confiscatory', seeking to finance additional expenses during an electoral year and compensate the deterioration of the government's fiscal position.

The importance of emergency tax to shore up the increased level of public spending in 2007—expanded cash-transfer programmes, transport and energy subsides, and sponsored additional rises in salaries—is laid bare in Figure 5.1: the public sector would have been in deficit for the first time since the crisis if it were not for transfers from the recently reformed pension system and the contributions of emergency taxes, which reached 4.7 per cent of GDP (Bonvecchi and Giraudy, 2007; Ministerio de Hacienda, 2021).

Furthermore, as the change in rationale for the export taxes was accompanied by the growing price of corn, wheat, and especially soy (which had started an upwards trajectory in 2006), this too heightened the criticism that was being levied by the rural producers' associations, which labelled this modification to the export tax strategy as nothing more than a programme of rent-seeking because of these price increases. There was growing pressure on the government to increase collection as the fiscal burden of the redistributive model of the state (especially through energy subsidy provision) was rising, along with inflation, and therefore, the government required augmented revenue collection to continue funding the energy policy and its welfarist model (Kulfas, 2016), a point that was highlighted by the producers.

The increase in export taxes was so contentious that it instigated an immediate and coordinated response from the rural sector. Eduardo Buzzi, leader of the CRA, declared that 'it's a pity that they [the government] are using us as source of revenue to solve cash problems', and the head of the FAA stated that 'with the excuse of *sojización* ['sojistation'] they are turning to fiscalist and rent-seeking measures' (Colombres, 2008).[27] The fragile consensus that had been displayed thus far, and the willingness to support crisis response, was

[27] *Sojización* is the process of land diversification away from other crops to soy because of increasing prices. This, in turn, affects domestic prices of traditional crops, pushing up the price of food products.

replaced by a cohesive reply that managed to bridge the heterogenous interests of the four major rural associations. The day after the implementation the *Mesa de Enlace* (literally translates as 'linkage table' but more appropriate is an agricultural liaison committee) was assembled, which comprised all four rural associations, and it immediately denounced the confiscatory character of the taxes and called for a nationwide, open-ended agrarian strike, stopping all agricultural activities and sales. Bridging the heterogenous interests of the four associations was no easy feat, and therefore it highlights the level of opposition that the taxes engendered:

> Kirchnerismo managed something that hadn't been seen previously, something that nobody had been able to do, they united groups within *el campo*. The SRA united with the FAA, it hadn't been seen, that hadn't been done for over 100 years.
> **(Interview, former secretary in Ministry of Agriculture, 2019)**

The conflict rapidly escalated as self-organized rural actors mobilized and set up roadblocks and picket lines across the main agrarian regions of the country. The opposition was initially surprised at the tax reform for two main reasons: first, because the tax hike was not in the producers' plans; and second, producers were angered because, in March 2008, a record crop was expected in both yield and international price. The timing of this change was viewed negatively as the policy—through the perspective of the producers—appeared to be rent-seeking due to the opportunistic way that it was implemented while there were high international prices, reaching over US$600 per tonne for soybeans (Figure 5.2).

Political parties that had been swept aside with the President's emphatic victory in October 2007, grasped the opportunity to consolidate their collective support behind the *Mesa de Enlace* and this consolidation had the intended outcome of further increasing the pressure on the government during this highly contentious period. The conflict witnessed outbreaks of violence and a destabilizing effect on the availability of products—following the blockades of key routes. The conflict lasted from March through until 18 July 2008. During this period, there were major protests both for and against the taxes, one of the biggest (anti-government) taking place on 25 March in Buenos Aires. The farmers and producers initiated sector-wide strikes and roadblocks, which affected the supply of staple foods (meat, poultry, milk, fruit, and vegetables) to supermarkets nationally and led to a lock-out of Buenos Aires. Pro-government rallies in response highlighted Cristina Kirchner's class argument. The government derided the farmers as 'protesters of abundance', with the President arguing that the farmers should act 'as part of a country, not as owners of a country' (Mcdonnell, 2008).

However, the taxes not only instigated a 'traditional' sectoral opposition from interest groups and their supporters but also managed to consolidate support in other groups; both the urban middle classes and upper classes joined the rural sector protests. The tax hike initiated a widespread intersectoral response (Fair Rzezak, 2008). Self-organized actors (known as *autoconvocados*)—comprising the more heterogenous group of new rural tenants, professionals, and small and medium-sized investors that had proliferated since the nineties (Gras and Hernández, 2009)—also mobilized and set up roadblocks and picket lines throughout the country. An interviewee writing for CEPAL highlighted that the conflict was at such a level that it raised awareness of export taxes in societal groups that he questioned would even have known they existed previously:

> Outside of economists, academics and the rural sector, nobody in Argentina even knew what *retenciones* were before [Resolution] 125, why would they? They [export taxes] weren't so political before the revolt; they were afterwards.
>
> **(Interview, CEPAL, 2023)**

The discussion of how an idea of export taxes became embedded with the statist model of Kirchnerismo and permeated into other socio-economic groups is explored in more detail in Chapter 7. What is important to highlight here is that the policy had become so contentious that the strategy was being rejected outside of the rural sector.

The roadblocks were only lifted when the resolution was sent to Congress. The administration's aim was to achieve legitimacy for its augmented export tax level by rallying unions, the unemployed, and influential FPV figures behind a proposal to have Congress enact the reform into law (Calvo and Murillo, 2012). However, and reflective of the level of contention, even though there was a strong FPV majority, the vote was not reflective of this in Congress because there was no real consensus between deputies and senators aligned to the government of how to address the agrarian conflict, and internal political wrangling would become salient within the ongoing situation.

Various sectors within the government argued for an orderly exit from the crisis through a negotiated drop in the level of the tax that was being levied, while still respecting the general framework of the mobile withholdings and, with it, demonstrating support for an increased overall tax burden on the sector (Kulfas, 2016). Senators who relied on the vote from agricultural provinces negotiated with rural actors directly and not in line with the administration's narrative. An interview with the former president of the National Foreign Trade Commission highlighted this perspective and said that 'there was great pressure on congress people and other public actors especially on those who were up for re-election' (interview, former president National Foreign Trade Commission, 2019).

Showing the deep contention that export taxes engender, the mobile tax resolution narrowly cleared the Chamber of Deputies by 129 to 122 votes, and the resolution then travelled to the Senate where, after eighteen hours of deliberation, the vote was tied, with many senators from the ruling party voting against the government's proposal, partly due to the fear of electoral reprisals from their constituents (Giraudo, 2017). The revocation of Resolution N.125 came on 17 July 2008, when the president of the Senate and vice-president, Julio Cobos, voted against Resolution N.125, and with this loss for the government, export taxes returned to pre-crisis levels (Giraudo, 2017).[28]

However, the utilization of emergency taxation through export taxes continued post conflict, albeit not in its variable mechanism. Export taxes had now been levied continuously from January 2002 and, as highlighted earlier, had been intrinsic in lifting the overall tax burden, which was funding increased public spending and redistribution, which reached a level of 32.6 per cent of GDP in 2008 (Figure 5.1). But the loss of the vote in the Senate was a seminal moment and was seen as a crushing blow for the executive. Through the initiation of the conflict, the farmers, producers, and their associations had withdrawn agreement for paying higher levels of extraordinary taxes—effectively putting a limit on how much fiscal revenue the government could extract from the sector. The wave of political popularity that had seen Cristina Kirchner and the FPV elected less than six months earlier had been eroded when the opposition transcended the rural sector. And with this erosion, the political space to implement further reforms diminished.

Ex-government officials and actors involved in the creation of the mechanism pointed to the fact that as the mechanism of Resolution N.125 was poorly communicated, this was a salient factor in explaining why the policy initiated such resistance. Although, as earlier highlighted, actors in the rural sector criticized the policy as rent-seeking, conversely, these interviewees pointed to the fairness of the mechanism and argued that when

[28] Julio Cobos was not a Kirchnerist or Peronist but was part of the UCR. He was part of Néstor Kirchner's 'transversal' movement under which he tried to unite progressive Peronists and non-Peronist leftists (Levitsky and Victoria Murillo, 2008).

prices dropped, farmers and producers would actually have been better off as the level of tax fell from the fixed rate export tax level that was in place by the time Néstor Kirchner stepped down as president (interview, CEPAL, 2019; interview, former president National Foreign Trade Commission, 2019; interview tax expert from AFIP, 2019). There was a belief in official circles that miscommunication was an important factor in triggering the conflict. There was a sense that it was poor articulation of the banded taxation system that was the real catalyst for conflict. As the response was instantaneous, it became problematic for the architects of the policy to explain this to the actors over whom the tax was levied. The former official highlighted that

> Producers, when scrutinising the bands of tax payable would see a tax rate of 95 per cent payable when the price of soy exceeded $USD600 per ton. This was contentious because what wasn't sufficiently explained was the fact that 95 per cent tax would be solely levied on the portion of the product that exceeded $USD600 not on the first $USD600. It was not well communicated.
>
> **(Interview, CEPAL, 2019; interview former government minister, 2019)**

Fairfield (2015) also argues that the 95 per cent rate of tax acted as a red flag. She highlights that because the tax rates were pegged to international prices, the producers felt that 'the state would take everything' (Fairfield, 2015: 211). Moreover, as Giraudo (2017: 172) indicates, by this point, many agricultural actors lacked trust that the government would keep its side of the fiscal bargain so that they would be 'sharing the profits but not the loses', and considering their recurrent side-lining, saw revolt as the only avenue left to defend their interests. So, what was seen as a level of miscommunication in government circles was viewed as an issue of mistrust by rural elites. The mistrust between the producers and the government had been steadily growing before 15 March 2008 hike and started with the two rises in 2007, with many in the sector feeling a sense of frustration at two increases in ten months, especially at the one that was implemented two days after the election of Cristina Kirchner. The 2007 hikes consolidated discontent among rural elites in a scheme that offered them limited economic or political benefits (Fairfield, 2015). A former government minister highlighted that

> Producers were very angry at the timing of the rise, and they felt powerless to complain as there was no official government in place. As the price of soy was increasing [to them] this amounted to a rent-seeking strategy.
>
> **(Interview, former government minister, 2019)**

What this conflict shows is that the government lost the support of the rural producers to increase taxes on exports; the associations' earlier hopes of improving relations had been lost.[29] The government lost the support of the producers because it didn't have the legitimacy to tax for an interventionalist state. Furthermore, by implementing the modification to the tax design through presidential decree, it shifted the fiscal contract by pursuing a hegemonic process that rejected any horizontal bargaining. The 2008 protest laid bare the limits of the government's strategy to embed this fiscal contract via a hegemonic coalition between civil society and certain elite sectors, such as industry, that would envelop the rural sector, marginalize its more powerful actors, and guarantee its fiscal subordination. The leader of the CRA also noted the ideological character of the fiscal bargain targeting and the lack of horizontal fairness by indicating that other sectors that were enjoying similar levels of 'rent' (profit) were not being targeted—a comment targeted towards bankers and industrialists who were present during the announcement of the mobile tax scheme, who 'clapped that the government was taking someone else's money' (Infocampo, 2008).

After the protests, the relationship between the government and the rural sector would turn openly adversarial, characterized by low trust and minimal communication and making any form of fiscal negotiation impossible.[30] Moreover, the strategy assumed by government to polarize the conflict in partisan terms eroded any space left for vertical and horizontal solidarity, particularly when deep-rooted political cleavages in society were laid bare, setting the government, unions, and its traditional working-class support base, against an emerging but disarticulated alliance between the rural sector, multiple opposition parties, and urban middle and upper classes (Catterberg and Palanza, 2012). This was a pivotal moment in Kirchnerist governance as its programme of enhanced interventionalist state capacity-building would both deepen and become more problematic, ultimately with policy choices consolidating support both for and against the Kirchnerist statist model.

Conclusion

The nexus of socio-political and socio-economic factors that was prevalent in Argentina post crisis afforded the President enhanced political and legislative space to govern through emergency policies in a post-crisis regime.

[29] The rural associations accepted that direct action would be pointless in 2007 and held out hope that Cristina Fernández de Kirchner's campaign promise to improve relations with the sector would come to fruition (La Nación, 2007; Fairfield, 2015).

[30] Interviewing a soy trader, Giraudo (2017: 173) notes that the view of the government after the protests was that agribusiness was administering wealth that did not belong to it and that its role was to contribute hard currency to the national budget.

The return of an export tax strategy framed as part of a wider basket of emergency taxes to ameliorate the dire state of social and economic indicators in post-crisis Argentina meant that there was a temporary consensus around these taxes; emergency had bestowed legitimacy on them in the eyes of the rural producers and associations. However, this legitimacy was temporary and only for crisis response, and the contention around these taxes quickly resurfaced when the rationale changed and questions of tax for whom and tax for what resurfaced in early 2008.

The third tax increase in fifteen months over some of Argentina's major agricultural exports demonstrated the importance of export taxes to the redistributive development model of Kirchnerismo, but it was also an increase too far. The hike was enough to bridge the heterogenous interests between the previously fragmented rural associations and crystallized support against the government. The variable tax mechanism was the catalyst for a cohesive sectoral response, which would ultimately pressurize the government to pass the vote to Congress, which would rescind the mobile export tax strategy and return the burden to pre-agrarian crisis levels. Export taxes that previously had legitimacy for emergency response lost legitimacy when they supported a programme of state capacity-building for an interventionist state, which, in turn, presented a major fiscal challenge for the government to continue its redistributive agenda with diminished resources.

Critically, even though the variable mechanism was not finally implemented, contention was at such a level that the policy became a fault line and crystallized an idea of this tax strategy directly with the ideology of Kirchnerismo and its brand of state-led development, which would endure beyond the export tax debate. In Chapter 6, the ramifications of this loss of tax revenue are discussed, alongside further concessions made to the agricultural provinces and what this meant for the redistributive development project of Kirchnerismo.

6
Commodity Price Volatility and Fiscal Entrapment

Introduction

This chapter introduces the vicissitudes of development strategies that rely on natural resource commodity extraction and export-led pathways during periods of low commodity prices. It highlights the challenges and limited options that the government of Cristina Kirchner had to finance public spending following the tax revolt in 2008. In doing so, this chapter, in conjunction with Chapter 7, shifts the focus away from a discussion centred around 'just tax' to locate the tax debate in the wider political economy and development challenges. The chapters address different elements of the tax debate, and I trace two narratives separately for the sake of clarity.

In this chapter, I show how, when the productive capacity of the Argentine economy failed to meet the popular economic aspirations of Argentine society, government attempts to continue spending to try and meet these aspirations resulted in growing societal opposition because the tax revolt had highlighted opposing ideas of tax and of state (Gerchunoff, Rapetti, and De León, 2020). I explore the economic challenges that had beset the government since there had been a further loss of legitimacy to tax agricultural producers in 2008 and from volatility in export revenues. Moreover, I demonstrate how concessions that were made to agricultural provinces and producers meant that the federal government was, fiscally, giving away a *bigger slice of a smaller pie.*

In Chapter 7, I then analytically trace how the rising social tensions that resulted from these macroeconomic challenges would fuel and become embedded in opposing ideas about export taxes. I argue that, during this period, social conflict no longer revolved solely around tax; but an idea of taxation was part of a contested vision about the nature of the state and the nature of development, and it was reflected in other issue areas that then accentuated the conflicts over tax. Export taxes became the fault line, but

Taxing for Development. Matt Barlow, Oxford University Press. © Matt Barlow (2025).
DOI: 10.1093/9780198923220.003.0006

sitting behind this were vast ideological differences about the nature and purpose of the state itself and its relationship with the market.

This chapter engages empirically with redistributive government policies that, I argue, locked the government in a gathering financial crisis when contingent macroeconomic factors made policies more expensive while income into the state decreased. There were key structural developments during this period of Kirchnerismo; for the first time, there were deficits in both the fiscal and current account balances. However, I show that while fiscal space was contracting, public spending was increasing, resulting in the financial entrapment whereby it was increasingly difficult for the government to deliver its progressive agenda. The chapter details some of these key social policies that contributed towards the decaying position of the twin balances that trapped the government. Policies including subsidy reforms, pension reforms, institutional interventions, and reforms underpinned income redistribution to clearly highlight that the policies were entrenched in an interventionalist vision of the state, and it required funding, which represented a major challenge as external factors were making this more expensive and putting increasing pressure on the government while international currency reserves were deteriorating.

I show that, during this period, while the weight of fiscal challenges was growing, the export tax strategy that had supported Argentine economic recovery ten years earlier was not expanded. Export tax percentages were either levied at the same level or reduced. However, this period is marked by both volatile and record commodity prices, but the government was not able to capitalize upon these record prices, even though revenue was scarce. Therefore, it shows that because the government had built a support base that depended on the redistribution of revenues, and as the government could not influence the producers to contribute further to this vision of a more interventionalist state, the government had trapped itself when macroeconomic pressures challenged the viability of this model.

Redistributive tensions: Expansive policies and reducing headroom, 2008–2011

This section briefly highlights the general economic environment in Argentina to provide context for policy implementations and to support the argument that the President was entering into a more generalized debate about the model of the state that was being pursued. During this period, the government would encounter increased fiscal challenges due to expansive

Table 6.1 Key economic and social indicators, 2008–2011

Year	2008	2009	2010	2011
GDP (US$) (2007 = 100) *Source*: World Bank	126	116	147	184
GDP growth increase (percentage) *Source*: World Bank	4.5	−5.9	10.1	6.0
Poverty rate—urban conglomerates (percentage of population) *Source*: National Institute of Statistics and Census of Argentina (INDEC)	15.3	13.2	9.9	6.5
Poverty level (percentage) *Source*: Universidad Católica Argentina	–	–	–	24.7
Inflation (percentage) *Source*: INDEC	7.2	10.6	10.9	9.5
Inflation (percentage) *Source*: Argentine Congress	–	–	–	22.6
Unemployment (percentage) *Source*: International Labour Organization (ILO)	7.8	8.6	7.7	7.2
Current account balance (percentage of GDP) *Source*: World Bank	1.5	2.2	0.3	−0.4
Fiscal account balance (percentage of GDP) *Sources*: Circular Economies Innovation Communities (CEIC), Organisation for Economic Co-operation and Development (OECD)	1.2	−0.6	0.2	−1.4
Total tax revenue (ARSm) (2007 = 100) *Source*: Ministerio de Hacienda, Argentina*	135	153	205	270
Total tax burden (percentage of GDP) *Source*: OECD	27.6	28.9	29.1	29.3
Emergency tax burden (percentage of GDP) *Source*: Ministerio de Hacienda, Argentina	5.7	5.0	5.1	4.9
Emergency tax (percentage of total tax revenue) *Source*: Ministerio de Hacienda, Argentina	20.6	17.25	17.6	16.7

Note: *Poverty level based on the ability to purchase a basic basket of goods.

spending and decreasing revenue collection, which would put pressure on export taxes (Table 6.1). Furthermore, additional funds would be required to address how increasing inflationary pressures would detrimentally affect the value of any collection.

In 2008, global economies were entrenched in a financial crisis and credit crunch that negatively impacted on global confidence and the liquidity of capital flows and reduced borrowing options (Brunnermeier, 2009). This global downturn did detrimentally affect Argentine economic output through reduced global demand for its exports, but the downturn was both shallow and short-lived. The Argentine economy bounced back relatively quickly, buoyed by the renewed growth in the price of soybeans and strong Chinese demand for them, meaning that export taxes continued to contribute significantly to the Argentine tax burden.[1] Table 6.1 shows both the economic contraction to −5.9 per cent in 2009 and the strong rebound to 10.1 per cent a year later, which maintained strong growth of 6 per cent through 2011. The value of this rebound was phenomenal, equivalent to a near 50 per cent increase on the value of the economy in 2007. Furthermore, Figure 6.1 highlights concomitant strong growth in the tax burden throughout this period, a key indicator of enhanced productivity and a growing economy.

The level of tax collected by the *Administración Federal de Ingresos Públicos* (AFIP) (Tax Collection Agency)[2] doubled during this period, with 2007 = 100; the tax burden doubled from 135 in 2008 to 270 by 2011.[3] However, although the level of emergency taxes significantly contributed to the growing tax burden and, overall, the absolute amount that they contributed grew year on year, as a percentage, this level started to fall following its peak at 20.6 per cent in 2008—this peak was buoyed by the tax hike in late 2007 and strong exports, which increased from US$55.7 billion in 2007, to US$70 billion in 2008 (World Bank, 2021a). However, paradoxically, even during a period of strong growth, emergency taxes remained levied and still represented 16.7 per cent of total taxes in 2011.[4] Demonstrating that the government did not increase the emergency tax base, it dropped as a share of tax take by 3.9 per cent in four years, and the share of export taxes within this take dropped by 5 per cent. The government did not push the agricultural producers any further to expand export taxation to fund its programme of redistribution.

[1] Soy peaked at US$603 per tonne in June 2008 (Cboe, 2020).

[2] Following his election in 2023, President Javier Milei changed the name of the Argentine tax collection agency from the *Administración Federal de Ingresos Públicos* (AFIP) to *Agencia de Recaudación y Control Aduanero* (ARCA) (Revenue Collection and Customs Control).

[3] $ARS269,351 million to $ARS540,138 million (Ministerio de Hacienda, 2021).

[4] These included export taxes and banking taxes on credits and debits.

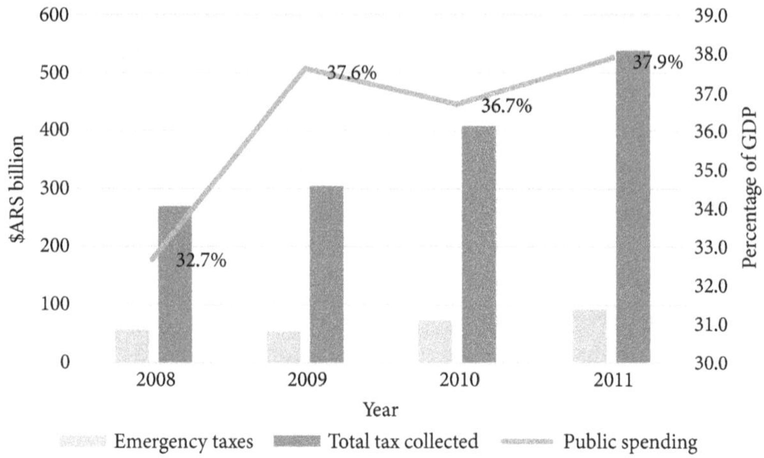

Figure 6.1 Total and emergency tax collection and public spending, 2008–2011 (% GDP)

Source: Ministerio de Hacienda (2021). Graph by author.

What Figures 5.1 and 6.1 do clearly illustrate is that through redistributive policies, the level of government spending was increasing. The fiscal surplus of 1.1 per cent in 2008 was the sixth consecutive annual fiscal surplus since 2003. However, this preceded the first fiscal deficit of Kirchnerismo of −0.6 per cent in 2009, which (aside from a slight bounce back in 2010) set the trend for consistent fiscal deficits for the reminder of the President's time in office. More striking was the fact that tax collection was at a record high, but this enhanced collection could still not keep pace with the level of government spending. This tension had deepened by 2011, when government spending reached a high of 37.9 per cent of gross domestic product (GDP), 5.2 percentage points higher over the course of the presidential mandate. Damill, Frenkel, and Rapetti (2015: 27) referred to this as the 'expansionary phase of the populist strategy', while other commentators were not so forgiving; economist Miguel Bein (2014) labelled the programme of enhanced spending with reduced domestic resources a 'macrocide'.[5]

Materially, government strategies under Cristina Kirchner to redistribute revenues through welfare projects *did* have a significant impact on the reduction of poverty levels in Argentina. Table 6.1 shows the consistent decline in the level of poverty from 15.3 per cent in 2008 to 6.5 per cent in 2011. But, as the *Instituto Nacional de Estadísticas y Censos de la República Argentina* (INDEC) had been intervened in 2007, The *Universidad Católica Argentina* (Catholic University of Argentina) (UCA) began presenting its own data

[5] Referring to what the economist saw as *macroeconomic suicide*.

series in 2011. This series challenged the official figures, as its estimates of domestic poverty were significantly higher. In 2011, UCA data suggested that 24.7 per cent of Argentinians lived in poverty. Politically, these disparities would fuel the claims of corruption levied against the President, which fed into wider and growing discontent but which will be discussed more fully in Chapter 7.

Important to note here is that while the Argentine government was spending its way into a deeper fiscal deficit, because of increasing inflationary pressures, the value of the redistribution was also being eroded as inflation was on the rise. Even when taking documented interference and manipulation into the INDEC into account, inflationary figures were consistently higher than the levels that were reported under Néstor Kirchner and rising: the rate of inflation in 2010 was more than 4 per cent higher at 10.9 per cent than the 6.1 per cent level recorded in 2004. These growing inflationary pressures eroded the effectiveness of any redistributive policies, which led to increased redistribution to maintain value, which, in orthodox monetary policy canon, fuelled the very inflation that it was trying to ameliorate. There were early signs that, after a brief interlude, Argentina's long and unenviable relationship with inflation had returned.

In short, government spending and inflation were increasing during this period, but post 2008, even when revenue was required, the relative share of the emergency export taxes began falling as the government had lost legitimacy to raise more taxes over them during the revolt. Moreover, the level of the tax revolt, and the fact it permeated into other sectors of society, shifted the debate from being one about tax to one that was more ideological. It was embedded in the Kirchnerist statist vision, but a vision that required funding and that had lost an important financing stream. Not only that, but also the revenue that was being collected was now, post conflict, subject to a concessionary sharing strategy from the federal government to the agricultural provinces from where the export taxes revenues were extracted.

Federalism, extraordinary taxation, and conflict

Argentina is a federal state, but the president retains substantial powers over the provinces—which are consolidated further in emergency scenarios—because constitutionally, the executive branch of government has the ultimate authority over the discretionary collection and redistribution of some fiscal resources (Rose-Ackerman, Desierto, and Volosin, 2011). Provincial governments have autonomous tax collection capacity over four main taxes: *impuesto inmobiliario* ('real estate tax'), *impuestos sobre los ingresos brutos* ('gross income tax'), *impuestos a los sellos* ('stamp tax'), and *impuesto a los automotores* ('automobile tax') (Argañaraz et al., 2019).[6] These tax receipts cover, on average, 40 per cent of the provinces' expenditure, with the remaining 60 per cent financed through federal government transfers and provincial debt (Cetrángolo and Gómez Sabaini, 2010). As the provinces rely on federal subsidies, those who manage the subsidies in turn hold a great deal of power and influence over the provinces (Manzetti, 2014). So, when governments have restricted any federal transfers, it has generated historic tensions between central governments and provincial leaders.

The framework under which the collection of fiscal revenue is redistributed to the provinces began its first iteration in 1935, with the *Evolución de los coeficientes legales de distribución primaria*.[7] This framework of redistribution was subsequently modified throughout the 1950s and 1960s, where additional smaller taxes were added to the redistributive formula under three legal mechanisms for redistribution, but all of which were underpinned by the notion of reimbursement.

The federal government would reimburse those jurisdictions in line with how it had contributed towards national fiscal collection: those that contributed more would receive more—inevitably the provinces with the largest populations (Cetrángolo, Jiménez, and Vega, 1998). In 1973, the three original mechanisms were amalgamated under one more simplified law: *Régimen Federal de Coparticipación* (Law N.20.221), which, crucially, was passed with key clauses that allowed the government to modify redistribution to the provinces when there were extraordinary reasons for this. And some of these clauses created tensions with the core concept of reimbursement because there were inbuilt mechanisms to circumvent this. Enshrined into law, the first of these clauses stated that all national revenues would be subject to redistribution *apart from* those taxes arising from foreign trade and those that had been levied for a specific reason (Cetrángolo, Jiménez, and Vega, 1998: 298). And it is through the ambiguity in the wording of 'specific reason' that governments have been able to modify the amount of fiscal resources that are available for redistribution to provinces. Moreover, as natural resource exports have historically underpinned Argentine economic production, the fiscal revenues from this specialized activity were already available to the

[6] The National Constitution, Article 75, subsection two, clearly defines federal and provincial tax powers by stating that indirect taxes, with the exception of import and export fees, which are exclusively federal are shared by both levels of government. However, direct taxes fall exclusively under the auspices of the provinces, but the federal government is not precluded from levying direct taxes during a limited term and on condition that national security and defence requires this.

[7] With the passing of laws: 12.139, 12.143, and 12.147, the mechanism for the redistribution of collected tax was created. Other supplementary tax laws were created on both sales and yields following the initial passing of these laws.

federal government and not automatically subject to the redistribution mechanisms and subject to historic contention because the provinces from where the majority of production occurred were not guaranteed to be reimbursed.

And while the volatile economic and political situation in Argentina in the 1980s meant that there were further modifications to *Coparticipación*, these modifications did not alter or repeal the exemption of taxes on exports from the redistribution mechanism,[8] a point that would give the government policy headroom in the aftermath of the 2001 crisis but that also deepened political cleavages between President(s) Kirchner, rural provinces, and agricultural producers until the same mechanism was used post 2008 tax revolt to bargain with rural actors.

Concessions through the soy fund

Under the presidency of Néstor Kirchner, there was a centralizing shift in the distribution of fiscal resources under emergency governance (Richardson N., 2009). The level of fiscal receipts that were held by the government between 2001 and 2006 increased during this period by 5.4 per cent up to 57.8 per cent, while transfers to the provinces fell to 23.1 per cent (Richardson N., 2009: 38). This framework, whereby the national tax burden increased but transfers to the provinces diminished, meant that any surplus tax revenue was retained by the government and not redistributed between the provinces, and it became deeply political because of perceived unfairness in this design. But it was through the *Coparticipación* mechanism that Cristina Kirchner made significant concessions to the agricultural provinces in the aftermath of the rural revolt, when some concessions around soy were offered, which was seen by many as a way of trying to repair some of the damaged relationships with agrarian subnational levels of government (interview, former secretary in the Ministry of Agriculture, 2019).

Before this point, the Kirchners had been able to discipline agrarian provinces by withholding the redistribution of federal revenues, through the framework of *Coparticipación* (Cetrángolo, Jiménez, and Vega, 1998; Bonvecchi and Lodola, 2011). Export taxes that were collected from provinces

[8] The law was modified once more in 1984, in response to shortfalls in pensions funds and the deteriorating general macroeconomic environment, which Latin American countries were enduring at this time (Bulmer-Thomas, 1995), and then again in 1988. The 1988 law (N.23.548) modification included changes to the transitory level of funds between the nation and province; 42.34 per cent was retained by the National Government and 54.66 per cent was to be distributed between the provinces. A further 2 per cent was retained between the Provinces of Buenos Aires, Chubut, Neuquén, and Santa Cruz, with 1 per cent destined for the *el Fondo de Aportes del Tesoro Nacional a las provincias* (National Treasury Contribution Fund to the Provinces).

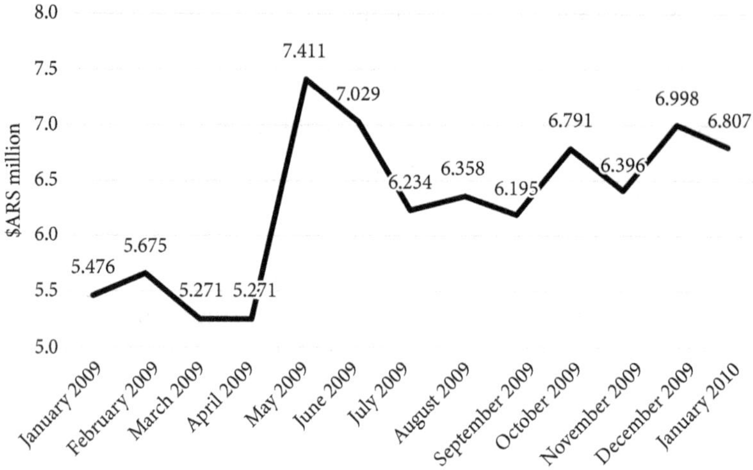

Figure 6.2 Evolution of redistributed revenue via *Coparticipación Federal*, January 2009–2010
Source: CIFRA CTA (2010). Graph by author.

where agribusiness was prevalent were not distributed back to them, allowing the government to exert authority over those subnational administrations (Giraudo, 2017). Post 2008, the government agreed to include some revenues from soy exports within the redistribution mechanism from March 2009, while other export taxes remained exempt (CIFRA CTA, 2010). This move to redistribute 30 per cent of collected soy export tax had a huge effect on the amount of revenues that the executive lost to the provinces through this framework (Figure 6.2).[9]

This concession demonstrated the influence that agricultural producers had on subnational levels of government and further underpinned the distributive conflict between both the producers and the President and federal and provincial levels of government. It also demonstrated the complexity of the challenge of trying to pursue a social redistributive programme while collection streams were diminishing. The challenge for the Treasury was to balance the increasing programme of social redistribution while sharing 30 per cent of soy taxes with the provinces. Table 6.1 highlights the scale of this challenge and points to this attrition in both the level of emergency taxes collected over the mandate and the share of these as a burden, the former dropping from 20.6 per cent to 16.7 per cent (with the share of export taxes within the emergency tax scheme dropping from 65 per cent to 60

[9] The amount of tax that is shared between the provinces varies depending on the price that the producers receive and the amount that is exported, hence the fluctuations.

per cent) while the latter reduced from 5.7 per cent to 4.9 per cent (Ministerio de Hacienda, 2021). What this meant was that the government was collecting less export tax revenues and redistributing more of the revenue it had collected, which was demonstrating some of the challenges that would beset the interventionalist model in the not-too-distant future. With diminished opportunities to tax the producers further, the vicissitudes of natural resource commodity dependence would create significant barriers for President Cristina Kirchner to continuing the redistributive governance that had so far been the hallmark of Kirchnerismo.

Deepening of the fiscal deficit, 2011–2015

After 2011, the macroeconomic challenges that had started to gather pace post 2008 became more problematic, creating social and political tensions and challenging the sustainability of the Kirchnerist statist model. This section points to the deteriorating macroeconomic environment and how policies emblematic of the vision of the state pursued by the Kirchners met an influx of macroeconomic factors that reduced the state's capacity to spend, leading to a social crisis that ultimately had an impact on tax questions and the government's ability to tax exports to fund the redistributive model, even after Cristina Fernández de Kirchner had been emphatically returned by the Argentine electorate with a very strong presidential mandate.

Cristina Kirchner was re-elected in 2011, taking 54.11 per cent of the vote. Her closest rival, Hermes Binner of the *Partido Socialista* (Socialist Party) obtained only 16.8 per cent of the vote (Ministerio del Interior, 2011; Página 12, 2011). It was not only the popularity of the president and her policies that achieved this level of victory but also a weak opposition, which simultaneously contributed towards the scale of the re-election (Freytes and Niedzwiecki, 2016). This victory, which represented the highest vote share since the return of democracy in 1983 (which would only be surpassed by the election of Javier Milei in 2023), should have given the President a strong mandate to push forward with tax collection and redistribution. However, the government was unable to persuade the agricultural producers to contribute more towards its vision of an interventionalist state.

In the following sections, I argue that as the government had already lost legitimacy—to increase taxes over the rural producers—in 2008, the deteriorating macroeconomic environment, the continuation of government spending on welfare and subsidies, and an inability to raise more resources from the rural sector economically trapped the government. To argue this,

I begin by drawing on macroeconomic indicators, which highlight the pattern and trajectory of a deteriorating economic landscape and the challenges to continuing redistributive governance.

Table 6.2 traces the erratic deterioration of key macroeconomic indicators during this period and clearly highlights that from 2012—the first full year of the President's new mandate—economically, this period would be more challenging for the government to finance welfare redistribution. This represented a point of departure from when President Fernández de Kirchner assumed the presidency in 2008. Then, GDP was growing at 4.06 per cent; now, economic output was contracting. GDP growth, as shown in Table 6.2, had already entered negative growth, and it would continue an erratic pattern throughout the mandate (World Bank, 2021b). This inconsistent growth pattern was accompanied by a deepening of the fiscal deficit from −2.5 per cent to −5.4 per cent GDP in 2015, demonstrating that government spending was outstripping domestic resource collection (Thomas and Cachanosky, 2016).

A dual and deepening problem was that Argentina was simultaneously entering into a current account deficit whereby it was importing more goods than it was exporting and, thus, eroding the levels of hard currency (Peña and Barlow, 2021), essential to finance these imports—especially energy, which is discussed in more detail later in the chapter.[10] Taken together, these deteriorating data converged and pointed towards fewer pathways through which the government could pursue its model of redistribution. In short, the commodity boom that had been prevalent in Argentina and that had been the driver for government extraction and redistribution had now abated, and it left the funding of a redistributive model much more problematic.

Another critical and perennially challenging indicator in Table 6.2 is the Argentine level of inflation. The growth in inflation measured by both the INDEC and Congress corroborated the fact that the inflationary position was worsening, with general prices rising—peaking in 2014 at 38.53 per cent and 23.9 per cent, respectively—and negating the real-term impact of welfare payments, thus, necessitating further increases to redistributive payments in an attempt to ameliorate the inflationary effect of them. Furthermore, trust in the official agency to correctly publish inflationary figures was deteriorating because the range between the figures that were provided by the INDEC and

[10] This has been a long-standing challenge in Argentina and the same one that created limitations to the industrialization process in the 1950s as the first Perón government struggled to purchase imports to facilitate the process of industrialization due to low levels of hard currency (Skidmore, 1978).

Table 6.2 Key economic and social indicators, 2011–2015

Year	2011	2012	2013	2014	2015
GDP (US$) (2010 = 100) *Source*: World Bank	125	128	130	124	140
GDP growth increase (percentage) *Source*: World Bank	6.0	−1.0	2.4	−2.5	−5.4
Poverty rate—urban conglomerates (percentage of population) *Source*: INDEC*	6.5	5.4	4.7	–	–
Poverty level (percentage) *Source*: Universidad Católica Argentina**	*24.7*	*26.2*	*27.4*	*28.7*	*29*
Inflation (percentage) *Source*: INDEC	9.5	10.2	10.6	23.9	14.3
Inflation (percentage) *Source*: Argentine Congress	*22.6*	*25.2*	*28.3*	*38.5*	*26.9*
Unemployment (percentage) *Source*: ILO	7.2	7.2	7.5	7.3	7.8
Current account balance (percentage of GDP) *Source*: World Bank	−0.4	−0.2	−0.7	−1.7	−3.0
Fiscal account balance (percentage of GDP) *Source*: CEIC, OECD	−1.4	−2.1	−1.9	−2.4	−5.1
Total tax revenue (ARSm) (2010 = 100) *Source*: Ministerio de Hacienda, Argentina	131	166	209	285	375
Total tax burden (percentage of GDP) *Source*: OECD	29.3	30.6	31.2	31.1	31.5
Emergency tax burden (percentage of GDP) *Source*: Ministerio de Hacienda, Argentina	4.9	4.7	4.2	4.4	3.4
Emergency tax (percentage of total tax revenue) *Source*: Ministerio de Hacienda, Argentina	16.7	15.5	13	13.7	11.1

Note: *INDEC did not provide poverty figures to the World Bank in 2014–2015. **Poverty level based on the ability to purchase a basic basket of goods.

by Congress was becoming greater (Wylde, 2016; Daniel and Lanata Briones, 2019).[11] This disparity was fuelling wider political contention, which in turn was creating this growing mistrust in the official agency's figures (interview, Economic Journalist La Nación, 2019). While I engage with the politics of this contention later in the chapter, the key takeaway here is to highlight that that growing inflation was negatively impacting further upon the government's fiscal capacity.

The government approached the deterioration of macroeconomic indicators with a counter-cyclical strategy whereby spending was increasing even though the space to do so was contracting. Moreover, and critically, the government did not seek to increase the export tax strategy even while some commodity prices were benefiting from a record, albeit temporary and volatile, spike. The level of emergency taxes as a percentage of the tax burden fell by 4.4 per cent in this period (2012–2015) alone, with export taxes falling by 14.8 per cent even though the price of soybeans reached highs of US$684 per tonne in 2012—before quickly falling again after this high (Cboe, 2020). Furthermore, in a point of departure from historical Argentine exchange rate policies, a currency devaluation implemented in 2014 was not, for the first time, accompanied by an increase in the export tax regime. Moreover, the composition of total exports clearly demonstrates that there was strong growth in primary commodity exports between 2011 and 2015. The percentage of primary commodities that were exported from Argentina in 2011 was 52.5 per cent; this had reached a level of 62.7 per cent by 2015 (CEPAL, 2017). There was a clear fiscal need, and export levels were growing, but the state didn't tax these more. The fact that the government didn't increase export taxes suggests that it didn't have sufficient political support to tax the producers further. It lacked the legitimacy to do this in the eyes of the producers; this had deteriorated since the 2008 revolt (interview, ex government minister, 2019). This loss of support from the producers is evident with the drop in level of export taxation collected as a percentage of tax take. This drop occurred at a time when increased resources were required to fund an expansive state spending programme; fiscally, this would become problematic for the government.

What this started to clearly point towards was the level at which post-crisis governments in Argentina had relied upon the extraction of revenues from agricultural commodities to support their redistributive agenda, which

[11] From 2011 onwards, Congress has produced its own inflation figures, comprising figures from eight independent consultants (Wylde, 2016).

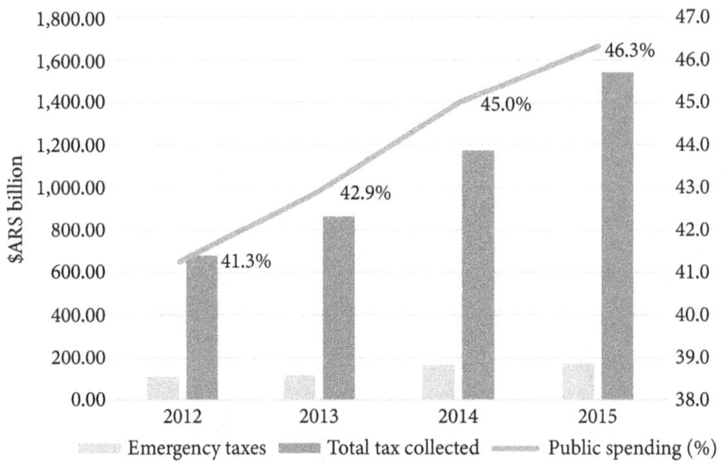

Figure 6.3 Total and emergency tax collection and public spending, 2012–2015 (% GDP)
Source: Ministerio de Hacienda (2021). Graph by author.

had previously been presented as an emergency package. Now, this started to reveal some tensions within the statist model and pointed towards future limitations when continued state spending, without the revenue to fund this, would fiscally trap the government (Figure 6.3). In the following sections, I highlight that the maintenance of some and the expansion in scope of other key welfare policies during this period would increase the pressure on the fiscal balance and eat into deteriorating currency reserves, thus deepening the crisis of entrapment.

Squaring the circle: The politics of redistributive commitments

The government had, quite successfully, built a support base of voters that relied on revenue redistribution, but social and economic aspirations had increased with this (Peña and Barlow, 2021). Therefore, the withdrawal of this redistribution would be politically difficult, what Bril-Mascarenhas and Post (2015) called the 'policy trap'. One of the most costly of these policies, and the first I discuss, was the continued utilization of 'emergency' transport and energy subsidies, which would detrimentally impact both the fiscal and trade accounts, while the measures that the government implemented to try and address this deteriorating position, paradoxically, ended up costing it more.

The subsidy programme implemented in the aftermath of the 2001 crisis had, up until this point, been a key policy area that was overwhelmingly emblematic of the redistributive generosity of Kirchnerismo (interview, expert working on tax evasion, 2019). But it was also a policy area that was contributing significantly to the deteriorating fiscal position and, by 2010, represented 1.7 per cent of GDP.[12] In energy alone, the value of these subsidies meant that gas and electricity bills in Argentina had been consistently around one-third of the bills that had been paid in other Latin American countries since initiating the price controls as response to crisis (Moffett, Parks, and Turner, 2012).

By late 2011, the sustainability of the strategy was creating significant fiscal tensions for the government, and in recognition, President Fernández de Kirchner mooted a strategy to gradually withdraw the subsidies offered across utilities and transport. It was part of a raft of policies aimed at reducing fiscal expenditure and was presented as a process of *Sintonía Fina* ('fine-tuning') rather than as cuts to redistribution (Clarín, 2012b). The withdrawal of energy subsidies to banks and industry was announced first in late 2011. It was then forecast to be rolled out to the wealthier suburbs of Buenos Aires in 2012, before encompassing other residents after that, but that stage would then include the demographic of the government's core support. And this was the difficult circle to square for the President; the government needed to ameliorate its fiscal position but was reticent about initiating policy reforms that would be undoubtedly unpopular and would negatively affect those in the urban areas that were the traditional core supporters of the *Frente para la Victoria* (Victory Front) (FPV).

In early 2012, there had already been indications about how this would be received in relation to transport subsidies. Initially, ticket price controls were withdrawn in January 2012, resulting in a 127 per cent price increase per transit ($ARS2.50) on the Buenos Aires *Subte* (Metro), which instigated significant pushback, not only from opposition figures and media outlets but also from government supporters, including from unions whose members would be impacted by hikes in the cost of public transport in Buenos Aires (Bril-Mascarenhas and Post, 2015). The pushback meant that the President had to argue that her plan to reform energy and transport prices, which

[12] The level of state intervention through energy subsidies actually grew throughout the first and second Kirchnerist mandates, which coincided with the period of strong economic growth from 2003 to 2008 (SGE, 2019). The subsidies rose from a level of 0.1 per cent of GDP in 2001 to 1.7 per cent of GDP in 2010 (Vagliasindi, 2012). The greatest increase in the level of subsidies came in the first year of President Fernández de Kirchner's mandate (2007–2008), where they increased sharply by 0.6 per cent of GDP following tariff reforms (Vagliasindi, 2012).

would have reduced state intervention in the economy, was not a *plan de ajuste* ('plan for austerity') but a process of fine-tuning through all government departments (La Política Online, 2012). In the end, it was a project that was not finally implemented: the economic fine-tuning policies were shelved. Some observers remarked that following the 2008 rural revolt, it was an argument that the President did not want to enter into—the government did not have the political support to carry out the reforms (interview, CEPAL, 2019). But not doing so was costly: the World Bank estimated that the government spent US$5 billion in Buenos Aires on transport subsidies in 2012 alone (Avner et al., 2017).

Through its attempt to instigate a programme of fiscal consolidation vis-à-vis the economic 'fine-tuning', the President had acknowledged that the cost of the subsidies was becoming too expensive and had acquiesced to policies to try and ameliorate the situation. Broad-based utility subsidies, as Bril-Mascarenas and Post (2015) highlight, had quickly become a 'policy trap', and

> [presidents] Kirchner received several proposals from their economic ministers and energy and transport and energy secretaries to exit broad-based subsidies gradually in order to avoid fiscal strains in the future. The Kirchners, however, rejected all of these policy proposals, arguing that such a move would entail unnecessary political risk in the context of fiscal abundance.
>
> **Bril-Mascarenas and Post (2015: 112–113)**

But the problem was now that as commodity prices were no longer growing strongly and consistently, there was not fiscal abundance, and the President was trapped. The fact that, ultimately, this was repealed because of the contestation that the policy engendered, demonstrates both that redistributive policies continued to be polemical and that the government was trapped in this spending cycle, a cycle that was shoring up the government's core supporters but at the same time spending vast amounts on those who were not supporters:

> The government had trapped itself; it had created a base of voters that depended on the resources that were redistributed to them. The Kirchners had been very generous in terms of spending, and it would have been very unpopular to reduce or remove the subsidies.
>
> **(Interview, expert working on tax evasion, 2019)**

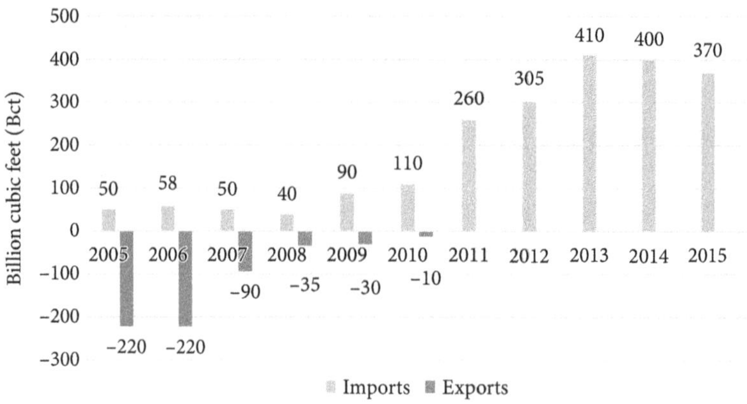

Figure 6.4 Natural gas imports and exports, 2005–2015

Source: Ministerio de Energia y Minería (2021). Graph by author.

But the government had to act, and in place of lifting price controls on energy, it implemented a plan that enhanced state intervention in the economy through the renationalization of the largest oil and gas-producing company in Argentina; *Yacimientos Petrolíferos Fiscales* (YFP). YPF had been originally privatized in 1992 during the presidency of Carlos Menem, when, as part of a raft of market-friendly policies, the Electricity Regulation Act sought to stimulate competition while benefiting consumers in terms of quality and service (Vagliasindi, 2012). However, now, the government saw the renationalization of YPF as a pathway to addressing the increased prices that it was paying to import energy—to cover the increased usage under the subsidy programme—a cost it blamed directly on a lack of investment into YPF while in private ownership. The energy price controls that had been in place since 2002 had been a major contributing factor to the lower levels of investment in the Argentine energy sector by Spanish company REPSOL, which had owned the controlling stake in the YPF until the renationalization of the company in 2012 (Vagliasindi, 2012). And this underinvestment was significant: a failure to sufficiently invest into the energy industry meant that the increased usage post 2002 due to both the widespread subsidy programme and growing employment and enhanced economic activity meant that, within a decade, the Argentine government began importing energy; as a result, it ultimately shifted Argentina from a position of a net exporter of natural gas in the early 2000s to a net importer by 2011, putting increasing fiscal pressure on the government, the trajectory of which can be traced in Figure 6.4.

Quantifying this shift: from 2005 to the end of the presidency of Cristina Kirchner, oil production in Argentina fell by 30 per cent, and between 2004

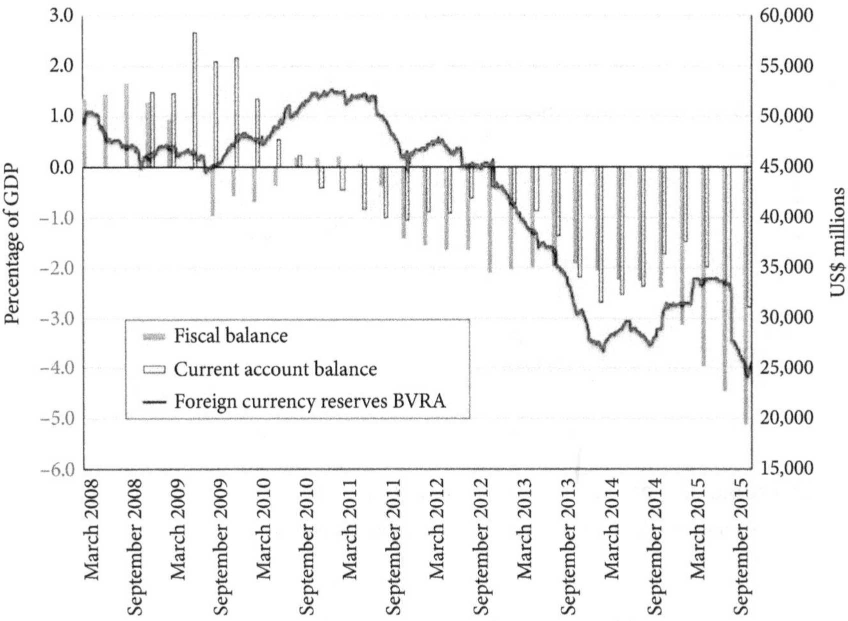

Figure 6.5 Currency reserves and fiscal and current balances, 2008–2015
Source: BCRA (2021). Graph by M. Barlow and A. Peña.

and 2013, the production of natural gas fell by 20 per cent (Kulfas, 2016). This shift put further fiscal pressure on to the Argentine government as the cost of importing energy between 2010 and 2013 (including natural gas from Bolivia) was estimated to be US$22,135 million (Kulfas, 2016). As the imports of energy are paid for in hard currency (US$), this negatively impacted the level of Argentina's US$ currency reserves. Figure 6.5 demonstrates the rapid decline in hard US$ from 2011 onwards, when imports of gas were growing and consumption surpassed domestic production, as seen in Figure 6.6. What this shows is that importing energy was pushing Argentina into a deeper trade balance crisis, which was eating into its level of currency reserves.

The exponential growth in energy consumption meant that electricity demand doubled between 2003 and 2013: consumption increased from 86,440 to *c.* 130,000 GWh per year. This growth in demand and consumption was underpinned by the cheaper energy through price control mechanisms and subsidies that were first implemented in response to the crisis situation: consumption increased from 86,440 to *c.* 130,000 GWh (gigawatt-hour) per year. The price of electricity pre-crisis was US$0.07 per KWh (kilowatt-hour); following the emergency reforms, this dropped to US$0.02 in 2002. By 2009, the continuation of the subsidies meant that the price of electricity had

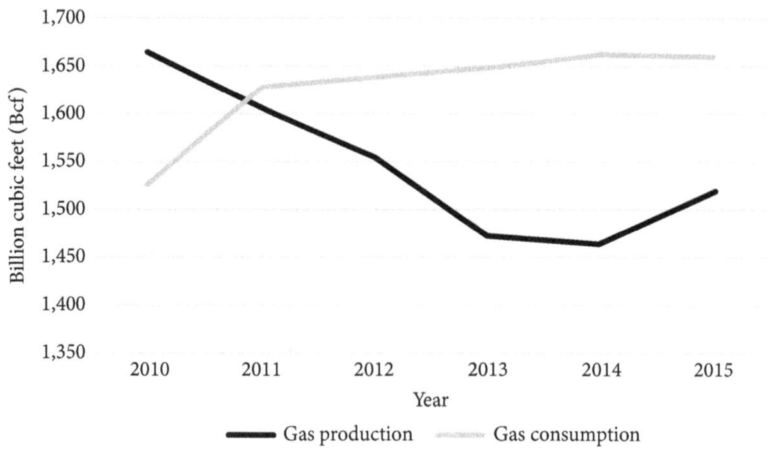

Figure 6.6 Gas production and consumption, 2010–2015
Source: Ministerio de Energia y Minería (2021). Graph by author.

only reached US$0.035 (Vagliasindi, 2012), thus demonstrating the level of burden that was placed on the Argentine government to continue with costly emergency policies when the economy had left the emergency period behind.

Therefore, the renationalization of YPF was an attempt to 'consolidate the role of the state in the economy and re-ignite energy investment and thus reduce the levels of imported energy' (Wylde, 2016: 335). This enhanced role for the state was costly and feeding into a more generalized conflict because the government was initially placing more burden on the state through costs to expropriate the controlling stake. Bringing YPF back into public ownership won widespread support in the Argentine Congress.[13] And this level of congressional support reflected wider public feelings about YPF, given the strong presence the company retained in the national collective imaginary. The decision was widely praised and was celebrated as contributing to a way to recover part of the national patrimony, lost during the Menem years. And as Lupu (2016) argues, it demonstrated that there was still a high level of support in Argentina for state-owned enterprises. Moreover, this shift inextricably links to the wider debate between the state and free market policies, and it underscores the opprobrium that is felt by many Argentines who attribute the privatizations of the 1990s with the growing level of debt that eventually led to the 2001 default (Wylde, 2016).

[13] The Argentine Senate approved the bill by sixty-three to three to renationalize a 51 per cent stake in YPF from REPSOL. This cleared Congress following the Chamber of Deputies, which voted emphatically by 207 to 32 to uphold the bill in April 2012 (Clarín, 2012a).

While the renationalization of YPF was a move that enhanced the state's role in the energy sector and the wider economy, because of growing inflationary pressures, deteriorating fiscal and current account balances, falling currency reserves, and the federal sharing of soy *retenciones* with the provinces, the financing of this policy, including the exploration and extraction of the recently discovered shale gas reserves at Vaca Muerta—the world's third largest unconventional hydrocarbon reserve was discovered in Argentina's western Neuquén province (Manzetti, 2016)—would become challenging and problematic for the government because the cost of the exportation of REPSOL from its YPF assets significantly increased pressure on already strained public finances. Moreover, the debt negotiations that were still ongoing as a fallout of the 2001 default added an additional layer of complexity.

Economy minister Axel Kicillof (2013–2015), who had overseen the renationalization of YPF in his former position (2011–2013) of secretary for economic planning and development, was responsible for the compensation negotiations that accompanied the political fallout of the renationalization of YPF (Wurgarft, 2012). As part of wider debt negotiations with holdout creditors through negotiations with the Paris Club of creditor nations, Minister Kicillof came to an agreement with REPSOL in November 2013 on a deal that represented US$5 billion of ten-year corporate bonds, half of the amount of compensation that was originally sought by REPSOL (Mander, 2014).[14] These negotiations preceded the culmination of the long-outstanding debt negotiations with the Paris Club of creditor nations, which resulted in agreement on the terms to pay back US$9.7 billion of outstanding debt over a period of seven years, which would begin in July 2014 with a payment of US$650 million, before a second payment of US$500 million was due in May 2015 (Mander, 2014). Although these payments would add to the already increasing pressure on the fiscal balance, they were essential to try and reconstruct investor confidence in Argentina and attract foreign investment (Hébert and Schreger, 2017). All of this was important as it was at a time when hard currency was required as the dollar reserves were being eroded by the high level of imports, especially energy, a pattern that can be seen in the negative distortion of the current account balance in Figure 6.5. However, it was not just through a raft of subsidies that the government of

[14] This renationalization of YPF had international connotations as the stake in YPF that was being expropriated was Spanish owned. This policy attracted heavy criticism from the Spanish prime minister, Mariano Rajoy (2011–2018), who labelled the reform as nothing more than resource nationalism (Lucas, 2012). Criticism was also echoed by the European Union and the G20, which argued that this move went against assurances that Argentina had offered to promote transparency and fight protectionism (Clarín, 2012c).

Cristina Kirchner was trying to square its redistributive commitments; the President's signature *Asignación Universal por Hijo* (Universal Child Benefit) (AUH) policy was expanded during this presidential mandate, adding to the government's fiscal burden of obligations.

Asignación Universal por Hijo: Universal child benefit

One of the biggest expansions to welfare during this period was the AUH, a key President Fernández de Kirchner policy that was initiated by presidential decree in November 2009 and expanded during the final Kirchnerist mandate. The design of the policy was an attempt to widen the scope of the social security programme through ensuring that the children of parents who were employed informally were also captured and covered by the scheme (Murillo, 2015). Payments were initially made under the plan of $ARS180 per month and reached nearly 4 million children (Grugel and Riggirozzi, 2012).[15] This payment level continued and progressively increased over the remaining period of Kirchnerist governance. Table 6.3 shows the evolution of the social security programme, whose final payment figure reached $ARS837 in June 2015 (Di Santi, 2015). This represented a 30 per cent increase from the previous payment in 2014.

The high level of annual increases (which were between 26 and 40 per cent in the period 2012–2015) for this programme cannot be explained wholly by commitment to income redistribution. These increases were also an attempt to ameliorate the effects of inflationary pressures that were eroding the payments. Table 6.3 highlights both the nominal rises and then the real amount of the welfare payments, when adjusted for inflation at the prevailing rate. In short, the welfare payments were costing the government more, and this was increasing pressure on an already problematic balance-of-fiscal- payments

Table 6.3 Evolution of Universal Child Benefit, 2009–2015

Year	2009	2010	2011	2012	2013	2014	2015
Monthly amount $ARS	180	220	270	340	460	644	837
Increase (%)	–	22	23	26	35	40	30
Monthly $ARS real	180	179	178	181	196	201	207

Source: CIFRA CTA (2020).

[15] Decree No. 1602/09 (InfoLEG, 2021).

position, which was reducing the fiscal space available to the government to continue its programme of welfare redistribution.

But while the president argued that the policy had tangible impact and significantly contributed towards reducing the high level of poverty, quantifying this was politically charged. By 2011—through welfare and increased employment—it was estimated by the government that poverty had been reduced from a level of 57.5 per cent in 2002 in the aftermath of the crisis, to 6.5 per cent in 2011 (INDEC, 2012). However, as earlier highlighted, because of the accusations of government intervention and data manipulation into the INDEC, post 2007 these figures were contested and should be treated with some caution (interview, Economic Journalist La Nación, 2019) and from 2010 onwards, poverty figures based on urban samples and measured by the capacity of individuals to purchase a basic basket of goods were simultaneously published by the UCA, which challenge those of the official government figures (Salvia and Vera, 2016).

These contradictory data are highlighted in Figure 6.7, and importantly, they not only show asymmetries in the level of the data series, but also they clearly highlight a pattern of continuous growth in the level of poverty post 2011. The level of poverty starts to increase in a steady growth trajectory to reach a level of 29 per cent by 2015. What all this translates into is that the government was spending more through welfare payments, as clearly demonstrated in Figure 5.1 (Chapter 5)—the level of public social spending increased from 25.6 per cent of GDP in 2011 to 30.3 per cent of GDP in 2015—and, as highlighted in Table 6.2, even though the cash transfers were

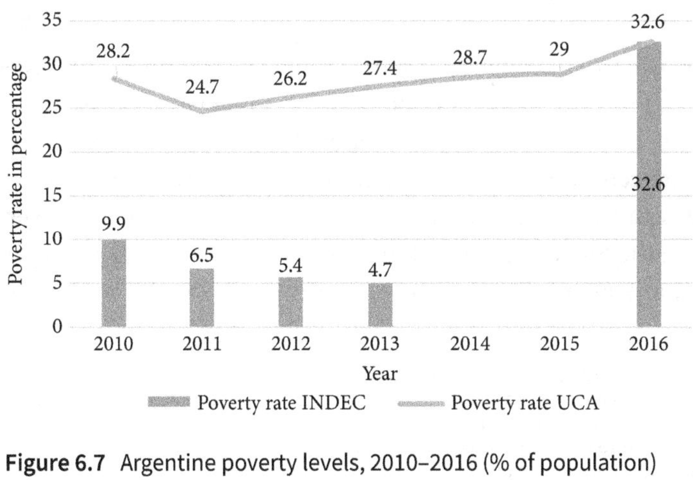

Figure 6.7 Argentine poverty levels, 2010–2016 (% of population)

Source: Salvia and Vera (2016); INDEC (2020). Graph by author.

becoming more costly, the impacts of these payments were not manifesting in a reduction in the poverty level, highlighting a clear tension in the model.

During this period, despite the fact that the fiscal space was contracting, the policy continued to play a prominent role in the redistributive model, even though the export taxes that had been integral to supporting earlier social redistribution strategies were now diminishing. The continuation of this policy while funding streams reduced demonstrated the 'personal importance to the president of widening the child benefit programme to families not covered by earlier support plans' (interview, CEPAL, 2019). It was a signature policy that the president implemented within the first year of assuming office and is one that fits squarely and highlights saliently the 'redistributive generosity' of Kirchnerismo. It was a policy that continued the pattern of spending that was seen in the post-crisis government of Néstor Kirchner and importantly, it appeared to 'speak directly to the Kirchner's core supporters' (interview, former government minister, 2019). The deteriorating fiscal balance did not prevent the government from implementing further welfare reforms to support its progressive agenda.[16] However, redistribution in the context of a deepening fiscal deficit (Figure 6.5), falling currency reserves, and growing inflation meant both that the sustainability of these policies was becoming fragile and the effectiveness of the programmes was diminishing; still, the government chose not to ask agricultural producers to contribute more to its progressive vision through export taxes because the politics of the strategy were proving politically contentious.

Export tax fatigue

The increasingly challenging economic environment that had besieged the Argentine government meant that a wide range of policies were implemented, including those that were aimed at shoring up the level of US$ held by the central bank. Unpopular currency controls[17] and programmes aimed at repatriating capital offshore, without criminal charges, were rolled out during the mandate, but with little success (Hébert and Schreger, 2017). However, any attempt to return to, and expand, export tax strategies was

[16] Additional redistributive measures were implemented through an additional social security programme; *ProgresAr* (Progress) was implemented in January 2014, guaranteeing $ARS600 for unemployed or informally employed eighteen to twenty-four-year-olds to complete secondary education and support this demographic through university (La Nación, 2014).

[17] The currency controls were operationalized through a*cepo cambiario* ('exchange clamp'), which was implemented by the AFIP on 28 October 2011. This was underpinned by General Resolution 3210/11 (InfoLEG, 2021).

avoided, even while increasing extraction from the agricultural producers could have helped ameliorate its economic position, especially as 2013 saw a record soy harvest and the government had entered its third year of a negative balance (Bronstein, 2014).

But export tax strategies had become embedded in an idea of extraction and redistribution, and politically, the strategy had also become embedded with an idea of unfairness. This idea was part of a more widespread political conflict that intersected with actors outside of both the government and the rural sector. And this wider debate ultimately had an impact on the government's capacity to collect export taxes. In this final section of this chapter, I argue that even when Cristina Kirchner had been emphatically re-elected and the government needed to mobilize more domestic resources, it didn't push export taxes further because the idea of them was at the forefront of conflict and redistribution, which had negative connotations that had spread to the Argentine middle classes, a point discussed in greater detail in Chapter 7. Not only were the taxes not expanded during this mandate, but also, in early 2015 (the election year), export taxes were actually reduced for some agricultural producers, showing how politicized and delegitimized they had become and how they were reduced to reflect a fairer fiscal strategy.

The level of Cristina Kirchner's electoral victory in 2011 had meant that opposition party challengers who had historically supported the agricultural community were not returned, and there would continue to be a significant lack of political representation for the rural sector. Moreover, representatives from major rural associations who had run for office in 2011 were also unsuccessful, leaving the sector with no political representation (De Santis, 2011). Without representation, this political landscape created an environment where the rural sector remained an easier target for the government to extract resources, especially because it had lost informal and personalized forms of access to government since the arrival of Néstor Kirchner in 2003 (Hora, 2010). Moreover, post crisis, there remained no institutionalized political mechanism through which the producers could officially protest and object against government policies (Freytes and O'Farrell, 2017): 'the sector was an easy target' (interview, ex government minister, 2019).

However, this political weakness was not capitalized upon. When the government required more resources, it did not ask the producers to contribute more. There was a perspective that the newly elected president was weaker because of the 2008 tax revolt, and although strongly elected in 2011, with the worsening economic environment, influential actors in the rural sector started to regain some power by the mid-term elections in 2013 (Freytes and

Niedzwiecki, 2016).[18] It was a problem of legitimacy: the government didn't have the legitimacy to tax the producers further; moreover, because of price volatility, producers were hoarding soybeans, and the government could not persuade them to export the products while prices were lower because they would lose more of their sale price through taxes to welfare redistribution (Bronstein, 2014). Therefore, export taxes lost their salient position within the tax basket to such an extent that, in 2013, this was the first year since 2002 that taxes on debits and credits surpassed the collection of export taxes ($ARS56,514 against $ARS55,465) (Ministerio de Hacienda, 2021), further highlighting the loss of space that the government had to extract more tax, even though there was a significant need for revenue.

In 2014, Argentina's vulnerabilities through its integration as a natural resource exporter into global commodity came to the fore when the soy commodity boom that had been responsible for supporting increased public spending during Kirchnerismo abruptly ended, with the price of soybeans dropping by 40 per cent (Freytes and Niedzwiecki, 2016; World Bank, 2021a). However, it did not affect all the producers in the same way; it was the smaller and medium producers that were more adversely affected by the drop in prices as the larger traders had mechanisms to pass on the impact of the export taxes that remained.

Therefore, there was a sense within the Ministry of Agriculture that, with the general drop in international commodity prices, there should be a drop in the export tax on the commodity, especially to the smaller-sized producers, who were being unfairly impacted by the export tax policy. In an interview with a former secretary in the Ministry of Agriculture, who was part of Minister Kicillof's team and had a direct reporting line to the Minister's office (Bertello, 2015a), he highlighted that there was an understanding and a growing sense that 'there was inequality in the rural sector between small and large producers, with smaller producers being adversely affected through export taxation' (interview, former secretary in the Ministry of Agriculture, 2019). There was now an acknowledgement that a segmented approach to the sector may be more sustainable.

The Ministry of Agriculture was therefore responsible, with the Ministry of Economy, for implementing a mechanism to reduce the tax burden for small producers only. One of the architects of the mechanism first highlighted the difficulties in the implementation of a policy that is fair to all

[18] From 2013 onwards, the rural associations have had a political presence with the election of former *Federación Agraria Argentina* (Argentine Agrarian Federation) leader Alfredo Luis De Angeli as senator for Entre Ríos (Senado Argentina, 2020).

producers because they have different interests (interview, former secretary in the Ministry of Agriculture, 2019). This fits squarely with Fairfield's (2015) argument, where she highlights that because of the heterogenous interests of the four main associations, there was fragmentation within the rural sector, which, as I argued earlier, had hindered a cohesive response pre-rural revolt in 2008 (Fairfield, 2015). Smaller producers are concentrated in the most fertile provinces, therefore they extract more product per hectare and, consequently, are taxed more, leading to lower margins overall (Rodríguez and Arceo, 2006; Cufré, 2007). The former secretary highlighted that

> When it comes to tax, it is very difficult to produce a policy for those who have lots of hectares and those who do not. There are different factors involved and when prices started to fall in 2014, the smaller producers were at greater risk from these falls than the larger ones and we needed something to protect them.
>
> **(interview, former secretary in the Ministry of Agriculture, 2019)**

Therefore, when prices of commodities began to fall, a subsidy programme was implemented to support producers of certain commodities.[19] This was operationalized in 2015 through Resolution N.126/2015 and applied solely to producers whose product level output was less than 700 tonnes annually (InfoLEG, 2021).[20] This system *retenciones segmentadas* was designed by the Agriculture Ministry to try and re-engage with the smaller producers, who had been those that had initiated the uprisings in 2008 (interview, former secretary in the Ministry of Agriculture, 2019). This subsidy mechanism ameliorated the tax position of the corn and wheat producers so much that, in 2015, the small producers ended up paying nothing as the international price of corn and wheat had dropped to such a level that no tax was levied on their products.[21] Furthermore, a medium-sized producer would pay half of the tax that they had been paying previously. However, this segmented sectoral reform, which was aimed at improving the relationship between government and producers to try and re-legitimize the tax, was implemented in a period when increased revenue was required to help fund government spending, and therefore, this policy increased the pressure on the government's fiscal position. This presented the government with further balance-of-payment problems: a revenue stream that at its height had represented nearly 13 per

[19] The resolution affected the fiscal position of soybean, wheat, corn, and sunflower producers.

[20] This was increased to 1,000 tonnes with Resolution 615/2015 in July 2015 (InfoLEG, 2021).

[21] Wheat prices fell from US$175 to US$127 and corn from US$298 to US$162 over the period 2013–2015 (Cboe, 2020).

cent of total tax collection now represented less than 5 per cent (Ministerio de Hacienda, 2021). Commodity dependency and lack of legitimacy were creating significant barriers to financing the Argentine state.

Conclusion

This chapter has analysed how, following the tax revolt in 2008, the government had to make concessions to the provinces to try and ameliorate some of the political damage that had beset Cristina Kirchner's government. The concessions over taxes on soy weakened the government's fiscal position at a time when its redistributive programme was expanding, which created a deepening fiscal position, especially into the President's second term in 2011. The return of lower prices for key agricultural commodities converged with a deteriorating fiscal and trade balance, which created a 'policy trap' for the President.

Throughout the chapter, I argued that there was a growing weight of fiscal challenges during this period, and because of this, the continuation of key redistributive policies trapped the government in a fiscal cycle that would exacerbate the economic situation further. I have shown that, even in times when the balance of payments in both the fiscal and current account indices was negative, the government did not seek to ameliorate this position by increasing export taxation over the agricultural producers, even when soy prices reached record levels. I have argued that the government lacked the producers' support to tax agricultural exports further; legitimacy to do so had been lost.

This chapter introduced the vicissitudes of development funded by natural resource export-led economic models. It argued that positive economic phenomena that had been prevalent since Néstor Kirchner's presidency were no longer the driving force of the Argentine economy; the commodity price boom had become more volatile; and the sustained growth that was concomitant and serendipitous during the post-crisis period could no longer sustainably fund public spending, even though spending continued. Growing inflation, less revenue collection, erratic commodity prices, deteriorating currency reserves, and outstanding debt restructuring all impacted upon the capacity of the state to maintain its programme of redistribution. The shift of Argentina from a net exporter to a net importer of energy contributed to a generalized situation whereby there was a growing balance-of-trade deficit. As imports are purchased in dollars, this produced a decaying situation in the amount of national hard currency reserves, which added further pressure as there were fewer dollars to exchange for pesos to address the growing balance-of-payment deficit.

I have argued that these indicators constituted a policy trap or fiscal entrapment because pressures were increasing on the capacity of the state to continue the model, but the government was in a situation that it had built up a strong voter base on the back of the redistributed revenues, and politically, it would be very costly to rescind them. Maintaining the policies was becoming more challenging because of the contingent factors that were adding downwards pressure on both balances. However, because of the deteriorating fiscal position and the fact that redistribution had, up to this point, been funded by emergency taxes levied over the rural sector, the debate now became more than tax, but it had an effect on tax questions as this debate was rooted in the export tax revolt. Export taxes as a percentage of emergency tax burden fell below those of financial transaction taxes for the first time since 2000. There was a need for tax, but the government didn't tax the producers further, displaying an acknowledgment that, following the 2008 revolt, it did not have the legitimacy to hike export taxes, even when commodity prices were high. The redistributive model that was being pursued was conflated with the export taxes, and there was a fatigue around export taxes as a driver of the Kirchnerist state model; the government was trapped as it could not extract more money from the sector. Fiscal policy during this period became complicated, but it was not only entrapment in an economic sense but also in a political one. The politics of tax came to the fore and an idea of what export taxes represented became a fault line that was wrapped up in wider discontents. The fiscal entrapment manifested itself in a politically polarizing sense as the government was being attacked by a strengthened opposition that had managed to regroup around policies that had been implemented to try and deal with this fiscal entrapment, which I engage with Chapter 7.

7
Embedded Ideas of Taxation, Wider Conflict, and Political Polarization

Introduction

This chapter extends the tax and development discussion beyond one that is centred just on tax. It does so to highlight how politically polarizing and conflict-inducing tax can be, and, in turn, highlights how this polarization can impact upon and shape wider ideas of development. The 2008 hike in export tax collection generated tensions between the government and the rural sector because of the change in rationale of these taxes from one that responded to crisis to a tax supporting a model of redistribution that affected the producers' interests. At this point, these taxes became crystallized in the political imaginary of both actors in support and against the taxes. However, the chapter shows that these taxes became politically polarizing not only because they were the cause of conflicts over material interests but also because of opposing ideas of development and, more explicitly, the state's role in this development. The tax question sits squarely in the centre of the debate about government economic interventionism and about the role of the state and the market in national development. Therefore, this chapter situates this growing political polarization around tax in a wider political economy of development debate.

Export taxes were emblematic of the period of Kirchnerist governance, but over the decade, they became viewed very differently by supporters and opponents of the Kirchners. They are simultaneously evidence of an extractive form of taxation for actors in the rural sector and conservative politicians and of state funding of a generous programme of subsidies and welfare distribution for government supporters. Export taxes were politically polarizing precisely because they aggravated and amplified wider socio-economic tensions and conflict, which then became embedded in debates about the Kirchnerist tax design. These socio-economic tensions themselves added to growing political polarization because the 2008 tax hike had been so contentious, drawing parallels with how Hall (1993) described the process of

Taxing for Development. Matt Barlow, Oxford University Press. © Matt Barlow (2025).
DOI: 10.1093/9780198923220.003.0007

ideas becoming embedded in policies through third-order changes when there is a paradigm shift or punctuated equilibrium. Therefore, the debate spilled over from one centred just on tax to become muddled in a wider political and economic debate where the statist model of Kirchnerismo itself became the source of conflict. Taxes became part of a bigger political cleavage that polarized politics and hardened positions.

This chapter, then, analyses how this political polarization hardened positions for reasons including the fact that it solidified opposition to the government's model of state-led welfare and development. And importantly, when it became fiscally problematic for the government to sustain this model of state, as explored in Chapter 6, this too polarized viewpoints. In other words, intense political polarization wasn't only the result of Cristina Kirchner's determination to pursue an interventionalist state model but also because the government could not sustain its model when macroeconomic indicators deteriorated. This also contributed to growing political and social levels of discontent and overall challenges to deliver development.

Conflict around ideas of development: A confluence of factors aggravated by tax

From 2011 onwards, the debate about export taxes became relatively subsidiary. But the way that the variable tax regime had been rejected in 2008 had crystallized the perception of this tax design within Kircherismo itself. From 2008 onwards, these taxes became enmeshed with the Kirchnerist statist vision and sat squarely with opposing ideas of the state's role in development. I use this section to elaborate this argument and to explain why the change to the mobile export taxes in 2008 had the polarizing effect that it did, when export taxes hadn't engendered this level of contention previously; more concretely, why it hadn't permeated into other sectors of society. Whilst export taxes had been utilized at different levels throughout the twentieth century, and they had been contentious for actors in the rural sector, they had not managed to polarize society or engendered the level of response that they did in 2008. Kirchnerismo brought with it a vision of Argentine development and a clear idea about how the state should work for citizens, in which export taxes played a salient role in the funding of this vision. But this vision, and these taxes, aggravated long-standing political cleavages between opposing visions of liberal, market-orientated models of development and those in which the state maintained a greater role.

In this sense, although the debate about export taxes itself died down post 2008, the association it crystallized with the Kirchenrist statist model did not; this endured. And as it was embedded within the model, it aggravated a number of wider factors that were characterized by opposing ideas of development but were always associated with the 2008 tax hikes and the rural revolt. This was acknowledged by an ex-government minister in Cristina Kirchner's first government:

> This variable tax system is now explicitly associated with the Kirchners and the export taxes have put them in a different perspective especially for the middle-classes. For many, the Kirchners are associated with export withholdings and corruption. Kirchnerismo was born during the tax revolt.
>
> **(Interview, ex government minister, 2019)**

Many interviewees from across the political divide agreed that 'when you think of Kirchnerismo, you think of *Retenciones*' (interviews, former president National Foreign Trade Commission, 2019; expert on tax evasion, 2019; CEPAL, 2019; former secretary of public revenue, 2019; Journalist Página 12, 2019; Journalist La Nación, 2019). This was also noted in academic circles by many authors, including Baud (2013) and Kulfas (2016), who acknowledged that many things changed for the government following the 2008 tax hikes. The rejection of the variable tax system in 2008 is widely referred to as a fault line that created a polarization between pro- and anti-Kirchnerist supporters, which had been unseen since the first decade of Peronism (De Luca and Malamud, 2010). The taxes had become a political watershed moment for both sets of supporters, which had led to a polarization that had its roots in opposing visions of the state model. Therefore, as the Kirchners' redistributive model was associated with export taxation, both facets became interlinked, and opposition to the interventionalist state model could not be separated from the opposition to export taxation, which translated into political polarization.

There was a confluence of factors that was driving political polarization (which is explored throughout this chapter), but sitting underneath this confluence was a fundamental dispute about who should have to pay tax and how much. It is a normative fault line between supporters of liberal and interventionalist types of state and economy. Tax is problematic because while it affects the profits of some actors, it creates the foundations of redistributive programmes for others. In this case, while representatives of the rural associations may not explicitly have said this, and it was packaged up in a wider argument with other factors, at the core of the problem, from their perspective, the tax reduced their profits and affected their interests. The president of the *Sociedad Rural Argentina* (Argentine Rural Society) (SRA), Luis Miguel Etcevehere, acknowledged that there had been reduced production in the sector because of the export taxes, and without the taxes, production would increase: 'the elimination of the export taxes will spill over into the production of food [without them] we can return to sell to the world' (Galli, 2015). What the SRA president was saying (without actually saying it) was that the sector would return to being more profitable; the taxes did not present an insurmountable barrier to export, but they did reduce profits.

It was this insistence on profitability that Cristina Kirchner focused on during the 2008 protests, where she derided the producers as 'greedy profiteers who are obsessed with their own earnings' (Mcdonnell, 2008) or as 'rural oligarchs' who were unpatriotically not sharing their profits (Balch, 2008). During the 2008 rural protests, Ricardo Rouvier, an international political analyst in Buenos Aires, summed up the fault line that the tax had become: 'she [the President] continues to pursue a policy that quickly establishes groups as either friends or enemies' (Balch, 2008). This fault line endured, and at the opening of the *Exposición Rural* (Rural Farm Show) in Palermo Buenos Aires in 2013, the SRA president demonstrated the level of anger that was still felt within the sector, both because the export taxes remained levied and because their use underpinned an interventionalist state model.[1] He argued that

> The national government wasted opportunities and misspent subsidies with cheap politics, corruption and populist actions. [. . .] They subsidise and benefit those that have the most while those who get up each morning at five to earn a living are forced to pay an exaggerated income tax. Your government has to understand, once and for all, that the policy of expropriating farm income has failed on a global scale, [. . .] you must put an end to market regulation, 'outdated' price controls and the ridiculous export barriers and bans.
>
> **(MercoPress, 2013)**

Here, the taxes were directly conflated with wider subsidy programmes connecting the two issues for the SRA president: the export taxes, and a rejection of the Kirchnerist statist model, whose elements cannot be separated. The following year, in a presentation at the 2014 Rural Farm Show

[1] The SRA's *Exposición Rural* in Palermo is the largest agricultural event in Argentina, but it is also politically and sociologically significant. First held in 1886, it has evolved from solely being a traditional upper-class social event to encompassing politics (CABA, 2021). And who is in attendance is often seen as a measure of political feeling in Argentina (MercoPress, 2013).

in Palermo, Martín Lousteau—the architect of the mobile tax mechanism, Resolution N.125—argued his justifications as ex-economy minister for the mobile export taxes, when he said at the time, 'I was trying to reduce inflation, [...] we needed to resolve a fiscal emergency, this was our answer, and it could have been much worse' (Bertello, 2014). With this statement, the ex-minister highlighted that others in government (Guillermo Moreno, the interior minister) had suggested to tax much higher at a fixed rate of 65 per cent (Kulfas, 2016). This response from the SRA delegates to the ex-minister helps corroborate the point that the tax remained a problem, and it was then caught up with, and reflected, wider conflicts:

> I don't like this example, I don't even like the idea that 35 or 63 [per cent] is acceptable. [. . .] and what about corruption? It has degraded Argentina. Accept that you were part of a corrupt government and accept that you were Minster of the Economy in this government.
>
> **(Bertello, 2014)**

Here, representatives of the SRA were protesting not only at the level of tax but also at the very concept of export tax. And they conflated this directly with wider dissatisfactions; in doing this, it moved the argument beyond tax. In a Página 12 interview with the ex-director of the *Federación Agraria Argentina* (Argentine Agrarian Federation) (FAA), Pedro Peretti acknowledged that the rejection of the tax was at such a level that from that point onwards, political opposition towards the government began to strengthen around this point:

> The coordinated unionist response that was born [out of a need] to protect the small and medium producers ended up transforming into a political party with an agrarian orientation whose central objective was the defeat of this government.
>
> **(Cufré, 2015)**

Why, then, did this tax engender extreme polarization outside of the rural sector? This, in part is because of how the opposition crystallized towards the export taxes during the rural revolt in 2008. Smink (2015) argued that '*la grieta* entirely polarised Argentine society'. During the 2008 agrarian protests, the President argued that the taxes were to the benefit of the poor by both supporting redistribution and vis-à-vis the protection of prices in the consumption basket, which, in essence, expanded the class argument. In 2008, Cristina Kirchner argued, 'higher tax will help fight inflation and poverty and keep farmers from abandoning less profitable wheat, corn and beef production' for the more profitable soybeans (Ortiz, 2008). The class argument was seized upon by government supporters, who organized pro-government protests at the time because, as they highlighted to a *Guardian* journalist, they had a 'visceral hatred of the Argentine oligarchy' (Ortiz, 2008). As one economic observer for an Argentine daily newspaper succinctly put it, '[Resolution] 125 reignited the grand fight between classes in Argentina' (interview, Journalist Página 12, 2019). And, although this perspective was highlighted by Página 12, a Kirchner government-supporting media outlet, there was a strongly held view across party lines that this episode was a shift in relationship between pro- and anti-Kirchnerists (Baud, 2013). Therefore, export taxes sat within wider development debates, but as this quote highlights—which was one of many articulating the same opinion—the taxes were embedded within what many interviewees associated with Kirchnerist governance because of the polarization that this engendered—to such an extent that a tax expert told me that, in their view,

> There were lots more things to criticize them [the Kirchners] for, but the *retenciones* turned into a political crisis that they couldn't escape. The middle-classes associated them [export taxes] with extraction and redistribution; ultimately with Kirchnerismo.
>
> **(Interview, former secretary of public revenue, 2019)**

Here, although this interviewee points (in their view, which was a widely held one in both periods of fieldwork) to how exports taxes were associated with Kirchnerismo, the perspective of whether these were viewed as either *rent-seeking* and extractive or, alternatively, as necessary to address the needs of the state would fit with opposing visions about how tax shapes ideas of development. An economic adviser working with a number of trade federations, including the *Unión Industrial Argentina* (Industrial Union of Argentina) (UIA), discussed the relationship between the taxes and the form of state:

> The taxes were an expression of the type of state, it was a state with a certain level of control over external markets, and a state that intervened into the economy by taking rents from *el campo*. [. . .] it was the redistribution of the rents that was the part that led to inevitable conflict, the tragedy of Kirchnerismo was that it placed us all in a redistributive dilemma.
>
> **(Interview, trade union economist, 2019)**

What all of this meant is that opposition—whose composition I explore in detail later in the chapter—that had originally solidified around a programme of export taxation extended beyond this and became muddled in other factors; the rejection of the taxes aggravated and became embedded in other policy areas. It became a defining pillar of Kirchnerismo and would feed into the argument around contested visions of the state, some of which were structural and would remain unresolved. Increasing state intervention into economic, social, and political life was accompanied by a claim that state-sponsored welfarism was clientelist in its orientation, which hardened opposition towards an interventionalist model. As Gaggero, Gaggero, and Rua (2015) argue, opposition was growing towards state spending that was concentrated on welfare provision at the expense of other areas of public spending, including infrastructure investment—which I engage with in the following section.

Beyond taxes: A wide-ranging and muddled debate

In 2011, Cristina Kirchner had been rewarded with a growing economy from the broad supporter base that had been constructed post 2003, composed of

> middle-class voters who had seen the worst economic crisis in Argentine history spiral into riots just 18 months earlier, and lower income voters who had rewarded the Kirchners for their redistributive policies.
>
> **(Calvo and Murillo, 2012: 151)**

However, volatility in commodity prices threatened the redistributive generosity that had helped secure the government's strong political standing thus far. Political polarization would grow along with these heightened economic challenges. The task for the government would be to continue delivering the programme of social redistribution that had elevated social expectations to a level where citizens relied on these payments (as evidenced when the President tried, unsuccessfully, to withdraw the energy subsidies), and in some cases, they were expected (Lupu, 2016). Furthermore, these policies had been popular at the polls; it was pointed out that through redistribution, the Kirchners had consolidated a large voter base:

> They [Kirchners] wanted to consolidate power through a political system that heavily distributed resources to the poor. It gave them tremendous power and a lot of votes. They wanted to implement different public projects that benefitted the poor. They were a very generous government in terms of spending.
>
> **(Interview, expert working on tax evasion, 2019)**

Not only that, but also these policies had been economically beneficial for many citizens. The signature *Asignación Universal por Hijo* (Universal Child Benefit) (AUH) and wider programmes implemented through the

Administración Nacional de la Seguridad Social (National Social Security Service) (ANSES); meant that the number of low-income families without some form of social security coverage for children dropped from 48 per cent when the AUH was implemented to less than 9 per cent nationally (Kulfas, 2016), In 2014, the government was spending 16 per cent more on social security payments than in 2011 (Kulfas, 2016), pushing the economy into a bigger balance-of-payments crisis and deeper fiscal deficit, while exacerbating a growing opposition to this type of redistributive policy. The cost of broad-brush implementation of transport and energy subsidies was recognized as problematic in 2011, and the tension was laid bare when the government tried to rescind these subsidies in early 2012. However, because the subsidies had become so entrenched in the government's policy basket, the subsidies were not withdrawn, which further increased the balance-of-payment problems (Bril-Mascarenhas and Post, 2015; IMF, 2016). As explored in detail throughout Chapter 6, this state spending, which was increasing the national debt, was highlighting tensions implicit in the statist model when spending levels exceed collection. As this social redistribution had been contingent on the productive capacity of the economy delivering surpluses for the government to redistribute, when these streams diminished along with the legitimacy to tax the rural sector, this became deeply problematic, which would lead to a new polarization and social tensions rising (Gerchunoff, Rapetti, and De León, 2020), including pitting the President against the largest media conglomerate in the country: Clarín (De Luca and Malamud, 2010).[2] And the growing openly adversarial attacks on other non-government-supporting outlets, including *La Nación*, meant that conflict was being played out publicly and hardening political positions.

This political polarization began to harden around cleavages and perspectives that questioned the overall legitimacy of the redistributive development programme of Kirchnerismo. The first of these cleavages was centred around the Kirchnerist state vision and its model of economic development. But now, the model was coming under increasing pressure because of deteriorating economic indicators, explored in Chapter 6. Therefore, when the commodity boom receded and stagnation became the prevailing economic context, the *retenciones* became entangled within an expanded narrative that resonated amongst opposition and wider sectors of the population that were being hit

[2] The chief executive officer of the Clarín Group, Héctor Magnetto, supported the rural sector during the conflict, and thus he argued that taking this position led the government to begin its attacks against the media group: 'we took the lead in the conflict and from there, the government tried to destroy us' (Perfil, 2008). The government sought to deregulate the power of Clarín by introducing the *Ley de Medios* (Audio-Visual Media Law, Law N.26.522), which was intended to deregulate the power that media giants had held since 1980 by effectively selling the licences held by Clarín (De Luca and Malamud, 2010).

by this stagnation. What all of this meant was that contingent factors became part of, and widened, this polarized narrative (that included economic mismanagement and calls of corruption), which contributed to dissatisfaction on the part of a growing opposition.

The opposition argument that redistributing through social policies rather than investment into other areas of the economy, including infrastructure, was tantamount to economic mismanagement became a target for the opposition towards government policies. By this, I mean that both government spending on welfare and the controls implemented to ameliorate the deteriorating currency levels were seized upon by opposition parties to be causal factors that directly contributed towards two national tragedies where welfare spending in place of infrastructure spending was argued to be the root cause of the disasters. Fifty-one people lost their lives in the *Once* train disaster in Buenos Aires on 22 February 2012, while ninety-one people died in floods in Greater La Plata between 1 and 3 April 2013 (Gilbert, 2013; Barreiro, 2017). The opposition argued that the deaths of these people was a direct result of underfunding in infrastructure spending and because of limitations on provincial governments to accessing World Bank financing streams, and directly blamed the implementation of government currency controls in 2011.[3] From this perspective, while the government was spending on welfare, it was neglecting infrastructure spending.

For opposition parties, interventionist policies were now being directly blamed for creating situations where citizens were losing their lives—adding to growing political polarization. In response to the *Once* train disaster, Kirchnerist spending came under attack from numerous opposition forces within Congress; Ricardo Alfonsin of the *Unión Cívica Radical* (Radical Civil Union) (UCR) argued that the disaster was a result of 'underinvestment and a lack of state control in services that are under the orbit of the national government'. He continued that 'the government are incapable of both protecting the lives of citizens, and sufficiently funding the railway'. Senator Ernesto Sanz of the UCR went further by directly blaming the amount of money spent on a programme of re-nationalizations as attributing to the disaster: 'the money that the Kirchners have spent on renationalising Aerolíneas [Argentinas] in place of servicing the trains, highlights an unfortunate lack of budgetary responsibility'. Elisa Carrió added to this opposition by conflating the tragedy

[3] Deteriorating dollar reserves led to the implementation of currency controls by the *Administración Federal de Ingresos Públicos* (Tax Collection Agency) (AFIP) on 28 October 2011 through a *cepo cambiario* ('exchange clamp'). This was underpinned by General Resolution 3210/11 (InfoLEG, 2021), which placed controls on the level of foreign reserves that could be held in both a domestic and business capacity. Authorization to hold higher levels of foreign currency was needed from the AFIP and was dependent on the company's balance sheet or financial position of the individual.

with growing calls of corruption and mismanagement in public spending: 'hopefully we Argentines can understand once and for all that corruption kills' (La Nación, 2012). This was also seized upon by the SRA president, who utilized the Kirchnerist supporters' slogan of the 'won decade' to argue that the government had misspent money for years:

> For many the 'won decade' is the lost decade, because they even lost their lives, when the train did not stop at *Once*, or when the flood swept everything in its path in La Plata, because no one did anything to prevent this, for many, many years.
>
> **(MercoPress, 2013)**

However, the spending policies that characterize the Kirchnerist state that were coming under increasing pressure need to be put into some context. The policies that were now attracting opposition criticism were, by and large, the same policies that had been praised in the previous mandates. The government was not only being attacked by a hardening opposition for its redistribution, but it was also being punished for not being able to continue to deliver this redistribution as it had done previously (Lupu, 2016). In this sense, while it was still an attack on the policies, the direction of the attack had shifted to the wider economic consequences that these policies engendered. Policies were now attracting criticism because the economy was showing signs of stagnation and contraction, which set the context for opposition to the development model of Kirchnerismo to crystallize and grow stronger. Kirchnerist state intervention into the economy to redistribute revenues was not only widely accepted when the economy was growing, but also it was viewed as a good thing by a vast swathe of society who were benefiting from the redistribution:

> For a lot of people Kirchnerist intervention seemed a good thing whilst the economy was growing. When the economy stopped growing, the same policies that were responsible for earlier popularity were instantly blamed. From then on, for a lot of people Kirchnerist state intervention became a bad thing.
>
> **(Interview, heterodox economist, 2019)**

For anti-government actors and the hardening opposition, Kirchnerist state intervention became bad for the economy because of commodity price volatility; now there was economic stagnation, and now the statist model could be attributed to this, with economic commentators across different sectors arguing whoever was elected president in 2015 would have to cut social programmes and subsidies, liberal observers arguing that 'things can't carry on as before' (Prange, 2015). However, before the economic decline, the intervention was generally accepted, and this became increasingly polarizing because of the economic context; the model was crystallizing polarization into supporters and opponents (Prange, 2015). A policy that sat squarely with this increasing polarization concerned the currency controls that were implemented to try and address the current account deficit and the purchasing price of the peso. This engendered social conflict and strengthened polarization because it affected the interests of middle-class savers, who both blamed the government for the policy and the model of the state that it was following for making this necessary (Goni and Watts, 2012).

Attacks were levied because of a perceived lack of investment in the energy industry by the Kirchners and the costs of the expropriation of *Yacimientos Petrolíferos Fiscales* (YPF) from REPSOL, which meant that importing energy became necessary: 'The state's intervention into the energy wholesale market sapped profits from producers which resulted in [their] chronic underinvestment and a consequent decline in energy production' (Simioni, 2019). This would be a direction of attack that would increase over the course of the third Kirchnerist mandate, with journalist Carlos Pagni (2013) denominating the continued use of energy subsidies while there was an energy deficit as the 'energy demagogy' of Kirchnerismo. Energy would occupy a prominent position in the opposition's 2015 electoral manifesto:

> We will take care of all our natural resources including our energy sources. In the last ten years, Argentina has ceased to be self-sufficient in energy because of erroneous public politics.
>
> **(CAMBIEMOS, 2015)**

Furthermore, the currency controls that had inadvertently created a distorted exchange rate added further pressure to the peso through the creation of the black-market dollar, shifting the official exchange rate from US$1 to $ARS9.6 to a rate of US$1 to $ARS16 (Murillo, 2015). What all this meant was that it was the model of a redistributive state that impacted upon other areas of the economy that added to a growing articulation of the opposition as policies were deemed inefficient and the economy mismanaged. In addition, price controls and exchange rate manipulations that were instigated during this period—in an attempt to control inflation—did not yield the intended results, and with the contested inflation rate peaking in 2014 at between 23.9 and 38.53 per cent, this increased the polarization that was gathering pace.

The disparity between these sets of figures produced by the *Instituto Nacional de Estadísticas y Censos de la República Argentina* (INDEC) and those of the Argentine Congress would themselves triangulate with wider factors in the growing argument of another controversy during this final Kirchnerist period that were all too often conflated with the export tax revolt: allegations of government corruption. This argument gained traction when the Argentine government became the first ever recipient of a censorship motion by the International Monetary Fund (IMF) against a member country for data manipulation (Webber, 2013). Allegations of corruption were levied by opposition actors in response to the policy that enabled US dollars previously held offshore to be repatriated into Argentina without reprisals. This drew staunch criticism from the opposition as being another interventionalist policy that benefited government supporters (interview, tax expert, 2019; interview, Journalist El Cronista, 2019). Some prominent tax experts preferred to highlight the fact that the policy posed wider questions of tax (un)fairness between citizens, and thus further created problems of legitimacy:

> Perhaps we should reflect on whether it is fair for two employees [. . .] who receive the same renumeration, who have the same family responsibilities, to pay the same income tax if one of them also obtains [tax] exempt income from financial investments when this positions the person in a stronger taxable capacity than those who do not obtain this income.
>
> **(Rapisarda, 2016)**

Others were keen to focus on the issue that drew the loudest criticism, which was the fact that the 2013–2015 law had no outright tax collection objective, which fed into the increasing polarization and growing calls of corruption levied at the government (Sued, 2013). While the official justification for the policy was to avoid a devaluation with the currency, some opponents of the Kirchners saw this policy as a way for businesses—some of which were being investigated for corruption—and individuals affiliated to the government to repatriate capital without threat of fines or tax. It was politically polarizing and even generated tension from within the *Partido Justicialista* (Justicialist Party) (PJ) itself with Peronist party politicians arguing against the bill during the final debate in Congress by pointing to this corruption:

> Tomorrow, there will be champagne in Panama, in Puerto Madero, Río Gallegos and Santa Fe. But at the same time, there will continue to be unemployment in thousands of homes [around the country].
>
> **(Sued, 2013)**[4]

[4] The vote cleared the Chamber of Deputies on 29 May 2013 by 130 votes for the policy with 107 against (Sued, 2013).

The debate drew attention to the business relations that the President had, and it was argued that it was a way for the government to look after its wealthy friends. By presenting the President and the government in this light, it allowed the opposition to focus its criticisms effectively. Elisa Carrió argued the point that it was a policy that was designed to guarantee impunity from tax evasion. She argued that the dollars that would be repatriated back into Argentina were from wealthy businesses associations of the Kirchners, who would gain influence from this:

> The most serious problem is the businesses that are setting up. Behind these if I am not mistaken, there are people who are going to put in dollars [. . .] but here are people who are going to own a lot of land in Argentina. And if I'm not mistaken, behind Elsztain [Eduardo] is Soros [George].
>
> **(Carrió, in Sued, 2013)**

Furthermore, it was a policy that was controversial because the government was operating a fiscal deficit, and this was bypassing an opportunity for revenue collection while offering an amnesty from fines for previously undeclared offshore investments and dollar reserves. This was another way in which tax collection became politicized and fed into this opposition; a point highlighted in an interview with a tax expert:

> The fact that close Kirchner allies were offered a way to avoid tax highlights again how politics was coming into tax administration. You can't have politics being the face of tax administration. The Kirchners confused the parameters between what is administrative and what is political.
>
> **(Interview, former secretary of public revenue, 2019)**

This perspective is important as although calls of corruption against the government were growing—including Vice-President Amado Boudou (2011–2015) being charged with corruption—which it refuted, it shows that polarization along traditional political cleavages was also growing, which would spill over into other areas (BBC, 2014).[5] Attempts at constitutional change to allow Cristina Kirchner to stand for a third term generated significant backlash, with opposition politicians joining an estimated half a million people at an anti-government protest in 2012 for what they saw as attempts to consolidate power and corruption. The *Coalición Cívica* (Civic

[5] Amado Boudou was charged with using his influence, during his time as economy minister (2009–2011), to award a contract for printing Argentine currency to a company he allegedly controlled (BBC, 2014).

Coalition) (ARI) senator María Eugenia Estenssoro argued that 'People are saying "enough" enough corruption, enough lies. It will be very hard for her to change the constitution after tonight' (Goni and Watts, 2012). What this shows is the level of growing opposition on several fronts in a confluence of dissatisfactions. All these incidents of economic mismanagement and corruption were politically polarizing and were now being attacked by the growing centre-Right opposition as part of a broader conflict towards Kirchnerist rule.

Growing opposition and the offer of a different vision of state

Initial opposition to Kirchnerist rule—as discussed in Chapter 5—came from a small pool of actors within the rural sector, but there was limited political opposition because of weak and fragmented parties to oppose it. Since 2002, there had been a lack of strong political opposition to the Kirchners. Initially, within the rural sector, there was an ambivalence around the tax response; an historic structural opposition to export taxes and a lack of formal political channels through which the rural sector could protest meshed with an acknowledgement that there was a need to fund the fallout from the 2001 crisis. Whilst this acknowledgement (detailed in Chapter 5), provided temporary legitimacy to the taxes between 2002 and March 2008, the ambivalence came from the fact that the taxes were firmly rooted within the argument about who the profits belonged to when international prices rose:

> They [the producers] weren't originally opposed [to the taxes] because there was an understanding about state needs. But what it did was to bring back debates about rents and whether these rents that essentially come from the 'ground' are public owned.
>
> **(Interview, former president National Foreign Trade Commission, 2019)**

Moreover, during early Kirchnerismo, outside of the rural sector, the government had strong popular support, it had benefited from high commodity prices, which enabled a robust social redistribution emergency programme to become normalized, and which in turn bolstered political support for the Kirchners. As Huber and Stephens (2012) pointed out, it was both the favourable economic conditions and the universal character of social policies that drove poverty and extreme poverty levels down. Not only did this redistributive programme and falling poverty help cement the position of Néstor Kirchner as one of the most popular outgoing presidents in Argentina's history, but also, the rising levels of employment through a growing economy ameliorated the lives of many Argentinians and added to this high level of popularity (Levitsky and Murillo, 2008). Therefore, at the changeover of presidential power in 2007, the opposition was unable to mount an effective challenge to the election of President Fernández de Kirchner, who secured the presidency in the first round, not only because of some of the overarching positive factors already highlighted, and an acknowledgement by rural actors that initially they had to pay the taxes to meet the post-crisis challenges, but also because of a weak opposition (Freytes and Niedzwiecki, 2016).

First, as Fairfield (2015) argues, aside from the 2008 rural revolt, there was not a coordinated and coherent opposition from the rural sector, with different associations representing heterogenous member interests making this difficult (Fairfield, 2015). Furthermore, she highlights that there was a lack of political representation within the sector, which meant that following the implementation of the export taxes under President Duhalde, even if the emergency situation had not bestowed a level of legitimacy, an effective coherent response to the government would have been more difficult as the sector lacked formal channels of influence. With the arrival of Kirchnerismo, the sector lost even more formal and informal pathways of influence, with few officials in the Ministry of Economy (under which the Secretary of Agriculture was subsumed) having relevant ties with the sector, while contrary to other countries, rural actors and producers lacked a strong grounding among opposition parties and suffered lasting difficulties in establishing coalitions with influential urban actors (Hora, 2010; Freytes and O'Farrell, 2017).

Since interest group representation by the big producers was weak or ineffective, there was a clear lack of a political channel through which the rural sector could protest the taxes, which was coupled with the fact that the traditional anti-Peronist factions had failed to regroup and mount a coherent challenge themselves to Kirchnerismo before the 2007 and 2011 elections. In the case of the first elections, the UCR politicians were still struggling from the substantial loss of political support they suffered in the 2001 uprisings when they, and President De la Rúa were on the receiving end of the *Cacerolazos* rallying cry (Gold and Peña, 2019).

However, during this period, the party-political face was changing and a future political opposition to the government was growing, signalling the emergence of a 'new right'. The *Propuesta Republicana* (Republican Proposal) (PRO) was created in 2005 and would represent a platform for the centre-Right to coalesce around to mount a future challenge. However, the popularity of the PRO was slow to gather momentum because, initially, there wasn't a coherent opposition narrative to Kirchnerismo, and therefore, there was a lack of a centre around which opposition groups could crystallize a narrative.[6]

A deteriorating economic landscape meant that post 2011, there was political created space for the opposition parties to formulate a narrative against the Kirchnerist statist model, which hardened the opposition. The model of the Kirchnerist state was a central tenet of an increasingly more unified attack and it was around this political cleavage that the UCR joined with the ARI to create the centrist coalition the FAUNEN *(Frente Amplio UNEN)* in 2013, which would join with the PRO in 2015 to mount a coherent challenge to the Kirchnerist vision of state through the wide-reaching centre-Right political party *Cambiemos* (Freytes and Niedzwiecki, 2016). Mauricio Macri, mayor of Buenos Aires (2007–2015), who headed this newly created party, argued that it was only the Argentine Right that was capable of representing a broad range of demands for change. Macri called for the reordering of the economy and the defence of democratic institutions, and with it, he agitated a 'moral panic' against the potential 'Venezuelisation' of the country (Morresi and Vommaro, 2014). The appeal of this centre-Right vision began to resonate with more voters than it had in 2011. The PRO party returned three senators and eighteen deputies in the 2013 legislative elections (Ministerio del Interior, 2013). The political opposition towards the government was reconstructing. However, the *Frente para la Victoria* (Victory Front) (FPV) maintained its majority in Congress, but the continued downturn in macroeconomic indicators meant that the opposition to the Kirchnerist model of governance would reach such a level that it would enable opposing parties to crystallize their positions into a unified opposition by 2015.

Macri campaigned focusing on wide-ranging issues that related to the vision of the state. His policies promised to reduce its influence within the economy. Policies included abolishing export taxes, export quotas, and price controls; removing capital controls; and reducing institutional intervention but also strengthening institutions because he argued that weaker institutions had enabled corruption (Semán, 2015). Macri drew attention to the fact that the intervention into the INDEC had damaged Argentina's international image, 'lying about and hiding the state of the economy had tarnished Argentina's reputation worldwide' (Associated Press, 2015). The centre-Right vision was presented to Argentines in a number of electoral promises: zero poverty, an influx of foreign investment, lower inflation, improved dialogue

[6] The popularity of PRO was slow to gather momentum during times when the government enjoyed solid popularity, especially in peripheral provinces, and as such, early support for PRO was based in the city of Buenos Aires (Levitsky and Murillo, 2008).

between politicians and citizens, and the strengthening of national institutions. He promised better relationships with the rural sector by removing taxes, which would increase production. All this was underpinned by what opposition politicians argued was a root cause of Argentina's economic problems—Kirchnerist spending—for which they promised a *reducción drástica del gasto público* 'significant cut in state spending' (Kollmann, 2016). The election fault lines had been drawn, and they were around policies that were politically polarizing and underpinned by ideas of what the state should be. While the accusations of corruption levied at the government hardened opposition, they also solidified support with pro-Kirchneristas by reinforcing voters' prior opinions (Lupu, 2016). The accusations of corruption were one point of attack but a point of attack that paled into insignificance when compared to the preoccupation of voters around the ability of the government to manage the economy (the most important of which was the reduction in inflation), reduce poverty, reduce crime, reduce wealth inequality, and fight corruption (Kollmann, 2016).[7]

The increasing partisanship of this opposition crystallized around a polarized cleavage that proposed an alternative to Kirchnerismo, a more market-friendly economic model, the type of which was blamed by Kirchner supporters for the economic challenges that led to the debt default in 2001 (Wylde, 2016). In an interview with PRO's chief of communications and general secretary of the city of Buenos Aires, Marcos Peña, he acknowledged that the market would play a central role in the new type of state:

> It is clear that we do not believe in hollowing out the state or in building the state by the state itself, our logic is based on tackling concrete problems with a strong state and a private sector that works together.
>
> **(La Nación, 2015)**

The wider set of policies that was championed by the opposition was built around a framework of deregulation, free-trade, and a reversal of part of the programme of nationalizations, all of which demonstrate that opposition was both growing and coalescing around visions of the state. Furthermore, embedded within this framework was the promise of a shift in the fiscal contract between the government and the producers through major tax reforms, which would reduce the burden not only on the rural sector but also on all

[7] At this point, President Kirchner's vice-president, Amado Boudou, was on trial for taking bribes, but still only 9 per cent of respondents from the Argentine Panel Election Study (APES) thought that corruption was the overriding problem in Argentina (Lupu, 2016).

Argentinians (Mangonnet and Murillo, 2020). The high tax burden was the underpinning rationale for a growing call from the opposition for tax reform through gradual reductions, which Mauricio Macri argued would increase opportunities for all (Marelli, 2015). This campaign promising to abolish the export withholdings, which, he argued, would result in increased production, more employment, and increased national consumption (Marelli, 2015). In a meeting with 300 producers, the Macri campaign argued its case for the lifting of the export taxes:

> When taxes are removed, there will be a reorientation and an optimisation of public spending to be able to meet the levels of investment that the country needs [. . .] the national government must improve its link with and facilitate the growth of this [rural] sector rather than impeding it.
>
> **(Infobae, 2015)**

This argument demonstrates that although the debate had transcended tax, export taxes remained salient and a fault line within these discussions and was at the intersection of opposing arguments about open and closed models of economic development and about the role of the state as regulator and intervener of these markets. Political debates were becoming more polarized and because of the continued deterioration of the Argentine economy, the opposition to the Kirchnerist state model was regrouping around a new breed of political party, which was offering voters an alternative narrative to that of Kirchnerismo and a different vision of state.

Loss of legitimacy to govern

The inflationary pressures and the negative current account balance, which was a contributing factor to the currency controls, were now not only affecting the middle classes but also adding to growing voter discontent in public-sector workers. In 2013, both police and teachers protested through strikes, unhappy about the limits to wage increases and the erosion of their pay under the pressures of rising inflation (The Economist, 2013). This growing discontent, which had now reached the public sectors, shows that following years of generous state spending, when the funding tap started to close, the government started to face increasing incidences of social unrest, dissatisfaction amongst the middle classes, and direct challenges from both opposition and labour forces. The President's approval level fell from 50 per cent to 30 per cent between June and September 2012 (Schiumerini and Steinberg, 2020).[8] Furthermore, there were growing calls of mismanagement of public spending within the popular and lower-income sectors, because it was these groups of workers who had been adversely impacted by the *Once* train disaster as the train was utilized primarily by lower-middle classes and workers (Barreiro, 2017).

This position was exacerbated further when, in his role as mayor of Buenos Aires, Mauricio Macri argued that underinvestment in the province of Buenos Aires had directly contributed towards lives lost during the 2013 floods in Greater La Plata and Greater Buenos Aires (Gilbert, 2013). With these incidences, the legitimacy of government spending on welfare and subsidies rather than on infrastructure (which was partly funded by, but inextricably associated with, an idea of export taxes) came to the fore, and the question transcended the traditional tensions between the producers and the government to envelop wider societal classes (Wylde, 2017). Furthermore, in a worsening economic climate, with capital being scarce, Argentina technically defaulted again on US$29 billion (31 July, 2014) when a US judge's ruling found in favour of the holdout companies who had rejected the debt haircut (Thomas and Cachanosky, 2016; Hébert and Schreger, 2017).

These interventions, which were concentrating power in the executive, were expanding the narrative of perceived mismanagement of public spending, which, in turn, was adding to a growing crisis of legitimacy built around spiralling inflation, currency controls, and a general downturn in economic indicators. This ultimately led to increased social tensions and widespread discontent through large national protests that began at the end of 2012 and early in 2013. While the opposition was not explicitly associated with the protests (as highlighted by interviewees in Gold and Peña, 2019), with estimates of half a million people protesting, the scale of these protests does show that there was growing public discontent against the government; after twelve years of Kirchnerismo, the conflict surrounding the vision of the state that the Kirchners were building had not been resolved, but the political polarization had increased, which, in turn, affected the legitimacy of the Kirchnerist statist model. And again, some of the protesters directly linked their wider discontent back to taxes. Ozarow (2019: 128) points to the continuing ideological rejection of *retenciones* because of the association with

[8] The authors consider that black currency markets are particularly unpopular in high–middle income countries like Argentina, as the middle-class sectors with savings in foreign currency is significant. Because the black-market premium is akin to a tax rate, and due to the additional risk incurred in buying in the black market, buyers will develop a negative view of the government responsible for creating the market (Schiumerini and Steinberg, 2020: 1219).

the type of state that Cristina Kirchner was pursuing. He cites an interviewee from Piedras Blancas: 'this government is giving out money, left, right and centre; Take, take, take from the hardworking taxpayers.' He went on to highlight that 'they are fed up with paying so that others can live for free'.

Post 2011, the government had trapped itself in a programme of state redistribution that was negatively impacted by contingent economic factors—in short, policy programmes that were expensive and becoming more so—and the government had limited options to fund them. Opposition was growing, and the challenge for the government was to address this growing and organized opposition in the October 2015 election with a new candidate, Daniel Scioli, who was viewed as a moderate who would reverse many Kirchnerist interventionalist policies (Lupu, 2016).[9] After twelve years in government, the FPV lost the presidential elections in October 2015 and Mauricio Macri was sworn in as president in December 2015. But even after all this growing opposition to Kirchnerismo, it was not an emphatic result, and after the opposition had mobilized and created a broad political base—which, in part, spoke to some of the Kirchner voters through a tamed conservative voice—Macri secured the vote with a 51.5 per cent vote share against 48.5 per cent share (Ministerio del Interior, 2015). Although, for all the reasons I have highlighted, the Argentine electorate did return a president from the Right in December 2015, but the close result demonstrated that this structural tension and the political cleavages that coalesced around opposing state visions remained. After twelve years of Kirchnerist governance, nearly half of the electorate was still willing to vote for the Kirchnerist candidate, highlighting that issues remained unresolved, and the fault line over which this contention had been built would remain contentious into the following administration.

Conclusion

This chapter has analysed factors and policies that moved Peronist government opposition from its traditional opponents within the rural sector to envelop other sectors of society, which ultimately led to a rejection of the Kirchnerist vision of the state. It has argued that the programme of redistribution through welfare and subsidies, which continued (and in some cases was enhanced) following the 2008 rural revolt, where legitimacy to tax exports was lost, was both a factor in government support and created a pathway towards hardening government opposition. It highlighted that this model

[9] Constitutionally, Cristina Fernández de Kirchner could not stand for re-election a third time.

of redistribution through state intervention into the economy came under increasing pressure following President Fernández de Kirchner's landslide victory in the 2011 election. Contingent economic factors that were explored in Chapter 6 accelerated a process of political polarization both for supporters and opponents of the government, which translated into accusations of economic mismanagement and growing corruption. During this period, political positions hardened in the run-up to the election.

Apart from the macro-level political economic story engaged with in this chapter, it has also explored factors at the micro level. These have helped to trace the trajectory of conditions around a hardening political polarization and the regrouping of the opposition. The Kirchnerist vision of the state and the policies that are emblematic of this state intervention—that had been vaunted in the post-crisis growth period of the early 2000s—now became a central focus for attack and a catalyst that allowed the opposition to centralize around this. The chapter has shown how conflict around tax became more than tax. Conflict built around opposing visions of the state, between opposing views of liberal markets and state-led interventionist policies. And, although this was a debate beyond tax, it had implications for tax as export taxes were embedded in this historic and structural debate between the Peronists and non-Peronists; the two were intertwined, and the debate was endemic in the relationship between organized actors in the rural sector and urban working classes. However, it has shown how muddled the debate became as the taxes aggravated and amplified wider socio-economic tensions and conflict that then became embedded in the Kirchnerist tax design and model of state.

Export taxes became the fault line around which the right coalesced because they were inextricably linked with Kirchnerismo; therefore, ideas of export taxes (and the rural revolt) were embedded in an interventionalist state and a redistributive state model because export taxes were driving this model. The export taxes could not be considered as a separate fiscal issue because they were so embedded within Kirchnerismo. Therefore, when tax became relatively subsidiary in this period, it was still a prominent focus of attack for the growing opposition, along with the model of the Kirchnerist state, because of the taxes. Tax became a fault line around which polarization manifested strongly, which, in turn, brought in other factors that it touched and aggravated; the debate transcended just tax to bring in wider dissatisfactions. This led to the return of the Right in Argentina. However, this was not the end of the debate, and explaining that the issue was structural and unresolved is important as this debate continued into the following presidential mandate. *Retenciones* are associated with Kirchnerismo, but the polemic of them continued to play out into President Marci's term in office, when, because of Argentina's specialized integration into the global economy as an exporter of agricultural commodities, and the fact that challenges to fund the state remained, the newly elected president was unable to reduce the burden on the agricultural producers as he had promised during the election campaign.

8
Conclusion

Contested Ideas of Tax and State

Introduction

The road to delivering progress on the United Nation's Sustainable Development Goals (SDGs) has faced significant barriers since 2020. The COVID-19 pandemic of 2020/2021 pushed back twenty-five years of equitable and inclusive development progress in twenty-five weeks (Gates Foundation, 2020), exacerbating many of the inequalities they were created to ameliorate in the process. The Russian invasion of Ukraine in early 2022 brought a cataclysmic series of events: spikes in energy prices, sustained and stubbornly high inflation, and challenges to food security, all of which detrimentally impacted on already fragile and heavily indebted (more so since COVID-19) economies across the Global South. Rising geopolitical tensions, increasingly polarized politics, unresolved debates on climate finance packages, and colonial reparations are all interwoven with eyewatering amounts of domestic tax receipts that are lost to offshore tax havens and the reticence of the Organisation for Economic Co-operation and Development (OECD) to sufficiently close these loopholes, which the Tax Justice Network calls 'tax misgovernance' (Tax Justice Network, 2024). What all these global challenges substantively mean is that the need for governments across the Global South to mobilize domestic resources has never been more important than it is now. It constitutes a key pillar of the SDGs to sustainably finance state spending and development strategies, but progress towards raising the tax burden and moving away from reliance on volatile commodity markets has remained slow, weak, and partial. Essentially, across much of the developing world, collecting more tax remains overwhelmingly aspirational, with progress frustratingly elusive.

Latin America is emblematic of these challenges to mobilize domestic resources to sustainably fund state expenditure and public services. Latin American countries account for some of the lowest tax-to-gross domestic product (GDP) burdens on the planet, with high levels of informality and increasing levels of evasion creating major hurdles for governments to

Taxing for Development. Matt Barlow, Oxford University Press. © Matt Barlow (2025).
DOI: 10.1093/9780198923220.003.0008

finance state spending to meet obligations. I have argued throughout the book that regionally, weak, and fragmented tax strategies should be viewed in a longer historical arc because they have their deepest roots in both colonialism and the subsequent instability following early independence and early integration into the global economy as providers of natural resources. This lineage is directly responsible for framing three macroeconomic phenomena concomitant with the region today: first, low levels of domestic resource mobilization are a historical legacy of Spanish and Portuguese colonial tax strategies, where the focus was less on building strong tax collection capacity and more firmly on cementing mercantilist trading policies to secure access to the abundance of primary commodities—factor endowments (Engerman and Sokoloff, 1994)—that were driving the wealth of Iberian empires.

Second, early independence and integration into global supply chains introduced new Latin American republics to international capital—predominantly British capital—which both negated the need to build legitimate and strong tax collection capacities and set a precedence for borrowing as a substitute for domestic resource mobilization, with capital provided by British and latterly US banks as a pathway to gain, and maintain, access to these markets.

Third, it crystallized the importance of natural resources to the region as a driver of economic development, while simultaneously cementing wealth and power with landowning elites that were the owners of economic production in these industries. And this generated a complex dynamic whereby governments were overly reliant on these sectors for economic production, but their autonomy to extract from them was not guaranteed, in many cases, because of landownership legacies that had cemented power with landed and not political elites. Moreover, the concomitant boom and busts of volatile commodity markets have highlighted the vulnerabilities of an over-reliance on these strategies of export-led development, especially in the context of low levels of domestic resource mobilization.

To this day, in Latin America, national economies remain reliant on the extraction and export of natural resources on which their economies remain integrated into the global economy. And the state's role in these industries remains a hotbed of scholarly debate. A recent title in this book series, Nem Singh's *Business of the State* (2024), discusses why state ownership matters for growth strategies based on critical mineral extraction and resource governance in Brazil and Chile. Taking a global view, Alami and Dixon (2024: 230) point to an increasing role for the state as 'promoter, supervisor, investor, and owner of capital across the spaces of the world economy'. But in Latin America, not all governments have sufficiently embedded themselves into these industries. Some progressive governments have struggled, historically, to permeate into specialized exporting sectors to extract and to redistribute at times of high commodity prices because of how different power structures have been built around natural resource ownership by influential elites, and because of how political coalitions have created a barrier to building consensus around the extraction of this revenue (Johnson et al., 2024). One of the remaining strategies available to governments in this context is the utilization of export taxes. But it is a political choice for the state to intervene into these sectors and markets, to mobilize domestic resources from them, and to redistribute to other areas of the economy, and in this sense, I have shown how they become ideological.

One of the key considerations for governments is the dilemma of who they should raise tax from and how much of the burden each taxpayer should pay. But this is not only an economic strategy for funding government but also, overwhelmingly, a political choice. Tax strategies not only require the infrastructure to enable tax collectors to raise revenue in the first place, but also they require significant political will and power to push through policy choices (Bird, 1989); which, in many cases, are grounded in political ideologies and designed to deliver economic benefits to supportive socio-economic groups. In democracies, tax is the most frequently occurring interaction between state and society, and because of this, it is the policy area most likely to generate tension, so governments need to try and build broad-based legitimacy around tax strategies to maximize resource mobilization and thus provide public services that legitimize the collection. So, how to legitimize tax strategies across societies for any government is both complex, because of opposing ideologies, and essential. Democratic governments across the globe align tax policies with political support, and the burden of this tax has been shouldered interchangeably between both capital and labour, with left-leaning strategies falling traditionally on the interests of capital, and right-leaning strategies falling more heavily over labour (Castañeda and Doyle, 2019). But these ideologies, I have shown, can become embedded in the tax policies themselves, and ideas of what the tax represents, can permeate into other socio-economic groups that oppose an idea and ideology, rather than their interests being directly and negatively impacted. So, politics matters for framing ideas of tax—what the revenue is collected for and redistributed to—and tax ideas matter for delivering political agendas, especially in the context of fewer options to raise revenue, and the problems of getting this wrong have all too often been played out with increasing political conflict and debt-led solutions.

Limitations of the Argentine export tax regime

This book provides a novel analysis of tax debates under Argentina's pink tide governments (2003–2015) and has offered insights into the challenges governments in low- and middle-income countries face in trying to legitimize changes in fiscal extraction, especially when tax changes adversely affect a small pool of actors who nonetheless enjoy considerable political resources, the use of the tax itself is contested, and the tax spend does not align with the interests of those taxed. Ultimately, through the utilization of an Argentine case study, I have demonstrated the way in which conflicts over tax mesh with conflicts over wider processes of, and ideas about, development where the role of state is a fault line and a deep political cleavage.

Empirically, the starting point for this book was the reimposition of export taxes as part of an emergency tax strategy which underpinned Argentina's recovery from the 2001 financial crisis. These taxes played a key role in this recovery. Their collection represented nearly one-quarter of all national tax collection in the aftermath of the crisis. Their continued utilization subsequently helped drive the national tax burden to its highest ever level: 31.5 per cent of GDP by 2015 (Ministerio de Hacienda, 2021). Strong commodity prices and the growth in tax collection enabled consecutive governments post 2001 to pursue a programme of social and economic redistribution that fitted with wider regional development projects of the post-neoliberal era (Grugel and Riggirozzi, 2012). These projects depended on enhanced state intervention into national economies to redistribute away from natural resource-extracting sectors to social welfare programmes to shift the dial towards delivering more equitable and inclusive development outcomes. As such, in Argentina during the Kirchnerist governance, export taxes were levied through one iteration or another for twelve years, consecutively collecting, on average, US$18 billion annually (Giraudo, 2020; FAOSTAT, 2021).

The reimplementation of a fiscal strategy that had be so contentious throughout the twentieth century was made necessary because of the emergency in which Argentina found itself post 2001 but which also bestowed legitimacy on the *retenciones* strategy. Emergency meant that the export taxes that were implemented under President Duhalde were temporarily legitimized (or at least accepted) in the eyes of the rural producers. This was the case because the debt default and the need for fiscal resources to underpin national recovery was at such a level that the interests of the producers became subsidiary to those of the state. As such, given the overwhelming necessity to raise and redistribute resources due to levels of poverty that reached 57.6 per cent in 2002 (INDEC, 2020), ideas about development also briefly aligned. Importantly, this was contingent on the crisis.

However, it was not only the context of emergency that had bestowed an initial legitimacy in the eyes of the producers but also a confluence of wider factors. First, the Argentine currency devaluation from 1:1/US$ in December 2001 to 3:1/US$ by March 2002 was instrumental in driving the profits of the rural producers and softening the blow of any tax hikes (Rodríguez and Arceo, 2006). Second, by the end of 2003 (Figure 5.2, Chapter 5) strong commodity prices and growing international demand for Argentine agricultural resources ameliorated the fiscal position of the producers, and therefore, the tax was not such an afront to their interests; it came at less of an economic cost than might initially appear. This is an important point: even though export taxes were implemented, the strong upwards cycle of commodity prices created an emollient economic landscape that offset losses for the producers, an economic position that would continue after the emergency government of President Duhalde into the presidency of Néstor Kirchner. There was a relative fiscal peace because under Néstor Kirchner, the Argentine government maintained an emergency discourse—consolidated in 2005 with gains in the mid-term elections—and his mandate was viewed by many as one of post crisis with debt renegotiations still outstanding (Wylde, 2012a). Therefore, policies implemented under crisis were still accepted as such. Moreover, the president did not increase the fiscal burden over the producers for most of his term in office; export taxes remained levied at the same rate until 2007 with minimal social conflict.

However, while the crisis had given the illusion of a consensus around these taxes, it was both temporary and fragile, and when, under President Fernández de Kirchner, taxes shifted towards supporting increased state spending, this fragile legitimacy finally cracked. In 2007, there were already signs pointing to the fragility of this export tax strategy as the context of emergency faded, but taxes were twice hiked over exports—in the space of ten months, there were increases of 18.5 per cent on sunflower exports and 21.5 per cent on soybean exports (Kosacoff, 2007). Now, the rural producers came to view the tax burden on them in a different light, considering this underpinned a long-term interventionalist model of the state where the rural sector would be subservient to the developmental and distributive priorities of the state: they were seen as confiscatory and discriminatory. And with this change in discourse, the government no longer had the support, or at least the acquiescence, of the rural producers' associations.

At the end of 2007, with the election of President Cristina Fernández de Kirchner, Kirchnerismo passed into its second phase, an epoch characterized by the return of political conflict, a deepening of the statist model, and early indications of the economic challenges that would beset the government for the next eight years (Kulfas, 2016). In the first three months of the presidency of Cristina Fernández, the third tax increase in the space of fifteen months provided the catalyst for a social uprising that reignited conflicts based on different state visions and entirely polarized Argentine society. The rejection of Resolution N.125 was a seminal moment, with opposition to it at such a level that it managed to bridge heterogenous and competing rural elites' interests. The suggested mechanism first crystallized a cohesive sectoral response by bringing together actors from all four rural producers associations (Fairfield, 2015). The tax hikes were not acceptable to rural producers and were viewed as a tax grab because of the strong growth in commodity prices, especially for soybeans. Now no longer for emergency, they were supporting a redistributive agenda and the polemic that began in *el campo* quickly transcended the government–rural sector cleavage encompass other socio-economic sectors because it was representative of a contested vision of state, which meant that the conflict moved from one centred in a rural oligarchic and popular classes cleavage to igniting discontent within the Argentine middle classes.

This, I conclude, was underpinned by a politically polarizing reading of the *retenciones* by both supporters and opponents of the government. The increase in export taxes became the fault line around which wider political polarization hardened because it reflected fundamentally different views of the role of the state. As a result, tax became embroiled in wider redistributional conflicts. The debate around tax thus became more than a tax conflict between the Kirchners and actors in the rural sector; it spread out to other social sectors and was accompanied by a regrouping and hardening of the Kirchnerist opposition. Export taxes became the cleavage around which a new regrouping of the right coalesced. We cannot therefore consider the *retenciones* as a separate or technical narrow fiscal issue because they are so embedded within Kirchnerismo. Tax remained a prominent focus of attack for the growing opposition, along with the model of the Kirchnerist state because they were considered part of the same argument. Conversely, for the government, tax was defended because it made its redistributional policies possible. However, sitting underneath this expanded argument is the fact that, once again, export tax questions had not been addressed. The question of the legitimation of this taxation model was not fully resolved: no consensus was formed, either with the sector in question or with opposition actors. It therefore remained unresolved and contentious.

This was problematic because the government had come to rely on this revenue—which, in 2011, still represented 10 per cent of total tax take (Ministerio de Hacienda, 2021). And when a nexus of contingent economic factors, including growing debt, deteriorating currency reserves, negative fiscal and current account balances, and growing inflation, all meshed together, this resulted in a macroeconomic dynamic in which the government had trapped itself because the capacity to fund redistribution had vastly diminished. A productive structure heavily reliant on natural resource exports that came under pressure from falling commodity prices post 2010, and a lack of investment into this productive structure because of a focus on social redistribution through welfare policies in lieu of other areas of public spending, began to challenge the statist model. These factors contributed towards an economy that was no longer able to provide the level of generous spending that had characterized Kirchnerist governance thus far. As the taxes had become inextricably enmeshed with the Kirchnerist interventionalist state, the statist model itself was coming under attack by a strengthened opposition that had managed to regroup around policies that had been implemented to try and deal with this fiscal entrapment: foreign currency limits, (attempted) removal of subsidies, public-sector wage freezes, and an opposing vision of the state.

This accelerated a process of political polarization both for supporters and opponents of the government. Polarization, as Peruzzotti and Waisbord (2021) argue, is long-standing and embedded in Argentina, but now that the export taxes no longer represented such a large share of the fiscal intake, socio-economic and political contention spilled over into a wider conflict. The export taxes had touched and aggravated long-standing divisions and became embedded within opposing ideas of the state. The conflict around tax became something bigger, and it coalesced around opposing visions of the state and the economy.

In October 2015, the Argentine electorate returned Mauricio Macri from *Propuesta Republicana* (Republican Proposal) (PRO) as its president, and with his election, Argentina shifted back (until 2019, with the election of Alberto Fernández of Frente de Todos) towards the centre-Right. At the time, this shift fitted in with a wider regional pattern whereby left-of-centre governments that had been elected in the early part of 2000s were replaced by governments from the Right or centre-Right. The pink tide ebbed away in the mid- and late 2010s, bringing with it major political change and the return of neoliberal ideas with right-of-centre governments not only returning in Argentina but also in Brazil (2016), Ecuador (2017), and temporarily in Bolivia between 2018 and 2020. Scholarly attention that has focused on the retrenchment of the Left during this time has done so by reigniting debates about the 'dependency' of Latin American states through the perspective of an exhaustion of the resource boom, which presented limitations to strong redistribution programmes (Ruckert, Macdonald, and Proulx, 2017), or through an inability to enact structural reforms that would sufficiently change the mode of production and break dependency on export revenues (Rojas, 2017; Grugel and Riggirozzi, 2018). Other authors have argued that it was a rejection of economic interventionalism (Ellner, 2019), or it was the process of funding populist policies through the redistribution of revenues that was responsible for this shift back towards the Right (Mazzuca, 2013; Castañeda, 2015).

Throughout all of these perspectives, the cyclical nature of this dependant relationship is embedded within this literature, and it is acknowledged as providing a paradox of opportunities: first, for the funding of left-wing progressive policies when there is a commodity 'boom' and then for creating limitations to the continuation of them, when prices experience a 'bust', resulting in political change. Argentina is representative of an exhaustion of the interventionist high-spending model of governance that came to the fore in the early 2000s, and it sits squarely with other Latin American distributive conflicts that ushered in political change in the mid-2010s.

The end of the commodity boom saw major political and social conflict in two other countries that previously had a limited history of social mobilization and distributive conflict under democracy: Brazil and Chile. For Brazil, the unprecedented increase in social redistribution seen during the Lula years added to anti-Workers' Party grievances once the bonanza subsided, resulted in an even more dramatic shift to the Right (Alonso and Mische, 2017: 122), while in Chile, there was a redistributive conflict of a different kind. Following the completion of President Bachelet's second term (2014–2018), President Piñera (2018–2022) was faced with a redistributive challenge not because the economy did not allow for social redistribution but because the government chose not to pursue social redistribution. In the case of Chile, there was capacity to implement social redistribution, but instead, the government chose not to do this, which led to the mass revolts of 2019–2020, revealing the extent of social discontent with the neoliberal socio-economic model inherited from the Pinochet dictatorship (Rozas Bugueño and Somma, 2020).

However, there was not the same level of redistributive conflict in all Latin American countries. Less affluent countries with less developed social states, such as Bolivia, Paraguay, and even Peru, have more 'tolerant' societies, and instead of distributive conflicts, these countries have favoured macroeconomic and political continuity (Duckworth, 2015). While

Argentina demonstrates asymmetries to these latter countries because of the prevalence of redistributive conflict, it also demonstrates asymmetries to Brazil and Chile because of its long-standing history with redistributive conflicts. Why, therefore, are redistributive conflicts more prevalent in Argentina? Natanson (2018: 30) offers an explanation for this whereby he argues that, in some countries (such as Chile), there are enough export resources to avoid the entrapment that was witnessed in Argentina post 2011, and in other countries, they have societies that have 'less "European" consumption patterns that also limits the needs for imports'. Exploring this statement further draws attention to some of the underpinning facets of these long-standing redistributive conflicts, which are associated with particularities in Argentine political economic history. Citizens have high expectations, especially on left-wing governments, which tend to be committed to redistribution, but governments have relied on volatile commodities to deliver these expectations. Early patterns of development meant that for much of the twentieth century, Argentina was the richest country in the region, with the highest wages and the largest consumption-orientated middle class. Furthermore, it was a country where a workerist popular political movement had dominated democratic politics since the mid-1940s, which helped shape an Argentine 'society little tolerant to resign what it considers acquired social rights' (Gerchunoff, Rapetti, and De León, 2020: 320), even when delivery of these social rights became more problematic because of structural economic challenges. So, while Argentina's shift back to the Right in 2015 was representative in some ways, it was a shift with Argentine particularities, but the challenges of export-led growth in the context of low tax collection did not end with Kirchnerismo.

The election of President Macri did little to resolve the long-running structural tensions around tax that had been evident under the redistributive programmes of Kicrhnerismo. The model of the state that was the centre for attack built around contested tax policies actually continued, albeit in a more diluted fashion. There were continuities within this change. Welfare programmes that were associated with 'more state' were not rescinded and re-nationalizations implemented under Cristina Kircher were not reversed (Semán, 2015). However, there were changes alongside these continuities, in line with the new agrarian business-friendly government narrative: export quotas were abolished, currency controls lifted, the peso devalued by 30 per cent, and the majority of export taxes were abolished. Importantly, whilst tax on soy remained—although this was reduced from 35 to 30 per cent—the rationale had changed. The reason for the maintenance of this tax was because the national finances the government had inherited were in such a bad state that the continuation of tax on soy was necessary, for now, but it was forecast to reduce by 5 per cent each year, depending on the fiscal situation (Bertello, 2015b). Moreover, because of contingent macroeconomic factors in Argentina, these were not abolished, and they became increasingly embedded in the tax basket, but the polemic these taxes engendered resurfaced when export taxes were expanded over a wider range of commodities in 2018 (Selman, 2018).

Under President Macri, export taxes were no longer framed as a redistributive tool whose burden fell on the producers of abundance; rather, the new president apologetically considered the partial reintroduction (tax on soy was already in place) as a bad policy but one that was necessary due to the deteriorating macroeconomic climate. They were once again necessary because of the persistence of emergency, and the tax was framed as a response to this emergency (El Cronista, 2018). High inflation and debt returned, and the Argentine state sought financing and, with reduced options, turned back to international borrowing. Seventeen years after the default, Argentina secured a US$57 billion loan, which represented the largest International Monetary Fund (IMF) loan in the institution's history, with the associated conditions requiring shrinking the state and achieving a zero deficit by 2019 (Goñi, 2018). With high debt levels, this time, the government could not turn to emergency export taxes to tax its way out of the crisis as emergency taxes had been normalized within the wider fiscal programme and with this, its effectiveness as an emergency tool, diminished. Deteriorating macroeconomic indicators and President Macri's deal with the IMF contributed to his resounding electoral defeat in 2019, with Argentine voters returning the Peronist candidate, whose campaign promised an expansion of redistributive policies for which export taxes would be increased to fund them, in doing so, directly (re)conflating export taxes with an idea of an interventionalist developmental state.

Theoretical contributions

I have argued throughout this book that ideas of taxation, which are a much understudied conceptual approach in both political economy of taxation and development studies literatures, offers us an analytical framework through which to understand tax conflict when tax strategies and burdens do not fall over a particular group of taxpayers, but they have the ability to generate conflict, nonetheless. Whilst not seeking to discount the concept of interests, which are undoubtedly the dominant approach to which scholars have pointed as the challenge to raise taxes across the Global South, or weak institutional capacity to collect, I have argued the salience of ideas alongside these approaches and strongly point out that they should not be discounted. Moreover, I have situated this tax-for-development debate in a rich empirical discussion that demonstrates an over-reliance on natural resource commodities and fiscal revenues from volatile commodity markets and a politically charged reading of the export tax regime. Therefore, what are the wider theoretical contributions of this book? I see three significant theoretical contributions that I discuss here but also point to wider opportunities for the application of this work at the end of this chapter.

Embedding ideas of tax with contested ideas of state

The first theoretical contribution that I make is by highlighting the link that exists between raising taxes, conflict, and ideas of development because underpinning all these discussions is the question of how to make 'taxes politically palatable' (Flores-Macías, 2019: 3). By exploring this link theoretically, I demonstrate the theoretical salience of tax ideas to development literatures because these ideas can become embedded in other areas of policy. Drawing from Hall's seminal (1993) paper, the processes of embedding ideas in policy occurs in three stages, his first- to third-order processes (see Chapter 2). And it is this idea of third-order processes, where a critical juncture or punctured equilibrium can embed ideas in policy, that is especially valuable for the theoretical contributions of this book. However, while in Hall's framework, ideas become embedded in the creation of policies as a response to crisis situations, I have argued that ideas can also become embedded in the policies themselves ex post. *Retenciones* were levied as a response to a particular emergency in 2002; they accompanied a significant devaluation of the Argentine peso and growing commodity prices and were one of a few polices that were available to the emergency government to try and rebuild the state after default. However, the attempted implementation of the variable tax mechanism whose value would trace the international price of commodities engendered a widespread conflict that would entirely polarize Argentine society. Why was it, then, that a fiscal strategy that was levied over the agricultural exports in 2008 led to a deep political cleavage that engulfed and polarized Argentine society? I have argued that because these taxes represented an ideology of an interventionist state and redistributive and progressive government, they became emblematic of Kirchnerismo, of taxing wealth and redistributing to popular classes through social welfare transfers, and this type of state is deeply contentious and reflects opposing political views, of state, market, and what the role taxation should play within this.

And this was the fault line; it was a rejection of the export taxes and, simultaneously, a rejection of an interventionist state. Whilst export taxes had supported programmes of subsidies that had benefited the middle classes more than they had the popular classes, the idea of Kirchnerismo was rejected. Moreover, when the economy was no longer able to provide the fiscal space for the government, conceptually, this idea of export taxes was held responsible for this. It became embedded in areas of wider conflict and became inseparable from wider government policies. An idea of export tax had become completely embedded with Kirchnerismo, and a political cleavage manifested around this idea. So theoretically, while the interests of agricultural exporters drove the initial uprising and there were worries in some organized labour groups outside of the sector asking if 'they could do it to the rural sector, will they come for me?' (interview, trade union economist, 2019), the way it completely enveloped other socio-economic groups is attributed to opposing ideas of what the taxes were being levied for and to whom they were being redistributed. And it is exactly this point that fed into class conflict because the export taxes were being used to ameliorate the living conditions of popular classes at the expense of the interests of the rural elites (Elbert and Pérez, 2018). Here, the tax debate becomes tense and politically polarizing as it is inextricably linked to the contention surrounding what is acceptable intervention into an economy and what tax revenues are redistributed to once they are collected.

State autonomy and extractivism: The conflict-inducing compensatory state

The process of how these ideas can generate wider socio-economic conflict I also attribute to the lack of autonomous state capacity into specialized extractive industries to manage resource booms. Highlighted in Figure 2.1 (see Chapter 2), I build a theoretical model through which I demonstrate how the different modalities of revenue resource extraction can frame high intersectoral social conflict. In this framework, the processes of how developmental states—with the state as the actor of development—manage resource booms is traced and delineated between the various degrees of autonomy that states have in natural resource-exporting sectors from state-owned enterprises to high/embedded state autonomy and weak state autonomy. I argue through this framework that in operations where there are either state-owned enterprises or a high/embedded autonomy, the processes employed to manage resource booms—increased sales revenue, special share schemes, and royalty schemes—are unlikely to result in social conflict. However, when there is weak state autonomy, and the state lacks official channels to permeate into extractive sectors, export taxes represent a pathway to manage the revenues from commodity booms through the concepts of state interventionism or resource nationalism. Moreover, by introducing the concepts of interests and contested ideas to export taxes, it traces the pathway of how high social conflict is generated in exporting sectors because of negatively impacted interests but also points to intersectoral social conflict because of contested ideas. So, state autonomy, resource governance, and contested ideas of export taxes are all inextricably linked in this framework, which, rather than solely offering a material-based explanation for social conflict, introduces ideas into the mix.

Furthermore, this framework has wider theoretical implications and contributes to both widespread understandings of development under progressive governments of Latin America's pink tide and the concept of post-neoliberalism and to Gudynas's (2016) concept of the compensatory state discussing the same period (late 1990s–mid-2010s). First, while widely acknowledged that the social redistribution that forms a central plank of post-neoliberalism (which I have discussed in detail in this book in relation to Argentina and which took place in other regional countries that voted in governments with the promise to redistribute: Bolivia, Brazil, Chile, Ecuador, Mexico, and Venezuela) was fuelled by taxes and royalty schemes during a super cycle of commodity prices, the collection of these is overwhelmingly assumed. Literatures have not thus far engaged with the politics of this tax collection, and therefore, the tensions that these strategies engendered and the bargaining role of the state as mediator to natural resource industries to try and legitimize extraction schemes are subsidiary. This book makes significant inroads into addressing these points.

In relation to the conceptual argument of the compensatory state, Gudynas (2016, 2018, 2020), the state is a critical actor that acts as a harmonizing force to correct the imbalances and inequalities of capitalism in extractive and export-led economies under progressive governments. Under resource nationalism, Gudynas argues that the state is characterized by first, the contradictions the state seeks to promote the liberalization of capital processes while ameliorating its negative impacts; second, the equilibria involved in balancing the concessions offered to, and the limitations imposed, upon capital; and third, the compensatory role of the state that intervenes into capital markets and redistributes economic compensation to reduce social conflict and maintain electoral support. However, while these characterizations elucidate the complexities and competing roles of the state in intervening into resource sectors to redistribute to reduce social conflict, they do not consider how contested ideas of these compensation strategies can themselves cause conflict, and state autonomy to carry out these processes is largely assumed. The arguments I have made throughout the book add a level of nuance to this conceptual understanding of state, thus foregrounding its theoretical contributions.

Emergency, legitimacy, and fiscal bargaining

The third substantive theoretical contribution that I make in the book is a contribution to the vast corpora of work in historical sociology and new fiscal sociology by bringing these into conversation with development studies literatures. I contribute to our understanding of the processes of building legitimacy around tax strategies in emergency situations and demonstrate under what circumstances legitimacy can be lost and how this can impact upon funding development processes. More concretely, I have argued that while legitimacy is difficult to build, emergency and crisis situations have the impact of providing temporary legitimacy because of the positive effect on building social consensus around national emergencies and shared socio-economic challenges. In this context, the emergency acts as a harmonizing force to build legitimacy around tax strategies, even in situations where the design negatively impacts upon interests and is incompatible with taxpayers' ideas. However, and importantly, when the context of emergency fades, the fragility of legitimacy becomes evident because the rationale for taxpayers to comply with emergency tax strategies is granted only because of the emergency context and should the rationale change, legitimacy is quickly lost (Barlow and Peña, 2022).

Moreover, while the emergency context had provided temporary legitimacy, in doing so, it had negated the process of legitimacy-building through fiscal bargaining. In this essential part of the process, governments bargain with taxpayers over the public services that they will provide for the taxes that they collect, thus building a fiscal contract and legitimizing tax strategies. In the context of emergency, this process becomes subsidiary and, temporarily, unnecessary. Emergency has created the context to bypass the normal processes of fiscal bargaining, but I have highlighted the trap of failing to build legitimacy when the emergency fades. Finally, in relation to tax bargaining, this book contributes theoretically to the historical work by Grafe and Irigoin

(2006), Frankema (2010), Gardner (2012), and McClure (2023), who argued against the concept of absolutist rule under the British, French, and Spanish Empires and foregrounded the requirements for colonial administrators to bargain with indigenous elites and populations over the collection of taxes. By bringing these historical narratives around tax bargaining together, across empires, Chapter 3 provides a novel account that demonstrates the importance of the tax bargaining for all Western empires, and because of the imposed and brutal governance structures of colonialism, building legitimacy was complex. Therefore, indirect taxes on commerce, imports, and exports were understood to be less confrontational, and their utilization across the Global South set in process some of the collection strategies that are still used today to avoid difficult tax questions—export taxes being one of these strategies that I have discussed in detail throughout the book. Finally, in making its contribution to these literatures, the book simultaneously draws attention to the complexities of building and legitimizing fiscal contracts in developing-country contexts, when not all in society are taxed equally. It shows that by leaving these tax questions unanswered and funding developing states through natural resource revenues or borrowing, tax strategies not only suffer in terms of legitimacy but also may turn openly contentious, with the ability to engender mass social and political conflict and disrupt policy consensus and developmental programmes.

Commodity dependence and challenges in the twenty-first century

In the opening chapter of this book, I began by introducing some of the contentious politics around the utilization of export taxes in Argentina by drawing attention to some of the small-scale producer protests that a recent hike of export taxes (2022) had instigated under President Alberto Fernández's administration (2019–2023). Moreover, I pointed to the President's tongue-in-cheek acknowledgement at the time that they would generate some sectoral conflict: as I have shown, this was because of deeply embedded historical cleavages over their utilization in Argentina. Less than two weeks after President Fernández's inauguration in December 2019, a congressional bill passed that included, as part of a package of reforms, increases in export taxes. The tax on soybeans was augmented by three percentage points to a total of 30 per cent (Bertelli, 2019), with the concomitant response of strikes from the rural sector's associations the following March (Martínez, 2020).

But the expansive and redistributive economic policies of the Fernández administration negatively converged with several global shocks: the COVID-19 pandemic, a three-year drought that impacted upon agricultural yields in the Pampas, and the global energy price shocks caused by Russia's invasion of Ukraine, all of which had a significant detrimental effect upon Argentina's domestic economy, with government policies to ameliorate the situation pushing annual inflation to 210 per cent in 2023.

The Argentine electorate, weary of lurching from one economic crisis to another, put their faith, resoundingly—with the biggest vote share since the return to democracy in 1983—in far-Right Libertarian and highly unorthodox candidate Javier Milei, who was elected president of the Republic in 2023, promising to eviscerate the Argentine state as part of his political dogma and, in doing so, garnering broad support from the rural associations because of his commitment to abolishing export taxes.

However, a year into his presidency, export taxes remain levied, demonstrating both their salience to the Argentine economy and their importance as a mechanism to extract from specialized industries when the state lacks the autonomy to benefit from natural resource export-led production through other means. In August 2024, soybean producers paid a 33 per cent export tax (Ruralnet, 2024), and although President Milei had reinstated his desire to abolish the taxes a month earlier, they remain levied, causing growing tensions with producers' associations. At the Rural Expo 2024, which Milei attended, representatives of the Argentine Rural Confederation lamented the slow progress on abolishing the taxes, which they described as an 'unfair, arbitrary, and distortive tax on agricultural exports', which, it argued, 'suffocates our producers' (Independent, 2024). President Milei was emphatically elected and given a platform to reduce state intervention into the lives of Argentines; thus far, the inability to abolish the export tax strategy above all highlights the continued importance of these exports to the Argentine economy to fund state obligations, even under a libertarian president who is ideologically opposed to them, and who built their abolition front and centre into his presidential campaign.

Contested ideas of export taxes, state, and the state's role in development have formed the theoretical and empirical core of this book. But the insights that it has provided in relation to natural resource export over-reliance, governance of resource booms, and weak and partial tax strategies are applicable to other countries in Latin America and in other regions of the Global South. I see these as interrelated facets of natural resource-led development, with progressive governments relying on resource wealth, through whichever mechanism, to redistribute to other sectors of society when prices are on the ascendency, and debt as a substitute for this when they are not. The role of the state is central to this, and the contention around this policy reflects fundamentally different views of what role the state should play in national development and in resource markets, and how this extraction is legitimized is essential. And with the race to secure access to critical minerals opening new resource frontiers, this continues to be a salient and timely debate.

In Latin America's lithium triangle (Bolivia, Chile, and Argentina), governments have taken different approaches to maximizing revenue from the 'surge in demand of battery metals' (Johnson et al., 2024: 9) to try and break historic oligopolies in the lithium industry but which have been shaped by historical institutional legacies of 'nationalizations and social mobilizations' (Johnson et al., 2024: 9), with Johnson et al. (2024) highlighting the politics that surround the states' role in these industries.

In Chile, the state has moderated the demands of economic nationalists by securing the interests of *Sociedad Química y Minera* (SQM), *Corporación Nacional del Cobre* (National Copper Corporation of Chile) (CODELCO), and *Empresa Nacional Minera* (ENAMI), thereby maintaining Chile's corporatist model of export-led development. In Argentina, the state has all but relinquished its control over the sector, further liberalizing what was an already liberal investment regime. Finally, Bolivia has adopted a model of resource nationalism that reflects the interests of a fragile coalition between regional organizations and the central state.

The authors conclude that while the government of Alberto Fernández had promised to make lithium a priority, movements to nationalize the industry never gathered pace. And while Bolivia, Chile, and Argentina have divergent approaches to managing lithium extraction with different levels of autonomy, what all three strategies have in common is a deepening of reliance on natural resource export-led growth, diminishing again the role of these countries to providers of primary commodities.

The arguments I have made in this book offer a theoretical framework that will help analyse any future social mobilizations over fiscal extraction schemes that will be implemented during the inevitable commodity price booms. Understanding the processes of legitimation, and how an idea of state can become embedded in an idea of tax, adds value for governments that are seeking to increase domestic resource mobilization to reduce dependence on natural resource exports.

And it is related to this very point that I conclude this chapter, and the book, by drawing from this dependence to offer some insights to Kaldor's (1962) seminal question: will underdeveloped countries learn to tax? While the politics of tax, as I have argued, is overwhelmingly a barrier to mobilizing domestic resources in the Global South, and political will is essential for governments to implement tax strategies to finance national development, what remains the dominant economic framework for countries across the Global South is that they continue to be embedded in an unequal relationship within the global economy. Peripheral states continue to be entrenched in an unequal economic relationship as exporters of natural resources to metropolis states in the Global North. And because of a continued reliance on the exportation of natural resource commodities, domestically, tax issues have not been addressed; they are development challenges that represent two sides of the same coin. Addressing the dependent development that is still illustrative of the economic production of many countries in the Global South is simultaneously a monumental structural challenge, but making progress towards one will help shift the dial on the other.

References

Acosta, A. (2013). 'Extractivism and Neoextractivism: Two Sides of the Same Curse'. *Beyond Development: Alternative Visions from Latin America*, *1*, 61–86.

Acosta, P. A., Lartey, E. K., and Mandelman, F. S. (2009). 'Remittances and the Dutch Disease'. *Journal of International Economics*, *79*(1), 102–116.

Acuña, C. H., Galiani, S., and Tommasi, M. (2007). 'Understanding the Political Economy of Structural Reform: The Case of Argentina'. Working Paper No. 91, Departamento de Economia, Universidad de San Andres.

Adebayo, E., Lashitew, A. A., and Werker, E. (2021). 'Is Conventional Wisdom about Resource Taxation Correct? Mining Evidence from Transparency Reporting'. *World Development*, *146*, 105597.

Alemann, R. (1989). *Breve historia de la política económica Argentina, 1500–1989*. Buenos Aires: Editorial Claridad.

Alami, I., and Dixon, A. D. (2024). *The Spectre of State Capitalism*. Oxford: Oxford University Press.

Alonso, A., and Mische, A. (2017). 'Changing Repertoires and Partisan Ambivalence in the New Brazilian Protests'. *Bulletin of Latin American Research*, *36*(2), 144–159.

Alvaredo, F. (2010). 'The Rich in Argentina over the Twentieth Century 1932–2004'. In Atkinson, A. B., Anthony, B., and Piketty, T. (Eds), *Top Incomes: A Global Perspective*. Oxford: Oxford University Press, p. 776.

Alt, J. E. (1985). 'Party Strategies, World Demand, and Unemployment in Britain and the United States, 1947–1983'. *Political Behavior*, *7*(1), 7–36.

Ames, E., and Rapp, R. T. (1977). 'The Birth and Death of Taxes: A Hypothesis'. *Journal of Economic History*, *37*(1), 161–178.

Amengual, M., and Dargent, E. (2020). 'The Social Determinants of Enforcement'. In Brinks, D., Levitsky, S., and Murillo, M. V. (Eds), *The Politics of Institutional Weakness in Latin America*. Cambridge: Cambridge University Press, pp. 161–182.

Anderson, C. W. (1978). 'The Logic of Public Problems: Evaluation in Comparative Policy Research'. *Comparing Public Policies: New Concepts and Methods*, *4*, 24–26.

Andersson, P. F. (2023). *Ideology and Redistribution: Left-Wing Tax Policy 1870–1945*. Stockholm University.

Andrenacci, L., Falappa, F., and Lvovich, D. (2004). 'Acerca del Estado de Bienestar del peronismo clásico (1943–1955)'. In Bertranou, J. Palacio, J. M., and Serrano, G. M. (Eds), *El país del no me acuerdo.(Des) memoria institucional e historia de la política social en Argentina*. Buenos Aires: Promote Lib's, pp. 83–114.

Antía, F. (2019). 'The Political Dynamic of Redistribution in Unequal Democracies: The Center-Left Governments of Chile and Uruguay in Comparative Perspective'. *Latin American Perspectives*, *46*(1), 152–166.

Argañaraz, N., Barraud, A., Castro, C., et al. (2019). *Vademecum de Tributos Argentina 2019: 163 impuestos nacionales, provinciales y municipales, muchas veces superpuestos*. Buenos Aires: Instituto Argentino de Analysis Fiscal.

Armendáriz, B., and Larraín, B. F. (2017). *The Economics of Contemporary Latin America*. Cambridge, MA: Massachusetts Institute of Technology (MIT) Press.

Associated Press. (2015). 'Argentina: New President Macri Promises Major Changes and Honesty'. NBC News, 10 December. Available at: https://www.nbcnews.com/news/latino/argentina-new-president-macri-promises-major-changes-honesty-n477966. Accessed 12 June 2021.

ATAF (African Tax Administration Forum). (2024). 'Africa's Role in the Push for Inclusive and Effective Global Tax Governance'. 16 May. Available at: https://www.ataftax.org/africa-s-role-in-the-push-for-inclusive-and-effective-global-tax-governance. Accessed 12 June 2021.

Austin, G. (2007). 'Reciprocal Comparison and African History: Tackling Conceptual Eurocentrism in the Study of Africa's Economic Past'. *African Studies Review*, *50*(3), 1–28.

Austin, G. (2008). 'The "Reversal of Fortune" Thesis and the Compression of History: Perspectives from African and Comparative Economic History'. *Journal of International Development: Journal of the Development Studies Association*, *20*(8), 996–1027.

Auyero, J. (2000). 'The Logic of Clientelism in Argentina: An Ethnographic Account'. *Latin American Research Review*, *35*(3), 55–82.

Avner, P., Mehndiratta, S. R., Viguié, V., et al. (2017). 'Buses, Houses or Cash? Socio-Economic, Spatial and Environmental Consequences of Reforming Public Transport Subsidies in Buenos Aires'. Policy Research Working Paper No. 8166. Washington DC: World Bank.

Aworawo, D. (2010). 'Bitterness on a Sugar Island: British Colonialism and the Socio-Economic Development of Jamaica (1655–1750)'. *Lagos Notes and Records*, *16*(1), 189–214.

Azevedo, J. L. de (1973). *Épocas de Portugal Econômico*. Lisbon: Livraria clássica editora de A. M. Teixeira & c.a (filhos) (reprint of the 1928 edition).

Baffes, J., and Temaj, T. (2022). 'Food Prices Continued their Two-Year-Long Upward Trajectory'. *World Bank*, 25 May. Available at: https://blogs.worldbank.org/opendata/food-prices-continued-their-two-year-long-upward-trajectory. Accessed 24 April 2025.

Bak, J. L. (1985). 'Political Centralization and the Building of the Interventionist State in Brazil: Corporatism, Regionalism and Interest Group Politics in Rio Grande do Sul, 1930–1937'. *Luso-Brazilian Review*, *22*(1), 9–25.

Balch, O. (2008). 'Argentina Turns against New President as Strike Worsens'. *The Guardian*, 25 May. Available at: https://www.theguardian.com/world/2008/may/25/argentina. Accessed 12 June 2021.

Bambaci, J., Saront, T., and Tommasi, M. (2002). 'The Political Economy of Economic Reforms in Argentina'. *Policy Reform*, *5*(2), 75–88.

Barlow, M. (2023). 'Export Taxes in Argentina: Embedded Ideas of State Interventionism'. *Economy and Society*, *52*(4), 602–625.

Barlow, M., and Peña, A. M. (2022). 'The Politics of Fiscal Legitimacy in Developmental States: Emergency Taxes in Argentina under Kirchnerism'. *New Political Economy*, *27*(3), 403–425.

Barreiro, R. (2017). 'Argentina: La tragedia de Once, cinco años después: "Me angustia no poder imaginar cómo sería Lucas hoy"'. *EL PAÍS*. 22 February. Available at: https://elpais.com/internacional/2017/02/22/argentina/1487718220_257164.html. Accessed 12 June 2021.

Barsky, O., and Dávila, M. (2008). *La rebelión del campo. Historia del conflicto agrario argentino*. Buenos Aires: Penguin Random House.

Baud, M. (2013). 'State and Society in Argentina: Change and Continuity under the Kirchners'. *European Review of Latin American and Caribbean Studies*, 95, 114–123.

BBC. (2014). 'Argentine Vice-President Boudou Charged in Corruption Case'. *BBC News*, 28 June. Available at: https://www.bbc.co.uk/news/world-latin-america-28069089. Accessed 12 June 2021.

BCRA (Central Bank of Argentina). (2021). 'Informe de Política Monetaria'. Available at: http://www.bcra.gov.ar/PoliticaMonetaria/IPOM0118.asp. Accessed 12 June 2021.

Bebbington, A., and Humphreys Bebbington, D. (2011). 'An Andean Avatar: Post-Neoliberal and Neoliberal Strategies for Securing the Unobtainable'. *New Political Economy*, *16*(1), 131–145.

Becerra, M. A., and Mastrini, G. (2010). 'Crisis. What Crisis? Argentine Media in View of the 2008 International Financial Crisis'. *International Journal of Communication*, *4*, 611–629.

Bein, M. (2014). 'La pax cambiaria, antes y después'. *Instituto Argentino de Ejecutivos de Finanzas*, *236*, 31–34.

Beramendi, P., and Rueda, D. (2007). 'Social Democracy Constrained: Indirect Taxation in Industrialized Democracies'. *British Journal of Political Science*, *37*(4), 619–641.

Bergman, L., and Gray, K. (2007). 'Argentine First Lady to Run for President'. *Reuters*, 9 August. Available at: https://www.reuters.com/article/us-argentina-politics/argentine-first-lady-to-run-for-president-idUSN0127423120070702. Accessed 12 June 2021.

Bergman, M. (2019). 'Economic Growth and Tax Compliance in Latin America'. In Flores-Macías, G. A. (Ed.). *The Political Economy of Taxation in Latin America*. New York: Cambridge University Press, pp. 53–75.

Berins Collier, R., and Handlin, S. P. (2005). 'Shifting Interest Regimes of the Working Classes in Latin America'. Institute for Research on Labor and Employment (IRLE) Working Paper No.122-05, August. Available at: http://repositories.cdlib.org/iir/iirwps/iirwps-122-05.

Bernstein, H. (1971). 'Modernization Theory and the Sociological Study of Development'. *Journal of Development Studies*, *7*(2), 141–160.

Bertello, F. (2014). 'Lousteau fue a la Rural, oyó quejas por la 125 y dijo que el plan de Moreno era peor'. *La Nación*, 26 July. Available at: https://www.lanacion.com.ar/economia/lousteau-fue-a-la-rural-oyo-quejas-por-la-125-y-dijo-que-el-plan-de-moreno-era-peor-nid1713241. Accessed 12 June 2021.

Bertello, F. (2015a). 'Agricultura gastó $ 8,4 millones en el auspicio de fiestas populares'. *La Nación*, 7 April. Available at: https://www.lanacion.com.ar/economia/campo/agricultura-gasto-84-millones-en-el-auspicio-de-fiestas-populares-nid1782190. Accessed 12 June 2021.

Bertello, F. (2015b). 'Ponen en duda una nueva rebaja de las retenciones de soja'. *La Nación*, 16 December. Available at: https://www.lanacion.com.ar/economia/campo/ponen-en-duda-una-nueva-rebaja-de-las-retenciones-de-soja-nid1854573. Accessed 12 June 2021.

Bertello, F. (2019). 'El Gobierno cambió el esquema de retencionas y decidió aumentarlas'. *La Nación*, 15 December. Available at: https://www.lanacion.com.ar/economia/campo/el-gobierno-cambio-esquema-retenciones-decidio-aumentarlas-nid2315733. Accessed 12 June 2021.

Bértola, L., and Ocampo, J. A. (2012). *The Economic Development of Latin America since Independence*. Oxford: Oxford University Press.

Bértola, L., Lara, C., and Martínez, C. (2023). 'Natural Resources Wealth and Fiscal Institutions in Latin America since Independence'. In Fehling, P., and Burchart, H.-J. (Eds), *Taxation and Inequality in Latin America*. London: Routledge, pp. 25–48.

Bethell, L. (Ed.). (1985). *The Cambridge History of Latin America*, Vol. III. Cambridge: Cambridge University Press.

Bethell, L. (Ed.). (1991). *The Cambridge History of Latin America*, Vol. VII. Cambridge: Cambridge University Press.

Bethell, L. (1993). *Argentina since Independence*. Cambridge: Cambridge University Press.

Bianchi, E., and Szpak, C. (2017). 'Soybean Prices, Economic Growth and Poverty in Argentina and Brazil'. Available at: https://www.fao.org/publications. Accessed 12 June 2021.

Bird, R. M. (1989). 'The Administrative Dimension of Tax Reform in Developing Countries'. In Gillis, M. (Ed.), *Tax Reform in Developing Countries*. Durham, NC: Duke University Press, pp. 315–346.

Bird, R. (2010). *Taxation and Development.* Washington, DC: World Bank.

Bird, R. M., and Zolt, E. M. (2004). 'Redistribution via Taxation: The Limited Role of the Personal Income Tax in Developing Countries'. *University of California Los Angeles Law Review, 52*, 1627.

Boix, C. (1998). *Political Parties, Growth and Equality: Conservative and Social Democratic Economic Strategies in the world Economy.* Cambridge: Cambridge University Press.

Bock, K. (1979). 'Theories of Progress, Development, Evolution'. *A History of Sociological Analysis*, 39–79.

Bonvecchi, A., and Giraudy, A. (2007). 'Argentina: Crecimiento económico y concentración del poder institucional'. Santiago: Revista de ciencia política.

Bonvecchi, A., and Lodola, G. (2009). *The Dual Logic of Intergovernmental Transfers. Territorial Coalition-Building in Argentina.* In Meeting of the Latin American Studies Association, Rio de Janeiro, June, pp. 11–14.

Bonvecchi, A., and Lodola, G. (2011). 'The Dual Logic of Intergovernmental Transfers: Presidents, Governors, and the Politics of Coalition-Building in Argentina'. *Publius: The Journal of Federalism, 41*(2), 179–206.

Booth, A. (1980). 'The Burden of Taxation in Colonial Indonesia in the Twentieth Century'. *Journal of Southeast Asian Studies, 11*(1), 91–109.

Bouët, A., and Laborde, D. (2010). 'The Economics of Export Taxes in a Context of Food Security'. In OECD Trade Policy Studies Series (Ed.), *The Economic Impact of Export Restrictions on Raw Materials.* Paris: OECD, pp. 59–78.

Brambilla, I., Galiani, S., and Porto, G. (2018). 'Argentine Trade Policies in the XX Century: 60 Years of Solitude'. *Latin American Economic Review, 28*(4). 1–30.

Bräutigam, D. (2002). 'Building Leviathan: Revenue, State Capacity, and Governance 1'. *Institute of Development Studies Bulletin, 33*(3), 1–17.

Bräutigam, D. (2008). 'Introduction: Taxation and State-Building in Developing Countries'. In Bräutigam, D., Odd-Helge, M. M., and Fjeldstad, O. H. (Eds), *Taxation and State-Building in Developing Countries: Capacity and Consent.* Cambridge: Cambridge University Press, pp. 1–33.

Bräutigam, D., Fjeldstad, O. H., and Moore, M. (Eds). (2008). *Taxation and State-Building in Developing Countries: Capacity and Consent.* Cambridge: Cambridge University Press.

Bräutigam, D. A., and Knack, S. (2004). 'Foreign Aid, Institutions, and Governance in Sub-Saharan Africa'. *Economic Development and Cultural Change, 52*(2), 255–285.

Bresser-Pereira, L. C. (2008). 'The Dutch Disease and Its Neutralization: A Ricardian Approach. *Brazilian Journal of Political Economy, 28*, 47–71.

Bril-Mascarenhas, T., and Post, A. E. (2015). 'Policy Traps: Consumer Subsidies in Post- Crisis Argentina'. *Studies in Comparative International Development, 50*(1), 98–120.

Brinks, D. M., Levitsky, S., and Murillo, M. V. (2020). *Understanding Institutional Weakness: Power and Design in Latin American Institutions.* Cambridge: Cambridge University Press.

Broms, R. (2017). 'Colonial Revenue Extraction and Modern Day Government Quality in the British Empire'. *World Development, 90*, 269–280.

Bronstein, H. (2014). 'Record Argentine Soy Crop to Pump Exports Despite Hoarding'. *Reuters*, 24 March. Available at: https://www.reuters.com/article/us-argentina-soy-hoarding-analysis/record-argentine-soy-crop-to-pump-exports-despite-hoarding-idUSBREA2N0M520140324. Accessed 12 June 2021.

Brunnermeier, M. K. (2009). 'Deciphering the Liquidity and Credit Crunch 2007–2008'. *Journal of Economic Perspectives, 23*(1), 77–100.

Buescu, M. (1974). *Evolucao económica do Brasil*, 2nd edn. Rio de Janeiro: APEC Editora.

Bulmer-Thomas, V. (1995). *The Economic History of Latin America since Independence.* Cambridge: Cambridge University Press.

Bulmer-Thomas, V. (2003). *The Economic History of Latin America since Independence*. Cambridge: Cambridge University Press.

Burchardt, H. J., and Dietz, K. (2014). '(Neo-)Extractivism—a New Challenge for Development Theory from Latin America'. *Third World Quarterly*, *35*(3), 468–486.

Burgess, R., and Stern, N. (1993). 'Taxation and Development'. *Journal of Economic Literature*, *31*(2), 762–830.

Bush, B., and Maltby, J. (2004). 'Taxation in West Africa: Transforming the Colonial Subject into the "Governable Person"'. *Critical Perspectives on Accounting*, *15*(1), 5–34.

Calogeras, J. (1939). *A History of Brazil*. Chapel Hill, NC: University of North Carolina Press.

Calvo, E., and Murillo, M. V. (2012). 'Argentina: The Persistence of Peronism'. *Journal of Democracy*, *23*(2), 148–161.

CAMBIEMOS. (2015). 'Plataforma electoral Cambiemos'. 21 September. Available at: https://www.slideshare.net/infodine/plataforma-electoral-cambiemos. Accessed 12 June 2021.

Castañeda, J. G. (2015). 'The Tides of Latin American Populism'. *Project Syndicate*, 22 December. Available at: https://www.project-syndicate.org/commentary/latin-america-rejection-leftist-governments-by-jorge-g--casta-eda-2015-12?barrier=accesspaylog. Accessed 12 June 2021.

Castañeda, N., and Doyle, D. (2019). 'Progressive Tax Policy and Informal Labor in Developing Economies'. *Governance*, *32*(4), 595–618.

Catterberg, G., and Palanza, V. (2012). 'Argentina: Scattered Opposition and the Rise of Cristina Fernández de Kirchner'. *Revista de Ciencia Política*, *32*(1), 3–30.

Cavalcanti, A. (1989). 'Finances'. In de Santa-anna Nery, F. J. (Ed.), *Le Bresil en 1889*. Paris: Librairie Charles Delagrave, pp. 317–347.

Cavallo, A., Cruces, G., and Perez-Truglia, R. (2016). 'Learning from Potentially-Biased Statistics: Household Inflation Perceptions and Expectations in Argentina'. National Bureau of Economic Research Working Paper No. 22103, Cambridge, MA.

Cboe. (2020). 'Cboe Global Markets'. Available at: https://www.cboe.com. Accessed 12 June 2021.

Centeno, M. A. (1997). 'Blood and Debt: War and Taxation in Nineteenth-Century Latin America'. *American Journal of Sociology*, *102*(6), 1565–1605.

Centeno, M. A. (2002). *Blood and Debt: War and the Nation-State in Latin America*. University Park, PA: Penn State Press.

Centeno, M. A., and Portes, A. (2006). 'The Informal Economy in the Shadow of the State'. In Fernández-Kelly, P. and Shefner, J. (Eds), *Out of the Shadows: Political Action and the Informal Economy in Latin America*. Pennsylvania: Pennsylvania State University Press, pp. 23–48.

CEPAL (United Nations Economic Commission for Latin America and the Caribbean). (2014). *Anuario Estadístico de América Latina y el Caribe*. Santiago de Chile: Naciones Unidas.

CEPAL. (2017). *Manufactura y cambio estructural: Aportes para pensar la política industrial en la Argentina*, Abeles, M., Cimoli, M., and Lavarello, P. (Eds). Santiago de Chile: Naciones Unidas.

CEPALSTAT. (2021). 'CEPALSTAT'. Available at: https://estadisticas.cepal.org/cepalstat/portada.html?idioma=español. Accessed 12 June 2021.

Cetrángolo, O., and Gómez Sabaini, J. C. (2010). 'Tax Policy in Argentina: Between Solvency and Emergency'. In Gordon, R. H. (Ed.), *Taxation in Developing Countries: Six Case Studies and Policy Implications*. New York: Columbia University Press.

Cetrángolo, O., Jiménez, J. P., and Vega, D. (1998). 'Algunas reflexiones sobre el federalismo fiscal en la Argentina. Apuntes para el diseño de un nuevo sistema de coparticipación federal de impuestos'. *Desarrollo Económico*, *38*, 293.

Cheibub, J. A., and Limongi, F. (2011). 'Legislative–Executive Relations'. In Ginsburg, T., and Dixon, R. (Eds), *Comparative Constitutional Law*. Cheltenham: Edward Elgar Publishing, pp. 211–233.

CIFRA CTA (Centro de Investigación y Formación de la República Argentina). (2010). 'Coparticipación Federal'. Available at: http://www.centrocifra.org.ar. Accessed 12 June 2021.

CIFRA CTA. (2020). 'CIFRA—Centro de Investigación y Formación de la República Argentina'. Available at: http://www.centrocifra.org.ar. Accessed 12 June 2021.

Clarence-Smith, W. G. (1983). 'Business Empires in Equatorial Africa'. *African Economic History*, 12, 3–11.

Clarín. (2005). 'El "Rodrigazo", un ajuste que dejó su huella en los argentinos'. Available at: https://www.clarin.com/ediciones-anteriores/rodrigazo-ajuste-dejo-huella-argentinos_0_S1WN56uyAKg.html. Accessed 12 June 2021.

Clarín. (2010). 'Qué son los superpoderes?' 25 June. Available at: https://www.clarin.com/gobierno/superpoderes_0_ryomddlCPmx.html. Accessed 12 June 2021.

Clarín. (2012a). 'Con amplio apoyo, el Senado aprobó la estatización de YPF'. 26 April. Available at: https://www.clarin.com/politica/amplio-senado-aprobo-estatizacion-ypf_0_ByVma2V2vXe.html. Accessed 12 June 2021.

Clarín. (2012b). 'En la renuncia a los subsidios, Cristina perdió por goleada: sacó el 0,25%'. 5 November. Available at: https://www.clarin.com/politica/gente-siguio-cristina_0_BJhBvl0sDXx.html. Accessed 12 June 2021.

Clarín. (2012c). 'La Unión Europea tomará medidas "en los próximos días" contra Argentina'. 7 May. Available at: https://www.clarin.com/politica/union-europea-medidas-proximos-argentina_0_SJEWsIE2PQg.html. Accessed 12 June 2021.

Clarín. (2023). 'Dura cata de Mauricio Macri contra al Gobierno: "Nunca quisieron bajar la inflación"'. 14 May. Available at: https://www.clarin.com/politica/dura-carta-mauricio-macri-gobierno-quisieron-bajar-inflacion-_0_bhaEqnEnpn.html. Accessed 12 June 2021.

Coatsworth, J. H. (1978). 'Obstacles to Economic Growth in Nineteenth-Century Mexico'. *American Historical Review*, *83*(1), 80–100.

Coatsworth, J. H. (2008). 'Inequality, Institutions and Economic Growth in Latin America'. *Journal of Latin American Studies*, *40*(3), 545–569.

Cogneau, D., Dupraz, Y., and Mesplé-Somps, S. (2021). 'Fiscal Capacity and Dualism in Colonial States: The French Empire 1830–1962'. *Journal of Economic History*, *81*(2), 441–480.

Collier, R. B., and Collier, D. (1979). 'Inducements versus Constraints: Disaggregating "Corporatism"'. *American Political Science Review*, *73*(4), 967–986.

Collier, R., and Collier, D. (2002). *Shaping the Political Arena*. Notre Dame, IN: Notre Dame University Press.

Colombres, M. (2008). 'Indignación en las entidades rurales'. La Nación, 12 March.

Colussi, J., Schnitkey, J., and Cabrini, S. (2022a). 'Argentina and Brazil Could Expand Wheat Production Due to the War in Ukraine'. *Farmdocdaily*, 8 April. Available at: https://farmdocdaily.illinois.edu/2022/04/argentina-and-brazil-could-expand-wheat-production-due-to-the-war-in-ukraine.html. Accessed 12 June 2021.

Colussi, J., Schnitkey, G., and Cabrini, S. (2022b). 'Wheat Outlook after Five Months of War in Ukraine'. *Farmdocdaily*, *12*, 112.

Conklin, M., and Davidson, D. (1986). 'The I.M.F. and Economic and Social Human Rights: A Case Study of Argentina, 1958–1985'. *Human Rights Quarterly*, *8*, 227.

Cornia, G. A. (2013). 'Income Distribution under Latin America's New Left Regimes'. In *Employment, Inequality and Globalization*. London: Routledge, pp. 83–112.

Cortés Conde, R. (1956). *Economía Política*. Cambridge: Cambridge University Press.

Craig, A. (1976). 'Perón and Peronism: Personalism Personified'. *International Journal, 31*(4), 703–717.

Craviotti, C. (2008). 'Empleo agrario y ruralidad ampliada'. *Revista de Estudios Geográficos, 4*(4), 1–18.

El Cronista. (2018). 'Macri confirmó que vuelven las retenciones'. 3 September. Available at: https://www.cronista.com/economiapolitica/Macri-confirmo-que-vuelven-las-retenciones-20180903-0025.html. Accessed 12 June 2021.

Cufré, D. (2007). 'Un aumento que busca parar la inflación'. August. Available at: https://www.pagina12.com.ar/diario/economia/2-94306-2007-11-08.html. Accessed 12 June 2021.

Cufré, D. (2015). 'Economía: A siete años de la 125'. *Página 12*, 12 March. Available at: https://www.pagina12.com.ar/diario/economia/subnotas/267962-71902-2015-03-12.html. Accessed 12 June 2021.

Damill, M., Frenkel, R., and Rapetti, M. (2015). 'Macroeconomic Policy in Argentina during 2002–2013'. *Comparative Economic Studies, 57*(3), 369–400.

D'Arcy, M. (2011). 'Why Do Citizens Assent to Pay Tax? Legitimacy, Taxation and the African State?', Afrobarometer Working Paper No. 126, Dublin.

Dalponte, F. (2009). 'La necesidad de decretar la urgencia'. *PoliticaArgentina.com*, 12 November. Available at: https://web.archive.org/web/20110715102325/http://www.politicargentina.com/analisis-politico/632-la-necesidad-de-decretar-la-urgencia. Accessed 12 June 2021.

Danermark, B., Ekström, M., and Karlsson, J. (2019). *Explaining Society: Critical Realism in the Social Sciences*. London: Routledge.

Daniel, C. J., and Lanata Briones, C. T. (2019). 'Battles over Numbers: The Case of the Argentine Consumer Price Index (2007–2015)'. *Economy and Society, 48*(1), 127–151.

Datz, G. (2009). 'State of Change: Global Turmoil and Government Reinvention'. *Public Administration Review, 69*(4), 660–667.

Davis, L. E., and Huttenback, R. A. (1986). *Mammon and the Pursuit of Empire: The Political Economy of British Imperialism, 1860–1912*. Cambridge: Cambridge University Press.

Dborkin, D., and Feldman, G. (2008). 'Los ingresos públicos'. In Filc, G. (Ed.), *Las políticas fiscales en la Argentina: Un complejo camino hacia la equidad y la eficiencia*. Buenos Aires: Center for the Implementation of Public Policies Promoting Equity and Growth (CIPPEC), pp. 195–236.

Debre, I. (2024). 'President Milei Renews His Vow to Scrap Export Taxes as Argentina's Powerful Farmers Get Impatient'. *The Independent*, 29 July. Available at: https://www.independent.co.uk/news/ap-argentina-buenos-aires-president-chinese-b2587406.html. Accessed 23 April 2025.

De Janvry, A. (1981). *The Agrarian Question and Reformism in Latin America*. Baltimore, MD: Johns Hopkins University Press.

De Luca, M., and Malamud, A. (2010). 'Argentina: Turbulencia económica, polarización social y realineamiento político'. *Revista de Ciencia Política, 30*(2), 173–189.

De la Torre, A., Yeyati, E. L., and Schmukler, S. L. (2002). 'Argentina's Financial Crisis: Floating Money, Sinking Banking'. National Bureau of Economic Research (NBER) Conference Paper, 3 June, pp. 1–26.

de Paiva Abreu, M., and Do Lago, L. A. C. (1997). 'Property Rights and the Fiscal and Financial Systems in Brazil: Colonial Heritage and the Imperial Period'. No. 370. Pontifícia Universidade Católica do Rio de Janeiro (PUC-Rio), Departamento de Economia, Rio de Janeiro.

De Santis, J. P. (2011). 'En el corazón del campo, el candidato de la Mesa de Enlace quedó último'. Available at: https://www.lanacion.com.ar/economia/en-el-corazon-del-campo-el-candidato-de-la-mesa-de-enlace-quedo-ultimo-junto-al-partido-obre-nid1417418/. Accessed 12 June 2021.

De Zwart, P., and Van Zanden, J. L. (2015). 'Labor, Wages, and Living Standards in Java, 1680–1914'. *European Review of Economic History*, *19*(3), 215–234.

Díaz Alejandro, C. (1975). *Ensayos sobre la historia económica argentina*. Buenos Aires: Amorrortu.

Diaz-Alejandro, C. (1979). 'Southern Cone Stabilization Plans'. Center Discussion Paper No. 330, Yale University, Economic Growth Center, New Haven, CT.

Di John, J. (2006). 'The Political Economy of Taxation and Tax Reform in Developing Countries'. WIDER Research Paper No. 2006/74.

Di Santi, M. (2015). 'La evolución de la AUH desde que se implementó'. *Chequeado*, 2 February. Available at: https://chequeado.com/el-explicador/la-evolucion-de-la-auh-desde-que-se-implemento. Accessed 12 June 2021.

Donghi T. H. (1985). 'Economy and Society in Post-Independence Spanish America'. In Bethell. L. (Ed.), *The Cambridge History of Latin America*. Cambridge: Cambridge University Press, pp. 297–346.

Dornbusch, R., and Carlos De Pablo, J. (1989). 'Debt and Macroeconomic Instability in Argentina'. In Sach, J. D. (Ed.), *Developing Country Debt and the World Economy*. Chicago, IL: University of Chicago Press. pp. 37–56.

Downward, P., and Mearman, A. (2007). 'Retroduction as Mixed-Methods Triangulation in Economic Research: Reorienting Economics into Social Science'. *Cambridge Journal of Economics*, *31*(1), 77–99.

Duckworth, C. (2015). 'President Lugo and the Indigenous Communities of Paraguay'. In Tidwell, A. C., and Zellen, B. S. (Eds), *Land, Indigenous Peoples and Conflict*. London: Routledge, pp. 78–92.

Dunn, R. S. (1969). 'The Barbados Census of 1680: Profile of the Richest colony in English America'. *William and Mary Quarterly: A Magazine of Early American History*, *26*, 4–30.

DuRivage, J., and Priest, C. (2014). 'The Stamp Act and the Political Origins of American Legal and Economic Institutions'. *Southern California Law. Review*, *88*(4), 875.

The Economist. (2013). 'Looting in Argentina—Law and disorder'. 11 December. Available at: https://www.economist.com/americas-view/2013/12/11/law-and-disorder. Accessed 12 June 2021.

Edwards, A. D. 2017. 'Grenville's Silver Hammer: The Problem of Money in the Stamp Act Crisis'. *Journal of American History*, *104*(2), 337–362.

Edwards, S. (1994). 'Trade and Industrial Policy Reform in Latin America'. National Bureau of Economic Research (NBER) Working Paper No. 4772.

Eichengreen, B., and Portes, R. (1989). 'Dealing with Debt: The 1930s and the 1980s'. National Bureau of Economic Research (NBER) Working Paper No. 2867, Cambridge, MA.

Elbert, R., and Pérez, P. (2018). 'The Identity of Class in Latin America: Objective Class Position and Subjective Class Identification in Argentina and Chile (2009)'. *Current Sociology*, *66*(5), 724–747.

elEconomista. (2007). 'Argentina aumenta impuesto a exportación de granos, como temían agricultores'. *elEconomista*, 7 November. Available at https://www.eleconomista.es/empresas-finanzas/noticias/309163/11/07/Argentina-aumenta-impuesto-a-exportacion-de-granos-como-temian-agricultores.html. Accessed 12 June 2021.

Ellis, F., and Biggs, S. (2001). 'Evolving Tthemes in Rural Development 1950s–2000s'. *Development Policy Review*, *19*(4), 437–448.

Ellner, S. (2019). 'Pink-Tide Governments: Pragmatic and Populist Responses to Challenges from the Right'. *Latin American Perspectives*, *46*(1), 4–22.

Engerman, S. L., and Sokoloff, K. L. (1994). *Factor Endowments: Institutions, and Differential Paths of Growth among New World Economies*. Cambridge, MA: National Bureau of Economic Research.

È Nziem, N. (1998). *Isidore. Histoire Général du Congo: De l'Héritage Ancien á la République Démocratique*. Brussels: Duculot.

Ervasti, H., and Hjerm, M. (2012). 'Immigration, Trust, and Support for the Welfare State.' In Ervasti, H., Andersen, J. G., and Ringdal, K. (Eds), *The Future of the Welfare State*. Northampton, MA: Edward Elgar Publishing, pp. 153–171.

Etchemendy, S., and Collier, R. B. (2007). 'Down But Not Out: Union Resurgence and Segmented Neocorporatism in Argentina (2003–2007)'. *Politics & Society*, *35*(3), 363–401.

Evans, P. (1995). *Embedded Autonomy: States and Industrial Transformation*. Princeton, NJ: Princeton University Press.

Evans, P. (2004). 'Development as Institutional Change: The Pitfalls of Monocropping and the Potentials of Deliberation'. *Studies in Comparative International Development*, *38*, 30–52.

Expo Rural. (2025). 'Exposición Rural Country Show'. Available at: https://www.exposicionrural.com.ar/. Accessed 4 August 2025.

Fair Rzezak, H. (2008). 'El Conflicto entre el Gobierno y el Campo en Argentina. Lineamientos Políticos, Estrategias Discursivas y discusiones teóricas a partir de un Abordaje Multidisiplinar'. *Iberóforum. Revista de Ciencias Sociales de la Universidad Iberoamericana*, *3*(6), 82–106.

Fairfield, T. (2010). 'Business Power and Tax Reform: Taxing Income and Profits in Chile and Argentina'. *Latin American Politics and Society*, *52*(2), 37–71.

Fairfield, T. (2011). 'Business Power and Protest: Argentina's Agricultural Producers Protest in Comparative Context'. *Studies in Comparative International Development*, *46*(4), 424–453.

Fairfield, T. (2015). *Private Wealth and Public Revenue in Latin America: Business Power and Tax Politics*, 1st edn. Cambridge: Cambridge University Press.

FAOSTAT (Food and Agriculture Organization of the United Nations). (2021). 'Food and Agriculture Data'. Available at: http://www.fao.org/faostat/en/#home. Accessed 12 June 2021.

Feldstein, M. (2002). 'Argentina's Fall: Lessons from the Latest Financial Crisis'. *Foreign Affairs*, *81*(2), 8–14.

Fehling. P., and Burchart, H.-J. (2023). 'Reorientating the Tax Debate'. In Fehling, P., and Burchart, H.-J. (Eds). *Taxation and Inequality in Latin America*. London: Routledge, pp. 1–21.

Fernández, C. (2008). 'Dicurso de Cristina contra el campo oligarca'. 25 March. Available at: https://www.cfkargentina.com/cfk-sobre-el-lock-out-patronal-del-campo-en-2008/. Accessed 12 June 2021.

Fernández-Milmanda, B., and Garay, C. (2020). 'A Multilevel Approach to Enforcement'. In Brinks, D. M., Levitsky, S., and Murillo, M. V. (Eds), *The Politics of Institutional Weakness in Latin America*. Cambridge: Cambridge University Press, pp. 183–207.

Filc, G. (2008). 'El gasto público en la Argentina'. In Filc, G. (Ed.). *Las políticas fiscales en la Argentina: Un complejo camino hacia la equidad y la eficiencia*. Buenos Aires: CIPPEC, pp. 107–158.

Fishlow, A. (1990). 'The Latin American State'. *Journal of Economic Perspectives*, *4*(3), 61–74.

Fjeldstad, O. (2005). 'Corruption in Tax Administration: Lessons from Institutional Reforms in Uganda'. In *International Handbook on the Economics of Corruption*. Chr. Michelsen Institute (CMI) Working Paper Series No. 2005: 10. Bergen: CMI, 484, pp. 1–22.

Fjeldstad, O. H., and Moore, M. (2005). 'Taxation and State-Building: Poor Countries in a Globalised World'. In *International Handbook on the Economics of Corruption*. Chr. Michelsen Institute (CMI) Working Paper Series No. 2007: 11. Bergen: CMI, pp. 1–22.

Fjeldstad, O. H., and Rakner, L. (2003). *Taxation and Tax Reforms in Developing Countries: Illustrations from Sub-Saharan Africa*. Bergen: CMI.

Flores-Macías, G. A. (2014). 'Financing Security through Elite Taxation: The Case of Colombia's "Democratic Security Taxes"'. *Studies in Comparative International Development*, *49*, 477–500.

Flores-Macías, G. A. (Ed.). (2019). *The Political Economy of Taxation in Latin America*. Cambridge: Cambridge University Press.

Fofack, H. (2015). 'The Idea of Economic Development: Views from Africa'. WIDER Working Paper No. 2014/093.

Ford. A. (1956). 'Argentina and the Baring Crisis of 1890'. *Oxford Economic Papers*, *8*(2), 127–160.

Frankema, E. (2010). 'Raising Revenue in the British Empire, 1870–1940: How "Extractive" Were Colonial Taxes?'. *Journal of Global History*, *5*(3), 447–477.

Frankema, E., and Buelens, F. (2013). *Colonial Exploitation and Economic Development*. London: Routledge.

Franko, P. M. (1999). *The Puzzle of Latin American Economic Development*. Lanham, MA: Rowman & Littlefield.

Frers, L. D. (2017). 'The Road to Budget Transparency in Argentina'. International Budget Partnership, September. Available at: https://www.internationalbudget.org/wp-content/uploads/the-road-to-budget-transparency-in-argentina-ibp-case-study-2017.pdf. Accessed 12 June 2021.

Freytes, C., and Niedzwiecki, S. (2016). 'A Turning Point in Argentine Politics: Demands for Change and Territorial Cleavages in the 2015 Presidential Election'. *Regional & Federal Studies*, *26*(3), 381–394.

Freytes, C., and O'Farrell, J. (2017). 'Conflictos Distributivos en la Agricultura de Exportación en la Argentina Reciente (2003–2015)'. *Desarrollo Económico*, *57*(221), 181–196.

Gaggero, J., Gaggero, A., and Rua, M. (2015). 'The Principal Characteristics and Macroeconomic Impact of Capital Flight in Argentina'. *Revista Problemas del Desarrollo*, *182*(46), 67–89.

Galli, E. (2015). 'Para el campo, ahora es el momento de la diversificación productiva'. *La Nación*, 16 December. Available at: https://www.lanacion.com.ar/economia/para-el-campo-ahora-es-el-momento-de-la-diversificacion-productiva-nid1854717. Accessed 12 June 2021.

Gardner, L. (2012). *Taxing Colonial Africa: The Political Economy of British Imperialism*. New York: Oxford University Press.

Gates Foundation. (2020). 'Covid-19: A global Perspective'. 2020 Goalkeepers Report, Bill and Melinda Gates Foundation.

Gerchunoff, P., and Antúnez, D. (2002). 'De la bonanza peronista a la crisis de desarrollo'. In Torre, J. C. (Ed.), *Nueva Historia Argentina*, Vol. VIII. Buenos Aires: Editorial Sudamericana, pp. 125–206.

Gerchunoff, P., and Díaz-Alejandro, C. (1989). 'Peronist Economic Policies, 1946–55'. In di Tella, G., and Dornbusch, R. (Eds), *The Political Economy of Argentina, 1946–83*. London: Palgrave Macmillan, pp. 59–88.

Gerchunoff, P., and Kacef, O. (2016). *Y ahora qué hacemos? La economía política del kirchnerismo*. No. 87. Instituto Universitario de Investigación en Estudios Latinoamericanos (IELAT), Universidad de Alcalá.

Gerchunoff, P., and Llach, L. (2004). *Entre la equidad y el crecimiento*. Buenos Aires: Siglo Veintiuno.

Gerchunoff, P., and Llach, L. (2009). 'Equality or Growth: A 20th Century Argentine dilemma'. *Journal of Iberian and Latin American Economic History*, *27*(3), 397–426.

Gerchunoff, P., and Llach, L. (2010). *El Ciclo de la Ilusión y el Desencanto*. Buenos Aires: Paidos.

Gerchunoff, P., Rapetti, M., and De León, G. (2020). 'La paradoja populista'. *Desarrollo Económico*, *59*(229), 299–328.

Gervasoni, C. (1998). 'Del distribucionalismo al neoliberalismo: Los cambios en la coalici6n electoral peronista durante el gobiero de Menem'. In Paper Prepared for Delivery at the 1998 Meeting of the Latin American Studies Association, The Palmer House Hilton Hotel, Chicago, IL, 24–26 September.

Gilbert, J. (2013). 'Argentina's Record Floods Kill Dozens'. *New York Times*, 3 April. Available at: https://www.nytimes.com/2013/04/04/world/americas/record-flooding-kills-dozens-in-Argentina.html. Accessed 12 June 2021.

Giraudo, M. E. (2017). *Uneven Development and the Governance of Agricultural Commodity Booms: The Case of Soybean in South America*. PhD thesis, University of Warwick, Warwick.

Giraudo, M. E. (2020). 'Taxing the "Crop of the Century": The Role of Institutions in Governing the Soy Boom in South America'. *Globalizations*, *18*(4), 516–532.

Giraudo, M. E., and Grugel, J. (2022). 'Imaginaries of Soy and the Costs of Commodity-Led Development: Reflections from Argentina'. *Development and Change*, *53*(4), 796–826.

Giraudy, A. (2007). 'The Distributive Politics of Emergency Employment Programs in Argentina (1993–2002)'. *Latin American Research Review*, *42*(2), 33–35.

Girvan, N. (2014). 'Extractive Imperialism in Historical Perspective'. In Petras, J., and Veltmeyer, H. (Eds), *Extractive Imperialism in the Americas*. Leiden: Brill, pp. 49–61.

Gold, T., and Peña, A. M. (2019). 'Protests, Signaling, and Elections: Conceptualizing Opposition-Movement Interactions during Argentina's Anti-Government Protests'. *Social Movement Studies*, *18*(3), 324–345.

Goldfarb, L., and van der Haar, G. (2017). 'The Moving Frontiers of Genetically Modified Soy Production: Shifts in Land Control in the Argentinian Chaco'. In de L. T. Oliveira, G., and Hecht, S. B. (Eds), *Soy, Globalization, and Environmental Politics in South America*. London: Routledge, pp. 312–332.

Goñi, U. (2018). 'Argentina Gets Biggest Loan in IMF's History at $57bn'. *The Guardian*, 27 September. Available at: https://www.theguardian.com/world/2018/sep/26/argentina-imf-biggest-loan. Accessed 12 June 2021.

Goñi, U., and Watts, J. (2012). 'Argentina Protests: Up to Half a Million Rally against Fernández de Kirchner'. *The Guardian*, 9 November. Available at: https://www.theguardian.com/world/2012/nov/09/argentiana-protests-rally-fernandez-kirchner. Accessed 12 June 2021.

Gordon, P. H. (1993). *A Certain Idea of France: French Security Policy and Gaullist Legacy*, Vol. XLII. Princeton, NJ: Princeton University Press.

Gough, I. (2004). 'Welfare Regimes in Development Context: A Global and Regional Analysis'. In Gough, I., and Wood, G. (Eds), *Insecurity and Welfare Regimes in Asia Africa and Latin America*. Cambridge: Cambridge University Press, pp. 16–45.

Grafe, R., and Irigoin, M. A. (2006). 'The Spanish Empire and Its Legacy: Fiscal Re- distribution and Political Conflict in Colonial and Post-Colonial Spanish America'. Global Economic History Network (GEHN) Working Paper No. 23/06, London.

Gras, C., and Hernández, V. (2009). *'Son los piquetes de la abundancia': Actores y Estado en el conflicto agrario en Argentina*. Rio de Janeiro: Asociación de Estudios Latinoamericanos.

Gras, C., and Hernández, V. (2016). *Radiografía del nuevo campo argentino: Del terrateniente al empresario transnacional*. Buenos Aires: Siglo Veintiuno.

Greco, E. (2020). 'Africa, Extractivism and the Crisis This Time'. *Review of African Political Economy*, *47*(166), 511–521.

Griffith-Jones, S., and Sunkel, O. (1986). *Debt and Development Crises in Latin America: The End of an Illusion*. Oxford: Oxford University Press.
Grindle, M. S. (2009). *Going Local: Decentralization, Democratization, and the Promise of Good Governance*. Princeton, NJ: Princeton University Press.
Gross, J. P. (1993). 'Progressive Taxation and Social Justice in Eighteenth-Century France'. *Past & Present*, 140, 79–126.
Grugel, J. (1992). 'Populism and the Political System in Chile: Ibañismo (1952–1958)'. *Bulletin of Latin American Research*, *11*, 169–186.
Grugel, J., and Riggirozzi, M. P. (2007). 'The Return of the State in Argentina'. *International Affairs*, *83*(1), 87–107.
Grugel, J., and Riggirozzi, M. P. (2012). 'Post-Neoliberalism in Latin America: Rebuilding and Reclaiming the State after Crisis'. *Development and Change*, *43*(1), 1–21.
Grugel, J., and Riggirozzi, P. (2018). 'Neoliberal Disruption and Neoliberalism's Afterlife in Latin America: What Is Left of Post-Neoliberalism?'. *Critical Social Policy*, *38*(3), 547–566.
Gudynas, E. (2016). 'Natural Resource Nationalisms and the Compensatory State in Progressive South America'. In Haslam, P. A., and Heidrich, P. (Eds), *The Political Economy of Natural Resources and Development: From Neoliberalism to Resource Nationalism* London: Routledge, pp. 103–117.
Gudynas, E. (2018). 'Extractivisms: Tendencies and Consequences'. In Munck, R., and Wise, R. D. (Eds), *Reframing Latin American Development*. London: Routledge, pp. 61–76.
Gudynas, E. (2020). *Extractivisms: Politics, Economy and Ecology*. Black Point: Fernwood Publishing.
Haggard, S., and Kaufman, R. R. (1994). 'The Challenges of Consolidation'. *Journal of Democracy*, *5*(4), 5–16.
Hall, P. A. (1993). 'Policy Paradigms, Social Learning, and the State: The Case of Economic Policymaking in Britain'. *Comparative Politics*, *25*(3), 275–296.
Hébert, B., and Schreger, J. (2017). 'The Costs of Sovereign Default: Evidence from Argentina'. *American Economic Review*, *107*(10), 3119–3145.
Heclo, H. (1974). *Modern Politics in Britain and Sweden*. New Haven, CT: Yale University Press.
Herbst, J. (1990). 'War and the State in Africa'. *International Security*, *14*(4), 117–139.
Hesse-Biber, S. (2010). 'Qualitative Approaches to Mixed Methods Practice'. *Qualitative Inquiry*, *16*(6), 455–468.
Hibbs, D. A. (1977). 'Political Parties and Macroeconomic Policy'. *American Political Science Review*, *71*(4), 1467–1487.
Hibbs, D. A. (1992). 'Partisan Theory after Fifteen Years'. *European Journal of Political Economy*, *8*(3), 361–373.
Hoffmann, K., Vlassenroot, K., and Marchais, G. (2016). 'Taxation, Stateness and Armed Groups: Public Authority and Resource Extraction in Eastern Congo'. *Development and Change*, *47*(6), 1434–1456.
Hora, R. (2001). *The Landowners of the Argentine Pampas: A Social and Political History 1860–1945*. Oxford: Oxford University Press.
Hora, R. (2010). 'La Crisis del Campo del Otoño de 2008'. *Desarrollo Económico*, *50*(197), 81–111.
Hora, R. (2020). 'Qué es y qué quiere el campo argentino?' *Nueva Sociedad*, *287*(May/June), 11–23.
Huber, E., and Stephens, J. D. (2012). *Democracy and the Left: Social Policy and Inequality in Latin America*. London: University of Chicago Press.
Huillery, E., 2014. 'The Black Man's Burden: The Cost of Colonization of French West Africa'. *Journal of Economic History*, *74*(1), 1–38.

Hutchison, J. (1972). 'Foreign Agricultural Economic Report (FAER) Argentina'. United States Department of Agriculture, Economic Research Service. Available at: https://ideas.repec.org/s/ags/uersfe.html. Accessed 12 June 2021.

IMF (International Monetary Fund). (1967). 'Annual Report'. Available at: https://www.imf.org/external/pubs/ft/ar/archive/pdf/ar1967.pdf. Accessed 12 June 2021.

IMF. (2016). 'Argentina: Economic Developments; IMF Country Report 16/68; February 27, 2014'. Available at: http://www.imf.org. Accessed 12 June 2021.

IMF. (2022). 'War-Fueled Surge in Food Prices to Hit Poorer Nations Hardest'. Available at: https://www.imf.org/en/Blogs/Articles/2022/03/16/war-fueled-surge-in-food-prices-to-hit-poorer-nations-hardest. Accessed 15 April 2022.

INDEC (National Institute of Statistics and Census of Argentina). (2012). 'Encuesta Permanente de Hogares: Incidencia de la Pobreza y de la Indigencia: Resultados del segundo semestre 2011'. Available at: https://www.indec.gob.ar/ftp/cuadros/sociedad/pob_tot_2sem11.pdf. Accessed 12 June 2021

INDEC. (2019). 'INDEC: Instituto Nacional de Estadística y Censos de la República Argentina'. Available at: https://www.indec.gob.ar. Accessed 12 June 2021.

INDEC. (2020). 'INDEC: Instituto Nacional de Estadística y Censos de la República Argentina'. Available at: https://www.indec.gob.ar/indec/web/Institucional-Indec-InformesTecnicos. Accessed 12 June 2021.

InfoAgro. (2024). 'La Larga historia de las retenciones'. Available at: https://www.infocampo.com.ar/la-historia-de-las-retenciones-en-la-argentina-los-gobiernos-que-mas-recaudaron-y-los-minimos-historicos. Accessed 1 August 2025.

Infobae. (2004). 'Reunidos con Kirchner, ruralistas apoyaron retenciones'. Available at: https://www.infobae.com/2004/08/19/133937-reunidos-kirchner-ruralistas-apoyaron-retenciones. Accessed 12 June 2021.

Infobae. (2015). 'Macri prometió "eliminar las retenciones a las exportaciones" si gana las elecciones en 2015'. Available at: https://www.infobae.com/2014/05/18/1565346-macri-prometio-eliminar-las-retenciones-las-exportaciones-si-gana-las-elecciones-2015. Accessed 12 June 2021.

Infocampo. (2008). 'La dirigencia del campo pidió que no se use la excusa del gasto social para aplicar impuestos confiscatorios al agro'. Available at: https://www.infocampo.com.ar/la-dirigencia-del-campo-pidio-que-no-se-use-la-excusa-del-gasto-social-para-aplicar-impuestos-confiscatorios-al-agro. Accessed 12 June 2021.

InfoLEG. (2021). 'Infoleg—Información Legislativa y Documental'. Available at: http://www.infoleg.gob.ar. Accessed 12 June 2021.

Ireland, D. (2019). 'What Marxist Tax Policies Actually Look Like'. *Historical Materialism*, *27*(2), 188–221. Available at: https://doi.org/10.1163/1569206X-00001543.

Irigoin, A., and Grafe, R. (2008). 'Bargaining for Absolutism: A Spanish Path to Nation-State and Empire Building'. *Hispanic American Historical Review*, *88*(2), 173–209.

James, D. (1988). *Resistance and Integration: Peronism and the Argentine Working Class, 1946–1976*. New York: Cambridge University Press.

Janaway, C. (Ed.). (1998). *Willing and Nothingness: Schopenhauer as Nietzsche's Educator*. Oxford: Oxford University Press.

Johnson, C. A., Clavijo, A., Lorca, M., and Andrade, M. O. (2024). 'Bringing the State Back in the Lithium Triangle: An Institutional Analysis of Resource Nationalism in Chile, Argentina, and Bolivia'. *The Extractive Industries and Society*, *20*, 101534.

Johnson, H. B. (1987). 'Portuguese Settlement, 1500–1580'. In Bethell, L. (Ed.), *Colonial Brazil*. Cambridge: Cambridge University Press, pp. 1–38.

Kaldor, N. (1962). 'Will Underdeveloped Countries Learn to Tax?' *Foreign Affairs*, *41*(2), 410–420.

Kay, C. (1989). *Latin American Theories of Development and Underdevelopment*, 1st edn. London: Routledge.

Kay, C. (1991). 'Reflections on the Latin American Contribution to Development Theory'. *Development and Change*, *22*(1), 31–68.

Kedar, C. (2013). *The International Monetary Fund and Latin America: The Argentine Puzzle in Context*. Philadelphia, PA: Temple University Press.

Kelly, K, G. (2017). 'Sugar Plantations in the French West Indies: Archaeological Perspectives from Guadeloupe and Martinique'. In Scott, E. M. (Ed.), *Archaeological Perspectives on the French in the New World*. Gainesville, FL: University Press of Florida, pp. 230–251.

Kiguel, M. (2015). *Las crisis económicas argentinas: Una historia de ajustes y desajustes*. Buenos Aires: Sudamericana.

King, N. (2004). 'Interviews in Qualitative Research'. In: Cassel, C., and Symon, G. (Eds), *Essential Guide to Qualitative Methods in Organizational Research*. London: Sage, pp. 11–22.

Kirchner, N. (2003). 'Discurso Del Señor Presidente De La Nación, Doctor Néstor Kirchner, Ante La Honorable Asamblea Legislativa'. 25 May. Available at: https://www.casarosada.gob.ar/informacion/archivo/24414-blank-18980869. Accessed 12 June 2021.

Knight, A. (1996). 'Latin America: Political Economy and Geopolitics since 1945'. *Oxford Development Studies*, *24*(2), 145–168.

Kollmann, R. (2016). 'Promesas sobre el bidet'. *Página 12*, 22 February. Available at: https://www.pagina12.com.ar/7949-promesas-sobre-el-bidet. Accessed 12 June 2021.

Kosacoff, B. (Ed.). (2007). Crisis, recuperación y nuevos dilemas. La economía Argentina, 2002–2007. Buenos Aires: CEPAL.

Kulfas, M. (2016). *Los Tres Kirchnerismos*, 1st edn. Buenos Aires: Siglo Ventiuno.

Lerner, D. (1968). 'Modernization: Social Aspects'. *International Encyclopedia of the Social Sciences*, *10*, 386–395.

Levi, M. (1988). *Of Rule and Revenue*. Oakland, CA: University of California Press.

Levitsky, S. (2003a). 'From Labor Politics to Machine Politics: The Transformation of Party–Union Linkages in Argentine Peronism, 1983–1999'. Latin American Research *Review*, *38*(3), 3–36.

Levitsky, S. (2003b). *Transforming Labor-Based Parties in Latin America: Argentine Peronism in Comparative Perspective*. Cambridge: Cambridge University Press.

Levitsky, S., and Murillo, M. V. (2003). 'Argentina Weathers the Storm'. *Journal of Democracy*, *14*(4), 152–166.

Levitsky, S., and Murillo, M. V. (2008). 'Argentina: From Kirchner to Kirchner'. *Journal of Democracy*, *19*(2), 16–30.

Lewis, C. M. (1975). 'Anglo-Argentine Trade 1945–1965'. In Rock, D. (Ed.), *Argentina in the Twentieth Century*. London: Gerald Duckworth & Co. Ltd, pp. 114–134.

Lewis, C. M. (2002). *Argentina: A Short History*. London: Oneworld.

Lieberman, E. (2001). 'National Political Community and the Politics of Income Taxation in Brazil and South Africa in the Twentieth Century'. *Politics & Society*, *29*(4), 515–555.

Lilleker, D. G. (2003). 'Interviewing the Political Elite: Navigating a Potential Minefield'. *Politics*, *23*(3), 207–214.

Lizardo, O., and Stoltz, D. S. (2018). 'Max Weber's Ideal versus Material Interest Distinction Revisited'. *European Journal of Social Theory*, *21*(1), 3–21.

López Cámarra, F. (1967). *La estructura económica y social de México en la época de la reforma*. Ciudad de México: Siglo XXI.

López Gallo, M. (1967). *Economía y política en la historia de México*. Ciudad de México: Grijalbo.

Lousteau, M. (2008). 'Anuncio de las retenciones moviles (1)'. 11 March. Available at: https://www.casarosada.gob.ar/informacion/archivo/16774-blank-23910970. Accessed 12 June 2021.
Lowy, M., Sader, E., and Gorman, S. (1985). 'The Militarization of the State in Latin America'. *Latin American Perspectives, 12*, 7–40.
Lucas, A. (2012). 'Nacionalización de YPF: los españoles que creen que la reacción es exagerada'. *BBC Mundo*, 18 April. Available at: https://www.bbc.com/mundo/noticias/2012/04/120417_espana_repsol_lucas_jrg. Accessed 12 June 2021.
Lupu, N. (2016). 'The End of the Kirchner Era'. *Journal of Democracy, 27*(2), 35–49.
Mahon Jr, J. E., Bergman, M., & Arnson, C. (Eds). (2015). *Progressive Tax Reform and Equality in Latin America*. Washington, DC: Wilson Centre.
Mander, B. (2014). 'Argentina Reaches Landmark Deal with Paris Club Creditors'. *Financial Times*. Available at: https://www.ft.com/content/212b0b1e-e722-11e3-aa93-00144feabdc0. Accessed 12 June 2021.
Malloy, J. M. (1993). 'Statecraft, Social Policy, and Governance in Latin America'. *Governance, 6*(2), 220–274.
Mangonnet, J., and Murillo, M. V. (2020). 'Protests of Abundance: Distributive Conflict over Agricultural Rents during the Commodities Boom in Argentina 2003–2013'. *Comparative Political Studies, 53*(8), 1223–1258.
Mann, M. (1984). 'The Autonomous Power of the State: Its Origins, Mechanisms and Results'. *European Journal of Sociology, 25*(2), 185–213.
Mann, M. (1986). *The Sources of Social Power*. Cambridge: Cambridge University Press.
Mann, M. (1988). *States, War, and Capitalism: Studies in Political Sociology*. Hoboken, NJ: Wiley Blackwell.
Manse, M. (2022). 'Two Sides of the Same Coin: Direct Taxation and Negotiated Governance in Colonial Indonesia. *Journal of Social History, 56*(2), 411–438.
Manzetti, L. (1992). 'The Evolution of Agricultural Interest Groups in Argentina'. *Journal of Latin American Studies, 24*(3), 585–616.
Manzetti, L. (2014). 'Accountability and Corruption in Argentina during the Kirchners' Era'. *Latin American Research Review, 49*(2), 173–195.
Manzetti, L. (2016). 'Renationalization in Argentina, 2005–2013'. *Latin American Politics and Society, 58*(1), 3–28.
Mares, I., and Queralt, D. (2015). 'The Non-Democratic Origins of Income Taxation'. *Comparative Political Studies, 48*(14), 1974–2009.
Marelli, F. (2015). 'Macri promete reducir "poco a poco" los impuestos y espera que el dólar esté "por debajo de los $16"'. *La Nación*, 8 November. Available at: https://www.lanacion.com.ar/politica/macri-promete-reducir-poco-a-poco-los-impuestos-y-espera-que-el-dolar-este-por-debajo-de-los-16-nid1843657. Accessed 12 June 2021.
Marichal, C. (1989). *A Century of Debt Crises in Latin America: From Independence to the Great Depression, 1820–1930*. Princeton, NJ: Princeton University Press.
Marichal, C. (2006). 'The Spanish-American Silver Peso: Export Commodity and Global Money of the Ancien Regime, 1550–1800'. In Topik, S., Marichal, C., and Frank, Z. (Eds), *From Silver to Cocaine: Latin American Commodity Chains and the Building of the World Economy*, 1500–2000, Durham, NC: Duke University Press, pp. 25–52.
Martin, G., 1985. 'The Historical, Economic, and Political Bases of France's African Policy'. *Journal of Modern African Studies, 23*(2), 189–208.
Martin, I., Mehrotra, A., and Prasad, M. (2009). 'The Thunder of History: The Origins and Development of the New Fiscal Sociology'. In Martin, I., Mehrotra, A., and Prasad, M. (Eds), *The New Fiscal Sociology: Taxation in Comparative and Historical Perspective*. Cambridge: Cambridge University Press, pp. 1–28.

Martin, P., and Trannoy, A. (2019). 'Taxes on Production: The Good, the Bad and the Ugly'. *Notes du Conseil Danalyse Economique*, 53(5), 1–12.

Martínez, B. (2020). 'Retenciones. Productores proponent en parode 15 días y una rebellion fiscal'. *La Nación*. Available at: https://es-us.noticias.yahoo.com/retenciones-productores-proponen-paro-15-210100640.html?guccounter=1&guce_referrer=aHR0cHM6Ly93d3cuZ29vZ2xlLmNvbS8&guce_referrer_sig=AQAAAJW3pQD66OlPjM8EyFhFmQS-Y9lRJDO_2xbbHdb6aF_UvkJUA9g_RjBQsXasReM3INDFJ2JxGOtSUhfFiM2tv_tm-fjT1p6IuxvWvT0jWm2WtDemExXAZS3w37TdC1ObI-74SU-AB9OYWzs1rMrIsI88RIkpCyhWtVDoAh-1JRUL. Accessed 12 June 2021.

Marx K., and Engels, F. (1970). *The German Ideology*. New York: International Publishers Co.

Masefield, S. C., Megaw, A., and Barlow, M. (2020). 'Repurposing NGO Data for Better Research Outcomes: A Scoping Review of the Use and Secondary Analysis of NGO Data in Health Policy and Systems Research'. *Health Research Policy and Systems*, *18*(1), 63.

Mayer, J. M. (1962). *El impuesto a los réditos y la destrucción de la clase media*. Buenos Aires: Libería del Colegio.

Mazzuca, S. (2013). 'The Rise of Rentier Populism'. *Journal of Democracy*, *24*(2), 108–122.

Mcdonnell, P. J. (2008). 'Mass Rally Backs Argentine President; Farmers Stand Firm'. *Los Angeles Times*, 2 April. Available at: https://www.latimes.com/archives/la-xpm-2008-apr-02-fg-farmers2-story.html. Accessed 12 June 2021.

McClure, J. (2022). 'Rethinking the Historic Models of the Role of Constitutions in Shaping Patterns of Inequality: Iberian Constitutionalism, Common Property, and Colonialism'. In Chadwick, A., Lozano-Rodríguez, E., Palacios-Lleras, A., et al. (Eds), *Markets, Constitutions, and Inequality*. Abingdon: London: Routledge, pp. 142–160.

McClure, J. (2023). 'Poverty and Ideology: Historic Pathways'. In Christiansen, C. O., Machando-Guichon, M. L., Hunt, O. B., et al. (Eds), *Talking about Global Inequality*. Cham: Palgrave Macmillan, pp. 21–29.

McNeish, J. A. (2018). 'Resource Extraction and Conflict in Latin America'. *Colombia Internacional*, *93*, 3–16.

Mendes, A. P. F., Bertella, M. A., and Teixeira, R. F. (2014). 'Industrialization in Sub-Saharan Africa and Import Substitution Policy'. Brazilian Journal of Political Economy, 34, 120–138.

Mendoza, E. G., and Oviedo, P. M. (2009). 'Public Debt, Fiscal Solvency and Macroeconomic Uncertainty in Latin America: The Cases of Brazil, Colombia, Costa Rica and Mexico'. *Economía mexicana. Nueva época*, *18*(2), 133–173.

MercoPress. (2013). 'Cristina Fernandez Administration Accused of Corruption and Waste by Farm Leaders'. 29 July. Available at: https://en.mercopress.com/2013/07/29/cristina-fernandez-administration-accused-of-corruption-and-waste-by-farm-leaders. Accessed 12 June 2021.

Ministerio de la Economía. (2021). 'Balances Energéticos'. Available at: https://www.argentina.gob.ar/economia/energia/hidrocarburos/balances-energeticos. Accessed 12 June 2021.

Ministerio de Energia y Minería. (2021). 'Homepage'. Available at: https://enermin.gob.ar. Accessed 12 June 2021.

Ministerio de Economía. (2019). Available at: https://www.argentina.gob.ar/economia/finanzas/graficos-deuda. Accessed 12 June 2021.

Ministerio de Hacienda. (2021). 'Recaudación'. Available at: https://www.argentina.gob.ar/economia/ingresospublicos/recaudacion. Accessed 12 June 2021.

Ministerio del Interior. (2003). 'Elecciones 2003. Available at: https://www.argentina.gob.ar/interior/dine/resultadosyestadisticas/2003. Accessed 12 June 2021.

Ministerio del Interior. (2005). 'Elecciones 2005'. Available at: https://www.argentina.gob.ar/interior/dine/resultadosyestadisticas/2005. Accessed 12 June 2021.

Ministerio del Interior. (2007). 'Elecciones 2007'. Available at: https://www.argentina.gob.ar/interior/dine/resultadosyestadisticas/2007. Accessed 12 June 2021.

Ministerio del Interior. (2011). 'Elecciones 2011'. Available at: https://www.argentina.gob.ar/interior/dine/resultadosyestadisticas/2011. Accessed 12 June 2021.

Ministerio del Interior. (2013). 'Elecciones 2013'. Available at: https://www.argentina.gob.ar/interior/dine/resultadosyestadisticas/2013. Accessed 12 June 2021.

Ministerio del Interior. (2015). 'Elecciones 2015'. Available at: https://www.argentina.gob.ar/interior/dine/resultadosyestadisticas/2015#8. Accessed 12 June 2021.

Moffett, M., Parks, K., and Turner, T. (2012). 'Era of Argentine Subsidies Ends'. *Wall Street Journal*, 6 January. Available at: https://web.archive.org/web/20160923115057/http://www.wsj.com/articles/SB10001424052970203513604577143000000536074. Accessed 12 June 2021.

Moore, M. (2004). 'Revenues, State Formation, and the Quality of Governance in Developing Countries'. *International Political Science Review*, *25*(3), 297–319.

Morresi, S., and Vommaro, G. (2014). 'Argentina: The Difficulties of the Partisan Right and the Case of Propuesta Republicana'. In Luna J. P., and Kaltwasser, C. R. (Ed), *The Resilience of the Latin American Right*. Baltimore, MD: Johns Hopkins University Press, pp. 319–345.

Morris, Z. S. (2009). 'The Truth about Interviewing Elites'. *Politics*, *29*(3), 209–217.

Munck, G. L., and Luna, J. P. (2022). *Latin American Politics and Society*. Cambridge: Cambridge University Press.

Munck, R. (2003). 'Neoliberalism, Necessitarianism and Alternatives in Latin America: There Is No Alternative (TINA)?' *Third World Quarterly*, *24*(3), 495–511.

Munck, R., and Wise, R. D. (Eds). (2018). *Reframing Latin American Development*. Routledge.

Murillo, M. V. (2015). 'Argentina Leans Right'. *Foreign Affairs*, 31 October. Available at: https://www.foreignaffairs.com/articles/south-america/2015-10-31/argentina-leans-right. Accessed 12 June 2021.

Murmis, M., and Portantiero, J. C. (2004). 'Estudioa Sobre los Orígenes del Peronismo'. Available at: https://condor-atlanta.org/wp-content/uploads/2024/02/36-Estudios-sobre-los-origenes-del-peronismo-Murmis-Portantiero.pdf. Accessed 12 June 2021.

La Nación. (2003). 'Para Kirchner llegó la hora de la verdad'. 24 May. Available at: https://www.lanacion.com.ar/economia/campo/para-kirchner-llego-la-hora-de-la-verdad-nid498244. Accessed 12 June 2021.

La Nación. (2007). 'La SRA, contra las retenciones'. 4 November. Available at: https://www.lanacion.com.ar/politica/la-sra-contra-las-retenciones-nid959177. Accessed 12 June 2021.

La Nación. (2012). 'La CGT expresó su solidaridad con las víctimas del choque'. 22 February. Available at: https://www.lanacion.com.ar/politica/schiavi-y-montenegro-en-la-estacion-de-once-nid1450642. Accessed 12 June 2021.

La Nación. (2014). 'ProgresAr, el nuevo plan del Gobierno para los jóvenes "ni-ni"'. 22 January. Available at: https://www.lanacion.com.ar/politica/progresar-el-nuevo-plan-del-gobierno-para-los-jovenes-ni-ni-nid1657619. Accessed 12 June 2021.

La Nación. (2015). 'En lo Estructural, no es un cambio de discurso'. Available at: https://www.google.com/search?q=Marcos+Pena+cristina+kirchner+2015&rlz=1C5CHFA_enGB883GB883&ei=iRCxYNuxKYeyUsC1sIAP&start=20&sa=N&ved=2ahUKEwibmuPU3OzwAhUHmRQKHcAaDPA4ChDw0wN6BAgBEEo&biw=1200&bih=650. Accessed 12 June 2021.

La Nación. (2022). 'Alberto Fernández habló sabre la posibilidad de subir las retenciones: "Necesito que el Congreso entienda el problem y acompañe'. 20 May. Available at: https://www.lanacion.com.ar/politica/alberto-fernandez-hablo-sobre-la-posibilidad-de-subir-las-retenciones-necesito-que-el-congreso-nid20052022. Accessed 25 January 2023.

La Nación. (2023). Available at: https://www.lanacion.com.ar/economia/inflacion-de-marzo-de-2023-fue-77-y-acumula-1043-en-12-meses-nid14042023. Accessed 11 July 2023.

Natanson, J. (2018). 'Mauricio Macri en su ratonera'. *Nueva Sociedad*, 276, 24–33.

Navarro, V. (2007). 'Neoliberalism as a Class Ideology; or, the Political Causes of the Growth of Inequalities'. *International Journal of Health Services*, *37*(1), 47–62.

Nem Singh, J. T. (2024). *Business of the State: Why State Ownership Matters for Resource Governance*. Oxford: Oxford University Press.

Nem Singh, J., and Chen, G. C. (2017). 'State-Owned Enterprises and the Political Economy of State–State Relations in the Developing World'. *Third World Quarterly*, *39*(6), 1077–1097.

Nem Singh, J. T., and Ovadia, J. S. (2020). 'The Theory and Practice of Building Developmental States in the Global South'. In *Developmental States beyond East Asia*. London: Routledge, pp. 1–23.

Nietzsche, F., 1977. *The Portable Nietzsche*. London: Penguin.

North, D. C., Summerhill, W., and Weingast, B. R. (1999). *Order, Disorder and Economic Change: Latin America vs. North America*. New Haven, CT: Yale University Press.

Ocampo, E. (2015). 'Commodity Price Booms and Populist Cycles. An Explanation of Argentina's Decline in the 20th Century'. *Serie Documentos de Trabajo*, 562, 1–35.

Odell, J. S. (2001). 'Case Study Methods in International Political Economy'. *International Studies Perspectives*, *2*(2), 161–176.

ODI Global. (2023). 'Four Expert Views on the Future of Tax for Development'. 7 February. Available at: https://odi.org/en/insights/four-expert-views-on-the-future-of-tax-for-development/#:~:text=Taxation%20is%20a%20key%20instrument,just%20financing%20for%20public%20budgets. Accessed 24 April 2025.

O'Donnell, G. (1993). 'On the State, Democratization and Some Conceptual Problems: A Latin American View with Glances at Some Postcommunist Countries'. *World Development*, *21*(8), 1355–1369.

OEC (Observatory of Economic Complexity). (2019). 'Argentina (ARG) Exports, Imports, and Trade Partners'. Available at: https://oec.world/en/profile/country/arg. Accessed 12 June 2021.

OEC. (2024). 'Wheat in Argentina'. Available at: https://oec.world/en/profile/bilateral-product/wheat/reporter/arg. Accessed 24 April 2025.

OECD (Organisation for Economic Co-operation and Development). (2017). *OECD Economic Surveys: Argentina 2017: Multi-dimensional Economic Survey*. Paris: OECD Publishing. Available at: https://doi.org/10.1787/eco_surveys-arg-2017-en. Accessed 12 June 2021.

OECD (2019). *Agricultural Policies in Argentina*. Santiago: Trade and Agriculture Directorate Committee for Agriculture, OECD.

OECD. (2020). 'Revenue Statistics in Latin America and the Caribbean 2020'. 7 May. Available at: https://doi.org/10.1787/68739b9b-en-es. Accessed 12 June 2021.

OECD. (2021a). 'OECD Tax Database'. Available at: https://www.oecd.org/tax/tax-policy/tax-database. Accessed 12 June 2021.

OECD. (2021b). *Revenue Statistics in Latin America and the Caribbean 2021*. Paris: OECD.

OECD. (2023). 'Base Erosion and Profit Shifting (BEPS) in Mining Programme'. Available at: https://www.oecd.org/tax/tax-global/work-on-extractive-industries.htm. Accessed 24 April 2025.

Omukuti, J. Megaw, A., and Barlow, M. (2021). 'The Value of Secondary Use of Data Generated by Non-Governmental Organisations for Disaster Risk Management Research: Evidence from the Caribbean'. *International Journal of Disaster Risk Reduction*, *56*, 102–114.

Ondetti, G. (2015). 'The Roots of Brazil's Heavy Taxation'. *Journal of Latin American Studies*, *47*(4), 749–779.

Ondetti, G. (2017). 'The Power of Preferences: Economic Elites and Light Taxation in Mexico'. *Revista mexicana de ciencias políticas y sociales*, *62*(231), 47–76.

Ondetti, G. (2021). *Property Threats and the Politics of Anti-statism: The Historical Roots of Contemporary Tax Systems in Latin America*. Cambridge: Cambridge University Press.

Ondetti, G. (2023). 'Redistributive Threats, Development Models, and Taxation in Latin America'. In Fehling, P., and Burchardt, H.-J. (Eds), *Taxation and Inequality in Latin America*. London: Routledge, pp. 157–175.

O'Rourke, K. H., de La Escosura, L. P., and Daudin, D. (2010a). 'Trade and Empire'. In *The Cambridge Economic History of Modern Europe*. Cambridge: Cambridge University Press, pp. 96–121.

O'Rourke, K. H., de la Escosura, L. P., and Daudin, G. (2010b). 'Trade and Empire, 1700–1870'. TEP Working Paper No. 0208, May. Available at: https://www.tcd.ie/Economics/TEP/2008/TEP0208.pdf. Accessed 12 September 2023.

Ortiz, A. D. (1971). *The Golden Age of Spain*. London: Weidenfeld & Nicolson.

Ortiz, F. (2008). 'Argentina's Fernandez Plays with Fire'. *The Guardian*, 1 April. Available at: https://web.archive.org/web/20080407011046/http://www.guardian.co.uk/feedarticle?id=7425706. Accessed 12 June 2021.

Ostiguy, P. (2000). *Peronism and Anti-Peronism: Class-Cultural Cleavages and Political Identity in Argentina*. Berkeley, CA: University of California in Berkeley.

Ozarow, D. (2019). 'Banging the Other Side of the Saucepan: Changing Political Activism and Performance of Citizenship among Argentina's Middle Class, 2001–2013'. In Montero-Diaz, F., and Winter, F. (Eds), *Citizenship in the Latin American Upper and Middle Classes*. London: Routledge, pp. 117–133.

Página 12. (2007). 'Repercusiones por la medida'. November.

Página 12. (2008). 'El país: Ella y el campo'. 19 June. Available at: https://www.pagina12.com.ar/diario/elpais/subnotas/106270-33525-2008-06-19.html. Accessed 1 November 2019.

Página 12. (2011). 'El país: CFK superó el 54 por ciento de los votos'. 4 November. Available at: https://www.pagina12.com.ar/diario/elpais/1-180493-2011-11-04.html. Accessed 12 June 2021.

Página 12. (2023). 'Ahora Mauricio Macri quiere dar consejos para bajar la inflación'. 15 May. Available at: https://www.pagina12.com.ar/549247-ahora-mauricio-macri-quiere-dar-consejos-de-bajar-la-inflacion. Accessed 24 April 2025.

Pagni, C. (2013). 'Una crisis con síntomas de simulacro'. *La Nación*, 19 December.

Paler, L. (2013). 'Keeping the Public Purse: An Experiment in Windfalls, Taxes, and the Incentives to Restrain Government'. *American Political Science Review*, *107*(4), 706–725.

Panizza, F. (2005). 'Unarmed Utopia Revisited: The Resurgence of Left-of-Centre Politics in Latin America'. *Political Studies*, *53*, 716–734.

Panizza, F. (2009). *Contemporary Latin America: Development and Democracy beyond the Washington Consensus*. London: Zed Books.

Parsons, T. (1937). *The Structure of Social Action*. New York: Free Press.

Payne, A., and Phillips, N. (2010). *Development*. Cambridge: Polity Press.

Pedreira, J. M. (2000). 'From Growth to Collapse: Portugal, Brazil, and the Breakdown of the Old Colonial System (1760–1830)'. *Hispanic American Historical Review*, *80*(4), 839–864.

Peña, A. M., and Barlow, M. (2021). 'Beyond the Boom: Dependent Development and Political Change in Argentina (2010–2015)'. *Frontiers in Political Science*, *3*, 705200.

Peralta-Ramos, M. (1992). *The Political Economy of Argentina: Power and Class since 1930*. Boulder, CO: Westview Press Inc.

Pereira, A. W. (1997). *End of the Peasantry: The Rural Labor Movement in Northeast Brazil, 1961–1988*, Vol. 349. Pittsburgh, PA: University of Pittsburgh Press.

Perfil. (2007a). 'Carrió pidió al Gobierno que deje "en paz" al campo'. November.

Perfil. (2007b). 'Hay actividades en crisis por retenciones del Gobierno'. December.

Perfil. (2008). 'Nosotros nos pusimos al frente del conflicto y a partir de allí, el Gobierno decidió destruirnos'. Council on Hemisphere Affairs, 19 February. Available at: https://www.coha.org/insufficient-media-reforms-in-latin-america-urgency-to-go-further. Accessed 12 June 2021.

Perochena, C., Rodríguez Rey, S., and Judzik, D. (2020). '2001 (parte 2): Del default al fin de la convertibilidad'. Available at: https://www.youtube.com/watch?v=ZLiBANb4jEo. Accessed 12 June 2021.

Peruzzotti, E., and Waisbord, S. (2021). 'Public Sphere and Post-Populism in the Covid-19 Pandemic: The Short Life of Depolarisation in Argentina'. *Javnost—The Public*, *28*(2), 1–16.

Phelan, J. L. (1960). 'Authority and Flexibility in the Spanish Imperial Bureaucracy'. *Administrative Science Quarterly*, *5*(1), 47.

Phillips, N. (2017). 'Doing Research in the Shadows of the Global Economy'. In Montgomerie, J. (Ed.), *Critical Methods in Political and Cultural Economy*. London: Routledge, pp. 115–120.

La Política Online. (2012). 'Cristina dijo que su gobierno no hace ajuste sino "sintonía fina"'. 25 January. Available at: https://www.lapoliticaonline.com/nota/nota-79672. Accessed 12 June 2021.

Ponce, A. F., and McClintock, C. (2014). 'The Explosive Combination of Inefficient Local Bureaucracies and Mining Production: Evidence from Localized Societal Protests in Peru'. *Latin American Politics and Society*, *56*(3), 118–140.

Porto, G. (2010). 'International Market Access and Poverty in Argentina'. *Review of International Economics*, *18*(2), 396–407.

Prange, A. (2015). 'Argentina Won't Likely Cry Much for Cristina Fernandez'. *Deutsche Welle*, 24 October. Available at: https://www.dw.com/en/argentina-wont-likely-cry-much-for-cristina-fernandez/a-18799764. Accessed 12 June 2021.

Prebisch, R. (1996). 'El desarrollo económico de la América Latina y algunos de sus principales problemas'. *El trimestre económico*, *63*(249(1)), 175–245.

Prichard, W. (2010). 'Taxation and State Building: Towards a Governance Focused Tax Reform Agenda'. *Institute of Development Studies Working Papers*, 341, 1–55.

Przeworski, A., and Wallerstein, M. (1988). 'Structural Dependence of the State on Capital'. *American Political Science Review*, *82*(1), 11–29.

Ramos, M. P. (2019). 'Una aproximación al análisis del peronismo'. *Realidad económica*, *48*(321), 85–107.

Randall, L. (1977). *A Comparative Economic History of Latin America*, 4 vols. Ann Arbor, MI: University Microfilms and Institute of Latin American Studies, Colombia University.

Rapisarda, M. J. (2016). 'Impuesto a las ganancias sobre dividendos. Reflexiones sobre seguridad jurídica'. El Cronista, 24 October. Available at: https://www.cronista.com/fiscal/Impuesto-a-las-ganancias-sobre-dividendos-Reflexiones-sobre-seguridad-juridica-20161024-0004.html. Accessed 12 June 2021.

Rasch, E. D. (2017). 'Citizens, Criminalization and Violence in Natural Resource Conflicts in Latin America'. *European Review of Latin American and Caribbean Studies*, 103, 131–142.

Regúnaga, M., and Tejeda Rodriguez, A. (2015). Argentina's Agricultural Trade Policy and Sustainable Development. Issue No. 55. Geneva: International Centre for Trade and Sustainable Development.

Reyes Abadie, W., and Vazquez Romero, A. (n.d.). *Crónica general del Uruguay*, Vol. III, *El Uruguay del siglo XIX*. Montevideo: Ediciones de la Banda Oriental.

Richardson, B. (2009). *Sugar: Refined Power in a Global Regime*. Cambridge: Polity Press.

Richardson, N. (2009). 'Export-Oriented Populism: Commodities and Coalitions in Argentina'. *Studies in Comparative International Development*, *44*(3), 228–255.

Río Negro. (2002). 'Retenciones: exportadores advierten efectos negativos.' Río Negro, 11 March. https://www.rionegro.com.ar/retenciones-exportadores-advierten-efectos-negativos-GEHRN02031117112002. Accessed 12 June 2021.

Robinson, W. I. (2008). *Latin America and Global Capitalism: A Critical Globalization Perspective*. Baltimore, MD: Johns Hopkins University Press.

Rock, D. (1987). Argentina, 1516–1987: From Spanish Colonization to Alphonsín. Berkeley: California University Press.

Rodríguez, J., and Arceo, N. (2006). 'Renta agraria y ganancias extraordinarias en la Argentina 1990–2003.' Documento De Trabajo De CENDA.

Rojas, R. (2017). 'The Ebbing "Pink Tide": An Autopsy of Left-Wing Regimes in Latin America.' *New Labor Forum*, *26*(2), 70–82.

Rose-Ackerman, S., Desierto, D. A., and Volosin, N. (2011). 'Hyper-Presidentialism: Separation of Powers without Checks and Balances in Argentina and Philippines.' *Berkeley Journal of International Law*, *9*(1), 101–188.

Ross, M. L. (2004). 'Does Taxation Lead to Representation?' *British Journal of Political Science*, *34*(2), 229–249.

Rostow, W. W. (1959). 'The Stages of Economic Growth.' *Economic History Review*, *12*(1), 1–16.

Rossignolo, D. (2016). 'Taxes, Expenditures, Poverty and Income Distribution in Argentina.' Working Paper No. 45, May. Available at: http://www.commitmentoequity.org/publications_files/Argentina/CEQ_WP45_TAXES_EXPENDITURES_POVERTY_AND_INCOME_DISTRIBUTION_IN_ARGENTINA.pdf. Accessed 12 June 2021.

Rossini, G., Arancibia, R. G., and Guiguet, E. D. (2017). 'Argentine Government Policies: Impacts on the Beef Sector.' *Agricultural and Food Economics*, *5*(1), 1–14.

Roxborough, I. (1979). *Theories of Underdevelopment*. London: Macmillan.

Rozas Bugueño, J., and Somma, N. M. (2020). 'Determinantes de la protesta juvenil en Chile.' *Revista mexicana de sociología*, *82*(3), 673–703.

Rueda, D. (2005). 'Insider–Outsider Politics in Industrialized Democracies: The Challenge to Social Democratic Parties.' *American Political Science Review*, *99*(1), 61–74.

Ruckert, A., Macdonald, L., and Proulx, K. R. (2017). 'Post-Neoliberalism in Latin America: A Conceptual Review.' *Third World Quarterly*, *38*(7), 1583–1602.

Ruralnet. (2024). 'Si bajaran las retenciones al 25%, ingresarían muchos más dólares a las arcas del estado.' 20 August. Available at: https://ruralnet.com.ar/2024/08/20/si-bajaran-las-retenciones-al-25-ingresarian-muchos-mas-dolares-a-las-arcas-del-estado. Accessed 24 April 2025.

Sachs, J. D. (1989). 'Social Conflict and Populist Policies in Latin America.' National Bureau of Economic Research (NBER) Working Papers Series. No. 2987, 1–33.

Saffon, M. P., and Bertomeu, J. F. G. (2020). 'What/Whose Property Rights?' In Brinks, D. M., Levitsky, S., and Murillo, M. V., (Eds), *The Politics of Institutional Weakness in Latin America*. Cambridge: Cambridge University Press, pp. 208–234.

Salvia, A., and Vera, J. (2016). *Pobreza y Desigualdad por Ingresos en la Argentina Urbana 2010–2015*. Buenos Aires: Documento de Trabajo/Informe Técnico.

Salvia, S. P. (2015). 'The Boom and Crisis of the Convertibility Plan in Argentina.' *Revista de Economia Política*, *35*(2), 325–342.

Sanchez, O. (2006). 'Tax System Reform in Latin America: Domestic and International Causes.' *Review of International Political Economy*, *13*(5), 772–801.

Sánchez-Sibony, O. (2019). 'Political Economy of Taxation in Latin America.' In *Oxford Research Encyclopedia of Politics*. Oxford: Oxford University Press. Available at: https://oxfordre.com/politics/view/10.1093/acrefore/9780190228637.001.0001/acrefore-9780190228637-e-1659. Accessed 11 August 2025.

Sánchez Román, J. A. (2012). *Taxation and Society in Twentieth-Century Argentina*. Basingstoke: Palgrave Macmillan.

Sánchez Román, J. A. (2015). 'Impuestos y terratenientes en la Argentina: Un balance'. *Anuario del Instituto de Historia Argentina*, *14*, 1–17.

Sanjurjo-Ramos, J. (2021). *In the Blood of Our Brothers: Abolitionism and the End of the Slave Trade in Spain's Atlantic Empire, 1800–1870*. Tuscaloosa, AL: University of Alabama Press.

Schiumerini, L., and Steinberg, D. A. (2020). 'The Black Market Blues: The Political Costs of Illicit Currency Markets'. *Journal of Politics*, *82*(4), 1217–1230.

Schmidt, K.-H. (2006). 'Schumpeter and the Crisis of the Tax State'. In Backhaus, J. (Ed.), *Joseph Alois Schumpeter*. Bonn, Germany: Kluwer Academic Publishers, pp. 337–351.

Schneider, A. (2012). *State-Building and Tax Regimes in Central America*. Cambridge: Cambridge University Press.

Schneider, B. R. (2004). *Business Politics and the State in Twentieth-Century Latin America*. Cambridge, MA: MIT Press.

Schneider, B. R. (2013). 'Institutions for Effective Business–Government Collaboration: Micro Mechanisms and Macro Politics in Latin America'. Inter American Development Bank (IDB) Working Paper Series No. 418. October. Available at: https://doi.org/10.18235/0011517.

Schoonenboom, J., and Johnson, R. B. (2017). 'Wie man ein Mixed Methods-Forschungs-Design konstruiert'. *Kolner Zeitschrift fur Soziologie und Sozialpsychologie*, *69*(2), 107–131.

Schumpeter, J. A. (1991 [1918]). *The Crisis of the Tax State. The Economics and Sociology of Capitalism*. Princeton, NJ: Princeton University Press.

Schwartz, S. B. (1987). *Plantations and Peripheries, c. 1580–c. 1750*. Colonial Brazil. New York: Cambridge University Press, pp. 67–144.

Seager, A. (2005). 'Argentina Says Debt Default Is Over | *Business*'. The Guardian, 4 March. Available at: https://www.theguardian.com/business/2005/mar/04/argentina.internationalnews. Accessed 12 June 2021.

The Seam. (2022). 'Global Sunflower Production Expected to Drop'. 13 July. Available at: https://www.theseam.com/global-sunflower-production-expected-to-drop. Accessed 24 April 2025.

Seers, D. (1963). 'The Limitations of the Special Case 1'. *Bulletin of the Oxford University Institute of Economics & Statistics*, *25*(2), 77–98.

Selman, C. (2018). 'Argentina Export Tax and Strike Risks'. S & P Global. Available at: https://www.spglobal.com/marketintelligence/en/mi/research-analysis/argentina-export-tax-and-strike-risks.html. Accessed 12 June 2021.

Semán, E. (2015). 'The Taming of the Argentine Right?'. *North American Congress on Latin America (NACLA)*, 2 December. Available at: https://nacla.org/news/2015/12/02/taming-argentine-right?utm_source=hootsuite. Accessed 12 June 2021.

Senado Argentina. (2020). 'Honorable Senado de la Nación Argentina'. Available at: https://www.senado.gov.ar/senadores/senador/438. Accessed 12 June 2021.

SGE (Secretaría de Gobierno de Energía). (2019). *Balance de gestión en energía 2016—2019*. Buenos Aires: Ministerio de Hacienda.

Shama, R. (2011). *Food Export Restrictions: Review of the 2007–2010 Experience and Considerations for Disciplining Restrictive Measures* Rome: Food and Agriculture Organization (FAO), pp. 1–12.

Sheild Johansson, M. (2018). 'Taxing the Indigenous: A History of Barriers to Fiscal Inclusion in the Bolivian Highlands'. *History and Anthropology*, *29*(1), 83–100.

Sikkink, K. (1997). 'Development Ideas in Latin America'. In Cooper, F., and Packard, R. M., (Eds), *International Development and the Social Sciences: Essays on the History and Politics of Knowledge*. Berkeley: University of California Press, pp. 228–256.

Simioni, E. (2019). 'Argentina's Electrifying Reforms'. *Wilson Center*, 13 September. Available at: https://www.wilsoncenter.org/article/argentinas-electrifying-reforms. Accessed 26 May 2021.

Sinnott, E., Nash, J., and De la Torre, A. (2010). *Natural Resources in Latin America and the Caribbean: Beyond Booms and Busts?*. Washington, DC: World Bank Publications.

Skidmore, T. E. (1978). 'A Case Study in Comparative Public Policy: The Economic Dimensions of Populism in Argentina and Brazil'. *Wilson Center*. Available at: https://www.wilsoncenter.org/sites/default/files/media/documents/publication/wp3_the_economic_dimensions_of_populism_in_argentina_and_brazil.pdf. Accessed 26 May 2021.

Skocpol, T. (1985). 'Bringing the State Back In: Strategies of Analysis in Current Research'. In Evans, P. B., Rueschemeyer, D., and Skocpol, T. (Eds), *Bringing the State Back In*. Cambridge: Cambridge University Press, pp. 3–38.

Smink, V. (2015). 'Qué ganó y qué perdió Argentina durante el kirchnerismo'. *BBC News Mundo*, 25 October. Available at: https://www.bbc.com/mundo/noticias/2015/10/151022_elecciones_argentina_kirchnerismo_vs. Accessed 12 June 2021.

Smith, W. C. (1991). 'State, Market and Neoliberalism in Post-Transition Argentina: The Menem Experiment'. *Journal of Interamerican Studies and World Affairs*, *33*(4), 45–82.

Sokoloff, K. L., and Engerman, S. L. (2000). 'History Lessons: Institutions, Factor Endowments, and Paths of Development in the New World'. *Journal of Economic perspectives*, *14*(3), 217–232.

Sourrouille, J. V, and Ramos, A. H. (2013). 'El Trigo y las Ganancias del IAPI entre 1946 y 1949: Miranda y la política económica en los inicios del Peronismo'. *Desarollo Económico*, *53*(209/210), 27–56.

Steinmo, S. (2003). 'The Evolution of Policy Ideas: Tax Policy in the 20th Century'. *British Journal of Politics and International Relations*, *5*(2), 206–236.

Sued, G. (2013). 'El kirchnerismo convirtió en ley el blanqueo de divisas'. *La Nación*. Available at: https://www.lanacion.com.ar/politica/el-kirchnerismo-convirtio-en-ley-el-blanqueo-de-divisas-nid1586803. Accessed 12 June 2021.

Sunkel, O. (1969). 'National Development Policy and External Dependence in Latin America'. *Journal of Development Studies*, *6*(1), 23–48.

Sunkel, O., and Paz, P. (1976). 'El subdesarrollo latinoamericano y la teoría del desarrollo'. Available at: http://repositorio.cepal.org/handle/11362/1912. Accessed 12 June 2021.

Swain, S., Evans, J., Phillips, D., and Grimshaw, P., 2003. *Equal Subjects, Unequal Rights: Indigenous People in British Settler Colonies, 1830–1910*. Manchester: Manchester University Press.

Swedberg, R. (2003). 'The Changing Picture of Max Weber's Sociology'. *Annual Review of Sociology*, *29*(1), 283–306.

Swedberg, R. (2018). *Max Weber and the Idea of Economic Sociology*. Princeton, NJ: Princeton University Press.

Swidler, A., and Arditi, J. (1994). 'The New Sociology of Knowledge'. *Annual Review of Sociology*, *20*(1), 305–329.

Tansey, O. (2007). 'Process Tracing and Elite Interviewing: A Case for Non-Probability Sampling'. *PS: Political Science & Politics*, *40*(04), 765–772.

Tanzi, V. (1997). 'The Changing Role of the State in the Economy: A Historical Perspective'. International Monetary Fund Working Paper No. 97/114.

Tanzi, V. (2000). 'Taxation in Latin America in the Last Decade'. Stanford Center for Intenrational Development Working Paper No. 76, 23 November 2022. Available at: https://kingcenter.stanford.edu/sites/g/files/sbiybj16611/files/media/file/76wp_0.pdf. Accessed 12 June 2021.

Tanzi, V., and Zee, H. H. (2000). 'Tax Policy for Emerging Markets: Developing Countries'. *National Tax Journal, 53*(2), 299–322.

Tanzi, V. Barreix, A., and Villela, L. (Eds). (2008). *Taxation and Latin American Integration*. Cambridge: Inter-American Development Bank.

Tax Justice Network. (2024). *State of Tax Justice 2024*. London: Tax Justice Network.

Taylor, L. (1991). 'Economic Openness: Problems to the Century's End'. *Economic Liberalization: No Panacea, 1989*, 99–147.

Tedesco, L. (1994). *The Crisis of the Argentinian State: Democratisation and Economic Restructuring 1976–1989*. Warwick: University of Warwick.

Teichman, J. (2008). 'Redistributive Conflict and Social Policy in Latin America'. *World Development, 36*(3), 446–460.

Teichman, J. (2019). 'Inequality in Twentieth-Century Latin America: Path Dependence, Countermovements, and Reactive Sequences'. *Social Science History, 43*(1), 131–157.

Thomas, C., and Cachanosky, N. (2016). 'Argentina's Post-2001 Economy and the 2014 Default'. *Quarterly Review of Economics and Finance, 60*, 70–80.

Tilly, C. (1985). 'War Making and State Making as Organized Crime'. In Evans, P., Rueschemeyer, D., and Skocpol, T. (Eds), *Bringing the State Back In*. Cambridge: Cambridge University Press, pp. 169–191.

Torgler, B. (2005). 'Tax Morale in Latin America'. *Public Choice, 122*(1), 133–157.

Tussie, D. (2009). 'Economic Governance after Neoliberalism'. In Grugel, J., and Riggirozzi, P. (Eds), *Governance after Neoliberalism in Latin America*. New York: Palgrave Macmillan, pp. 67–87.

UN. (2024). 'Goal 8: Promote Sustained, Inclusive and Sustainable Economic Growth, Full and Productive Employment and Decent Work for All'. Available at: https://sdgs.un.org/goals/goal8. Accessed 12 June 2021.

Vagliasindi, M. (2012). 'Implementing Energy Subsidy Reforms'. *World Bank*, Open Knowledge Repository. Available at: https://doi.org/10.1596/978-0-8213-9561-5.

Vaisey, S. (2009). 'Motivation and Justification: A Dual-Process Model of Culture in Action'. *American Journal of Sociology, 114*(6), 1675–1715.

Van der Meer, A. (2020). *Performing Power: Cultural Hegemony, Identity, and Resistance in Colonial Indonesia*. Ithaca, NY: Cornell University Press.

Varise, F. (2003). 'Kirchner dio una señal al agro, pero no bajará las retenciones'. *La Nación*. 5 August. Available at: https://www.lanacion.com.ar/economia/kirchner-dio-una-senal-al-agro-pero-no-bajara-las-retenciones-nid516902. Accessed 12 June 2021.

Vellacott, C. (2007). *Economic Policy Reform in Late Industrialisers: Argentina and Spain since 1950*. London: London School of Economics.

Veltmeyer, H., 2012. 'The Natural Resource Dynamics of Postneoliberalism in Latin America: New Developmentalism or Extractivist Imperialism?' *Studies in Political Economy, 90*(1), 57–85.

Venkatesh, V., Brown, S. A., and Bala, H. (2013). 'Bridging the Qualitative—Quantitative Divide: Guidelines for Conducting Mixed Methods Research in Information Systems'. *Management Information Systems Quarterly, 37*(1), 21–54.

Vilas, C. M. (2006). 'Neoliberal Meltdown and Social Protest: Argentina 2001–2002'. *Critical Sociology, 32*(1), 163–186.

Vom Hau, M., Peres-Cajías, J., and Soifer, H. D. (2023). 'No Taxation without Informational Foundation: On the Role of Legibility in Tax State Development'. *Journal of Institutional Economics, 19*(3), 426–443.

Von Haldenwang, C. (2008). *Taxation, Social Cohesion, and Fiscal Decentralization in Latin America*, Vol. I. Bonn: Dokuz Eylul University.

Von Haldenwang, C. (2010). 'Taxation, Fiscal Decentralisation and Legitimacy: The Role of Semi-Autonomous Tax Agencies in Peru'. *Development Policy Review*, *28*(6), 643–667.

Walker, G. J. (2016). *Spanish Politics and Imperial Trade, 1700–1789*. London: Macmillan Press.

Webber, J. (2013). 'IMF Acts over Flawed Argentine Economic Data'. *Financial Times*. Available at: https://www.ft.com/content/eb704c98-6cbe-11e2-953f-00144feab49a. Accessed 12 June 2021.

Weyland, K. (2001). 'Clarifying a Contested Concept: Populism in the Study of Latin American Politics'. *Comparative Politics*, *34*(1), 1–22.

World Bank. (2019). 'Inflation, Consumer Prices (Annual %)'. Available at: https://data.worldbank.org/indicator/FP.CPI.TOTL.ZG. Accessed 12 June 2021.

World Bank. (2021a). 'Commodity Markets'. Available at: https://www.worldbank.org/en/research/commodity-markets. Accessed 12 June 2021.

World Bank. (2021b). 'GDP (current US$)—Argentina'. Available at: https://data.worldbank.org/indicator/NY.GDP.MKTP.CD?locations=AR. Accessed 12 June 2021.

World Bank Commodity Price Data (The Pink Sheet). (2021). 'Monthly Prices in Nominal US Dollars, 1960 to Present'. Available at: https://thedocs.worldbank.org/en/doc/5d903e848db1d1b83e0ec8f744e55570-0350012021/related/CMO-Historical-Data-Monthly.xlsx. Accessed 12 June 2021.

Wurgarft, R. (2012). 'Kicillof dice que Argentina no debe pagar un centavo a Repsol por la expropiación'. *Elmundo.es*, 23 April. Available at: https://www.elmundo.es/america/2012/04/23/argentina/1335193213.html. Accessed 12 June 2021.

Wylde, C. (2011). 'State, Society and Markets in Argentina: The Political Economy of Neodesarrollismo under Néstor Kirchner, 2003–2007'. *Bulletin of Latin American Research*, *30*(4), 436–452.

Wylde, C. (2012a). *Latin America after Neoliberalism*. London: Palgrave Macmillan.

Wylde, C. (2012b). 'Neoliberalism or Developmentalism? The Political Economy of Brazil 2003–10'. In *Latin America after Neoliberalism*. International Political Economy Series. London: Palgrave Macmillan, pp. 161–183.

Wylde, C. (2016). 'Post-Neoliberal Developmental Regimes in Latin America: Argentina under Cristina Fernandez de Kirchner'. *New Political Economy*, *21*(3), 322–341.

Wylde, C. (2017). 'Argentina under the Kirchner Administrations'. In *Emerging Markets and the State: Developmentalism in the 21st Century*. London: Palgrave Macmillan, pp. 97–127.

Wylde, C. (2018). 'Twenty-First Century Developmental States? Argentina under the Kirchners'. *Third World Quarterly*, *39*(6), 1115–1132.

Young, C. (1994). *The African Colonial State in Comparative Perspective*. New Haven, CT: Yale University Press.

Zeigler, M., and Truitt Nakata, G. (2014). *The Next Global Breadbasket: How Latin America Can Feed the World: A Call to Action for Addressing Challenges & Developing Solutions*. Washington, DC: Inter American Development Bank.

Index

Tables and figures are indicated by an italic *t* and *f*, following the paragraph number.

For the benefit of digital users, indexed terms that span two pages (e.g., 52–53) may, on occasion, appear on only one of those pages.

A

Acosta, A., 54
Adebayo, E., 6
AFIP (*Administración Federal de Ingresos Públicos*/Tax Collection Agency), 147
Africa, 35, 36–37, 80–81
  Belgian Empire and, 62–63
  British Empire and, 56–58, 59–60
  French Empire and, 60–61
African Union, 5–6
agriculture
  agricultural export-led development, 127
  export taxes, 45–46
  Latin America: agricultural exports, 9–10, 45–46, 74–75
  state and agricultural resources, 45–46
  tertib, 60–61
  see also rural sector (Argentina)
Alami, I., 195–196
Alfonsín, Raúl, 106, 108–109
Alfonsín, Ricardo, 180–181
Alt, J. E., 8
Amengual, M., 37–38
Andersson, P. F., 80
ANSES (*Administración Nacional de la Seguridad Social*/National Social Security Service), 178–179
Argentina
  1955–1989 post-Peronist politics, 98–99
  2001–2002 financial crisis, 112–113, 132–133
  2001–2008 key economic and social indicators, 121–122, 123*t*, 129, 131
  Barings Crisis, 84–85
  Concordancia government, 87–88, 90, 93
  contested state visions, 89, 98–99, 103, 112
  Convertibility Plan, 108–110, 115–117
  década infame (infamous decade), 88
  direct taxes, 93, 95–96, 97*f*, 99, 102–103
  economic liberalization, 105
  El Corralito policy, 115
  export-led development, 127, 131, 170–171
  federalism, 149–150
  indirect taxes, 92–96, 97*f*, 99, 102–103
  industrialization, 87, 90, 91–92, 96–98
  inequalities, 85, 91–92, 96
  inflation, 2, 96–97, 102–103, 107–108, 111, 116, 129–130, 132–133, 136, 209
  interventionism, 82–83, 108, 112
  lithium triangle, 210
  macroeconomic problems, 98–99, 106–108, 111, 132, 187, 200, 202–203
  market-led development, 108–110, 160, 188–189
  nationalization/renationalization, 91–92, 160, 162–163, 180–181, 202–203
  neoliberalism, 3–4, 108–110, 114–115, 120–121
  Plan Primavera (Spring Plan), 107–108
  poverty, 111, 116, 129, 136, 148–149, 165*f*, 165–166, 185–186, 197–198
  privatization, 108–110, 160, 162
  public spending, 82, 95, 95*t*, 103, 119–120, 121–122, 122*f*, 125–127, 129, 137
  Rio de la Plata (River Plate), 70
  state terrorism, 105
  tax capacity, 12, 95–96, 117–118, 134–135
  tax debates, 11, 87–88, 93, 114–115, 143–144, 197, 205
  tax evasion, 102–103, 115, 117–118, 184
  tax reforms, 93, 95–96, 98–99, 117, 128–130, 188–189
  tax system, 92–93

tax system (*Continued*)
  see also Argentina post 2008 revolt; currency-related issues (Argentina); debt (Argentina); emergency taxes (Argentina); export taxes (Argentina); fiscal issues (Argentina); interventionalist state (Argentina); Kirchnerismo; Kirchnerist statist model; Peronism; polarization (Argentina); redistribution (Argentina); rural sector (Argentina); tax collection (Argentina); tax ideas/ideology (Argentina); tax legitimacy (Argentina); welfare (Argentina)
Argentina post 2008 revolt, 144–145, 170–171
  2008–2011 key economic and social indicators, 146*t*, 147, 148–149, 152–153
  2008–2011 tax collection, 147, 148*f*, 148, 152–153
  2011–2015 key economic and social indicators, 154–156, 155*t*
  AUH, 163–166, 178–179
  concessions, 144, 149, 151–153, 170
  contested state visions, 144–145, 149
  Coparticipación mechanism, 151–153, 152*f*
  currency reserves, 145, 156–157, 160–161, 161*f*, 163–164, 166, 170–171, 200
  debt, 163–164, 170–171, 178–179, 200
  emergency taxes, 147, 148*f*, 149, 152–153, 156, 157*f*, 171
  export taxes, 145–147, 156, 166–171
  export taxes, legitimacy of 144, 156, 167–168, 169–171
  fiscal deficit, 145, 148–149, 153–157, 163, 166, 178–179, 184, 200
  fiscal/financial trap, 145, 153–154, 156–157, 159, 170–171, 191, 200–202
  inflation, 145–147, 149, 154–156, 163, 164–165, 170–171, 182, 189–191, 200
  interventionalist state, 145, 153, 200
  macroeconomic problems, 144–145, 153–154, 155*t*, 156, 173, 187, 190–191, 200
  oil/gas, 160*f*, 160–161, 162*f*, 162–164, 170–171, 182
  poverty, 148–149, 165*f*, 165–166
  price volatility, 144–145, 167–168, 170–171, 178, 200
  public spending, 144–145, 147–148, 148*f*, 149, 153–154, 157*f*, 159, 178–179
  redistribution, 145–149, 151–154, 157, 159, 166, 170–171, 178–179
  repatriation of capital, 182–184
  subsidies, 157–160, 161–162, 163–164, 178–179
ARI (*Coalición Cívica*/Civic Coalition), 130, 184–185, 187
AUH (*Asignación Universal por Hijo*/Universal Child Benefit), 163–166, 178–179
  evolution of, 164–165, 164*t*

B

Baud,M., 174
Bein, M., 148
Belgian Empire
  brutal extractive methods, 62
  CFS (Congo Free State), 62–63
  head taxes, 62–63
  Leopold II (King), 62–63
  trade taxes, 62
Bergman, M., 103, 159, 166–167, 178
Bertello, F., 175–176
Bértola, L., 32, 70–71, 72–73
Bertomeu, J. F. G., 37–38
Bethell, L., 72–73
Binner, Hermes, 153
Bird, R. M., 7–8, 34, 37–39
Bolivia, 42, 201–202, 206
  expropriation of oil rights from foreign entities, 77
  lithium triangle, 210
Bräutigam, D., 27
Brazil, 71–72, 75–76
  agricultural exports, 9–10
  debt, 71–72
  Lula da Silva, Luiz Inácio, 201
  popular classes, 46
  Portuguese Empire, 64–65
  redistribution, 201, 206
  shift to the Right, 201
  state-led interventionalist development, 77
Bretton Woods institutions, 77–78, 91–92
Bril-Mascarenhas, T., 157, 159

British Empire
British-Franco imperial wars, 57
extraction and conflict, 56–59
Stamp Act (1763–1767), 57–58
tax bargaining, 59–60, 207–208
trade taxes, 59–60
Broms, R., 58
Bulmer-Thomas, V., 70–71, 74–75, 77
Burchardt, H. J., 47–48
Buzzi, Eduardo, 137–138

C
Calvo, E., 178
Cambiemos (political party, Argentina), 182, 187
capitalism, 54
material interests, 26–27
taxation and, 25–27
tax reform challenges: interest-based accounts, 25
Caribbean, the, 59–60, 66
Carrió, Elisa, 130, 180–181, 184
Castañeda, N., 8, 40–42
Cavallo, Domingo, 110, 115, 117
Centeno, M. A., 24, 71–72
CEPAL (*Comisión Económica para América Latina y el Caribe*/Economic Commission for Latin America and the Caribbean), 118, 135–136, 139
Cetrángolo, O., 119
CGT (*Confederación General del Trabajo de la República Argentin*/General Confederation of Labour), 107
Chile, 71–73, 75–76, 128
export-led development, 210
lithium triangle, 210
Piñera, Sebastián, 201
popular classes, 46
redistribution, 201–202, 206
Spanish Empire, 69
state-led interventionalist development, 77
Clarence-Smith, W. G., 62
Clarín Group, 178–179
class
2008 export tax revolt and (Argentina), 176–177, 205
development tax strategies and class, 8
elite/upper classes, 41, 69–70, 80, 139
export taxes and class conflict, 11
fiscal policies and, 8
interventionalist state, tax strategies and, 4–5, 42–43, 47, 80
Latin America, 46–47
middle classes, 8, 41, 46, 120–121, 139, 167, 189–190, 198–199, 201–202, 205
popular classes, 8, 41, 46–47, 50–51, 80, 88, 128–129, 198–199, 204–205
redistribution and, 41–42, 88, 204–205
Resolution N.125 and class conflict, 176–177
see also rural sector (Argentina)
Coatsworth, J. H., 69–70
Cogneau, D., 55–56, 61
Collier, D., 46
Collier, R., 46
Colombo, L., 86–87
colonialism, 30, 207–208
debt, 71
direct taxes, 66–68
extractivism, 53–55
indirect taxes, 52, 55, 59, 61, 66–67, 207–208
Latin America, 65–67, 76, 80–81, 194–195
legacies, 52–55, 76
taxation and, 6–7, 13, 19, 52
tax bargaining, 55–56, 64, 80–81, 207–208
tax capacity, 6–7, 55–56, 64, 80–81
tax collection, 60, 63, 66, 71
tax design, 52, 57, 67–69, 71, 81
tax legitimacy, 55–56, 64, 80–81
see also Belgian Empire; British Empire; Dutch Empire; French Empire; Portuguese Empire; Spanish Empire
commodity
commodity booms and export taxes, 10, 42–45, 205–206
commodity booms and export taxes (Argentina), 11, 13–14, 102, 114–115, 127, 137, 198
commodity dependence and challenges in the twenty-first century, 208–211
commodity production and development, 5, 13
CONINAGRO (*Confederación Intercooperativa Agropecuaria*), 106, 110
COVID-19 pandemic, 194, 209

CRA (*Confederaciones Rurales Argentinas*), 106, 110, 122–125, 130, 137–138, 142
Craig, A., 90
currency-related issues (Argentina)
  currency controls, 166–167, 180, 181–182, 189–191, 202–203
  currency reserves, 96–97, 145, 156–157, 160–161, 161*f*, 163–164, 166, 170–171, 200
  devaluation, 96–97, 101, 116–119, 126–127, 156, 183, 198, 202–203, 204–205
  exchange rate, 96–97, 131, 134–135, 182

D

Dargent, E., 37–38
debt
  Brazil, 71–72
  debt-led development, 34, 43–44, 52, 70, 112–113
  direct taxes and, 71–72
  Latin America, 70–73, 75*t*, 75–77, 195
  Mexico, 71–72
  natural resource-led development and, 209–210
  Uruguay, 71–72
debt (Argentina), 71–72, 91–92, 98, 102–105, 107–108, 110–111, 111*t*, 115, 162
  2001 IMF debt default, 3–4, 13–14, 111–114, 116, 162–163, 188, 197–198
  2014 debt default, 190
  debt restructuring, 129, 170–171
  export taxes and, 83, 103, 107–108, 112–113, 117, 197–198
  Kirchner, Néstor, 129, 131, 198
  Macri, Mauricio, 203
  post 2008 revolt, 163–164, 170–171, 178–179, 200
  public spending and, 103
  tax reform and, 117
  see also Argentina
De la Rúa, Fernando, 115, 186
De León, G., 201–202
democracies, 60
  taxation in, 28–29, 36–37, 196
De Paiva Abreu, M., 65
developed countries, 26–27, 29–30, 36
developing countries
  challenges of raising tax, 5–8, 210–211
  development dilemmas, 1, 33–34
  export taxes, 1
  indirect taxes, 19
  industrialization, 31
  natural resource exports, 1–2, 19, 54
  tax capacity, 6, 30
  tax evasion, 19
  tax system, 5–6, 19, 29–30, 40, 52
  see also Global South
development, 30
  agricultural export-led development, 127
  commodity production and, 5, 13
  debt-led development, 34, 43–44, 52, 70, 112–113
  development dilemmas, 1, 33–34
  export-led development, 53, 73–77, 80, 127, 131, 170–171, 195, 210
  export taxes and, 4–5, 10–13, 34–35
  industrialization/industrial development, 30–32
  interventionalist state and, 32–33
  Latin America, 32, 45, 47–48, 70
  market-led development, 47–48, 75–76, 108–110, 160, 188–189
  natural resource-led development, 209–210
  political economy of, 12, 16–17, 34, 172, 203–204
  state and, 43–44, 48
  taxation and, 5–8, 10, 16, 18–19, 22, 23–24, 34–35, 52–53, 80, 203–205, 210–211
  theoretical framework: tax and development, 30–34, 43*f*, 50–51
  underdevelopment, 30–31, 33, 38–39, 45, 210–211
  see also economic development; interventionalist state; Kirchnerismo; sustainable development
DGA (*Dirección General de Aduanas*/Argentine Customs Tax Agency), 126
DGI (*Dirección General de Impositiva*), 95–96
Díaz-Alejandro, C., 78
Dietz, K., 47–48
direct taxes, 38
  Argentina, 93, 95–96, 97*f*, 99, 102–103
  colonialism, 66–68

debt and, 71–72
Global South, 52
Latin America, 77
left/right-wing ideologies and, 8, 40–41
Dixon, A. D., 195–196
Do Lago, L. A. C., 65
Donghi T. H., 70–71
Doyle, D., 8, 40–42
Duhalde, Eduardo, 116, 119–120
export taxes, 3–4, 14, 114, 116–119, 121–122, 125–126, 186, 197–198
Dunn, R. S., 59–60
Dupraz, Y., 55–56, 61
Dutch Empire, 63–64
tax bargaining, 64

E
ECLA (Economic Commission for Latin America), 31
ECLAC (Economic Commission for Latin America and the Caribbean), 31
economic development
Latin America: export-led growth, 53, 73–77, 80, 195
state and, 43–44
taxation and, 25
see also development
Ecuador, 206
Eichengreen, B., 75
emergency taxes (Argentina), 117, 129, 136, 203
contribution of, 121–122, 130–131, 137
export taxes, 117, 118–119, 121–126, 136, 140, 142–143, 171
post 2008 revolt, 147, 148*f*, 149, 152–153, 156, 157*f*, 171
Engerman, S. L., 66
England (feudal), 26–27
Estenssoro, María Eugenia, 184–185
Etcevehere, Luis Miguel, 174–175
European Union, 6
export taxes
agricultural exports, 45–46
as 'bad tax', 44, 119, 203
challenges, 9
class conflict, 11
commodity booms and, 10, 42–45, 205–206
competitiveness and, 44
contentious nature of, 1–2, 10, 23, 44, 49
developing countries, 1
development and, 4–5, 10–13, 34–35
fiscal policies and, 1
Global South, 9, 22–23
importance of, 1
interventionalist state and, 1–2, 9, 32–33, 45, 50, 80
Latin America, 50, 195–196
natural resource exports, 1, 9–10
state *versus* markets conflict, 18–19, 23, 42–43, 45, 47, 49
tax ideology, 16, 23, 80, 195–196, 205–206
tax legitimacy, 42–43
theoretical framework, 22, 34–35, 42–44, 47, 49–50
use and functions of, 9, 44–45
export taxes (Argentina), 11–13
1965–1970 export tax levels on major exports, 101*t*, 101–102
1980s reintroduction of, 106–108
2001–2008 commodity prices and tax levels, 134*f*
2002 reintroduction of, 3–4, 116–118
2002–2007 evolution of, 125*t*
2002–2015 evolution of agricultural export taxes, 133–134, 135*t*
2022 protests, 3
abolition of, 3–4, 105, 106–108, 109–110, 117–118, 209
commodity boom and, 11, 13–14, 102, 114–115, 127, 137, 198
Congress and, 3
contentious nature of, 11, 82–83, 99–100, 102–104, 114, 130–131, 167
contested state visions, 91, 133–136, 144–145, 171
as crisis response, 3–4, 11, 13–14, 20, 114, 115–120, 130–131, 142–143, 185, 197–198, 203–205
debt and, 83, 103, 107–108, 112–113, 117, 197–198
Duhalde, Eduardo, 3–4, 14, 114, 116–119, 121–122, 125–126, 186, 197–198
as emergency taxes, 117, 118–119, 121–126, 136, 140, 142–143, 171
extractivism, 82–83, 167, 172–173

as fault line, 11–12, 15, 21, 83, 114–115, 143–145, 171, 174–175, 189, 192–193, 199, 205
Fernández, Alberto, 2–3, 4–5, 208
fiscal policies and, 2–3, 114, 121–122, 132–133
introduction of, 99–104
Kirchner, Cristina Fernández de, 198–199
Kirchner, Néstor, 3–4, 14, 114, 121–125, 126–130, 198
Kirchnerismo, 12, 121, 130–131, 136, 172–173, 197
Kirchnerist statist model, 3, 11–12, 14, 21, 114–115, 129–131, 137, 171, 192–193, 197–200
limitations of export tax regime, 21, 197–203
Macri, Mauricio, 188–189, 192–193, 202–203
Menem, Carlos, 109–110
Milei, Javier, 209
national development and, 16, 83
opposition to, 19, 83, 112, 119, 130
Peronism, 19, 82–83, 112, 192
political polarization, 83, 114, 172–174
post 2008 revolt, 145–147, 156, 166–171
redistribution, 12, 82–83, 103–104, 107, 121–126, 127–128, 130–131, 140, 171–174, 197
rent-seeking, 11
rural sector, 11, 14, 82, 99–100, 102, 106–108, 112, 129, 130–131, 167–169, 185, 197–198, 209
soybean and beef exports, 127–129
state *versus* markets conflict, 11–12, 14–15, 144–145
tax capacity, 12, 117–118
tax collection, 117–118, 121–122, 127–128, 167
tax design, 11, 15, 20, 83, 117–119, 122–125, 172–173
tax ideas/ideology, 144–145, 167, 171, 190–192
tax legitimacy, 11, 13–14, 20, 82–83, 112–114, 119, 122–125, 130, 142–144, 156, 167–168, 169–171, 197–198
taxpayers, 9–10, 20, 117–118
tax reforms, 128–130, 140–141
as temporary measure, 99–100, 119, 122–125
unfairness, 167–168, 171, 209
volatility of markets, 82–83
see also Argentina; export tax revolt (Argentina, 2008); *retenciones*; rural sector (Argentina)
export tax revolt (Argentina, 2008), 3, 4–5, 138–139, 198–199
barriers to domestic resource mobilization, 3, 10
class argument, 176–177, 205
contested state visions, 12, 15–16, 20–21, 172–173, 198–199, 204–205
impact of, 5, 144, 149, 171, 173–174, 176–177, 182–183, 192–193
intersectoral response, 14, 20, 139, 143, 198–199
key arguments, 13–16
Kirchner, Cristina Fernández de, 3–5
Kirchnerist opposition, 15, 20, 199, 205
Kirchnerist statist model, 11–12, 15–16, 20–21, 114–115, 139, 142–143, 175, 205
Mesa de Enlace, 137–139
mistrust between producers and government, 141–142
polarization, 10, 12, 15, 20–21, 114–115, 135–136, 142, 198–199, 204–205
protests, 138–139, 175, 176–177, 198–199
retenciones, 15–16
rural sector, 14, 20, 137–139, 140–142, 172, 175, 198–199
social conflict and, 114–115
social redistribution programme and, 4–5, 14–16, 20, 114–115, 137, 143, 172, 176–177, 198–199, 204–205
state/taxpayers conflictive relation, 13–15
strikes and roadblocks, 4, 138–139
tax ideology, 4–5, 12, 15, 20, 172–173, 204–205
taxpayers, 14–15
tax reform, 4, 14, 21, 132–136, 137–138
uneven redistribution of export tax revenues, 20
violence, 138–139
see also Argentina; export taxes (Argentina); Resolution N.125
Exposición Rural (Rural Farm Show, Palermo, Argentina), 174–176
extractivism

colonialism, 53–55
as development strategy, 54–55
export taxes (Argentina), 82–83, 167, 172–173
fiscal extractivism, 52–53, 62–63, 79–81, 83, 197, 210
Global South, 53–55, 80–81
Latin America, 47–48, 52–53, 70–74, 77, 79–80
nationalist extractivism, 48–49
neo-extractivism, 48
state autonomy and extractivism: compensatory state, 205–207
see also Belgian Empire; British Empire; Dutch Empire; French Empire; natural resource exports; natural resources; Portuguese Empire; Spanish Empire

F

FAA (*Federación Agraria Argentina*/Argentine Agrarian Federation), 85–86, 106, 110, 119, 130, 137–138, 176
Fairfield, T., 141, 168–169, 186
FAOSTAT (Food and Agriculture Organization of the United Nations), 2
FAUNEN (*Frente Amplio UNEN*), 187
Fernández, Alberto, 200–201, 203, 208–210
export taxes, 2–3, 4–5, 208
Fernández de Kirchner, Cristina, *see* Kirchner, Cristina Fernández de
FIEL (*Fundación de Investigaciones Económicas Latinoamericanas*/Latin American Economic Research Foundation), 118
fiscal issues
class ideology and fiscal policies, 8
export taxes and fiscal policies, 1
fiscal extractivism, 52–53, 62–63, 79–81, 83, 197, 210
see also tax reform
fiscal issues (Argentina)
2008 export tax revolt and, 4–5
export taxes and, 2–3, 114, 121–122, 132–133
fiscal deficit, 104*f*, 105, 119
fiscal surplus, 122, 122*f*, 129, 130–131, 132–133, 148
Peronism: fiscal deficit, 95, 95*t*, 96–98, 103–104
post 2008 revolt: fiscal deficit, 145, 148–149, 153–157, 163, 166, 178–179, 184, 200
post 2008 revolt: fiscal trap, 145, 153–154, 156–157, 159, 170–171, 191, 200–202
Fishlow,A., 79
Fjeldstad, O. H., 35
Flores-Macías, G. A., 34–35, 204–205
Fofack, H., 60
food security 1–2, 9, 44–45, 194
FPV (*Frente para la Victoria*/Victory Front), 120–121, 126–127, 136, 139, 158
2013 legislative elections, 187
2015 presidential elections, 191
redistributive agenda, 121–122
Frankema, E., 57–58, 59–60, 207–208
French Empire, 60–61, 207–208
capitation/head tax, 61
tax capacity, 61
trade taxes, 61

G

Gaggero, A., 177–178
Gaggero, J., 177–178
Gardner, L., 57–58, 207–208
GATT (General Agreement on Tariffs and Trade), 77–78
Gerchunoff, P., 91, 97, 102, 201–202
Giraudo, M. E., 141
global financial crisis (2007/2008), 132–133, 147
globalization, 41
Global South, 1, 194, 210–211
development and taxation, 52–53
direct taxes, 52
export taxes, 9, 22–23
extractivism, 53–55, 80–81
indirect taxes, 52, 207–208
natural resource exports, 22–23, 80–81, 210–211
taxation, 5, 19, 22, 52
tax collection, 30
tax evasion, 52
see also developing countries
Gómez Sabaini, J. C., 119, 176–177, 184
Gough, I., 47
Grafe, R., 69, 207–208

Great Depression (1929–1939), 63, 74–75, 77–78
Grugel, J., 48–49, 125–126
Gudynas, E., 11, 12–13, 18–19, 48–49, 54–55, 206–207

H

Haggard, S., 36–37
Hall, P. A., 39–40, 172–173, 204–205
Heclo, H., 39
Hesse-Biber, S., 16–17
Hibbs, D. A., 8
historical sociology, 18–19, 23–25, 26–28, 50–51, 207
Hora, R., 84–85, 86–87, 93
Huber, E., 185–186

I

IAPI (*Instituto Argentino de Promoción del Intercambio*), 90–91, 93, 98–101, 112
  disbanding of, 98–100
IDB (Inter-America Development Bank), 9
ideas/ideology
  policy and, 39–40
  see also tax ideas/ideology
IMF (International Monetary Fund), 5–6, 10, 41
  2001 IMF debt default (Argentina), 3–4, 13–14, 111–114, 116, 162–163, 188, 197–198
  Argentina and, 101, 103–104, 108, 109–110, 182–183, 203
INDEC (*Instituto Nacional de Estadísticas y Censos de la República Argentina*), 137, 154–156
  data manipulation, 129–130, 132–133, 148–149, 165, 182–183, 187–188
indirect taxes
  Argentina, 92–96, 97*f*, 99, 102–103
  British Empire, 57–59
  colonialism, 52, 55, 59, 61, 66–67, 207–208
  developing countries, 19
  Global South, 52, 207–208
  indirect trade taxes, 55, 59, 61, 66
  Latin America, 70
  left/right-wing ideologies and, 8, 40–41
  Spanish Empire, 68–69
Indonesia, 9, 63–64
industrialization, 54, 81
  Argentina, 87, 90, 91–92, 96–98
  developing countries, 31
  industrial development, 30–32
  state-led industrialization, 75–76
  see also ISI
Industrial Revolution, 73, 84
institutions
  institutional weakness, 36–37
  Latin America, 36–37
  politics of institutional tax capacity, 36–38
  taxation: institutional-based accounts, 7–8, 22–23, 36–38, 203–204
interests, 25–26
  challenges to interest-based theories, 39
  Latin America, 35–36, 39
  left/right-wing politics, 41
  material interests, 26–27
  taxation and, 26–27
  taxation: interest-based accounts, 7–8, 12, 18–19, 22, 25, 26–27, 34–36, 47, 203–204, 205–206
interventionalist state
  class, tax strategies and, 4–5, 42–43, 47, 80
  development and, 32–33
  export taxes and, 1–2, 9, 32–33, 45, 50, 80
  interventionalist developmental state, 48–49, 203
  Latin America, 46, 79–80
  natural resource exports, 12–13, 47–48, 205–206
  redistribution, 9–10, 41, 47, 79–80
  state-led interventionalist development, 77
  tax ideas/ideology, 40–41, 50
interventionalist state (Argentina), 82–83, 108, 112, 203, 205
  exhaustion of interventionist high-spending model, 201
  Peronism, 89–90, 112
  state-led interventionalist development, 77, 83
  see also Kirchnerist statist model
Irigoin, M. A., 69, 207–208
ISI (import substitution industrialization), 31–33, 75–76, 78–81

J

James, D., 88
Johnson, C. A., 210

K

Kaldor, N., 7–8, 30, 33–34, 38–39, 103, 210–211
Kaufman, R. R., 36–37
Kicillof, Axel, 163–164, 168
Kirchner, Cristina Fernández de
  2007-2011 first presidency, 130–131, 136, 185–186, 198–199
  2008 export tax revolt, 3–5
  2011-2015 second presidency, 153–154, 164, 167, 170, 178, 191–192
  2012 *Once* train disaster (Buenos Aires), 180–181, 189–190
  2013 floods in Greater La Plata, 180, 190
  corruption, 148–149, 179–181, 182–185, 187–192
  economic deterioration and commodity headwinds, 132–133
  'expansionary phase of populist strategy', 148
  infrastructure spending, neglect of, 180–181, 190
  interventionalist state, 145, 153, 173, 181
  loss of legitimacy to govern, 189–191
  popularity, 153
  redistribution, 4, 20, 132–133, 135–136, 145–149, 151–153
  Resolution N.125, 4, 135–136
  strikes and protests, 184–185, 189–191
  subsidies, 135–136, 153–154, 157–160, 161–162, 163–164, 175–176, 190, 205
  welfare, 164–166
  see also Argentina post 2008 revolt; export tax revolt (Argentina, 2008); Kirchnerismo; Resolution N.125
Kirchner, Néstor, 120–121
  2003-2007 First Kirchnerismo, 120–121, 131, 198
  debt, 129, 131, 198
  export taxes, 3–4, 14, 114, 121–125, 126–130, 198
  interventionalist state, 122, 126
  popularity, 131, 185–186
  redistribution, 12, 121–127, 130, 151–152
  subsidies, 119–120, 129, 158
  tax reforms, 128–130
  welfare, 119–120, 125–126
  see also Kirchnerismo
Kirchnerismo
  clientelism, 177–178
  emergency taxes, 136
  'energy demagogy', 182
  export taxes, 12, 121, 130–131, 136, 172–173, 197
  opposition to, 12, 15, 20, 130, 171, 173, 174–176, 177–178, 180–189, 190–193, 198–200, 205
  Peronism and, 120–121, 125–126
  polarization, 142–143, 151, 172–173, 174–182, 184–185, 190–192, 200
  redistribution, 4, 12, 130–131, 143, 152–153, 166, 178–180, 185–186, 192–193, 202–203
  Resolution N.125 and, 143
  retenciones, 15–16, 174, 190–191, 192–193, 199
  tax ideas/ideology and, 15, 21, 139, 149, 172–174, 175–185, 187, 190–191, 192–193, 204–205
  'won decade', 180–181
  see also Kirchner, Cristina Fernández de; Kirchner, Néstor; Kirchnerist statist model
Kirchnerist statist model, 142, 175–176, 187, 190–191
  2008 export tax revolt, 11–12, 15–16, 20–21, 114–115, 139, 142–143, 175, 205
  continuity into Macri's presidency, 202–203
  criticism, 180–183, 192, 199–200
  export taxes, 3, 11–12, 14, 21, 114–115, 129–131, 137, 171, 192–193, 197–200
  Kirchner, Cristina Fernández de, 145, 153, 173, 181
  Kirchner, Néstor, 122, 126
  post 2008 revolt, 145, 153, 200
  state-led development, 114–115, 120–121, 143
  see also Kirchner, Cristina Fernández de; Kirchner, Néstor; Kirchnerismo
Kulfas, M., 174

L

Lamberto, Oscar, 119
Lanata, J., 135
Lara, C., 70–71, 73–74

Lashitew, A. A., 6
Latin America
  agricultural exports, 9–10, 45–46, 74–75
  classes, 46
  colonialism, 65–67, 76, 80–81, 194–195
  customs taxes, 76, 76*t*, 77, 80–81
  debt, 70–73, 75*t*, 75–77, 195
  debt-led development, 70
  debt-to-export ratios, 75*t*, 75
  development, 32, 45, 47–48, 70
  direct taxes, 77
  export-led growth, 53, 73–77, 80, 195
  export taxes, 50, 195–196
  extractivism, 47–48, 52–53, 70–74, 77, 79–80
  indirect taxes, 70
  interventionalist state, 46, 79–80
  left-wing politics, 12–13, 78–81, 126, 200–201
  macroeconomy, 194–195, 201–202
  nation-state formation, 71, 73–74
  natural resource exports, 35–36, 42, 45, 47–48, 73–74, 78, 195–196
  neoliberalism, 78–79
  pink tide, 48, 50–51, 126, 197, 200–201, 206
  political economy, 38–39
  post-neoliberalism and return of the state, 48–50
  poverty, 72–73
  protectionism, 77–79
  redistribution, 47–48, 78–80, 200–202
  right-wing politics, 200–201
  state-building, 71
  structural change, 75–76, 78–79
  taxation: institutional-based accounts, 36–37
  taxation: interest-based accounts, 35–36
  tax collection, 71–72, 77, 194–195
  tax evasion, 36–37, 194–195
  tax ideas/ideology, 40, 42–43, 79–81
  tax legitimacy, 81, 195
  tax raising, challenges of, 5
  tax systems, 65, 80–81, 194–195
  trade liberalization, 78–79
  trade taxes, 38–39, 65–66, 73–74, 77, 80–81
  trade unions, 46
  Wars of Independence, 35–36, 45–46, 52–53, 70–73, 81
  wealth concentration, 41
  welfare, 46–48, 78–79
  see also Portuguese Empire; Spanish Empire
Latin American Development School, 32
left-wing politics
  Latin America, 12–13, 78–81, 126, 200–201
  Left turn, 50–51, 126
  redistribution, 41, 80
  social democratic governments, 8
  tax ideology, 8, 10, 40–41, 45, 50–51, 79–80, 196
  see also Peronism; politics
Lenicov, Jorge Remes, 119
Levi, M., 23–24, 28
Llach, L., 91, 97, 102
Lousteau, Martín, 133, 134–135, 175–176
Luna, J. P., 72–73
Lupu, N., 162

M

Macri, Mauricio, 187–190
  2015–2019 presidency, 191, 200–201, 202–203
  debt, 203
  export taxes, 188–189, 192–193, 202–203
  inflation, 203
  macroeconomic problems, 203
Mann, M., 23–24
Manse, M., 64
Manzetti, L., 106–107, 110
Martin, I., 28–29, 34–35
Martínez, C., 70–71, 73–74
Martínez de Hoz, José Alfredo, 105
Marx, K., 25–27
materialism, 7, 18–19, 22, 26–27, 205–206
McClure, J., 66–68, 207–208
Mehrotra, A., 28–29, 34–35
Menem, Carlos, 108, 111, 115, 120–121
  export taxes, 109–110
  reformist agenda, 108–111, 160, 162
MERCOSUR (Southern Common Market) 109–110
Mesplé-Somps, S., 55–56, 61
methodology, 16–18
  Argentina as case study, 16, 19, 21, 81, 82, 111–112, 197
  data, 16–18
  interviews, 17–18

mixed-methods research design, 16–17
qualitative analysis, 16–18
Mexico, 73, 206
debt, 71–72
expropriation of oil rights from foreign entities, 77
Spanish Empire, 66, 69
state-led interventionalist development, 77
Miguens, Luciano, 122–125
Milei, Javier, 209
Mitre, Bartolomé, 84
Moore, M., 28
Munck, G. L., 72–73
Murillo, M. V., 178

N
Nación, La (newspaper), 178–179
Napoleonic Wars, 70–71, 73
Natanson, J., 201–202
natural resource exports
dependency on, 21–23, 31, 35–36, 45, 73–74, 75–76, 170–171, 203–204, 209–211
developing countries and, 1–2, 12, 54
end of commodity booms, 201
Global South, 22–23, 80–81, 210–211
interventionalist state, 12–13, 47–48, 205–206
Latin America, 35–36, 42, 45, 47–48, 73–74, 78, 195–196
modalities of natural resource revenue extraction, 42–43, 43*f*, 205–206
redistribution and, 42
state-owned enterprises, 42, 205–206
transnational corporations, 47–48
see also export taxes; extractivism
natural resources
fiscal extractivism and, 52–53
natural resource-led development, 209–210
resource curse, 45–46
resource dependency, 5, 12, 33
resource nationalism, 12–13, 49, 205–207, 210
see also extractivism
Navarro, V., 4–5, 42
neoclassical economics, 32–34, 44–45
neo-developmentalism, 12–13
neoliberalism, 41, 47–48
Argentina, 3–4, 108–110, 114–115, 120–121
Latin America, 78–79
see also Washington Consensus
new fiscal sociology, 18–19, 27–28, 50–51, 207
Nietzsche, F., 26

O
Ocampo, E., 85
Ocampo, J. A., 32, 72–73
OECD (Organisation for Economic Co-operation and Development), 10, 33, 110–111, 194
tax governance, 5–6
O'Rourke, K. H., 55, 65
Ozarow, D., 190–191

P
Pagni, C., 182
Panizza, F., 48–49, 108–109, 126
Paraguay, 9, 201–202
Parsons, T., 26–27
Peretti, Pedro, 176
Perón, Isabel Martinez de, 101–102, 103–104
1976 deposition, 103–105
Perón, Juan Domingo, 87–88
1943 military coup, 87–88
1946–1955 first presidency, 87–89
1955 deposition, 97–98
1973–1974 second presidency, 101–102, 103–104
death, 103–104
Partido Laborista (Labour Party), 88
as secretary of labour, 88
Peronism, 13, 88–89, 99, 120–121
1952 *Plan de Emergencia*, 97–98
agrarian reform, 92
export taxes, 19, 82–83, 112, 192
extracting from landed elite, 88, 90–93
fiscal deficit, 95, 95*t*, 96–98, 103
interventionalist state, 89–90, 112
Kirchnerismo and, 120–121, 125–126
left-wing politics, 19
national economic independence, 91–92, 96
nationalization, 91–92
PJ, 89, 92–93

Peronism (*Continued*)
political cleavages, 85–86, 90–91, 112, 135–136
popular/working classes, 46, 88–90, 92–93, 103–104, 125–126
public spending, 95, 95*t*, 103
redistribution, 19, 83, 88–89, 90–93, 95–97, 112
rural sector, 87–88, 90–93, 99–100, 102, 112, 135
social justice, 89, 91–92
state-led development, 83
trade unions, 88
welfare, 89–90, 92–93, 125–126
see also Argentina
Peru, 42, 69, 73, 201–202
Peruzzotti, E., 200
Phillips, N., 17
PJ (*Partido Justicialista*/Justicialist Party), 89, 108, 110, 120–121
polarization (Argentina), 13, 98–99, 107–108, 200
2008 export tax revolt, 10, 12, 15, 20–21, 114–115, 135–136, 142, 198–199, 204–205
export taxes, 83, 114, 172–174
export taxes as fault line, 11–12, 15, 21, 83, 114–115, 143–145, 171, 174–175, 189, 192–193, 199, 205
Kirchnerismo/the Kirchners, 142–143, 151, 172–173, 174–182, 184–185, 190–192, 200
Peronism, 85–86, 90–91, 112, 135–136
retenciones 199
tax as fault line, 192–193, 199
tax ideology and, 172–173, 174–177, 200
political economy, 144
Argentina, 20, 132–133, 134–135, 201–202
of development, 12, 16–17, 34, 172, 203–204
Latin America, 38–39
of taxation, 6, 16, 18–19, 25, 34–35, 203–204
politics
institutional tax capacity and, 7–8, 36–38
political cleavages and tax ideologies, 38–43, 50, 196
taxation and, 7–8, 10, 34–35, 38–39, 184, 210–211
tax capacity and, 7–8
tax collection and, 103
taxing for development, 8
tax reform and, 7–8, 10, 38–39
see also left-wing politics; polarization (Argentina); right-wing politics
Portes, R., 75
Portuguese Empire, 64–65, 66–67, 194–195
Brazil, 64–65
tax bargaining, 65
tax collection, 71
trade taxes, 65
Post, A. E., 157, 159
post-neoliberalism, 48–51, 206
poverty, 44
Argentina, 111, 116, 129, 136, 148–149, 165*f*, 165–166, 185–186, 197–198
Latin America, 72–73
tax systems and, 33–34
Prasad, M., 28–29, 34–35
Prebisch, R., 31–33, 93
PRO (*Propuesta Republicana*/Republican Proposal), 186–187
2013 legislative elections, 187
2015 presidential elections, 188–189, 200–201
see also Macri, Mauricio
protectionism
Latin America, 77–79
trade liberalization *versus* protectionism, 77–80

R

Rakner, L., 35
Rapetti, M., 201–202
Rapisarda, M. J., 182–183
redistribution
Brazil, 201, 206
Chile, 201–202, 206
class and, 41–42, 88, 204–205
as conflictual, 47, 52–53
interventionalist state, 9–10, 41, 47, 79–80
Latin America, 47–48, 78–80, 200–202
left-wing policies, 41, 80
natural resource exports and, 42
natural resource-led development and, 209–210
'solidarity hypothesis,' 29
taxes and, 8–9, 22–23

theoretical framework, 22–23, 38, 41, 47
uneven redistribution, 20, 28, 38
see also welfare
redistribution (Argentina), 87–88
2008 export tax revolt and, 4–5, 14–16, 20, 114–115, 137, 143, 172, 176–177, 198–199, 204–205
Coparticipación mechanism, 20, 150–152
export taxes and, 12, 82–83, 103–104, 107, 121–126, 127–128, 130–131, 140, 171–174, 197
federalism and, 150–151
Kirchner, Cristina Fernández de, 4, 20, 132–133, 135–136, 145–149, 151–153
Kirchner, Néstor, 12, 121–127, 130, 151–152
Kirchnerismo, 4, 12, 130–131, 143, 152–153, 166, 178–180, 185–186, 192–193, 202–203
Peronism, 19, 83, 88–89, 90–93, 95–97, 112
post 2008 revolt, 145–149, 151–154, 157, 159, 166, 170–171, 178–179
redistributive conflicts, 201–203
tax ideas/ideology, 167, 174, 179–180, 190–191
see also redistribution
REPSOL S.A., 160, 163–164, 182
Resolution N.125, 4, 12, 133–136
banded taxation system, 133*t*, 140–141
class conflict, 176–177
Congress vote on, 139–140, 143
contentious nature of, 14–15, 134–136, 139–141, 143
implementation of, 134–136
Kirchner, Cristina Fernández de, 4, 135–136
Kirchnerismo and, 143
opposition to, 137–139, 140–141, 176, 198–199
presidential decree on, 136, 142
as progressive tax mechanism, 133–134
rent-seeking, 14, 135, 137–138, 139–142
revocation of, 140, 143, 176
Senate vote on, 140
tax capacity, 117–118, 134–135
tax design, 142
tax ideas/ideology, 175–177
tax legitimacy, 14–16, 134–135, 142
see also export taxes (Argentina); export tax revolt (Argentina, 2008)
Resolution N.126, 169–170
retenciones (withholdings, Argentina), 2–3, 99–100, 199, 204–205
2008 export tax revolt, 15–16
Kirchnerismo, 15–16, 174, 190–191, 192–193, 199
retenciones móviles, 133, 139–140, 142, 173, 175–176
retenciones segmentadas, 169–170
see also export taxes (Argentina)
Richardson, N., 44–45
Riggirozzi, M. P., 48–49, 125–126
right-wing politics, 80
Argentina, centre-Right, 184–185, 186–188, 191, 192–193, 200–202
Argentina, Libertarianism, 209
Brazil, 201
Latin America, 200–201
tax ideology, 8, 10, 40–42, 196
see also politics
Rodríguez Saá, Adolfo, 116
Rostow, W. W., 30
Rouvier, Ricardo, 175
Rua, M., 177–178
Rueda, D., 41
rural sector (Argentina)
1990s, 110–111
2008 export tax revolt, 14, 20, 137–139, 140–142, 172, 175, 198–199
agricultural commodities/exports, 9–10, 83–85, 90, 99, 109*t*, 109–110, 111–112, 116–117
Austral Plan, 107–108
Britain and, 86, 90
business leaders/UIA, 86–87
campo (countryside), 3
chacareros (smaller farmers), 85–86
class conflicts, 85–88, 92, 105
Concordancia government, 87, 90
conflicts in, 84–88, 90–91, 99–100, 105
contribution of, 90, 91*t*
extracting from landed elite, 88, 90–93, 99, 106–107, 111–112
extractivism, 116–117
'fiscal pact', 110–111
Grito de Alcorta rebellion, 85–86
Junta Nacional de Granos (*Grain Regulatory Board*), 90

rural sector (Argentina) (*Continued*)
landed elite/*estancieros*, 82–83, 84–88, 92, 99–100, 105, 111–112
land taxes, 87–88, 90
Menem: reduced conflict and rural-sector transformations, 110–111
Pampas, the, 82–85, 87, 92, 209
Peronism, 87–88, 90–93, 99–100, 102, 112, 135
political cleavages, 85–86, 90–91, 112, 135–136
Pronagro (national agricultural programme), 106
rural *versus* industrial cleavage, 106–107
US and, 86
see also export taxes (Argentina); FAA; IAPI; SRA
Russia, 128
2022 invasion of Ukraine 2, 194, 209

S

Saffon, M. P., 37–38
Sanchez, O., 13
Sánchez Román, J. A., 90, 93, 95, 100, 102–103
SAPs (structural adjustment programmes), 41
Saurrat, A., 60
Schneider, B. R., 101–102
Schopenhauer, A., 26
Schumpeter, J.A., 24
Scioli, Daniel, 191
SDGs (Sustainable Development Goals), 5–6, 33, 194
see also sustainable development
Singh, N., 195–196
Skocpol, T., 23–24, 37
Smith, A., 25, 61
Smith, W. C., 108–109
Sokoloff, K. L., 66
Spanish Empire, 66–70, 194–195
aduanas (customs duties), 68, 70
alcabalas (sales tax), 68–69
direct taxes, 68
indirect taxes, 68–69
tax bargaining, 66–68, 207–208
tax collection, 71
tax design, 67–69
tax inequality, 68–69
tax legitimacy, 67, 69
tax revolts, 69
trade taxes, 66
SRA (*Sociedad Rural Argentina*/Argentine Rural Society), 14, 84–85, 106, 110, 122–125
export taxes and, 106–108, 119, 126–127, 130, 174–176
members in government positions, 101–102, 107–108
upper class, 84–85
state
agricultural resources and, 45–46
compensatory state, 11, 18–19, 49–50, 205–207
development and, 43–44, 48
developmental state, 43*f*, 48–49, 203, 205–206
minimal state, 32–33, 40–41, 47–48
neoliberal state, 41
state-owned enterprises, 42, 162, 205–206
tax and state-building, 23–25, 71
tax and vision of state, 19, 22–23
see also interventionalist state
state capacity
Argentina, 20
strong state capacity, 37
taxation and, 27, 36–38, 41
tax collection and, 22–23
tax compliance and, 23–24, 37
tax enforcement, 23–24, 37
weak state capacity, 37–38
state/society relationship
Latin America, 45–46
post-neoliberalism, 48–49
taxes, 34–35, 196
tax legitimacy, 24–25, 27–29
Steinmo, S., 39–40
Stephens, J. D., 185–186
structural change, 1–2
Latin America, 75–76, 78–79
see also SAPs
structuralism, 31–33, 93
subsidies (Argentina), 107, 149–150
agricultural subsidies, 169–170
energy subsidies, 119–120, 129, 157–158, 160, 161–162, 178–179, 182
Kirchner, Cristina Fernández de, 135–136, 153–154, 157–160, 161–162, 163–164, 175–176, 190, 205
Kirchner, Néstor and, 119–120, 129, 158

post 2008 revolt, 157–160, 161–162, 163–164, 178–179
transport subsidies, 157, 158–159, 178–179
utility subsidies, 159
sustainable development, 1
see also SDGs

T

Tanzi, V., 6, 13, 44
taxation
capitalism and, 25–27
challenges of raising tax, 5–8, 24–25, 210–211
colonialism and, 6–7, 13, 19, 52
as conflictual, 52–53
in democracies, 28–29, 36–37, 196
development and, 5–8, 10, 16, 18–19, 22, 23–24, 30–35, 43*f*, 50–51, 52–53, 80, 203–205, 210–211
Global South, 5, 19, 22, 52
interventionalist state, class and, 4–5, 42–43, 47, 80
political economy of, 6, 16, 18–19, 25, 34–35, 203–204
politics and, 7–8, 10, 34–35, 38–39, 184, 210–211
redistribution and, 8–9, 22–23
roles of, 24, 27
state-building and, 23–25, 71
theoretical contributions, 203–211
war and, 24, 71
welfare and, 26–27, 30
tax bargaining, 6–7, 19, 24–25, 52–53, 66–67, 207–208
British Empire, 59–60, 207–208
colonialism, 55–56, 64, 80–81, 207–208
Dutch Empire, 64
Portuguese Empire, 65
quasi-voluntary compliance and, 28
Spanish Empire, 66–68, 207–208
tax capacity, 5, 68, 117–118, 196
Argentina, 12, 95–96, 117–118, 134–135
colonialism, 6–7, 55–56, 64, 80–81
developing countries, 6, 30
French Empire, 61
institutional capacity, 7–8, 22–23
lack of/weak capacity, 22–23, 80–81
political will and, 7–8, 196
politics of institutional tax capacity, 7–8, 36–38
theoretical framework, 23–25
see also tax collection
tax collection
administrative approach to, 36
barriers to, 7, 12, 35–37
colonial tax collection, 60, 63, 66, 71
Global South, 30
inequalities in, 66–67
Latin America, 71–72, 77, 194–195
low/poor tax collection, 30, 33–34, 37–38, 43–45, 71–72
politics and, 103
professionalized tax collection, 33
tax capacity and, 22–23
theoretical framework, 23
see also tax capacity
tax collection (Argentina)
1930s–1990s, 94*t*, 95–96, 99, 102–103
2008–2011, 147, 148*f*, 148, 152–153
export taxes, 117–118, 121–122, 127–128, 167
federalism, 149–150
tax compliance, 27–29
contractual/vertical 'fiscal exchange' models, 28–29
horizontal 'political community' models, 28–29
quasi-voluntary compliance, 28
state capacity and, 23–24, 37
tax legitimacy and, 28–29
tax debates, 25
Argentina, 87–88, 93, 114–115, 143–144, 171, 197, 205
tax design, 8, 18, 21
colonialism, 52, 57, 67–69, 71, 81
contentious tax design, 68
export taxes (Argentina), 11, 15, 20, 83, 117–119, 122–125, 172–173
Resolution N.125 (Argentina), 142
tax legitimacy and, 18–19
tax enforcement, 7, 23–24, 36–38, 58
taxes: types
automobile taxes, 149–150
capital, taxes on, 8, 40–41, 80
consumption taxes, 8, 38, 40–41, 93
corporation taxes, 8, 40–41, 95–96
customs taxes, 59–60, 65, 71, 76, 76*t*, 77, 80–81

taxes: types (*Continued*)
debits and credits, taxes on, 167–168
income taxes, 8, 33–34, 40–41, 93, 95–96, 149–150
land taxes, 87–88, 90, 110
property taxes, 110
real estate taxes, 149–150
sales taxes, 65, 68–70, 96
stamp taxes, 149–150
VAT, 110
see also direct taxes; emergency taxes; export taxes; indirect taxes; trade taxes
tax evasion, 27–28
Argentina, 102–103, 115, 117–118, 184
developing countries, 19
Global South, 52
Latin America, 36–37, 194–195
tax governance, 5–6
'tax misgovernance', 194
tax ideas/ideology
contested state visions, 40–41, 45, 204–205
development and, 21
development tax strategies and class, 8
export taxes, 16, 23, 80, 195–196, 205–206
importance of, 203–205
interventionalist state, 40–41, 47
Latin America, 40, 42–43, 79–81
left/right-wing politics, 8, 10, 40–42, 45, 50–51, 79–80, 196
modalities of natural resource revenue extraction, 42–43, 43*f*
political cleavages and tax ideologies, 38–43, 50, 196
politics of taxing for development, 8
state *versus* markets conflict, 23, 45
theoretical contributions, 204–207, 210
theoretical framework, 22–23, 28, 34–35, 38–43, 47, 50–51
tax ideas/ideology (Argentina), 11–12, 15, 81, 172–173
2008 export tax revolt, 4–5, 12, 15, 20, 172–173, 204–205
contested state visions, 12, 15, 172, 173–174, 175–176, 177–178, 179–180, 191–192, 204–205
corruption, 179–180
development, conflict around ideas of, 173–178, 179–181
export taxes, 144–145, 167, 171, 190–192
export taxes as fault line, 11–12, 15, 21, 83, 114–115, 143–145, 171, 174–175, 189, 192–193, 199, 205
interventionalist developmental state, 203, 205
Kirchnerism, 15, 21, 139, 149, 172–174, 175–185, 187, 190–191, 192–193, 204–205
lack of consensus around tax ideas, 12, 19, 112
political polarization, 172–173, 174–177, 200
redistribution, 167, 174, 179–180, 190–191
repatriation of capital policy, 182–184
Resolution N.125, 175–177
socio-economic tensions, 15, 144–145, 172–173, 178–179, 192
unfairness, 167
tax inequality
Spanish Empire, 68–69
tax collection inequalities, 66–67
uneven taxation burden, 28, 36, 38, 52, 63–64, 68–69, 71, 207–208
Tax Justice Network, 5–6, 194
tax legitimacy, 14, 16
accountability, 27–28
arguments for, 29
British Empire, 57–58
colonialism, 55–56, 64, 80–81
developed countries, 27
developing countries, 29–30
export taxes, 42–43
governance dividend, 28
importance of, 18–19, 196
Latin America, 81, 195
provision of public goods and, 27, 29–30, 42–43
Spanish Empire, 67, 69
state/society relationship, 24–25, 27–29
tax burden and, 28, 36, 38
tax compliance and, 28–29
tax design and, 18–19
tax reform and, 29–30
theoretical contributions, 207–208
theoretical framework, 27–30
war and, 24
tax legitimacy (Argentina)

export taxes, 11, 13–14, 20, 82–83, 112–114, 119, 122–125, 130, 142–144, 156, 167–168, 169–171, 197–198
post 2008 revolt, 144, 156, 167–168, 169–171
Resolution N.125, 14–16, 134–135, 142
taxpayers, 196
2008 export tax revolt (Argentina), 13–15
export taxes (Argentina), 9–10, 20, 117–118
Latin America, 36
tax burden in developed countries, 27, 36
taxpayer information, 6–7, 36–37
uneven taxation burden, 28, 36, 38, 52, 63–64, 68–69, 71, 207–208
tax reform
2008 export tax revolt (Argentina), 4, 14, 21, 132–136, 137–138
Argentina, 93, 95–96, 98–99, 117, 128–130, 188–189
challenges: institutional-based accounts, 7–8, 22, 36–37, 203–204
challenges: interest-based accounts, 7–8, 12, 18–19, 22, 25, 26–27, 34–35, 203–204
colonialism and, 6–7
export taxes (Argentina), 128–130, 140–141
politics and, 7–8, 10, 38–39
procedural legality of, 14
state/society contract, 28
tax systems
Argentina, 92–93
developed countries, 27, 29–30
developing countries, 5–6, 19, 29–30, 40, 52
Latin America, 65, 80–81, 194–195
politics and, 7–8
poverty and, 33–34
professionalized tax systems, 27, 29–31, 33
weak tax systems, 29–30, 36–37, 40, 43–44, 47, 52, 65
Taylor, L., 78–79
Teichman, J., 47
Tilly, C., 24
trade liberalization
Latin America, 78–79
trade liberalization *versus* protectionism, 77–80
trade taxes, 33–34, 38, 59–60, 63, 73–74, 77–78
Belgian Empire, 62
British Empire, 59–60
French Empire, 61
indirect trade taxes, 55, 59, 61, 66
Latin America, 38–39, 65–66, 73–74, 77, 80–81
politics of, 38–39
Portuguese Empire, 65
reducing trade taxes, 77–78
Spanish Empire, 66
trade unions
Argentina, 88, 105, 158–159
Latin America, 46
Tussie, D., 48–49

U

UCA (*Universidad Católica Argentina*/Catholic University of Argentina), 148–149, 165
UCR (*Unión Cívica Radical*/Radical Civil Union), 106, 180–181, 186–187
UIA (*Unión Industrial Argentina*/Industrial Union of Argentina), 86–87, 106–107, 177
UIF (*Unidad de Información Financiera*/Argentine Financial Information), 126
Ukraine: 2022 Russian invasion of, 2, 194, 209
UN (United Nations), 5–6
United Kingdom, 39–40, 71–72
Uriburu, José Félix Benito, 93
Uruguay, 71–72, 75–76

V

Vargas, Getúlio, 75–76
Venezuela, 206
Videla, Jorge Rafael, 103–105
Von Haldenwang, C., 36

W

Waisbord, S., 200
Washington Consensus, 47–48, 108–110, 114
see also neoliberalism
Weber, M., 25–27
welfare, 78–79
developed countries, 26–27

welfare (*Continued*)
 Latin America, 46–48, 78–79
 taxation and, 26–27, 30
 see also redistribution
welfare (Argentina), 89, 119–120
 Kirchner, Cristina Fernández de, 164–166
 Kirchner, Néstor, 119–120, 125–126
 Peronism, 89–90, 92–93, 125–126
 see also AUH
Werker, E., 6
World Bank, 5–6, 10, 106–108, 158–159
world history, 23–25
World War I, 74–75, 77, 86
World War II, 29–30, 77, 87, 90, 95–96
Wylde, C., 48–49, 115, 125–126, 162

Y
YPF (*Yacimientos Petrolíferos Fiscales*), 160, 162–164, 182
Yrigoyen, Hipólito, 93

Z
Zee, H. H., 6
Zolt, E. M., 34

The manufacturer's authorised representative in the EU for product safety is Oxford University Press España S.A. of el Parque Empresarial San Fernando de Henares, Avenida de Castilla, 2 – 28830 Madrid (www.oup.es/en or product.safety@oup.com). OUP España S.A. also acts as importer into Spain of products made by the manufacturer.

www.ingramcontent.com/pod-product-compliance
Lightning Source LLC
Chambersburg PA
CBHW060733181125
35524CB00076B/235/J

9780198923190